SEEKING A NEW MAJOR

SEEKING A NEW MAJORITY

The Republican Party and
American Politics, 1960–1980

*Edited by Robert Mason
and Iwan Morgan*

Vanderbilt University Press

NASHVILLE

© 2013 by Vanderbilt University Press
Nashville, Tennessee 37235
All rights reserved
First printing 2013

This book is printed on acid-free paper.
Manufactured in the United States of America

Library of Congress Cataloging-in-Publication Data on file

LC control number 2012018051
LC classification JK2356.S44 2012
Dewey class number 324.273409'046—dc23

ISBN 978-0-8265-1889-7 (cloth)
ISBN 978-0-8265-1891-0 (e-book)

CONTENTS

ACKNOWLEDGMENTS

This book grows out of a conference co-organized by the Institute for the Study of the Americas (ISA), part of the University of London's School of Advanced Study, and the University of Edinburgh's School of History, Classics and Archaeology. As editors, we would like to acknowledge the financial support that the conference received from ISA, the British Association for American Studies, and (with particular thanks to Tony Badger) the University of Cambridge's Mellon Fund. We are also grateful to colleagues at London and Edinburgh for their help with this project, and especially to Olga Jimenez, ISA events coordinator, for her customary efficiency in ensuring that the conference proceeded so smoothly. Because a book such as this is very much a collective venture, we would like to express our thanks to all the contributors for submitting their chapters in timely fashion and accommodating requests for amendments with such good grace.

We are very grateful, too, to all those at Vanderbilt University Press who contributed to the development of this book, to the press's anonymous reviewers for their insightful and thought-provoking comments, and especially to Eli Bortz for his enthusiastic support of the project.

INTRODUCTION

Republicans in Search of a New Majority

Robert Mason and Iwan Morgan

The 1960s and 1970s were a time of social, economic, and political tumult in the United States. The upheavals of this era had profound consequences for the nation's two main political parties. Having enjoyed majority status since the New Deal, the Democratic Party lost its clear-cut ascendancy in national politics. With the opposition in decline, the Republican Party had the opportunity to reestablish itself, for the first time since the 1920s, as the dominant force in the two-party system. Having recovered from the nadir of electoral catastrophe in 1964, the GOP (Grand Old Party) apparently entered a new era of power in 1980. Ultimately, Republican hopes of a realignment comparable to that which launched the New Deal political order in 1928–1936 turned out to be premature. This quest for a new majority did not result in the creation of a dominant electoral coalition. Measured by a different yardstick, however, it was a success. There may have been no majority party in American politics during the final years of the twentieth century, but the momentum lay with the GOP. In contrast to the mid-twentieth century, it was the Republicans rather than the Democrats who had the upper hand in shaping the nation's political course.[1]

This book offers a new exploration of the Republican revival. It is a subject that is central to any understanding of U.S. political history during the second half of the twentieth century, but has not in general reached the forefront of scholarly attention. In contrast, the development of American conservatism over the same period has attracted an unusually rich and creative historiography since the early 1990s. This topic is no longer "something of an orphan in historical scholarship," as Alan Brinkley put it in 1994.[2] Until recently, however, discussion of the Republican Party remained on the margins of this enterprise. *Seeking a New Majority* aims to redress this relative neglect by presenting fresh perspectives on the GOP revival from scholars working in this field. Their contributions to this volume signal the emergence of a new historiography that recognizes the significance of the Republican Party's revival both to the advance of American conservatism and to the broader development of U.S. politics in the late twentieth century and beyond.

The contributors to this study discourage a monocausal explanation of the Republican resurgence by emphasizing the complexity of the issues involved. Their analysis suggests that a number of factors underlay this development. It was partly dependent on contingency in the form of the Democratic travails that undermined the domination of the opposition party in the late 1960s and 1970s. It also reflected the GOP's capacity to fashion a positive, conservative response to the political, economic, and social changes of the era. In this sense, the Republicans were more successful than the Democrats in adapting to a changing America in which ideas of race, gender, and ethnicity were undergoing significant transformation, old economic orthodoxies were in decay, and Cold War foreign policy was being reassessed. Linked with this transformation of the policy debate, the GOP made significant organizational improvements in its national and state institutions that enhanced its capacity to respond to new electoral opportunities. Finally, this book makes clear that Republican progress from landslide defeat in the 1964 elections to success in the 1980 elections was anything but smooth and linear. There were many setbacks and false starts along the way.

The election of Ronald Reagan as president in 1980 was more a rejection of the unpopular Jimmy Carter than a mandate either for conservatism or for the GOP. Nevertheless, it marked the beginning of a right turn from the liberal course charted by Franklin D. Roosevelt when he became president in 1933 and sustained by his Democratic successors, Harry Truman, John F. Kennedy, and Lyndon B. Johnson, after 1945. For much of the half-century between Roosevelt's coming to power and Reagan's victory, American politics operated within the framework of what scholars have termed the New Deal order.[3] The organizing principles of political discourse and public policy in this era broadly accepted the capacity of an activist state to deal with domestic problems, the obligation of government to safeguard the rights of hitherto disadvantaged groups (notably labor unions in the 1930s and racial minorities in the 1950s and 1960s), and—with America's entry into World War II—the need for global activism to promote its international interests and enhance its national security.

During the early twentieth century, until the 1930s, the Democrats had been the minority party in American politics, with the white South as their most reliable bastion. Between 1928 and 1936, however, they achieved majority status thanks to the votes of predominantly urban and socioeconomically less privileged groups in the big industrial states with large numbers of electoral votes. In 1928, the presidential campaign of Alfred E. Smith, the first Roman Catholic to head the Democratic ticket, ended in heavy defeat but began the process of mobilizing ethnic Americans to support the national party. The Roosevelt elections of 1932 and 1936 brought blue-collar families, labor union members, low-income workers, and northern blacks into the Democratic coalition. The expansion of the Democratic base was such that FDR would have won the presidency in 1940 without carrying a single southern state.[4] However, white southerners retained considerable influence within the congressional wing of the party thanks to their ascendancy in the legislative committee system. They acted as a restraint on the liberal tendencies of the urban-oriented presidential wing of the party, but were mainly capable only of slowing liberal policy development rather than reversing it.[5]

With the support of the New Deal voter coalition, the Democrats won the presidency in eight of the twelve elections from 1932 through 1976 and enjoyed almost unbroken control of both houses of the legislature from 1933 through 1981; the exceptions to the record of Democratic legislative control were the 80th Congress (1947–1949) and the 83rd Congress (1953–1955). To challenge the opposition's hold on power, the GOP had the option of either holding fast to its conservative tradition or being in essence the "me-too" party of statist accommodation. Conservative champion Senator Barry Goldwater of Arizona famously characterized its dilemma as one of offering "a choice" or "an echo."

Without doubt, the GOP fared better in electoral terms in the postwar era when it manifested acceptance of the existing New Deal state than when it sought to roll this back. As Dwight D. Eisenhower remarked in 1954 to his hard-shell conservative brother, Edgar, "Should any political party attempt to abolish social security, unemployment insurance, and eliminate labor laws and farm programs, you would not hear of that party again in our political history."[6] Accordingly, the first GOP president since Herbert Hoover demonstrated his willingness not only to intervene against recession, expand Social Security, and launch the largest public works program hitherto in American history (the interstate highway system), but also to involve the state in new ventures, notably federal aid to education and civil rights legislation. Richard Nixon, the next Republican occupant of the White House, showed a similar proclivity for expanding programs in the New Deal tradition, notably entitlements, and undertaking initiatives in new fields, such as environmental protection and occupational health and safety.[7] Conversely, Harry Truman played on the anti–New Deal record of the GOP-controlled 80th Congress to win reelection against the odds in 1948. Most dramatically, Goldwater's conservative campaign for president in 1964 resulted in the lowest GOP popular vote share since 1936. The election consequently turned into an anti-Republican landslide that reduced the party's representation in Congress to its lowest level since 1941–1942.[8]

Some scholars have conjectured the existence of a liberal consensus in the two decades after World War II in recognition of the broad acceptance within the American polity of government activism at home and anticommunist containment abroad.[9] To be sure, such a consensus reflected the modifying influence of World War II–generated economic growth on New Deal liberalism.[10] Moreover, it did not mandate smooth progress toward domestic liberal ends or prevent the conservative congressional coalition of right-wing Republicans and southern Democrats from obstructing the development of new programs. Nor did bipartisan support for the Cold War stop foreign policy from being a major focus of political disagreement. Accusations by the opposition party, whether Republican or Democratic, that the administration in office was letting the Soviet Union gain the upper hand in the global struggle with the United States and its allies were a recurring feature of American politics from the late 1940s onward.[11] Nevertheless, the liberal consensus remains a valid descriptor of the fundamental course of American politics in the mid-twentieth century. Underlying this consensus was the remarkable prosperity and growth of the postwar economy. As historian Robert Collins has shown, the "growth liberalism" of this era rested on the belief that the state had the policy instruments and expertise to help the private economy achieve constant expansion. Initiated by the Truman administration, practiced with more restraint by the Eisenhower administration, and brought to its peak by the Kennedy and Johnson administrations, postwar economic growthmanship obviated the painful and divisive choices of redistributive politics.[12]

Lyndon B. Johnson's landslide victory of 1964 seemed to provide a mandate for a new expansion of liberalism. In its wake, Johnson pursued his Great Society of programmatic innovation, the greatest surge of state building since the New Deal. Before long, however, cracks in Democratic ranks suggested that the 1964 triumph represented the electoral high-water mark of the New Deal tradition rather than a fresh surge in its development. Urban upheavals, antiwar protest, white "backlash" against civil rights advances, and an emerging debate over values provoked by the sociocultural changes of the 1960s brought the big tent of consensus crashing down on LBJ. Democratic hopes of rebuilding it in the ensuing decade ran aground on the rocks both of stagflation, which ended the long postwar boom, and of foreign policy failures, which aroused fears of Cold War retreat.[13]

The travails of liberalism and its Democratic agents may encourage historians to assume that Republican Party advancement was consequently assured, that Barry Goldwater's unsuccessful 1964 presidential candidacy produced a conservative blueprint to ensure GOP ascendancy in the long term, and that Reagan's election in 1980 was the logical culmination of America's turn to the right, which had been in motion since the late 1960s. In reality, the Republican Party's history between 1960 and 1980 mirrored the broader tumult that the United States experienced as Republicans pondered how best to respond to changes that had shattered many of the assumptions of the postwar polity.

Far from being a linear progression toward political success, the GOP narrative involved setbacks as well as steps forward. Above all, there was an active and often bitter debate about the party's future. On the one hand, mindful of past wisdom, which held that frontal attacks on the New Deal state were suicidal, many Republicans saw a full-fledged embrace of conservatism as the sure route to the party's demise rather than its resurgence. On the other, believing the time was now ripe for the GOP to offer "a choice, not an echo," some on the right were increasingly confident that it could regain power through a renewal of the Goldwater crusade. In essence, therefore, there was no Republican consensus about how to build a new majority. In broad terms, party members from the so-called Sunbelt, initially the growth states of the Southwest and eventually the economic hotspots of the "New" South, favored the conservative course. In contrast, the presence of moderate Republicans who saw the center as the essential ground for political victory was stronger in other regions, particularly the Northeast, the Midwest, and the Pacific Northwest.

Even as the New Deal order showed signs of decline, electoral outcomes did not chart a consistent course of GOP advance. The 1960 presidential election effectively produced a dead heat between Richard Nixon and John F. Kennedy, but the Democrats retained a comfortable majority in Congress. This seemed to confirm the lesson of the 1950s that Republican presidential strength was greater than the party's fortunes as a whole. Four years later, however, the GOP Right's capture of the presidential nomination and the crushing defeat of its chosen standard-bearer encouraged speculation of the party's demise. "Goldwater may have given the Republican Party the *coup de grâce* as a genuine major-party competitor," commented historian Richard Hofstadter during the campaign itself. Even if this judgment smacked of hyperbole, the right wing of the party appeared to have suffered a fatal reverse. As two analysts of public opinion observed of Goldwater's emphasis on conservatism, "To the extent that Goldwater was interpreted along the lines that he wished to be understood—that is, ideologically—he suffered considerably as a consequence."[14]

Just two years on, however, the strong showing by Republicans in the midterms of 1966 placed the party clearly on the comeback trail. Another two years later, despite Nixon's narrow margin of victory in popular-vote terms and lack of coattails (he could not carry his party into control of Congress), his election as president generated speculation that a new Republican majority was at hand. Political aide Kevin Phillips captured the widespread expectation of electoral realignment in the GOP's favor in his strategic blueprint for its achievement, *The Emerging Republican Majority*, published in 1969.[15]

The Nixon administration pursued a serious effort to mobilize a new voter coalition that would keep the GOP in power for a generation, but success was equivocal. The 1970 midterms offered little evidence of electoral realignment. The landslide margin of Nixon's reelection in 1972 was more personal than partisan, but the Watergate crisis that destroyed his presidency threatened to do the same to his party. Pollster Robert Teeter told Republicans in late 1974 that "present trends indicate that in 20–30 years the party will be extinct."[16] As had happened a decade earlier, however, such gloomy predictions soon gave way to new optimism. Amid the woes of the Carter administration, the Republicans made progress in the 1978 midterms and scored their greatest electoral success since the 1920s two years later. The larger story, then, is one of failure and disappointments as well as moments of triumph and optimism—not a straightforward narrative of progress.

The complex and tortuous nature not only of the Republican revival but also of the Right's resurgence to gain leadership of the party is explored in Chapter 1 of this volume, by Donald Critchlow. He finds rich interactions between politicians and ideas, between principle and pragmatism, between organizations and voters, and between ambition and contingency. Crucial to the rise of the Right were its ability to generate new ideas about the nature of the individual and the good society, its capacity for organization—especially the establishment of new think tanks to provide the GOP with policy ideas and personnel in the 1970s—and the emergence of leaders such as Ronald Reagan who were able to articulate conservative principles to the larger electorate while also engaging in the compromises necessary to win power. The contingencies of politics also played no small part in the conservative triumph. Democratic miscalculations and misfortunes allowed the GOP to recover quickly after the disasters of the Goldwater campaign and Watergate. Reagan was fortunate to run for president in 1980 amid circumstances that favored the nonincumbent party. Four years earlier, the anti-incumbent mood of the nation had favored the Democrats. Had Reagan gained the Republican presidential nomination instead of Gerald Ford in 1976, he would likely have lost to Jimmy Carter, a defeat that would have reversed the Right's ascent in the party.

Casting further light on the complex chronology of the Republican resurgence, Timothy Thurber examines the role of race in the growth of the GOP in Chapter 2. This issue is conventionally regarded as pivotal in explaining Democratic decline and Republican advance, especially in the South. Thurber's analysis confirms the electoral salience of civil rights, but it also shows that the Republican debate about race long predated Goldwater-era divisions over the exploitation of "backlash" against the 1960s civil rights revolution. While historians have neglected the racially conservative impulse among Republicans during the 1940s and 1950s, and the GOP's ambition to make electoral progress based on it, they have equally underestimated the continuing strength within the party of liberalism on race during the 1960s and 1970s. In challenging the conventional chronology of the Republican resurgence, Thurber thereby complicates understandings of how the party's fragile Lincolnian inheritance evolved in the era of civil rights.

As Thurber's exploration of race reveals, the search for a new majority involved an extensive intraparty debate. When considering the Republican resurgence, historians have usually paid particularly close attention to the strategic choices of presidential candidates and presidents. Such a perspective, however, overlooks others in the party who contributed to the debate and to the majority-seeking effort. In Chapter 3, Joe Merton analyzes how Republicans responded to the rediscovery of white ethnic identity during the 1960s and 1970s. Many among them concluded that white ethnics, a traditionally Democratic bloc, were ready for successful Republican cultivation. The Nixon administration engaged in extensive efforts to capture their votes. So did independently minded officials on the Republican National Committee and in state and local parties, sometimes in ways that differed from parallel White House activities. To understand fully how Republicans sought a new majority, therefore, it is necessary to develop a perspective that moves beyond a presidential focus.

In Chapter 4, Catherine Rymph also explores the larger party and uncovers a lost debate about the importance of diversity to its future. She demonstrates that the relationship between the Republican search for a new majority and the revitalization of American conservatism was not a straightforward one. Indeed, some in the party identified conservatism as a hindrance to electoral success, rather than a help. As Rymph shows, the black freedom struggle helped to foster the conclusion that Republicans needed to offer an "open door" to those who previously considered themselves marginalized in a party dominated by white, wealthy, Protestant men. During the Nixon years, Republican activists flirted with the notion of quotas to ensure that their party convention was representative of American diversity. A fleeting moment of intraparty liberalism ultimately gave way, however, to a conservative counterreaction that demonized quotas as anti-individualistic. As Rymph's exploration of party dynamics shows, the Republican mood was decisively different in the late 1970s compared with the early 1970s. GOP engagement with the idea of a new majority had shifted from the embrace of diversity to the defense of individualism.

Analysis of the party's revitalization during the 1960s and 1970s often emphasizes a rightward turn in public opinion, but the style as well as the substance of GOP politics changed in this era. During the party's minority period, Republicans had endured a disadvantageous reputation as the representatives of a socioeconomic elite. According to Kevin P. Phillips in *The Emerging Republican Majority*, the Republican opportunity partly depended on the new image of Democratic leaders as the representatives of a liberal establishment rather than Franklin D. Roosevelt's "forgotten man," as had been the case during the New Deal era. In Chapter 5, Timothy Stanley discusses the efforts of Nixon political aide Patrick J. Buchanan to promote such populism as the route to electoral growth. Although he enjoyed only limited success in doing so during the 1970s, Buchanan became the archetypal proponent of the Republican need to recraft the party's message to appeal to "middle Americans" rather than WASP elites.

The South was a crucial region in the Republican resurgence. The vision for the party's growth that Phillips outlined in *The Emerging Republican Majority* was conventionally identified as synonymous with a "Southern Strategy" (misleadingly so, because he examined Democratic disaffection outside as well as within the region). As broadly understood, the Southern Strategy based its fundamental appeal on race whereby Republicans plucked white southerners from the Democratic Party through common alignment to prevent the further expansion of African American rights. Sean P. Cunningham's analysis of Texas Republicans in Chapter 6 both challenges and complicates such an assumption. He argues that developments internal to the state, as opposed to national trends, were especially important in fostering the growth of its GOP. Liberal-conservative tensions within the state Democratic Party created the opportunity for enterprising Republican John Tower to win a Senate seat and lay the foundations for his party's expansion in Texas. Moreover, if race was not insignificant in the Lone Star state, it was not always a conservative issue, because

Texas Republicans adopted progressive positions to cultivate electoral support among Latinos. In Cunningham's account, populism is also a theme that helps to explain the vicissitudes of the Republican experience in Texas. Opposition to a putatively out-of-touch Democratic elite initially helped Tower to win office, but he later became vulnerable to the populist critiques of opponents, both Republican and Democratic.

The search for a new majority involved a quest for alliances with and support from a variety of extraparty groups. The mid-1970s arrival of "New Right" organizations had enormous promise for this project, but connections with groups outside the party harbored dangers, too. Robert Freedman's exploration of the Religious Right in Chapter 7 demonstrates that these groups had an uneasy alliance with the GOP from the start. Steadfastly promoting their own political agenda, leaders of this movement expected Republican obeisance to their interests but did not guarantee loyalty in return. Conversely, many in the GOP recognized that the Religious Right agenda threatened to alienate some voters even while mobilizing others. Freedman's careful exploration of the movement's impact on the 1980 election also suggests that its leaders exaggerated its contribution to GOP success.

Some explanations for the Democrats' lack of success at the presidential level in the elections of the 1970s and 1980s emphasize how their party's divisions jeopardized efforts to field a successful candidate, even while its ideological breadth facilitated continuing congressional success.[17] In Chapter 8, Sandra Scanlon shows that ideological divisions also existed in the GOP, particularly over foreign policy, and that their resolution was essential to the quest for a new majority. Conservative reluctance to compromise principle for power was the crux of the problem. In Richard Nixon's view, one of his greatest political challenges was to be adequately conservative to maintain the commitment of right-wing activists while blurring conservative principles that might alienate the electorate as a whole. Such an approach infuriated leading conservatives, who expressed strong criticism of his foreign policy of détente. But conservatives themselves were beset by divisions, especially between those inside the party and those outside it. As Scanlon demonstrates, the Right eventually achieved unity over foreign policy and its ideas gained mainstream acceptance within the Republican Party as the 1970s progressed. Moreover, as détente faltered, the public's appetite for a more assertive brand of global anti-communism increased. As a consequence, the Republicans were in a position to reap electoral advantage from popular disenchantment with U.S. foreign policy failures in 1979–1980. Internal party dynamics were thus critical in Republican efforts to seek a new majority.

One of the challenges that scholars face in studying the GOP revival is to explain its differing fortunes in presidential contests and at other levels of political competition. As Robert Mason discusses in Chapter 9, the electoral role of foreign policy helps to provide an explanation. This chapter emphasizes foreign policy's significance, often underappreciated, in accounting for the party's revitalization. Although Richard Nixon initially had a wider-ranging project to boost GOP electoral fortunes, in reaching out to his "new American majority" of 1972 he largely relied on the politics of patriotism, which supported his Vietnam and détente policies. Especially because post-Vietnam divisions within the Democratic Party on the Cold War facilitated Republicans' efforts to depict their opponents as weak on foreign policy, patriotism, and an emphasis on strength in national defense, remained an important party appeal. Often powerful in building support at the presidential level, it was less powerful in boosting party fortunes at large, however. The size of this electoral advantage depended on geopolitical developments, thus jeopardizing the solidity of the new, enlarged Republican coalition. As Mason also discusses, the role of foreign policy in explaining the party's revitalization involves a theme of continuity as well as change. The reputation of the GOP as the party more skilled in foreign policy was not a new development in the Vietnam era and its aftermath, as it had actually developed during the earlier phase of the Cold War, but it had been an advantage that politicians could not usually exploit at the polls.

Nixon relied on foreign policy to build electoral support in part because he lacked confidence in economic issues as the foundation for victory. Far from making common cause with those challenging Keynesian orthodoxies, Nixon stimulated the economy to support his reelection in 1972 in order not to run afoul of voter concerns on unemployment—a key reason for his 1960 defeat against Kennedy, he thought. Still operating within the assumptions of the New Deal political order, he failed to anticipate the success that an updated version of economic conservatism would soon achieve in the stagnation-afflicted 1970s. In Chapter 10, Iwan Morgan analyzes an important transition that assisted Republicans in their quest for power. No longer seeing tax reduction as an adjunct to spending control and balanced budgets, they now promoted it as the recipe for economic growth, thereby stealing the Democrats' reputation as the party better able to promote prosperity. Such new ideas in economic policy became party policy through the work of political promoters like Ronald Reagan and Jack Kemp, policy entrepreneurs like Jude Wanniski, and congressional aides like Paul Craig Roberts. Despite Reagan's election victory, however, voters remained more concerned about inflation than tax cuts until the severe recession of 1981–1982 restored price stability. According to Morgan's analysis, low taxes were initially a party-building issue that benefited the GOP in the run-up to the 1980 election but were not a critical vote-winner until four years later.

Just as the chronology of the Republican resurgence needs revision, so too do understandings of its outcome. At first sight, this book concludes with the moment of GOP triumph, when Ronald Reagan, a conservative Republican in Goldwater's ideological mold, won the White House and the party took control of the Senate for the first time since 1952. As Dominic Sandbrook shows in the final chapter, however, the meaning of the 1980 elections was more ambiguous. Republican victories depended at least as much on Democratic problems as any party success in winning the political argument. Although there is no question that over the previous two decades the Republican Party had strengthened its position, the party had not consolidated the support of the "emerging Republican majority" that Phillips had forecast in 1969. During the 1980s, Richard Wirthlin, a key pollster for the Reagan administration and the Republican National Committee, referred to the Republicans as a "parity party," rather than the majority party.[18] The formulation suggested that the party was now on a more or less equal footing with the Democratic Party, and that it had not actually ascended to majority status. Such observations raise questions about the success that Republicans achieved in seeking a new electoral majority. In discussing the Republican resurgence, scholars need to qualify its extent, and they need to find explanations for its limitations as well as its strengths.

Nevertheless, the Republicans had unquestionably sought a new majority in an imaginative and multifaceted manner rather than simply being the beneficiaries of Democratic decline. Their long-term project in pursuit of electoral advance is a key element in modern American political history and its consequences have proved to be significant. The GOP clearly did not succeed in creating its own version of the once-dominant New Deal coalition. Nor as a consequence did a conservative consensus replace the now-vanished liberal consensus. The Republicans did gain ascendancy, however, in terms of moving the American polity rightward in the final decades of the twentieth century and beyond. As this book seeks to demonstrate, many factors rather than a single critical one underlay the Republican resurgence of the 1960s and 1970s and its progress was tortuous rather than straightforward. Central to GOP success was the growing influence of the conservative wing of the party. As such, the rise of the Republican Party also brought the GOP Right from the periphery to the center of American politics. This ensured that party politics in the late twentieth-century United States entered a new era of increasing partisanship, polarization, and ideological discord as conservative Republicanism sought to turn ideas into policy in a political system that traditionally favored incremental over radical change.

In some ways, the Tea Party movement that became a force in Republican politics in the run-up to the 2010 midterm elections suggests the continuation of this trend. Some interpreted the GOP's strong performance in those elections, in gaining control of the House of Representatives and slashing the Democratic majority in the Senate, as an indication that the shock troops of the Right were on the verge of the final assault to overthrow the citadel of big government. While allowing for the different structure and context of politics that existed a half-century ago, the history of the Republican revival in the 1960s and 1970s suggests that electoral politics produce more complex outcomes than the total victory pursued by contemporary conservatives. The Democrats discovered this to their cost in the 1964 election that was supposed to represent the ultimate triumph of New Deal liberalism but instead constituted its last hurrah. Whatever course American politics takes in the second decade of the twenty-first century, it is likely that contingency, compromise, and calculation will have greater significance on its trajectory than ideological clarity.

NOTES

1. One indication of this is that historians conventionally talk of the "Age of Reagan" to cover not only his presidency but also its prelude and postlude. See, for example, Steven F. Hayward, *The Age of Reagan: The Fall of the Old Liberal Order, 1964–1980* (Roseville, CA: Prima, 2001), and *The Age of Reagan: The Conservative Counterrevolution, 1980–1989* (New York: Crown Forum, 2009); and Sean Wilentz, *The Age of Reagan: A History, 1974–2008* (New York: Harper, 2008).

2. Alan Brinkley, "The Problem of American Conservatism," *American Historical Review* 99 (1994): 409. Examples of this new scholarship on conservatism include Lisa McGirr, *Suburban Warriors: The Origins of the New American Right* (Princeton, NJ: Princeton University Press, 2001); Jonathan M. Schoenwald, *A Time for Choosing: The Rise of Modern American Conservatism* (New York: Oxford University Press, 2001); Kevin M. Kruse, *White Flight: Atlanta and the Making of Modern Conservatism* (Princeton, NJ: Princeton University Press, 2005); Matthew D. Lassiter, *The Silent Majority: Suburban Politics in the Sunbelt South* (Princeton, NJ: Princeton University Press, 2006); Joseph Crespino, *In Search of Another Country: Mississippi and the Conservative Counterrevolution* (Princeton, NJ: Princeton University Press, 2007); Allan J. Lichtman, *White Protestant Nation: The Rise of the American Conservative Movement* (New York: Atlantic Monthly Press, 2008); and David Farber, *The Rise and Fall of Modern American Conservatism: A Short History* (Princeton, NJ: Princeton University Press, 2010).

3. See, for example, Steve Fraser and Gary Gerstle, eds., *The Rise and Fall of the New Deal Political Order, 1930–1980* (Princeton, NJ: Princeton University Press, 1989); Stephen Skowronek, *The Politics Presidents Make: Leadership from John Adams to Bill Clinton* (Cambridge, MA: Belknap Press, 1997), 287–406; and William Chafe, ed., *The Achievement of American Liberalism: The New Deal and Its Legacies* (New York: Columbia University Press, 2003).

4. Samuel Lubell, *The Future of American Politics*, 3rd rev. ed. (New York: Harper and Row, 1965); Carl N. Degler, "American Political Parties and the Rise of the City: An Interpretation," *Journal of American History* 51 (1964): 41–59; John Allswang, *The New Deal and American Politics: A Study in Political Change* (New York: Wiley, 1978); and David Plotke, *Building a Democratic Political Order: Reshaping Liberalism in the 1930s and 1940s* (New York: Cambridge University Press, 1996).

5. James MacGregor Burns, *The Deadlock of Democracy: Four-Party Politics in America* (Englewood Cliffs, NJ: Prentice Hall, 1963); James T. Patterson, *Congressional Conservatism and the New Deal: The Growth of the Conservative Coalition in Congress, 1933–1939* (Lexington: University Press of Kentucky, 1967); and Robert Garson, *The Democratic Party and the Politics of Sectionalism, 1941–1948* (Baton Rouge: Louisiana State University Press, 1974).

6. Dwight D. Eisenhower to Edgar Newton Eisenhower, November 8, 1954, in *The Presidential Papers of Dwight David Eisenhower*, ed. Louis Galambos and Daun van Ee (Baltimore: Johns Hopkins University Press, 1996), document 1147; republished at *www.eisenhowermemorial.org* by the Dwight D. Eisenhower Memorial Commission.

7. For the Eisenhower administration, see Alonzo Hamby, *Liberalism and Its Challengers: FDR to Reagan* (New York: Oxford University Press, 1985), 115–28; Robert Griffith, "Dwight D. Eisenhower and the Corporate Commonwealth," *American Historical Review* 87 (1982): 87–122; and Iwan Morgan, *Eisenhower versus "the Spenders": The Eisenhower Administration, the Democrats, and the Budget, 1953–1960* (New York: St.

Martin's Press, 1990). On Nixon, see Stephen E. Ambrose, *Nixon: The Triumph of a Politician, 1962–1972* (New York: Simon and Schuster, 1989); Allen J. Matusow, *Nixon's Economy: Booms, Busts, Dollars, and Votes* (Lawrence: University Press of Kansas, 1999); and Melvin Small, *The Presidency of Richard Nixon* (Lawrence: University Press of Kansas, 1999).

8. Gary Donaldson, *Truman Defeats Dewey* (Lexington: University Press of Kentucky, 1999); and Robert David Johnson, *All the Way with LBJ: The 1964 Presidential Election* (New York: Cambridge University Press, 2009).

9. The classic statement of this is Godfrey Hodgson, *In Our Time: America from World War II to Nixon* (New York: Knopf, 1978). See, too, Iwan Morgan, *Beyond the Liberal Consensus: A Political History of the United States since 1965* (New York: St. Martin's Press, 1994); James T. Patterson, *Grand Expectations: The United States, 1945–1974* (New York: Oxford University Press, 1996); and Rick Perlstein, *Before the Storm: Barry Goldwater and the Unmaking of the American Consensus* (New York: Hill and Wang, 2001).

10. Alan Brinkley, *The End of Reform: New Deal Liberalism in Recession and War* (New York: Knopf, 1995).

11. See, in particular, Alonzo Hamby, *Beyond the New Deal: Harry S. Truman and American Liberalism* (New York: Columbia University Press, 1973); M. J. Heale, *McCarthy's Americans: Red Scare Politics in State and Nation, 1935–1965* (Basingstoke, UK: Macmillan, 1998); David W. Reinhard, *The Republican Right since 1945* (Lexington: University Press of Kentucky, 1985); James L. Sundquist, *Politics and Policy: The Eisenhower, Kennedy, and Johnson Years* (Washington, DC: Brookings Institution, 1968); and Peter J. Roman, *Eisenhower and the Missile Gap* (Ithaca, NY: Cornell University Press, 1985).

12. Robert M. Collins, *More: The Politics of Economic Growth in Postwar America* (New York: Oxford University Press, 2000).

13. For Democratic travails, see Allen J. Matusow, *The Unraveling of America: A History of Liberalism in the 1960s* (New York: Harper and Row, 1984); Bruce J. Schulman, *Lyndon B. Johnson and American Liberalism: A Brief Biography with Documents* (Boston: Bedford, 1995); Ronald Radosh, *Divided They Fell: The Demise of the Democratic Party, 1964–1996* (New York: Free Press, 1996); and W. Carl Biven, *Jimmy Carter's Economy: Policy in an Age of Limits* (Chapel Hill: University of North Carolina Press, 2002).

14. "The Two-Party System: How to Help It Survive," *Life*, October 16, 1964, 4; and Jack Osgood Field and Ronald E. Anderson, "Ideology in the Public's Conceptualization of the 1964 Election," *Public Opinion Quarterly* 33 (1969): 392.

15. Kevin P. Phillips, *The Emerging Republican Majority* (New Rochelle, NY: Arlington House, 1969).

16. Quoted in Robert Mason, *Richard Nixon and the Quest for a New Majority* (Chapel Hill: University of North Carolina Press, 2004), 212.

17. William G. Mayer, *The Divided Democrats: Ideological Unity, Party Reform, and Presidential Elections* (Boulder, CO: Westview, 1996).

18. Quoted in Hedrick Smith, "Congress: Will There Be Realignment?," in *Beyond Reagan: The Politics of Upheaval*, ed. Paul Duke (New York: Warner, 1986), 162.

CHAPTER I

The Rise of Conservative Republicanism

A History of Fits and Starts

Donald T. Critchlow

One of the most significant developments in modern American political history was the rise of a self-identified conservative movement, which would turn the Republican Party into a voice of conservatism. Increasingly the Republican Party became a home to conservatives, driving out liberal Republicans, the so-called eastern wing of the party. This transformation came slowly, often by fits and starts, and with a good deal of bitterness, infighting, and recrimination. As conservatives slowly won their battle to make the Grand Old Party into their bailiwick, Republicans continued to battle the Democrats for political office. The struggle between the two parties involved its own political drama, and at no time was the outcome certain. The main lesson to be learned from the rise of conservative Republicanism is that whenever it appeared knocked down and out for the count as a political force, Democrats and the Left allowed it to get up off the canvas to go on for another round. In short, there was a good deal of fortune in the rise of the Right and its transformation of the GOP and an even greater deal of political miscalculation by the Left. This is to say that the course of the conservative movement was not preordained, nor was its political triumph through the agency of the Republican Party inevitable.

To presume that the conservative ascendancy was a linear development elides the circumstance of history and good political fortune. The GOP could have remained a party of moderation instead of becoming a force for conservatism, and conservative Republicanism could have been vanquished by the Democrats. Nonetheless, the GOP Right ultimately triumphed over its intraparty foes and put liberalism—both the New Deal variety and post-1970s progressivism—on the defensive. One indication of these changes was the political complexion of presidents. From 1932 to 1968, the only Republican to win the White House amid a quartet of liberal Democrats, Dwight D. Eisenhower, ran as a moderate rather than a conservative. Conversely, no Democrat won the presidency as a liberal between the victories of Lyndon B. Johnson in 1964 and Barack Obama in 2008. Any assumption that the latter's triumph heralded the restoration of the liberal ascendancy contravened the reality that approximately 35 to 40 percent of the electorate still identified itself as "conservative."

A successful political brand in the last third of the twentieth century and beyond, conservatism seemed a lost cause before then. Indeed, one of the challenges for the modern Right was to escape from the somewhat disreputable shadow cast by the old Right. Associated with intransigent reaction to the political changes of the 1930s, American conservatism manifested a peculiar crankiness and eccentricity that prevented it from developing a sustainable political movement until the 1960s. Still, much conservative criticism of the New Deal economic program—expressed by the likes of the Liberty League, University of Chicago economists, business organizations, and independent financial journalists—revealed a good deal of intellectual rigor and was by no means as nonsensical as political and ideological opponents then (or later) made it appear.[1] The Right's general, though by no means unanimous, pre–Pearl Harbor opposition to Franklin D. Roosevelt's policies to aid Britain in its war against Nazi Germany further allowed critics to dismiss it as outlandish. In particular, the anti-Semitic attitudes of some prominent anti-intervention leaders, including female ones, saddled conservatism with a reputation for bigotry.[2]

Postwar conservatives, most eminently William F. Buckley Jr., the founding editor of the nation's most influential conservative magazine, *National Review*, quickly disassociated their movement from isolationist foreign policy and anti-Semitic polemicists. Buckley's most significant initiative to this end was in breaking relations with the increasingly anti-Semitic *American Mercury* in 1951.[3] This set the foundation for the emergence of the Right in modern American politics. However, the growth of conservatism as an intellectual force and a political movement did not immediately endow it with respectability. Startled by its rapid development, which eventually culminated in the nomination of Barry Goldwater to head the Republican presidential ticket in 1964, liberals were not sure what to make of it.

Influenced by the fight against fascism in the 1930s and social science analysis of that ideology, some liberals envisaged American conservatism as a protofascist movement. In an influential critique, historian Richard Hofstadter framed the rise of the Right within what he called "the paranoid style" of American politics that gave voice to "status resentment" by groups undergoing economic and social displacement. In his assessment, their sense of powerlessness found expression in ire against established politicians, government officials, corporate leaders, intellectuals, and other experts. This framework enabled Hofstadter to group the Ku Klux Klan, Prohibitionists, nativists, and ordinary grassroots anticommunists in the 1950s into a tradition of populist anti-intellectualism.[4]

Other critics used similar approaches to depict the emergent conservative movement and conservative intellectuals as mentally and psychological disturbed. In *Danger on the Right: The Attitudes, Personnel, and Influence of the Right and Extreme Conservatives* (1964), journalists Arnold Forster and Benjamin R. Epstein warned that the so-called radical Rightists "constitute a serious threat to our democratic process."[5] In his etiological study of the modern Right, Harry Allen Overstreet, another popular writer of the early 1960s, diagnosed right-wing thinking as a mental disease. A succession of other studies presented unflattering images of conservatism that were perfectly encapsulated in their titles: *The Challenges of Democracy: Consensus and Extremism in American Politics*; *The American Ultras: The Extreme Right and the Military Industrial Complex*; *The Christian Fright Peddlers*; and *Men of the Far Right.*[6]

This backlash interpretation of American conservatism—the view that conservatives were reacting to modern society—held some truth. After all, William F. Buckley Jr. had announced in the opening pages of the first issue of *National Review* that a conservative is a fellow standing athwart history yelling, "Stop!" This typified the prevailing sentiment of conservatives—that they had witnessed enough "progress" under New Deal liberalism to last a lifetime. They wanted to draw the line against the continued expansion of the liberal state to prevent further erosion of constitutional principle, individual liberty, self-responsibility, and national capacity to confront Soviet communism abroad and at home. Notwithstanding its reactionary and antimodern aspects, however, idealism and projections of an alternative future (not just turning the clock back) lay at the core of postwar conservatism as a political and intellectual movement.

The backlash interpretation continued to hold a powerful, if not wholly dominant, influence on historians of American conservatism, especially with the rise of the so-called New Right in the 1970s. Scholars in the 1960s increasingly focused their attention on issues of race and of racial and gender inequality in America. As a consequence, many placed the conservative movement within the context of a white male backlash against the black civil rights movement and the feminist movement. This scholarship ushered in new understanding of the importance of race and gender in American society and their influence on modern American politics. An important example of it is Dan T. Carter's biography of Alabama segregationist George Wallace, *Politics of Rage* (1995). Based on extensive primary research, Carter's book argues that Wallace provided a conduit for turning white voters, upset about and fearful of gains made by the black civil rights movement, from being Democrats into Republicans.[7]

Carter's monochromatic linear account of the Republican capture of the South beginning in the 1970s was challenged by a younger generation of southern historians who offer considerably more nuanced interpretations of the ascendancy of the GOP in the South. Scholars such as Matthew D. Lassiter, Kevin M. Kruse, and Joseph Crespino, for example, maintain that Repubican strategists consciously and instinctively seized on white suburban voter discontent with affirmative action, school desegregation, and busing to win them for the GOP column.[8] Such interpretations exerted considerable influence on historical scholarship by generating debate over the importance of race in explaining the Republican takeover of the South.

According to political scientists Byron Shafer and Richard Johnston, however, GOP regional ascendancy was built on economics rather than race.[9] Their sophisticated analysis of voting behavior indicates that the Republican rise in the South had begun on the presidential level in the 1950s. It involved a gradual shift that commenced in the suburbs and then followed on the district level in statewide races in the 1960s. In Shafer and Johnston's assessment, suburban voters in the South were primarily concerned with issues such as low taxes, antiunionism, and family values. This burgeoning constituency went overwhelmingly Republican in 1980, and in the elections that followed, because the GOP stood for tax reduction and a smaller federal government. Especially interesting in this regard was the pattern of voting for third-party presidential candidate George Wallace in 1968 and Democratic presidential candidate Jimmy Carter in 1976 and 1980. In 1976, when Carter first ran for president, he won majorities in 79 percent of the districts in the South that had voted for Wallace in 1968, while gaining majorities in only 59 percent of the districts that had gone for Nixon in 1968. In the 1980 election, when Ronald Reagan swept the region, the majority of districts that voted for Carter had gone to Wallace in 1968. This suggests that Wallace was not a bridge candidate for white voters in the South into the Republican Party.

Variants of the backlash interpretation found expression in other studies of conservatism. Feminist scholars examining the role of women in conservative causes, such as opposition to the Equal Rights Amendment and abortion, and support for school prayer, maintained that many of the participants expressed traditional values resistant to the changing status of women within the workplace and society.[10] In his expansive survey of nativism and right-wing politics, *The Party of Fear* (1988), historian David H. Bennett offers a general assessment of the American Right as a movement founded on periodic expressions of anger and anxiety on the part of groups threatened by social and demographic change.[11] Other, more specialized studies of conservative groups also suggest reactionary missions. In *Invisible Hands* (2009), Kim Phillips-Fein argues that corporate and small business interests, threatened by the New Deal economic order and the rise of organized labor, funded and promoted the postwar conservative movement.[12] Meanwhile, Nancy MacLean, a historian of women in the Ku Klux Klan, argues that conservatism represented a reaction to changing roles of race, gender, and organized labor.[13]

Scholars interested in historicizing the conservative movement and the Republican Party by examining how conservatives and Republican activists and leaders perceived the world, and their motivations in acting on those perceptions, present a different side of the story. Particularly revealing in this regard is Lisa McGirr's pathbreaking *Suburban Warriors* (2001). In her study of California right-wing women, McGirr seeks to understand them on their own terms, while placing them within the context of the booming defense industry economy of Southern California.[14] This book helped to shape a new historiography of the American Right. By the end of the first decade of the twenty-first century, scholarly studies of the interior workings of the conservative mind, movement, and influence on the Republican Party had become so numerous that they became nearly impossible to keep up with.

Representative of the approach that sought to understand critically conservatism on its own terms is Jennifer Burns's insightful biography of Ayn Rand, *Goddess of the Market* (2009), which explores how the influential conservative thinker and novelist perceived the socialist threat to the free market.[15] Breaking with the liberal orthodoxy, economic historian Brian Domitrovic offers a positive assessment of supply-side economics and its intellectual origins in *Econoclasts* (2009).[16] Other studies offer engaging portraits of Friedrich Hayek, including works by Alan Ebenstein and Bruce Caldwell.[17] John E. Moser gives a perceptive account of libertarian thinker John Flynn in *Right Turn* (2005).[18] Research by Sean P. Cunningham on the ascent of the Republican Party in Texas, which he discusses in Chapter 6, shows how rising politicians such as John Tower won a segment of the Hispanic vote to the Republican Party.[19] Along similar lines, Laura Gifford in *The Center Cannot Hold* (2009) explores how party factionalism helped boost Republicans to power in South Carolina.[20] In a terse critical synthesis of prewar and postwar conservatism, *The Conservative Century* (2009), Gregory L. Schneider historicizes the protean character of American conservatism.[21]

These studies reveal a complex relationship between the Republican Party and the conservative movement. Furthermore, they demonstrate that modern liberalism proved to be a formidable opponent. The modern welfare and administrative state created in the Progressive era at the turn of the twentieth century, expanded during Roosevelt's New Deal and further enlarged by Lyndon B. Johnson's Great Society, was not easily dismantled by conservative Republicans coming to power. The modern American welfare state had become institutionalized. Moreover, as Republican candidates continued to discover in running for and then holding office, American voters tended to support federal programs, especially those that appeared to benefit the middle class—notably Medicare, Social Security, student loans, and federal aid to education.

This placed conservatives within the Republican Party in an ideological dilemma. While proclaiming the principles of small government, individual responsibility, and free enterprise as an alternative to modern liberalism, they recognized that voters generally accepted the essential role that federal programs had come to play in their lives. Electoral realities consequently impelled conservative politicians to voice support for the core elements of the modern welfare state. Those advocating privatization of Social Security, rising medical deductibles for Medicare, or cutting funds for education quickly discovered that such proposals alienated voters and projected ideological extremism. Indeed, Barry Goldwater's staff initially hesitated at having Ronald Reagan on television in support of the Republican presidential candidate in the last days of the 1964 campaign, because they feared that he might endorse Social Security privatization.[22] Although the Arizonan had won the GOP

nomination by running as a conservative, his aides tried to position him more toward the center in the general election campaign, hoping to recover the large numbers of Republican-leaning and independent voters alienated by the "Extremism in
defense of liberty is no vice!" remarks in his acceptance speech at the Republican
national convention in San Francisco.

Whatever the ideological tensions and contradictions conservatives faced in
gaining power, liberalism faced its own problems in holding on to it. Established
in the 1930s, the New Deal coalition—a polyglot alliance of urban voters in the
North, labor unions, ethnic and racial minorities, and southern whites—experienced considerable stress after World War II. Southern Democrats initially accepted the New Deal because it channeled federal funds into their underdeveloped
region and heavily subsidized its agricultural sector, but they became increasingly
concerned at the eventual pro-labor and pro-welfare orientation of Franklin D.
Roosevelt's program. Their particular fear was that the expansion of national government would eventually impinge on states' rights in matters of race. Signaling
the likelihood of growing divisions with liberal elements of the New Deal coalition
in the future, southern Democrats had blocked enactment of a federal antilynch-
ing law, integration of the House cafeteria, and other civil rights measures in the
1930s. Harry Truman's support for civil rights initiatives and the national platform's
endorsement of federal civil rights legislation provoked so-called Dixiecrats to contest the 1948 presidential election under the banner of the States' Rights party. The
rupture was not permanent, but the uneasy postelection truce within Democratic
ranks did not look like it would last. The defection of white southern voters toward the Republican presidential ticket in 1952 and 1956 marked the first signs of
regional realignment, but this would proceed in fits and starts. Dwight D. Eisenhower's 1957 intervention in Little Rock, Arkansas, in support of school integration
slowed the disintegration of the one-party South until the civil rights revolution of
the 1960s put it into fast gear once more.[23]

While racial-issue tensions were being played out in the Democratic Party, profound changes in the postwar economy not only eroded the foundations of the New
Deal coalition but also encouraged a political shift to the right within the Republican Party. Increasingly confronted by the pressures of a globalized marketplace,
American manufacturing enterprise began shifting from mass-production heavy industry to high-tech and defense companies that found better economic conditions
for growth in nonunionized, low-tax, pro-business Sunbelt states. This encouraged
regional migration from the old industrial areas of the North to the Southwest and
eventually the South. One result of this was that California replaced New York as
the nation's most populous state in 1963. Meanwhile, white-collar workers employed in the services and professions, a Republican-leaning constituency, overtook
blue-collar ones, a core Democratic constituency, as a proportion of the work force.
As a corollary, the increasing numbers of college-educated women now had greater

opportunity for careers in the nonindustrial sectors of the economy, but this had a significant impact on traditional family structures and gender roles.

After much testing, the GOP responded to these broad economic, social, and racial changes by becoming the party of low taxes, pro-business policies, strong national defense, preservation of family values (including regulation of social morality), and ultimately affirmation of equality of opportunity in opposition to preferential treatment based on race or gender. As a result, an expanded white middle class drifted toward the GOP, first at the presidential level and eventually at state and local levels.

In this profound economic and social shift, the Republican Right moved from the periphery of American politics to its center. This movement was by no means steady or linear. Instead, there were many twists and turns, and ups and downs, as the conservatives challenged their opponents within the Republican Party—tagged Rockefeller Republicans—and New Deal liberalism. The early conservative movement was built on a popular anticommunism that emerged on the grassroots level and found political voice through diverse Republican leaders, including Senator Robert Taft of Ohio, Senator (and later Vice President) Richard Nixon of California, and Senator Joe McCarthy of Wisconsin. While grassroots anticommunism set the stage for Barry Goldwater's nomination in 1964, his landslide defeat by liberal Democrat Lyndon B. Johnson was a significant setback for the GOP Right. This precipitated a purge of conservatives within the Republican National Committee staff and many state parties. It also set the stage for Richard Nixon's remarkable comeback after his defeats in the 1960 presidential election and the 1962 California gubernatorial election. Despite his early-career association with anticommunism, he now positioned himself between the party's conservative and Rockefeller wings, enabling him to appeal to both groups and to occupy the middle ground of politics apparently vacated by the Democrats in their haste to build the Great Society.[24]

Once in office, Nixon appeared to betray the right wing of the party through his abandonment of the gold standard, his declaration that he was now a Keynesian in economics, the imposition of wage and price controls, his support for new environmental regulation, his pursuit of arms control with the Soviet Union, and his opening of diplomatic relations with the People's Republic of China.[25] As such, the thirty-seventh president appeared to be part of the old liberal consensus that conservatism wanted to do away with. Even his landslide defeat of the ultraliberal George McGovern in the 1972 presidential election was the voters' endorsement of him as an individual, rather than a victory achieved through a partisan strategy, let alone a conservative one. Having done little to boost his party, Nixon left it in shambles when revelations of his Watergate wrongdoings impelled his resignation in 1974 to avoid impeachment. Conservatives found themselves once again a minority within a minority party.[26]

Elevated to the presidency without the benefit of a mandate, Gerald Ford tried to calm the nation by pursuing moderate domestic policies, continuing the Nixon foreign policy of détente, and pardoning his predecessor for any crimes committed while president. The pardon was his most controversial initiative—one that sent his poll numbers plummeting on its announcement, and proved instrumental in his failure to win reelection. In hindsight, however, Ford had faced a nearly insurmountable task as president because of the liberal orientation of Congress, his fractious relationship with the GOP Right, and the slow recovery of the economy from the severe recession of 1974–1975.

In the 1974 midterm elections, the Democrats gained forty-three seats in the House and three in the Senate.[27] The freshman House Democrats—the so-called Watergate Babies—were ideologically to the left of party leadership, and assumed senior positions in the congressional party in years to come. At the same time, moderate-liberal Republicans, such as Paul N. McCloskey Jr. of California, Gilbert Gude of Maryland, and Ronald A. Sarasin of Connecticut, largely survived the electoral wreckage and improved their relative strength in the House GOP. Conversely, the party lost ten seats in the South and fared badly in the Midwest. In the Senate, Barry Goldwater easily won reelection but conservative incumbents Peter H. Dominick and Marlow W. Cook lost in Colorado and Kentucky respectively. In Kansas, Bob Dole barely won reelection with 50.8 percent of the popular vote after an especially nasty campaign on both sides. A last-minute attack slamming his Democratic opponent as an abortion supporter was critical to this victory. Dole's use of this wedge issue signaled the coming shift to the right within the Republican Party, as social issues like abortion, the Equal Rights Amendment, and school prayer gained political salience.

Confronted by a hostile Congress in 1975–1976, Ford also faced a well-entrenched federal bureaucracy anxious to expand the liberal administrative state. His strategy to deal with these difficulties was essentially to hew to the center. To the outrage of conservatives, he appointed Nelson Rockefeller, the longtime symbol of the liberal eastern establishment—the so-called kingmakers within the Republican Party—as vice president. Furthermore, he relied on congressional moderates like Senator Charles Percy of Illinois and Senator Jacob K. Javits of New York for advice on legislative issues. Seemingly oblivious to the stirrings of the Republican Right, Ford calculated that the road to reelection lay in attracting moderate voters. As a consequence, he distanced himself from the conservative wing of his party through his appointments, his equivocation on abortion, his endorsement of the Equal Rights Amendment (which his wife, Betty, vociferously campaigned for), and his pursuit of another arms control agreement with the Soviet Union.

The economy presented Ford with further problems. As an oil crisis, runaway inflation, and a serious recession signaled the end of the long postwar boom, his administration seemingly lacked a vision for restoring prosperity. Its ultimate solution was to treat inflation as the number-one problem, but this entailed considerable pain for little immediate gain. That approach ran counter to the growth economics increasingly advocated by conservative Republican tax-cutters. Dissatisfaction with his foreign and economic policies also made Ford vulnerable to Ronald Reagan's challenge for the 1976 presidential nomination. Ford's narrow defeat by Democrat Jimmy Carter in a presidential election that saw both candidates vie for the center ground offered encouragement that a conservative alternative would do better four years later.

By the time Reagan ran for president in 1980, the Republican Right had gained the upper hand in the party. With the exception of Representative John Anderson of Illinois, who later bolted from the GOP to run as an independent, every serious candidate for the presidential nomination was a conservative. From this point onwards, every Republican presidential nominee over the next three decades—Reagan, George H. W. Bush, Bob Dole, George W. Bush, and John McCain—identified themselves as conservatives (even if the Right sometimes doubted whether Reagan's successors were true believers). And while the Republican Party became the voice of conservatism, the Democrats shifted to the middle ground. Between 1976 and 2008, their only successful presidential candidates, Jimmy Carter and Bill Clinton, were from the South and ran as centrists. Only in 2008, amid the worst economic crisis since the 1930s, were Democrats able to elect an identifiable liberal, Barack Obama.

The success of conservative Republicanism in the last half of the twentieth century is truly remarkable. Later historians will likely compare its ascent with that of the Jacksonian Democrats in the 1820s and 1830s and the Republican Party in the pre–Civil War era. Arguably the GOP Right's rise is explained in large part by three factors: first, its ability to generate new ideas; second, its capacity for organization, especially the establishment of new policy institutions; and third, the emergence of leaders such as Ronald Reagan who were able to articulate conservative principles to the larger electorate.

The invigoration of conservative ideas in the postwar period was initially the circumstantial result of the arrival in America of a group of intellectuals fleeing from fascism or communism in Europe. Among the most significant were Soviet novelist Ayn Rand, Austrian economists Friedrich Hayek and Ludwig von Mises, and German political theorists Eric Voegelin (Austrian-educated) and Leo Strauss.[28] Prior to their arrival on the American scene, conservative intellectual complaint was often polemical and generally without great philosophical depth.[29] The New Humanist movement promoted by Irving Babbitt drew on classical philosophy, but expressed a deep distrust of democracy. The Southern Agrarian school provided a critique of industrial capitalism, but its members were divided over antimodernist prescriptions.[30] The European intellectuals, in combination with a younger generation of conservative authors, transformed American conservatism to give it deep and enduring philosophical roots.

This small band launched a movement to stop the advance of what it deemed the collectivist state initiated by the New Deal. They were joined by anticommunist activists found throughout grassroots America.[31] These two forces, intellectual and popular, laid the foundations for the GOP Right in America.

The reinvigorated Right engaged in a battle of ideas after World War II with proponents of liberalism. This hitherto dominant doctrine, rooted in early twentieth-century European socialism and American Progressive thought, lacked freshness and innovative zeal by comparison. In addition to attacking liberal statism, the intellectual Right adapted its thinking to address new questions posed by the onset of the Cold War: Should it compromise small government principles in support of the global struggle against communism? Did the United States have the right to intervene militarily and politically in the affairs of another country to prevent a perceived communist takeover? Should government restrict the civil liberties of communists in the United States? The theorists' grappling with these issues enhanced the vibrancy of conservatism, boosting its appeal to a younger generation of students and activists no longer satisfied with Freudianism or French existentialism, the intellectual fads of the day. For many of these students and activists, their first introduction to conservative thought came from its two giants, Friedrich Hayek and Ayn Rand.

Hayek gained worldwide fame for his best-selling book *The Road to Serfdom*, first published in Britain in 1944 while he was a professor at the London School of Economics.[32] It advanced the argument that private ownership in a society was essential to freedom and that free-market capitalism was the foundation of democracy. Socialism, in any guise, would lead to a totalitarian state, even if it was brought about by democratic means. Seeing this belief system as inimical to liberty because it devalued individual rights, personal freedom, and economic choice, Hayek warned that it would condemn the individual to become little more than the means for realizing the schemes of a planner. The University of Chicago Press agreed to publish an American edition of *The Road to Serfdom*, which appeared six months after the British edition. It received wide attention in the American press. A *Reader's Digest* version of the book consequently appeared in 1945. After Hayek's opus was picked up by the Book-of-the-Month Club, sales skyrocketed to over 600,000.

In 1948, Hayek accepted a faculty position at the University of Chicago in the Committee for Social Thought program. The post was financed by the William Volker Fund, a foundation created by a Kansas City, Missouri, window shades manufacturer who had become a critic of the New Deal. Starting his new job in 1949, Hayek found many familiar faces in the coterie of free-market economists who had colonized the University of Chicago in the 1930s. Especially important were Henry Simon, Aaron Director, and the young Milton Friedman, who a decade later would publish his influential *Capitalism and Freedom* (1962). Director, who had landed a post at the University of Chicago Law School in 1946, introduced free-market economic analysis to legal studies. In 1958, he and Simon founded the *Journal of Law and Economics*, which changed the course of conservative legal thinking in the United States. Shortly after its establishment, Director brought Ronald Coase, an English economist and future Nobel laureate, to the university to help him coedit the journal. Their scholarly venture directly challenged Keynesian macroeconomics by introducing microeconomic analysis to legal studies. By the 1960s, many law schools had adopted their views, facilitated by the establishment of law and society centers sponsored by the Olin Foundation. Among the new generation of legal scholars influenced by Director and Coase were Robert Bork and Richard Posner.[33]

By the time Hayek left the University of Chicago in 1961 to resume teaching in Europe, *The Road to Serfdom* had become a classic in the canon of conservative thought and had influenced a generation of conservatives. Still, Hayek did not receive universal acceptance on the Right. Criticism came sometimes from unexpected quarters. Ayn Rand, a best-selling author and leading figure on the Right, considered Hayek "dangerous." She deemed him too middle-of-the-road because he accepted that government had the right and even the responsibility to regulate private industry. Rand also rejected Hayek's concept of "maximizing" liberty. For her, liberty was not a relative concept: it either existed or did not exist; similarly, private enterprise was either unfettered or it was not. While government had the responsibility to protect the rule of law and safeguard the nation from outside threats, Rand believed that the state by its very nature was an intrusion on the individual's liberty. Meanwhile, Hayek's rejection of tradition and custom as the basis of liberty was contentious to their conservative defenders.

These tensions between the differing perspectives among members of the Right grew apparent in a fierce and polemical debate that emerged in the 1950s. A group that became known as libertarians, most prominently represented by Rand and Murray Rothbard, clashed with traditionalists such as Russell Kirk and William F. Buckley Jr.[34] Libertarians considered themselves to be classical liberals upholding the Lockean tradition of property rights and contractual government. Traditionalists were Burkean advocates of long-standing custom, the rule of law, social order, and hierarchy as guiding principles of good government.

Cold War issues constituted another major bone of contention between the conservative disputants. Criticism of *National Review*'s hard-line foreign policy position was found throughout the libertarian Right in the 1950s and grew more strident during the Vietnam War in the 1960s.[35] In 1961, Ronald Hamowy, a former student of Hayek, publicly attacked Buckley in the pages of the *New Individualist Review*, a short-lived quarterly journal published at the University of Chicago. He asserted that Buckley and like-minded conservatives were leading "true believers in individual freedom down a disastrous path" and wanted to "turn America into an armed camp."[36] Buckley's rejoinder, which appeared in the same issue, was ironic and pointed. Urging libertarians to "face reality," he contended that freedom existed in the United States because "we have a formidable military machine which keeps the Soviet Union from doing to us what it did to the Hungarians." It was because

of the conservatives' disposition to sacrifice in order to withstand the enemy, Buckley sardonically concluded, that purists such as libertarians "were able to enjoy their
monasticism, and pursue their busy little seminars on whether or not to privatize
the garbage collectors."[37]

Buckley's position illustrated the dilemma facing Cold War conservatives.
While proclaiming small government as essential, they realized that the anticommunist crusade required the further expansion of government through a massive military buildup. Nevertheless, the libertarian-traditionalist debates enriched
conservatism in the 1950s and the 1960s, thereby strengthening the foundations
of the revolt against the state. The intellectual ferment on the Right helped inspire
the political revolt within the Republican Party that brought about the presidential
nomination of Barry Goldwater in 1964. For conservatives, his crushing election
defeat was a reversal in the battle to renew America's ideological soul, but not the
Appomattox that many liberals fondly imagined.[38]

Critical to the next stage of the revolt of the Right was the development of
institutional support for the conservative movement. The failings of the Goldwater
campaign and later on the ideological frailty of the Nixon administration revealed to
conservatives the need for more specific policy proposals to combat the hegemony of
liberalism in the policy arena and to present a case to voters (and Republican Party
leaders) that there were real alternatives to the status quo. Aware of the influence
that liberal think tanks (such as the prestigious Brookings Institution) and the liberal
academy had on policy makers and opinion makers, conservatives wanted to create
other sources for what Washington insiders called "policy innovation." Accordingly,
policy entrepreneurs began to institutionalize conservatism through research insti-
tutes, fellowships, student training programs, and new publications. They brought
to these endeavors a single goal: the erection of countervailing sources of power to
undermine the liberal establishment. The first fruit of this strategy was the expansion
under new leadership during the 1960s of the American Enterprise Institute (initially
established in 1943). This was followed in the next decade by the creation of new
policy research institutions, notably the Heritage Foundation, founded in 1973.[39]

The development of think tanks marked an important shift in the history of
conservatism and would have important implications for the shaping of the Republican Right in subsequent years. These organizations provided not only technical
expertise to the GOP but also personnel to fill key positions in the Reagan administration. Under their influence there arose a kind of "managerial conservatism" that
reoriented conservative thinking on actual governance and more readily accepted
the exertion of federal power acting within the broad principles of conservatism.

Coinciding with the emergence and expansion of conservative think tanks was
the disaffection of a group of liberal intellectuals and academics—the so-called neoconservatives—with the Democratic Party in the late 1960s and 1970s. Neoconservatives were not of one mind about politics or political ideology; many refused to
accept the conservative label, and many remained Democrats. Their ideas exerted a

subtle, if indeterminate, influence on American conservatism. The godfather of this credo was University of Chicago political theorist Leo Strauss. A trenchant critic of modern liberalism, even though it is impossible to derive any specific conservative ideology from his writings, he influenced two generations of neoconservatives, among them Irving Kristol and Kristol's son, William.[40]

Any understanding of neoconservatism must begin with the leftward shift of the Democratic Party that produced George McGovern's presidential nomination in 1972. The South Dakota senator beat back the challenge of a trio of Cold War liberals, Senators Hubert Humphrey of Minnesota, Edmund Muskie of Maine, and Henry Jackson of Washington, whose support came from the urban, blue-collar, labor-union wing of the party. To do so, he reached out to new constituencies, mostly young cultural leftists who were antiwar activists, feminists, and New Left sympathizers.[41]

The introduction of these groups into the Democratic Party moved it to the left. This transformation was made possible under the rule changes approved after the 1968 Democratic convention and implemented four years later in 1972. Proposed by a commission headed by McGovern, these changes aimed to democratize the party by ensuring a wider and proportional representation of ethnic minorities, women, and community activists among convention delegates. Before party regulars realized what had happened, McGovern forces, joined by feminists within the National Organization for Women and the National Women's Political Caucus, had seized control of the selection process and imposed a quota system. They came to the 1972 convention with an agenda that was anti-imperialist, antiracist, pro-feminist, pro-abortion, and pro-homosexual rights. McGovern's landslide defeat did not kill off the new politics any more than Goldwater's had put paid to conservatism. The long-term consequences were problematic for the Democrats, however. The so-called McGovernization of the party saddled it with an image of cultural liberalism that was out of step with the traditional values of the majority of voters.

This brings us to the third factor in explaining the rise of the GOP Right—the emergence of a charismatic conservative leader in the person of Ronald Reagan. Nevertheless, the significance of contingency in his success has to be acknowledged. To this end, it is interesting to speculate what might have happened had Reagan wrested the Republican nomination from Gerald Ford to run for president in 1976. In all likelihood, any Republican candidate would have lost to Jimmy Carter in an election affected by Watergate and recession (though Carter's poor campaign, which so nearly ended in defeat, prevents any certain assertion).[42] Had Reagan rather than Ford been the GOP loser, his political career would have ended. Moreover, the conservative wing of the party would have been set back years. A Reagan defeat combined with the Goldwater defeat in 1964 would have convinced the Republican leadership that conservatives just could not prevail in a general election. Instead, Ford's defeat by Carter paved the way for Reagan to win the GOP nomination in 1980. Contingency was again a factor in his presidential election success over Carter, however. The Democratic incumbent's woeful economic record and his foreign policy failures—notably the loss of ground in the Cold War signified by the Soviet invasion of Afghanistan, and the humiliations of the Iranian hostage crisis—undermined his case for reelection. Carter also led a party that was divided over his economic, foreign, and social policies. In contrast, the GOP was united in identifying him with the failures of liberalism, which legitimized its advocacy of a conservative alternative.[43]

Reagan's victory demonstrated how far the Republican Right had traveled since 1964 but it was not yet at the journey's end of complete triumph. Conservative Republican success in gaining control of the White House was not replicated in control of both houses of Congress during the 1980s. Control of the Senate, won in 1980, was lost in 1986 in line with the habitual anti-incumbent pattern in midterm elections in the sixth year of a presidency. Meanwhile, the recession of the early Reagan years had killed off GOP hopes of capturing the House of Representatives in 1982.

There was also dissension on the Right over the imbalance between economic and social conservatism in the fortieth president's governing agenda. In winning election, Reagan seized on sociomoral issues to mobilize support from white southern evangelicals in particular, but downplayed these in office to focus on economic and foreign policy. This led to criticism from both the Religious Right and liberals that he had exploited issues such as abortion and school prayer to win office in order to pursue his real agenda of tax reform and deregulation. In reality, Reagan never hid his prioritization of economic policy during the 1980 campaign, but discontent with his social agenda record indicated the difficulties of attaining the diverse goals of conservatism.[44]

There were also political tensions between conservative leaders that were manifested in the peculiar relationship between Barry Goldwater and Ronald Reagan.[45] When Reagan ran for California governor in 1966, he had looked toward the former presidential candidate as a mentor and often wrote him while in office, but his 1976 challenge for the Republican presidential nomination caused a rift. Tensions between them heightened when Reagan began criticizing Ford on the Panama Canal issue in the North Carolina primary. Negotiations to turn the canal back to Panama had begun in Richard Nixon's administration and continued in the Ford administration. The guiding hand in these negotiations belonged to Secretary of State Henry Kissinger, a man generally despised by the Right.[46] Worried that Reagan's statements could "needlessly lead this country into open conflict," Goldwater openly criticized his position on Panama to the press. In his own mind, his remarks were intended to help his onetime ally. As he explained in a lengthy letter to actor John Wayne, Reagan "was traveling the same road I traveled in 1964 when the press picked up remarks of mine, not nearly as strong as Ron's, and tied me to the cross of war monger." An irate Reagan replied to Goldwater, "Barry, I did not create the Canal issue—the people did."

The Arizonan's endorsement of Ford provoked a complete break between the two erstwhile friends. Reagan did not correspond with him again for fifteen months. When he finally did so, Goldwater responded, "It was a pleasure hearing from you and I hope someday the hatchet, if there is a hatchet, can be buried because it seems to me a strange world, having you a valued friend . . . and me feeling hesitancy in writing you." Reagan replied: "Maybe both of us thought there was a hatchet, [and] . . . the other one was swinging it. I will admit I was hurt and as a result, I suppose, felt the same hesitancy you did about writing. Maybe the press . . . provided the opportunity for us to find out there really needn't be any hatchet at all." Later, Goldwater wrote Nancy Reagan that he had made a mistake by endorsing Ford in 1976, and he would not make the same mistake twice. He endorsed Reagan in 1980 and continued to support him during Reagan's two terms in office.[47]

The story of the GOP Right's rise to ascendancy is one of ideological contradiction, political opportunism, and electoral triumph, but equally of deeply held beliefs about the nature of the individual and the good society. It also owes something to political contingency, particularly the travails of liberalism and the problems of the Democratic Party. This is not a cautionary tale of how principle was betrayed by practice or a celebration of light over darkness. Instead, it is about how conservative beliefs were translated into political power over time and how through a process of ideological and political compromise the GOP Right made history in its ascent to power.

NOTES

1. George Wolfskill and James Hudson, *All but the People: Franklin D. Roosevelt and His Critics, 1933–1940* (New York: Macmillan, 1969); and Robert M. Collins, *The Business Response to Keynes, 1929–1964* (New York: Columbia University Press, 1981), 23–52. Paradoxically, the most thorough and intellectually formed critique of the New Deal was found not on the Right but on the Left. In his 1937 book, *The Good Society*, columnist Walter Lippmann accused Roosevelt's program of betraying the principles of the Founding Fathers and their inherent distrust of centralized government. For insightful historical analysis of this study, see Gary Dean Best, "Introduction to the Transaction Edition," in Walter Lippmann, *The Good Society* (New Brunswick, NJ: Transaction, 2005), xxiii–xlvii. For an important discussion of Lippmann, see Ted V. McAllister, *Revolt against Modernity: Leo Strauss, Eric Voegelin, and the Search for a Postliberal Order* (Lawrence: University Press of Kansas, 1996).

2. June Melby Benowitz, *Days of Discontent: American Women and Right-Wing Politics, 1933–1945* (DeKalb: Northern Illinois University Press, 2002); and Glen Jeansonne, *Women of the Far Right: The Mother's Movement and World War II* (Chicago: University of Chicago Press, 1996). See also Justus D. Doenecke, *Storm on the Horizon: The Challenge to American Intervention, 1939–1941* (Lanham, MD: Rowman and Littlefield, 2000); Wayne S. Cole, *America First: The Battle against American Intervention, 1940–41* (Madison: University of Wisconsin Press, 1953); Wayne S. Cole, *Charles A. Lindbergh and the Battle against Intervention in World War II* (New York: Harcourt Brace Jovanovich, 1974); Ronald Radosh, *Prophets on the Right: Profiles of Conservative Critics*

of American Globalism (New York: Simon and Schuster, 1975); Leo P. Ribuffo, *The Old Christian Right: The Protestant Far Right from the Great Depression to the Cold War* (Philadelphia: Temple University Press, 1983); and Justin Raimondo, *Reclaiming the American Right: The Lost Legacy of the Conservative Movement*, 2nd ed. (Wilmington, DE: Intercollegiate Studies Institute, 2008).

3. For insight into the Far Right and the conspiratorial mind-set that prevailed within this small segment of extremists, see George Michael, *Willis Carto and the American Far Right* (Gainesville: University Press of Florida, 2008).

4. See Richard Hofstadter, *The Paranoid Style in American Politics, and Other Essays* (New York: Knopf, 1965); and his *Anti-Intellectualism in American Life* (New York: Knopf, 1963).

5. Arnold Forster and Benjamin R. Epstein, *Danger on the Right: The Attitudes, Personnel, and Influence of the Radical Right and Extreme Conservatives* (New York: Random House, 1964), xvii.

6. Harry Overstreet and Bonaro Overstreet, *The Strange Tactics of Extremism* (New York: Norton, 1964); Murray Havens, *The Challenges of Democracy: Consensus and Extremism in American Politics* (Austin: University of Texas Press, 1965); Irwin Suall, *The American Ultras: The Extreme Right and the Military Industrial Complex* (New York: New America, 1962); Brook Walker, *The Christian Fright Peddlers* (Garden City, NY: Doubleday, 1962); and Richard Dudman, *Men of the Far Right* (New York: Pyramid Books, 1963). For excellent discussion of this literature, see Richard Gid Powers, *Not without Honor: The History of American Anticommunism* (New York: Free Press, 1995), 273–318.

7. Dan T. Carter, *The Politics of Rage: George Wallace, the Origins of the New Conservatism, and the Transformation of American Politics* (New York: Simon and Schuster, 1995). Carter extended this analysis further in *From George Wallace to Newt Gingrich: Race in the Conservative Counterrevolution, 1963–1994* (Baton Rouge: Louisiana State University Press, 1996).

8. Kevin M. Kruse, *White Flight: Atlanta and the Making of Modern Conservatism* (Princeton, NJ: Princeton University Press, 2007); Matthew D. Lassiter, *The Silent Majority: Suburban Politics in the Sunbelt South* (Princeton, NJ: Princeton University Press, 2007); and Joseph Crespino, *In Search of Another Country: Mississippi and the Conservative Counterrevolution* (Princeton, NJ: Princeton University Press, 2009).

9. Byron E. Shafer and Richard Johnston, *The End of Southern Exceptionalism: Class, Race, and Partisan Change in the Postwar South* (Cambridge, MA: Harvard University Press, 2006).

10. For anti-ERA backlash, see Mary Frances Berry, *Why ERA Failed: Politics, Women's Rights, and Amending the Constitution* (Bloomington: Indiana University Press, 1986); on antiabortion women, see Michele McKeegan, *Abortion Politics: Mutiny in the Ranks of the Right* (New York: Free Press, 1992), and Tanya Melich, *The Republican War against Women: An Insider's Report from Behind the Lines* (New York: Bantam, 1996); and on evangelical women see, for example, Michael D'Antonio, *Fall from Grace: The Failed Crusade of the Christian Right* (New York: Farrar, Straus and Giroux, 1989).

11. David H. Bennett, *The Party of Fear: From Nativist Movements to the New Right in American History* (Chapel Hill: University of North Carolina Press, 1988).

12. Kim Phillips-Fein, *Invisible Hands: The Making of the Conservative Movement from the New Deal to Reagan* (New York: Norton, 2009).

13. Donald Critchlow and Nancy MacLean, *Debating the Conservative Movement, 1945 to the Present* (Lanham, MD: Rowman and Littlefield, 2009).

14. Lisa McGirr, *Suburban Warriors: The Origins of the New American Right* (Princeton, NJ: Princeton University Press, 2001).

15. Jennifer Burns, *Goddess of the Market: Ayn Rand and the American Right* (New York: Oxford University Press, 2009).

16. Brian Domitrovic, *Econoclasts: The Rebels Who Sparked the Supply-Side Revolution and Restored American Prosperity* (Wilmington, DE: Intercollegiate Studies Institute, 2009).

17. Alan Ebenstein, *Friedrich Hayek: A Biography* (New York: Palgrave, 2001); and Bruce Caldwell, *Hayek's Challenge: An Intellectual Biography of F. A. Hayek* (Chicago: University of Chicago Press, 2004).

18. John E. Moser, *Right Turn: John T. Flynn and the Transformation of American Liberalism* (New York: New York University Press, 2005).

19. See also Sean P. Cunningham, *Cowboy Conservatism: Texas and the Rise of the Modern Right* (Lexington: University Press of Kentucky, 2010).

20. Laura Jane Gifford, *The Center Cannot Hold: The 1960 Presidential Election and the Rise of Modern Conservatism* (DeKalb: Northern Illinois University Press, 2009).

21. Gregory L. Schneider, *The Conservative Century: From Reaction to Revolution* (Lanham, MD: Rowman and Littlefield, 2009).

22. Jonathan M. Schoenwald, *A Time for Choosing: The Rise of Modern Conservatism* (New York: Oxford University Press, 2001).

23. Earl Black and Merle Black, *The Rise of Southern Republicans* (Cambridge, MA: Harvard University Press, 2003); and Joseph Aistrup, *The Southern Strategy Revisited: Republican Top-Down Advance in the South* (Lexington: University Press of Kentucky, 1995).

24. Great insight into Nixon the politician is found in Irvin Gellman, *The Contender: Richard Nixon, The Congressional Years, 1946–1952* (New York: Free Press, 1999).

25. Conservative discontent with Nixon is found in William F. Buckley Jr., "Is Nixon One of Us?," in *Inveighing We Will Go* (New York: Putnam, 1972).

26. The best account of the political fallout of Watergate is found in Michael Barone, *Our Country: The Shaping of America from Roosevelt to Reagan* (New York: Free Press, 1990). See also Joan Hoff, *Nixon Reconsidered* (New York: Basic Books, 1994); Stanley Kutler, *The Wars of Watergate: The Last Crisis of Richard Nixon* (New York: Norton, 1990); and Herbert S. Parmet, *Richard Nixon and His America* (Boston: Little, Brown, 1990). Nixon's campaign strategy is discussed in Robert Mason, *Richard Nixon and the Quest for a New Majority* (Chapel Hill: University of North Carolina Press, 2004). For a critical assessment of Nixon's relations with China, see James Mann, *About Face: A History of America's Curious Relationship with China from Nixon to Clinton* (New York: Knopf, 1999).

27. "Politics: The 1974 Elections," *Congressional Quarterly* 30 (1974): 839–64; Barone, *Our Country*, 530–41.

28. The best account of conservative intellectuals remains George H. Nash, *The Conservative Intellectual Movement in America since 1945* (New York: Basic Books, 1976; thirtieth anniversary edition, Wilmington, DE: Intercollegiate Studies Institute, 2006).

29. For the prewar Right, see Schneider, *Conservative Century*; and Moser, *Right Turn*.

30. J. David Hoeveler Jr., *The New Humanism: A Critique of Modern America, 1900–1940* (Charlottesville: University Press of Virginia, 1977), and Irving Babbitt, *Democracy and Leadership* (1924; Indianapolis: Liberty Fund, 1979). For the Agrarian school, see Twelve Southerners, *I'll Take My Stand: The South and the Agrarian Tradition* (New

York: Harper, 1930), and Alexander Karanikas, *Tillers of a Myth: The Southern Agrarians as Social and Literary Critics* (Madison: University of Wisconsin Press, 1966). Also of interest are William Henry Chamberlain, *The Confessions of an Individualist* (New York: Macmillan, 1940), and Robert Crunder, *The Mind and Art of Albert Jay Nock* (Chicago: University of Chicago Press, 1964).

31. For the issue of communism in this period, see Harvey Klehr and John Earl Haynes, *The Secret World of American Communism* (New Haven, CT: Yale University Press, 1995); David Caute, *The Great Fear: The Anti-Communist Purge under Truman and Eisenhower* (New York: Simon and Schuster, 1978); and Powers, *Not without Honor*.

32. The influence of Hayek's book is discussed in Paul Gottfried and Thomas Fleming, *The Conservative Movement* (Boston: Twayne, 1988); Ebenstein, *Friedrich Hayek*, especially 115–46; and Caldwell, *Hayek's Challenge*. For libertarian criticism of Hayek, see Brian Doherty, *Radicals for Capitalism: A Freewheeling History of the Modern American Libertarian Movement* (New York: PublicAffairs, 2007).

33. Samuel Francis, *Beautiful Losers: Essays on the Failure of American Conservatism* (Columbia: University of Missouri Press, 1993). Chicago at this time is captured in McAllister, *Revolt against Modernity*.

34. There is a huge and growing literature on William F. Buckley Jr. and *National Review*. A reading of this literature should begin with John B. Judis, *William F. Buckley, Jr.: Patron Saint of the Conservatives* (New York: Simon and Schuster, 1988); Patrick Allitt, *Catholic Intellectuals and Conservative Politics in America, 1950–1985* (Ithaca, NY: Cornell University Press, 1993); Daniel Kelly, *James Burnham and the Struggle for the World: A Life* (Wilmington, DE: Intercollegiate Studies Institute, 2002); Kevin J. Smant, *Principles and Heresies: Frank S. Meyer and the Shaping of the American Conservative Movement* (Wilmington, DE: Intercollegiate Studies Institute, 2002); and Jeffrey Hart, *The Making of the Conservative Mind: "National Review" and Its Times* (Wilmington, DE: Intercollegiate Studies Institute, 2005).

35. Attempts to fuse the libertarian and traditionalist positions are discussed in Paul Gottfried, *The Search for Historical Meaning: Hegel and the Postwar American Right* (DeKalb: Northern Illinois University Press, 1986).

36. Ronald Hamowy, "*National Review*: Criticism," *New Individualist Review*, November 1961, 3–7.

37. William F. Buckley Jr., "Three Drafts of an Answer to Mr. Hamoway," *New Individualist Review*, November 1961, 7–10. For debates over liberty within *National Review*, see Frank S. Meyer, "Collectivism Rebaptized," *Freeman*, July 1955, 559–62; Russell Kirk, "Mills' 'On Liberty' Reconsidered," *National Review*, January 25, 1956, 23–24; and Frank S. Meyer, "In Defense of John Stuart Mill," *National Review*, March 28, 1956, 23–24.

38. Theodore White, *The Making of the President—1964* (New York: Atheneum, 1965); Robert Alan Goldberg, *Barry Goldwater* (New Haven, CT: Yale University Press, 1995); and Lee Edwards, *Goldwater: The Man Who Made a Revolution* (Washington, DC: Regnery, 1995). Also valuable, though it needs to be read cautiously, is Rick Perlstein, *Before the Storm: Barry Goldwater and the Unmaking of the American Consensus* (New York: Hill and Wang, 2001).

39. The discussion of think tanks in this chapter relies heavily on Donald T. Critchlow, *The Conservative Ascendancy: How the GOP Made Political History* (Cambridge, MA: Harvard University Press, 2007), 106–27. See also James Allen Smith, *The Idea Brokers: Think Tanks and the Rise of the New Policy Elite* (New York: Free Press, 1991), and Lee

Edwards, *The Power of Ideas: The Heritage Foundation at 25 Years* (Ottawa, IL: Jameson Books, 1997).

40. There is an extensive literature on Strauss and the neoconservatives. In addition to their own writings, see Alexander Bloom, *Prodigal Sons: The New York Intellectuals and Their World* (New York: Oxford University Press, 1986); Gary Dorrien, *The Neoconservative Mind: Politics, Culture, and the War of Ideology* (Philadelphia: Temple University Press, 1993); Mark Gerson, *The Neoconservative Vision: From the Cold War to the Culture Wars* (Lanham, MD: Madison Books, 1996); John P. East, *The American Conservative Movement: The Philosophical Founders* (Washington, DC: Regnery, 1987); Peter Steinfels, *The Neoconservatives: The Men Who Are Changing America's Politics* (New York: Simon and Schuster, 1979); and John Ehrman, *The Rise of Neoconservatism: Intellectuals and Foreign Affairs, 1946–1994* (New Haven, CT: Yale University Press, 1995). Justin Vaïsse, *Neo-Conservatism: The Biography of a Movement* (Cambridge, MA: Belknap Press, 2010), translated by Arthur Goldhammer, imparts many insights into the neoconservative response to American politics, culture, and foreign policy.

41. Byron E. Shafer, *Quiet Revolution: The Struggle for the Democratic Party and the Shaping of Post-Reform Politics* (New York: Russell Sage Foundation, 1983); and Bruce Miroff, *The Liberal Moment: The McGovern Insurgency and the Identity Crisis of the Democratic Party* (Lawrence: University Press of Kansas, 2007).

42. For an account of Carter's failure of leadership, see Laura Kalman, *Right Star Rising: A New Politics, 1974–1980* (New York: Norton, 2010).

43. The literature on Ronald Reagan and his presidency has become immense. A good starting point can be found in Steven F. Hayward, *The Age of Reagan: The Fall of the Old Liberal Order, 1964–1980* (Roseville, CA: Forum, 2001), and *The Age of Reagan: The Conservative Counterrevolution, 1980–1989* (New York: Crown Forum, 2009); and Robert M. Collins, *Transforming America: Politics and Culture in the Reagan Years* (New York: Columbia University Press, 2007). The 1976 election is discussed by Craig Shirley in *Reagan's Revolution: The Untold Story of the Campaign That Started It All* (Nashville: Nelson, 2005); Elizabeth Drew, *American Journal: The Events of 1976* (New York: Vintage, 1977); and Jules Witcover, *Marathon: The Pursuit of the Presidency* (New York: Viking, 1977).

44. Mark A. Smith, *The Right Talk: How Conservatives Transformed the Great Society into the Economic Society* (Princeton, NJ: Princeton University Press, 2007).

45. Relations between conservative leaders, notably those of Reagan with Goldwater and Nixon, are a fruitful but undeveloped area of research on the Republican Right.

46. Adam Clymer, *Drawing the Line at the Big Ditch: The Panama Canal Treaties and the Rise of the Right* (Lawrence: University Press of Kansas, 2008).

47. Barry Goldwater, memorandum, May 4, 1976; Goldwater to John Wayne, May 12, 1976; Goldwater to Nancy and Ronald Reagan, May 13, 1976; Ronald Reagan to Goldwater, June 3, 1976; Goldwater to Ronald Reagan, December 15, 1977; Ronald Reagan to Goldwater December 30, 1977; Ronald Reagan to Goldwater, February 3, 1978; and Goldwater to Nancy Reagan, August 21, 1978; all in Alpha Correspondence File, Barry Goldwater Papers, Arizona Historical Foundation, Arizona State University, Tempe, AZ.

CHAPTER 2

Race, Region, and the Shadow of the New Deal

Timothy N. Thurber

American politics in the early twenty-first century has become a mirror image of what it was a century ago. One reversal relates to region. The South, once overwhelmingly Democratic, constitutes the most loyal base of the Republican Party. During the presidency of George W. Bush, the conservative, southern, evangelical Christian wing of the GOP set the rhetorical tone and policy directions in the executive and legislative branches. Moderate northern Republicans felt marginalized and feared for the future of the GOP in their states. A second reversal relates to race. African Americans, who supported the Republicans for nearly seventy years following the Civil War, now strongly favor the Democratic Party. Richard Nixon won approximately 32 percent of the African American vote in 1960, and since then no Republican presidential candidate has garnered more than 15 percent. Few GOP candidates for Congress, or at the state and local level, have done much better.[1]

Scholarly and popular conventional wisdom about the relationship of the Republican Party to the South and to race often focuses on Senator Barry Goldwater of Arizona, the party's 1964 presidential nominee. Goldwater suffered a tremendous loss, but he supposedly charted a new, more conservative course for the Republicans on race through his vote against the 1964 Civil Rights Act and his focus on winning the support of white southerners—and, to a lesser extent, that of working-class whites in the North, who likewise harbored racial hostility toward African Americans. The "party of Lincoln" allegedly disappeared that year and has not been seen since; according to some observers, Republicans discovered in the mid-1960s that they could exploit a white backlash over race to win elections and have been using that formula ever since. In this characterization, 1964 marks a clean break between the party that existed before Goldwater and the party that developed afterward.[2]

While there is much in this analysis that is persuasive, the Republican Party's struggle to build an electoral majority, one that is rooted chiefly in the white South and largely bypasses African Americans, is marked by more contingency and a deeper history than the conventional wisdom suggests. Though the Goldwater campaign was indeed significant, the influence of 1964 should not be overstated. Instead, we must broaden our focus to understand more fully the dynamics of the politics of race, and the development of the Republican Party, in the post–World War II era. Concepts such as "white backlash" and a focus on the South did not suddenly emerge in the 1960s in response to race riots in the North or struggles for voting rights and equal access to public accommodations and schooling in the South. Race and the role of the South stood at the center of a twenty-five-year debate within the GOP over just what type of party it wanted to be. From the 1940s through the early 1970s, Republicans regularly wrestled over how they should deal with the South and civil rights issues. Battles raged between northern liberals such as Senator Jacob K. Javits of New York, who favored government taking a relatively active role in addressing racial inequality, and conservatives such as Goldwater, who wanted a more limited role for government in this area. These were policy debates over the role of the state in social, economic, and political affairs, but they were also sharp disagreements over electoral strategy. Both sides offered prescriptions for how to rebuild the Republican Party into a political force in the aftermath of the New Deal and the emergence of race as a national issue. In addition, assumptions about the GOP as the party of Lincoln prior to 1964 collapse under close scrutiny. Aside from a few liberals, Republicans in the pre-1964 period were largely indifferent or opposed to most civil rights legislation. The post-Goldwater period is, on the other hand, more ambiguous regarding civil rights, at least through the early 1970s. Nixon, as several scholars have recently shown, took a more liberal approach to civil rights policy in some respects than contemporary critics acknowledged.

To set the context for debates within the GOP during the post–World War II period, we need to look back to an earlier era. From 1896 to 1928, the Republicans won six presidential elections; the Democrats won two. From 1895 to 1933, the Republicans controlled the Senate for all but six years. The GOP enjoyed a majority in the House of Representatives for all but eight of those years. The two parties' fortunes reversed suddenly and dramatically starting in the 1930s. Democrats won a majority of presidential elections over the next thirty years and controlled Congress for most of that time. Between 1933 and 1995, the Republicans controlled the House of Representatives for just four years; they constituted a majority in the Senate for only four years between 1933 and 1981. Dwight D. Eisenhower appeared to signal a rebirth of the Republican Party as he swept to an easy victory in 1952 and then again in 1956, but the beloved war hero proved more popular than his party as the GOP experienced relatively few gains beneath the presidential level. Political analyst Samuel Lubell rightly observed that the Democrats were the "sun" in America's political solar system, whereas the Republicans were the peripheral "moon."[3]

The GOP's time in the political wilderness overlapped with the emergence of a new political landscape regarding race and region. The New Deal and World War II sparked a surge of African American activism. Membership in the National

Association for the Advancement of Colored People (NAACP) soared, and leaders such as A. Philip Randolph urged direct action protests. In Congress, legislation to establish a permanent Fair Employment Practices Commission (FEPC) with enforcement powers (also known as a compulsory FEPC because it would provide the federal government with authority to order companies to change employment practices) constituted the top priority of civil rights groups. Activists sought other legislative remedies, and reforms through the courts, related to education, voting rights, housing, and personal safety. Politically, the African American vote, which had crossed over to the Democrats starting in 1936, appeared to grow more significant as the black population of northern industrial states such as New York, Michigan, and Illinois expanded enormously. Certainly, civil rights groups wanted both parties to think so; they routinely invoked the "balance of power" argument when lobbying for reforms. According to this theory, African Americans constituted a sufficient proportion of the voters in electoral-rich northern and western states to determine which party captured the White House and ruled Congress. Both parties, black leaders contended, should therefore aggressively seek the black vote through outreach and policy proposals. The 1930s and 1940s also witnessed the growing disaffection of many white southerners toward the Democratic Party. The party of their forebears, many now complained, had become too beholden to labor unions, African Americans, and urban immigrants. Even so, white southerners continued to support their Democratic incumbents, and Roosevelt never lost a southern state in any of his four campaigns. Substantial fissures existed among members of the New Deal coalition, but those tensions had not reached the point of rupture. Republicans thus swam in a fluid political environment; any route to victory required making decisions about the role of the South and African Americans. With answers far from clear, many voices within the party weighed in with prescriptions.[4]

Debate over race and region had existed prior to the New Deal and World War II, but it intensified in 1948. Both parties appeared eager to pursue African American votes in the North. President Harry Truman had angered southern Democrats with his support for civil rights legislation; some went so far as to leave the party to support the States' Rights Party (Dixiecrat) candidate, Strom Thurmond, the governor of South Carolina. The nomination of Governor Thomas E. Dewey of New York instead of Senator Robert Taft of Ohio constituted a triumph for the GOP's more racially liberal wing. Black Republicans had strongly objected to the conservative Taft, largely because of his opposition to an FEPC with enforcement powers. The Ohioan supported some civil rights reforms but believed that employment discrimination would best be overcome through education and persuasion rather than federal law. Conservatives such as Taft saw opposition to an FEPC with enforcement authority as part of a broader struggle over the right of management to control labor policies. Employers, they feared, had been losing ground since the establishment of the National Labor Relations Board and other New Deal initiatives.[5]

Though Dewey had angered civil rights groups with his response to several issues, including equal employment opportunity, voting rights in the South, and segregation in the National Guard, he had a stronger record on race than any other governor of his era. During World War II, he had spoken of the need to combat racial discrimination, and while running for governor in 1942 he had told a Harlem crowd that if elected he would end discriminatory pay rates by the state government. Once in office, he named several African Americans to prominent posts. More important, in the spring of 1945 he had backed New York's compulsory FEPC law, the first such statute in the nation and, he proclaimed, "one of the great social advances of our time." Dewey had some private reservations about it, and some civil rights leaders soon questioned the committee's effectiveness and wondered whether the governor had appointed officials who were too timid in their enforcement efforts. Nevertheless, his support for the bill marked him as racially progressive. Dewey had taken other pro–civil rights steps as well. That fall, he had condemned the banning of an African American singer from a Washington, DC, concert hall and declared that the American Revolution had been "fought for the democratic principle that all men are created equal." Two months prior to the Republican convention, he had signed a law banning discrimination in higher education. Black Republicans felt the governor had a deeper reservoir of support among African Americans than any GOP nominee in decades. Heading into November, Dewey was confident he would be the next president. The governor was wrong. There were several factors behind Truman's surprise victory, but civil rights leaders contended that the black vote in the North was crucial. Democrats, moreover, regained control of both houses of Congress. Though Franklin D. Roosevelt had been dead for three years, the Democratic juggernaut rolled right along.[6]

Stunned, Republicans commenced a vigorous debate over their future. For some, the answer lay partly in bringing African Americans back to the party of Lincoln. According to this view, Dewey and other Republicans had failed to mount an aggressive effort to win black votes. Robert R. Church Jr., a prominent black Republican from Memphis, pointed out in August 1949 that the party had taken no action on civil rights when it had controlled Congress in 1947 and 1948 and had allied with southern Democrats earlier that year in battles over the filibuster rule in the Senate, compulsory FEPC, and other civil rights legislation. (Southern Democrats had long used the filibuster, or the threat of a filibuster, to block civil rights measures.) Church also chastised party leaders at the Republican National Committee (RNC) for ignoring a 1938 recommendation from Ralph Bunche, a prominent African American intellectual and civil rights activist, that more blacks be appointed to leadership positions in the party. A year later, Senators Irving Ives of New York, H. Alexander Smith of New Jersey, and Wayne Morse of Oregon trumpeted the 1949 election of Alfred Driscoll, a racial progressive, as governor of New Jersey as evidence that the party needed to be more liberal on civil rights to win in the North. Like Church, these senators urged fellow Republicans to get behind a compulsory FEPC bill and support reform of the filibuster rule.[7]

Few Republicans were eager to follow such a strategy, however. Most either ignored or downplayed civil rights matters both in politics and policy. In May 1949, the RNC identified twelve policy objectives that it believed would propel the GOP to victory in the 1950 and 1952 elections. Civil rights did not make the list. Three months later, the head of the RNC Subcommittee on Civil Rights indicated to party leaders that his group had not determined a stand on racial issues because members had not been able to meet. Moreover, he asserted that he and others were waiting for congressional action on this "difficult" problem. In February 1950, House Republicans released a statement of principles that contained a promise to "continue to sponsor and support legislation to protect the rights of minorities." Civil rights leaders, as well as liberal Republicans such as Ives and Javits, found this far too tepid.[8]

Other Republicans advocated a far different approach. They believed Dewey *had* made a strong bid for black votes and failed through no fault of his own. Michigan congressman Clare Hoffman told fellow Republicans in the summer of 1949 that they were "barking up the wrong tree" if they thought that supporting civil rights would mean more black votes for the GOP. The African American vote had been irrevocably lost, he claimed. Hoffman's argument echoed the theme of the "bought vote," a derisive term employed by some Republicans since the 1930s to argue that the New Deal had rallied voters, including African Americans, to the Democrats through federal spending. The 1950 election seemed to provide further support for Hoffman's view, for no part of the New Deal coalition remained more loyal to the Democrats than African Americans. Likewise, though Dewey had not done particularly well in the South in 1948, many Republicans were not giving up on the region. RNC chair Guy Gabrielson lamented at an RNC meeting a month after the election that the party entered presidential contests with a big deficit by conceding the South to the Democrats. He added that such a deficit "might not have been too serious at the time when we had solid Republican states north of the Mason-Dixon line, but some of those states that were at one time very solidly Republican are now becoming marginal areas, and if we are going to build towards a stronger Republican Party that can carry a national election we must do some effective and constructive work south of the Mason-Dixon line." For Gabrielson, the success of FDR and other Democrats in traditionally Republican industrial states such as Pennsylvania, Ohio, and Michigan had altered the political map; looking to the South was a defensive move driven by a search for a path to victory. Republicans, he contended, would not likely do well in the South in 1952, but immediate and sustained efforts might yield gains in 1956. Other RNC members echoed Gabrielson's analysis. "There are certain definite changes in our political horizons that an alert party must consider," one declared. At the same meeting, the RNC passed a resolution that a seven-member committee be named to boost the party's fortunes in Dixie. A month later, one member of the committee presciently forecast that the party might succeed in the 1952 election in Virginia, Tennessee, North Carolina, and Florida, but he also stressed that the party needed to organize across the entire region. Building a viable party in Dixie might take two decades or more, he indicated, but Republicans had to start immediately.[9]

Even some civil rights proponents in the Republican Party conceded that the GOP needed to look to the South to offset Democratic gains elsewhere. A July 1951 exchange between Representative Clifford Case of New Jersey and Senator Karl Mundt of South Dakota revealed the complexity of debate surrounding the future role of the South in the GOP. On the one hand, the conservative Mundt noted that the Democrats started with a huge advantage given their strength in the South. "It is mighty difficult to win a horse race with a three-legged horse," he observed. But even some of the three legs on the GOP horse were wobbly. Mundt highlighted recent Republican setbacks in the Northeast and Midwest. The GOP, he thus argued, would not be able to control Congress by conceding the South to the Democrats. He claimed that a new strategy was needed because the GOP had tried but failed to win African American support in the North. Though he did not expressly discuss making overt racial appeals to southern whites, he referred to the South as "the natural and logical source of new strength for the Republican Party" and urged the GOP to emphasize the theme of opposition to centralized authority. (Later that summer, Mundt proposed allowing southern Democrats to name the 1952 Republican vice presidential candidate and allowing them to retain their control of congressional committees should they pledge their support to the Republicans and the GOP win back control of Congress.) For Mundt, the chief political challenge of the day was to bring a greater degree of formality to the congressional alliance between southern Democrats and Republicans that had arisen in opposition to the New Deal in the late 1930s.[10]

Case, a civil rights supporter, offered both a practical and a philosophical rebuttal. He interpreted Mundt's argument as a call to cultivate support among segregationist whites alarmed over the racial liberalism of the New Deal and Truman administration. Case predicted that conservative, segregationist Democrats would continue to view Republicans with suspicion, just as they had since the Civil War and Reconstruction, and to resist GOP overtures for a more concrete alliance. Even if such a marriage could be arranged, aligning with these forces would be a "betrayal of our heritage," he insisted. But Case did not think that Republicans should ignore the South altogether. Instead, he believed Mundt and his fellow conservatives mistakenly saw southern politics as a zero-sum game. Predicting that segregation's days were numbered, Case urged instead that the GOP pursue what he saw as nascent progressives in agriculture, labor, and industry. These individuals favored the social and economic modernization of the region, and thus indicated that a more liberal South was emerging. The party's future in Dixie, then, lay in bringing in new voters rather than seeking crossovers from the ranks of traditional Democrats. Case's thinking reflected the common belief among many political elites and intellectuals that the South was fundamentally outside the mainstream of the nation's development but could be brought into step with other regions once it developed a vigorous two-party system.[11]

Case offered a second critique of Mundt's recommendations. Joining with segregationists in Dixie, he argued, would only worsen the GOP's situation in the North. Dewey's margins of victory in the large industrial states of New York, Michigan, and Pennsylvania in 1948 were dangerously thin, Case pointed out. Losing further ground among both liberal whites and blacks in those electoral vote–rich states by hewing to a more conservative stand on civil rights (as well as several other issues) to gain the relatively sparsely populated South thus would be a foolish trade.[12]

The triumph of Dwight D. Eisenhower in 1952 constituted a setback for Case and the liberals. Eisenhower won the large industrial states of the North, and Republicans narrowly took control of both houses of Congress, without substantial black support. The "balance of power" argument appeared to be a paper tiger. Eisenhower also cracked the Democratic South by winning four states in 1952 and five in 1956; in both elections, he came close to victory in several others. His opposition to a compulsory FEPC and emphasis on reform through education rather than federal law sat well with white southerners, and there were some areas where Eisenhower simply benefited from white hostility toward the Democrats' civil rights policies. However, as political scientists Byron Shafer and Richard Johnston have contended, class, not race, was the primary force behind the election results in the South. The former general ran best among more socioeconomically privileged whites in urban and suburban areas, where economic development since the New Deal had been greatest, and where relatively few African Americans resided. An emerging class of business leaders (some of whom were northern transplants) was starting to vote like their northern counterparts. Southern white protest against the Democrats' civil rights policies in 1948 was not the start of a linear shift of segregationist whites to the GOP, for many areas that had supported Thurmond now voted for Democratic nominee Adlai Stevenson. Eisenhower was more popular than his party in the South, however. He had no coattails in the region as Democrats continued to win nearly all congressional races as well as contests for state office. The Republican Party was still so weak organizationally that it was unable to field candidates in many races.[13]

Though Eisenhower did not aggressively seek African American votes, his performance among blacks in 1956 shot up by eighteen percentage points over his total four years earlier. Increased African American support helped the president carry Tennessee, Virginia, and Louisiana. Eisenhower's improvement, however, was more the result of African American anger at the Democrats than a love for the GOP. More important, his level of support among African Americans was not as significant as it first appears because sizable numbers of blacks, especially in the North, stayed home on Election Day. Southern African Americans showed stronger support for the president, but the Republican National Committee tempered enthusiasm over those results by noting that Democrats still far outnumbered Republicans in the region, most African Americans still did not or could not vote, the percentage of the African American population in many areas was declining, and any future increase in black support might easily be offset by greater white turnout for the Democrats. Though African Americans likely played a pivotal role in the victory of Republican Thruston Morton in the Kentucky Senate contest, black votes for the GOP in congressional races, especially in the populous areas of the North, showed no real change compared to 1952. Eisenhower was particularly disappointed that he and the GOP did not fare better among African Americans.[14]

Northern Republicans seized on the vote totals nevertheless as evidence that African Americans would return to the party of Lincoln if it took a strong civil rights stand. One boasted, "Give us a civil rights bill and by 1960, we will break the Roosevelt coalition of the large cities and the South, even without Eisenhower." These Republicans conceived of race as primarily a southern issue. Reform of the South, liberal Republicans believed, would pay political dividends in the North. Nearly all Republicans continued to oppose fair employment legislation and other economic measures of interest to African Americans in the North. Few had anything to say about housing discrimination or school segregation there. Neither did many Democrats, but given black voting patterns since the 1930s and Democratic support for unions, the key issue here is that the GOP did not offer African Americans sufficient reason to switch parties. In 1957 and 1960, Eisenhower and congressional Republicans were instrumental in passing civil rights legislation that focused primarily on protecting voting rights for African Americans in Dixie. Though many civil rights activists correctly predicted that these laws were too weak to substantially change the status quo there, Eisenhower sincerely believed the GOP had compiled a good civil rights record compared to the Democrats, whom he saw as hypocrites who talked about racial change but remained firmly under southern control.[15]

By 1960, racial conflict had intensified substantially. Angry over the lack of progress in many parts of the South, African Americans employed direct action techniques against racial oppression while whites continued to resist change. In the North, African Americans who protested discrimination in housing, schools, and employment were met by whites determined to preserve the status quo. Such an environment posed acute challenges to both presidential candidates. Republican nominee Richard Nixon had acquired a solid civil rights reputation as Eisenhower's vice president; he had earned the respect of many black leaders, including Martin Luther King Jr. and NAACP chief Roy Wilkins. Nixon first moved to the left by following New York governor Nelson Rockefeller's call for a liberal plank on civil rights and other issues. Rockefeller had been Nixon's chief rival for the nomination and remained convinced that a Republican victory in November required winning the large industrial states of the Northeast and Midwest. That would require substantial support from African Americans. Conservatives saw the plank as bad policy and bad politics, for they believed that Nixon could not win the North and thus needed to build on Eisenhower's success in the South. Barry Goldwater, the conservatives' champion, denounced the plank as the "Republican Munich."[16]

Having moved left to head off a perceived threat from Rockefeller, Nixon tacked back to the right that fall. He expended little effort to woo black voters. Nixon refused appeals from black Republicans to become involved in the controversy over the jailing of Martin Luther King Jr. in Atlanta. During the final two weeks of the campaign, he canceled appearances in northern African American neighborhoods. The GOP, he later confessed, remained weak organizationally there. Whereas Democrat John F. Kennedy mounted an extensive publicity campaign among black voters, Nixon and the Republicans failed to do so. Conversely, Nixon made numerous appearances across the South, where he drew large, enthusiastic, and nearly all-white crowds. The vice president was not a race baiter; he reached out to whites by emphasizing themes of local control of education, discussing issues other than race, accusing the Democrats of abandoning their traditional support for state autonomy, and contending that the Democrats took the South for granted. Republicans, he claimed, better embodied southern traditions and values. Like Eisenhower, he trumpeted his faith that racial progress would come slowly and mostly through educational efforts to change personal beliefs rather than laws and court rulings.[17]

Kennedy's narrow victory left both liberal and conservative Republicans convinced that had Nixon followed their advice he would have triumphed. Kennedy garnered 68 percent of the black vote, compared to 61 percent for Stevenson in 1956; black votes helped the Massachusetts senator carry South Carolina, North Carolina, and Texas, as well as Illinois, Michigan, Missouri, and New Jersey. Nixon won Tennessee, Virginia, and Florida, but overall he failed to expand on Eisenhower's success in the South because the presence of Lyndon B. Johnson on the Democratic ticket likely held several southern states for Kennedy. Nixon won a respectable 32 percent of the black vote nationwide, but prominent Republicans believed that African Americans had failed to reward Nixon for what they regarded was a strong GOP stand on race during the Eisenhower years. When Nixon, Eisenhower, and other Republicans gathered at the White House in December 1960 to examine the election results, Eisenhower claimed Nixon had lost North Carolina and South Carolina by being too liberal on race. African Americans, he added, "just do not give a damn" about the GOP. Nixon revived the "bought vote" argument, saying that progress in civil rights under Eisenhower meant little compared to social welfare programs that black voters associated with the Democrats. Thruston Morton bluntly declared that his attitude toward African Americans was "to hell with them."[18]

Party debates in the aftermath of Nixon's defeat resembled those following Dewey's loss. Believing that Nixon had blown the election by ignoring African Americans, black Republicans urged party leaders to boost their presence in black areas and give African Americans more prominent leadership roles. In 1961, the national committee named a fourteen-member task force to boost GOP support in the metropolitan areas of the North; Kennedy had crushed Nixon there. Concluding that the Republicans had been "outmanned, outorganized, outspent, and outworked" in most big cities, the group suggested greater outreach efforts to African Americans as one part of a broad urban effort that would also include union members, people from diverse religious traditions, and assorted ethnic groups. Presumably, they believed that the party had a better policy record on race than the Democrats. Yet many Republicans still seemed woefully out of touch with the concerns and aspirations of African Americans. In 1962, Eisenhower convened a meeting of party leaders to discuss political strategy. The former president created quite a stir when he told the audience, "I've talked to a Negro today, and what he told me would be of interest to all of us. We must hold more meetings and hear this story." Plans to build the party in urban areas of the North, however, largely failed to get off the ground as William Miller, a conservative congressman from upstate New York who became RNC chief in 1962, preferred to focus on the South.[19]

Miller's emphasis closely matched conservatives' desires to attract white southerners. The RNC had moved in this direction in 1957 when it created Operation Dixie. I. Lee Potter, the Virginian who headed the effort, wanted to downplay race and build the party among young, urban professionals on the basis of fiscal conservatism and good government. Positions on race, as well as whether to reach out to the still small but growing black electorate, would be left to local parties. Race remained central to southern politics, however, as civil rights protests mounted across the region in the early 1960s. Whites were determined to preserve the status quo and viewed the Kennedy administration as an ally of those seeking change. Republican candidates in the South tried to seize this opening. The Republican Party in Mississippi, for example, displayed the Confederate flag on its letterhead, and new GOP officials across the South tended to push out African Americans, the traditional party leaders in the region. "We can't build a Republican Party with rejects from the Democratic Party," one African American Republican lamented. "We don't need these reactionaries." Though black Republicans continued to urge the party to reach out to the growing African American electorate in the South, there was little to no effort to do so through Operation Dixie or the Minorities Division of the RNC. During the early 1960s, Operation Dixie, which had no blacks in prominent positions, received roughly three times more funds than the Minorities Division, which the RNC disbanded by 1963. Efforts to build the party in the South had yielded only modest fruit by the early 1960s, but Goldwater and other conservatives still saw the white voters there, not African Americans, as prime targets. "The Republican Party has not attracted Negro voters," Goldwater bluntly stated in 1961. "It is time to admit we cannot get them . . . so let's quite trying specifically to get them." Echoing the "bought vote" argument from earlier eras, he also bluntly asserted that the GOP could not "out-promise the Democrats" for black support.[20]

The 1962 elections sharpened the debate over the future of the party. Conservatives cheered what they saw as enormous progress in the South, where Republicans won four new House seats and improved their overall showing. Whereas Republican congressional candidates had won 16.3 percent of all votes cast in southern House races in 1958, four years later they received 31 percent. The party enjoyed substantial gains in gubernatorial contests as well, and in South Carolina and Alabama GOP Senate candidates nearly knocked off longtime Democratic incumbents. "Republicans in the South are no longer made to feel like skunks at a church social," Goldwater observed. "Republican influence in the South is growing in direct proportion to the South's moderation on the race issue," he declared, with the GOP core of support coming from "young, energetic and imaginative southerners" whose politics were rooted primarily in business concerns.[21]

The Arizona senator painted far too benign a picture. Race was not the only force in southern politics, to be sure, but it remained a core issue. In Alabama, for example, Republican Senate candidate James Martin tried to win support by stirring up white resentment over President Kennedy's approach to the Freedom Rides in 1961 and the integration of the University of Mississippi in September 1962. In South Carolina, GOP Senate candidate William Workman firmly backed segregation and accused the Democrats of fostering civil rights lawsuits and demonstrations. The *New York Times* observed that most of the Republican gains were made by candidates who favored segregation; Javits similarly believed that GOP House candidates in Alabama and South Carolina tried to outdo their opponents in their support for Jim Crow.[22]

Pro–civil rights Republicans in the North found such trends alarming. Senator Kenneth Keating of New York acknowledged that southern Republicans would likely favor segregation, but he warned that if they gained too much visibility and influence nationally the GOP would become "forever a minority party" due to losses in the North. "It's a matter of clear mathematics; a majority of the more populous states just do not favor [segregation]," he declared. The editors of *Advance*, a publication of young Republicans at Harvard University, chastised Goldwater, who headed the GOP Senate campaign committee, and other conservatives for "hitching the party wagon to the falling star of segregation." Such a strategy, they maintained, was "totally unacceptable, both morally and politically." The editors downplayed southern victories as "significant but hardly earthshaking events." They too wanted the party to succeed in Dixie, but through recruiting new, progressive candidates rather than by running segregationist ex-Democrats; they essentially repeated what Case had argued a decade earlier. They lamented that focusing on gains in the South obscured more noteworthy developments elsewhere, including the "dramatic" improvements registered by pro–civil rights Republican gubernatorial candidates George Romney, Nelson Rockefeller, and William Scranton among black voters in Michigan, New York, and Pennsylvania, respectively. Worried about the loss of four Republican Senate seats outside Dixie, which gave the Democrats their biggest majority since 1939, they called for "a new coach with a new approach" that focused primarily on the urban areas of the North and West.[23]

On Capitol Hill, meanwhile, Republicans remained opposed or indifferent to civil rights issues. Republican lawmakers were largely silent regarding civil rights demonstrations such as the Freedom Rides; the direct action campaign in Albany, Georgia; and the integration of the University of Mississippi. Only a few liberals, such as Javits, Keating, Rockefeller, and New York congressman John Lindsay, spoke in support. Bills to combat inequalities in voting, employment, education, and housing enjoyed the backing of a handful of Republicans, but most members of both parties, as well as the White House, showed little or no enthusiasm for legislative remedies. Kennedy did sponsor a mild voting rights bill in 1962, but Republican opposition to cloture helped ensure the bill's demise due to a filibuster by southern Democrats. Few Republicans backed efforts to reform the Senate filibuster rule. The only civil rights bill passed between 1961 and 1964 was a two-year extension of the Civil Rights Commission, a move civil rights groups denounced as far too tepid given the growing urgency of education, voting, employment, and housing concerns.[24]

Republican opposition to more substantial reforms stemmed from several factors, but politics clearly was part of the equation. During a 1962 debate over Kennedy's plan to create a department of urban affairs and name Dr. Robert Weaver, an African American, as its head, William Ayres, a congressman from northeast Ohio, implored his colleagues to vote against the bill by compiling a table showing that only 8 out of 150 Republicans in the House came from districts outside the South where African Americans formed 10 percent or more of the population. Claiming that the power of the African American vote in the North was "an inflated myth," he called on Republicans to ignore warnings from civil rights groups that rejecting the bill would mean defeat in November. Indeed, most Republicans could safely ignore the black vote; it was no coincidence that the strongest GOP voices on civil rights since the 1940s came from New York and other states with significant black populations, and that those individuals tended to be senators or governors who faced broader electorates than members of the House. The "balance of power" argument still failed to motivate most Republicans.[25]

The nomination of Goldwater in 1964 brought a new intensity to the conflict over the direction of the party. It was more a difference of degree than kind. Though he had voted for the 1957 and 1960 Civil Rights Acts and regularly said that he personally opposed segregation, Goldwater was one of just six Republican senators who opposed the 1964 Civil Rights Act. Insisting there was "no constitutional basis" for its provisions outlawing segregation in public accommodations and employment discrimination, Goldwater accused the bill's supporters of "political demagoguery" and warned of an impending "police state." Goldwater had also sided with southern segregationists on several civil rights votes in the early 1960s and by declaring that the Supreme Court had trampled on states' rights when it had outlawed legally segregated public schools in 1954. In 1962, he defended the right of Mississippi to maintain a segregated public university. Politically, he continued to challenge the Republican Party to adopt a southern strategy. A coalition of the South and West, Goldwater and his supporters believed, was the key to the White House. Goldwater still publicly insisted that Republican growth in the South was not the result of racism, though in private several advisers, as well as some of his southern supporters, acknowledged that white hostility toward the civil rights movement would benefit the candidate in both the South and the North. The first Republican ever to make winning the South essential to victory, Goldwater remained a hero to many white southerners for a host of reasons that included but were not limited to race. James J. Kilpatrick, a prominent intellectual leader in the drive to preserve white supremacy in Dixie, warmly described the senator in 1963 as "a symbol of everything the conservative South reveres" and favorably contrasted his approach to civil rights with that of the Kennedy brothers and Nelson Rockefeller, who had been sharply critical of Goldwater's racial views and stood as the Arizonan's chief rival.[26]

Goldwater arrived at the Republican convention as the enormous favorite to win the nomination. Rockefeller, Romney, Scranton, and other northern Republicans invoked the potential loss of the black vote in the North, as well as other concerns, in their failed last-minute bid to deny him that prize. The antiblack feeling on display by many Goldwater delegates alarmed black Republicans. "The floor of this convention feels like downtown Birmingham," one remarked. For them, a particularly revealing moment occurred when Goldwater expressed resentment that his integrity was being challenged by a lifelong black Republican who asked him how he would enforce civil rights laws. When the delegate persisted, Goldwater supporters hissed him. For the first time in its history, the NAACP jettisoned its nonpartisan status and urged African Americans to vote for Lyndon B. Johnson. Former baseball great Jackie Robinson, who sympathized with Republicans on many issues, wrote in his newspaper column, "I now believe I know how it felt to be a Jew in Hitler's Germany," while A. Philip Randolph accused Goldwater of showing "utter contempt" for African Americans.[27]

Civil rights (and foreign policy) had so divided the Republicans at their convention that Eisenhower, Nixon, and other party leaders convened a unity summit in early August. The race issue had become even more sensitive since the convention, as race riots occurred in several northern cities that summer. The riots came in addition to a surge in protests over jobs, housing, and education since the early 1960s. Pundits speculated that a "white backlash" against civil rights might hurt the Democrats. Eisenhower was so alarmed over the possibility of a wider conflagration that he privately indicated he would vote for Johnson if Goldwater played up racial animosities. Goldwater assuaged Eisenhower's worries, but he was less successful with several others. Romney pressed the senator to make a clear statement affirming the importance of "human rights" over states' rights. Not satisfied with the language Goldwater used in his press statement afterward, Romney refused to endorse the senator that fall. Goldwater's stand on civil rights was a significant factor behind the refusal of Javits, Rockefeller, Case, Keating, and Senator Thomas Kuchel of California, who had been central to getting the 1964 Civil Rights Act through the Senate, to back him as well. These Republicans found his approach to race morally troubling and feared it would prove politically damaging to the party in the North in federal as well as state and local elections.[28]

Goldwater won just six states and only 38.5 percent of the popular vote. He carried just sixty congressional districts in the entire nation; only sixteen of those were located outside the South. Five of those sixteen were in archconservative Southern California. Republican support at the presidential level declined from 1960 totals in thirty-three of thirty-six large cities. Goldwater, moreover, lost ground among several demographic groups. The "white backlash" failed to materialize, at least at the polls, as whites outside the South overwhelmingly supported Johnson. No group experienced a larger swing than African Americans; Goldwater received just 6 percent of black ballots. Republicans also suffered a net loss of thirty-eight House seats and two Senate seats. The percentage of votes won by Republicans in congressional and state house races declined from 1962 and 1960 levels.[29]

The one exception appeared to be the South, where Goldwater won five states. Each of the seven new Republican congressmen from the South also opposed the 1964 Act. Republican strength in the South correlated very closely with segregationist Strom Thurmond's success in 1948. But even in the South the picture was mixed at best, for though Goldwater boosted GOP totals among rural and small-town areas in the Deep South, he surrendered upper South and border states. Losses were especially severe in the fast-growing urban and suburban areas, where Nixon and Eisenhower had done well. The senator won only a minority of the region's electoral votes (47 of 128), fewer than either Nixon or Eisenhower had, and failed to win a majority of the popular vote (48.6 percent). African American support for the GOP, which had been respectable in 1956 and 1960, dwindled to almost nothing as black voters swung Florida and Virginia to the Democratic column for the first time in sixteen years and were critical to Johnson's victories in North Carolina, Tennessee, and Arkansas.[30]

The magnitude of the defeat sparked a robust discussion that echoed those from the 1940s. Race was at the center of this conversation. Though Goldwater did not explicitly appeal to bigotry during the campaign, his emphasis on states' rights and his calls for law and order carried racial overtones. Voters across the nation clearly saw him as the anti–civil rights candidate. Pro–civil rights Republicans felt their fears had materialized and worried that the party would continue to lose both white and black support in large industrial states unless it changed direction. Senator Hugh Scott of Pennsylvania demanded a purge of "southern scalawags," while one Maryland congressman called Goldwater's writing off the black vote "cynically short sighted." Asserting that the GOP was in worse shape than at any point since 1936, Javits forecast that the Republicans' tepid support for civil rights and appeal to law and order would give Democrats a political edge "for years to come." Massachusetts attorney general Edward Brooke, an African American, described the segregationist vote as "fool's gold" and urged the party to reject Goldwaterism by "[opening] its doors to . . . the great grandchildren of slaves." Romney wrote Goldwater a month after the election, expressing his concern over the civil rights issue and the "southern-rural-white orientation" of the Arizonan's campaign. Several Republicans who had lost congressional or state races pointed to miniscule black support as a critical factor in their defeat. Charles Percy, who narrowly lost the gubernatorial race in Illinois, insisted, "We have got to get the party away from being an Anglo-Saxon Protestant white party."[31]

These Republicans, a few of whom were southerners, considered a strong civil rights stand as integral to success in Dixie as well. They likely did not believe the GOP could win a majority of the black vote, but they were convinced that improvements over Goldwater's miniscule total were essential. Senator Thruston Morton of Kentucky stressed that future success depended on Republicans garnering at least 20 percent of the African American vote. This was true nationally, but especially in the South, where Morton expected the number of black registrants to increase dramatically. Insisting that the Republicans did not have to appeal to racism to win in the South, he dreamed of a biracial coalition similar to that which had formed briefly during Reconstruction. Pointing out that the Republicans had controlled Congress for just four of the previous thirty-four years, the Kentucky senator argued that writing off the South to the Democrats meant that the GOP faced the almost impossible task of triumphing everywhere else to establish a legislative majority or win the White House.[32]

Others echoed Morton's approach. The Ripon Society, an organization of liberal Republicans based in the Northeast, observed that by 1968 African Americans would likely constitute 20 percent of the southern electorate, enough to move the Goldwater states of Georgia, Louisiana, and South Carolina to the Democrats. Liberal Republicans also believed that southern whites were becoming more progressive on race. Southern politics, the Ripon Society predicted, would gradually move away from its traditional focus on race as the region continued its rapid economic development, and as a result a strategy based on the dying theme of racial supremacy "could have a price which will be paid back in costly installments over the next several generations." The defeated Republican candidate for governor in North Carolina similarly added, "I don't want this party to be a racist or a lily-white party. The quicker we admit that Negroes have a right to vote, the better it will be for us." Dean Burch, the outgoing chair of the RNC, urged Republicans to appeal to southerners' economic conservatism and their concerns over foreign policy. "You don't have to go down there and wave the Confederate flag," he observed.[33]

Southern Republicans dismissed the pro–civil rights approach as political fantasy. They saw no need to rethink the Goldwater strategy of ignoring black voters. Congressman Albert Watson of South Carolina, who became a Republican in 1964, advised his new colleagues to refrain from a bidding war with the Democrats for black voters. "You can't outdo the president," he counseled. Others maintained that fears of an expanding black electorate leading to Republican defeats were vastly overblown because whites constituted the majority in most parts of Dixie. Alabama party chief Manyon Millican contended that there was "no justification for an attempt to go after the Negro vote"; his state party released a statement arguing that any targeting of black voters was reverse discrimination. The platform of the Republican Party in Mississippi, meanwhile, announced that segregation was "absolutely essential."[34]

As the racial crisis intensified in both the North and the South between 1965 and 1968, Republicans continued to spar over policy and their political future. Racial tensions were clearly hurting the Democrats, but Republican electoral success was far from certain. Romney, Javits, Rockefeller, and other liberals called for increased federal spending to alleviate ghetto poverty and backed legislation to combat housing discrimination, but Republican leaders in Congress ignored their pleas. Open housing measures failed to pass in 1966 and 1967. Republicans also largely refused to back legislation, co-sponsored by Javits, Kuchel, and other liberals, to boost the enforcement powers of the Equal Employment Opportunity Commission. Conservatives such as Goldwater and Thurmond demanded stiffer jail terms and blamed Democrats, black leaders, permissive judges, and the media for encouraging a spirit of anarchy. Neither side was able to gain control of the party, however. Liberals continued to argue that cozying up to southern segregationists might yield short-term gains but would fail in the long run. They urged the RNC and other party leaders to be more assertive in reaching out to black voters and welcoming blacks into leadership ranks. Conservatives still countered that the black vote was lost and that playing to white middle-class anger was good politics and policy.[35]

Both sides claimed vindication following the 1966 elections. Liberals noted that the African American vote for Republican candidates in several large cities of the North and West jumped substantially and that William McCulloch, the Ohio congressman who had led the 1964 Civil Rights Act through the House, won despite his opponent's attempts to use that issue against him. Conservatives pointed to further gains for the party in the South, where Republicans won eight House seats, and how white backlash over racial matters helped Charles Percy defeat liberal Democratic senator Paul Douglas in Illinois and Ronald Reagan win the governorship of California. GOP advances tended to be lowest in the Northeast, strongest in the South and West. Yet the southern GOP was no monolith regarding civil rights. In Florida, Claude Kirk campaigned for the governor's seat with a slogan, "Your Home is Your Castle—Protect It," that unmistakably signaled his opposition to open housing reforms. On the other hand, Howard Baker won a Senate seat in Tennessee as a racial moderate; he received between 15 and 20 percent of the

African American vote. In Arkansas, Republican Winthrop Rockefeller, brother of Nelson Rockefeller, ran against a staunch segregationist Democrat and won a majority of the black vote. Overall, Republicans elected to the House tended to be conservatives, but five of the six new Republican senators were liberals or moderates who had enjoyed respectable support from African Americans. They included Massachusetts's Edward Brooke, the first African American elected to the Senate since Reconstruction.[36]

The battle reached a resolution with the nomination of Nixon in 1968. Romney's and then Rockefeller's efforts to carry the flag for liberal Republicanism fell flat for reasons that had nothing to do with race, but so too did Ronald Reagan's drive as the champion of conservatism. Nixon's acute political sensibilities led him to chart a middle course between the liberals and conservatives on racial issues. Nixon wisely concluded that repeating Goldwater's stand on civil rights would be a mistake. He reached out to whites in both the North and the South with conservative language about limiting the power of the courts, preserving local autonomy regarding schools, and maintaining law and order. Black Republicans found such rhetoric alarming; one commented that Nixon "had prostituted himself to get the southern vote." Yet Nixon also talked in surprisingly liberal terms about the need to extend economic opportunity to poor African Americans. He told reporters that ghetto residents "have got to have more than an equal chance," and that they should be given a "dividend" to be able to participate fully in the social and economic life of the nation. He did not elaborate on just what that meant, though he did briefly sketch a program of "Black Capitalism."[37]

Republicans from the late 1960s through the early 1970s also repudiated Goldwaterism on several policy matters. Republican lawmakers backed the 1968 Fair Housing Law (though Dirksen and other GOP leaders helped weaken its enforcement provisions, as they had done with the 1964 Civil Rights Act), and in the early 1970s Republicans, especially those in the Senate who hailed from the Northeast and West, provided crucial support in the drive to expand the power of the Equal Employment Opportunity Commission and substantially increase the number of workers who fell under federal protections against employment discrimination. Likewise, driven in part by conviction as well as political concerns over losing black votes, they were crucial to defeating attempts by southern lawmakers to weaken the enforcement provisions of the Voting Rights Act. As president, Nixon offered some surprisingly liberal policy initiatives on civil rights, including support for affirmative action and increased funding for African American educational institutions.[38]

Following Nixon's resignation, the Republicans' debate over civil rights receded. The party grew more homogeneous on race and many other issues. Rockefeller, Romney, and Javits disappeared from the national stage, and no liberals took their place. That the conversation occurred, however, indicates that the history of the Republican Party in the three decades after World War II was marked by considerable tension. It points to the power of the New Deal to shape subsequent political developments, for this debate was essentially over how the party should respond to forces that had taken root in the 1930s.

Liberals, however, mostly failed in their thirty-year quest to chart a racially progressive direction for the GOP. There were several reasons for that outcome. First, they faced a considerable hurdle in trying to change the impressions African Americans had formed of the GOP during the 1930s. Given the swing of black voters to the Democrats during the New Deal, it fell to the Republicans to persuade them to come back to the party of Lincoln. Voters do change loyalties, but such shifts are infrequent and require the confluence of several variables that never materialized for the GOP. Civil rights efforts by Democrats such as John F. Kennedy and Lyndon B. Johnson mattered, but much of the GOP's failure was self-inflicted. Internal developments within the party, some of which had nothing to do with race, had racial effects. Liberals never occupied positions of power to set the tone on race. Rockefeller and Romney never won the Republican presidential nomination, in part because of personal flaws but also because they lacked sufficient organizational strength to challenge Goldwater and Nixon. Instead, most of the party's nominees were moderates at best who offered relatively little to African Americans, especially regarding economic matters. Political outcomes also result from strong organization, but here, too, liberals never occupied positions of power in party structures where decisions about voter outreach were made. RNC officials sometimes talked about the need to build stronger organizations in black communities, but they rarely followed through. Instead, party leaders focused more heavily on white southerners and suburbanites, most of whom were also white, across the nation.

This lack of attention stemmed from how Republican leaders conceptualized race and politics. Most Republican Party leaders and lawmakers considered the black vote as simply not necessary for victory. Republican lawmakers tended to come from districts or states where there were few black voters. Eisenhower, Nixon, and then Reagan and the two Bushes showed that the GOP could, contrary to the claims of the NAACP and other civil rights organizations, capture the White House with little or no African American support. Black leaders tried to woo Republicans into supporting civil rights legislation with the hope of black votes, but most electoral outcomes, which stemmed from many factors not necessarily tied to race, undermined their "balance of power" argument.

Winning elections obviously motivates lawmakers to behave in certain ways, and ideology also matters. Republicans' political and policy decisions about race were rooted to a considerable degree in their conceptions about how American society operated. Their faith that the free market, self-help, reliance on state and local power (rather than federal authorities), and educational efforts to cure white racism would lead to black progress was not entirely wrong, but it struck African Americans as woefully insufficient. Their historical experience had taught them that hard work often led to minimal economic gains, employers discriminated, and state and local authorities (especially in the South) wanted to keep them out of the voting booth. The record of the Democrats and the federal government was far from spot-less on race, but for most blacks it was preferable to the Republicans' alternative.

Looking closely at the struggle to build the Republican Party in the aftermath of the New Deal and World War II not only sharpens scholars' understanding of history, but also puts contemporary developments into a larger context. Barack Obama's triumph in 2008 triggered a debate among Republicans that closely re-sembles that which occurred from the 1940s through the early 1970s. Obama's suc-cess was primarily rooted in several demographic trends that have transformed the American electorate, the most important being the substantial turnout of and sup-port from African Americans and Latino voters. Whites are a declining portion of the electorate. Like their predecessors, modern conservatives insist that the GOP will win again by hewing to a more conservative line. They show little interest in outreach to nonwhites. Others echo liberals from the past as they warn that ignor-ing racial and ethnic minorities and taking strong conservative positions will con-demn the party to minority status for a generation or more.

Demographics are not destiny, for those who might be inclined to support a particular party must be mobilized. Demographics create a structural framework, however, that offers substantial advantages to one party or the other. Liberal Repub-licans were wrong in many of their assumptions about the South and the politics of race. White registration far outpaced black registration in Dixie in the 1970s and 1980s, and the reservoir of racial goodwill among white northerners was not nearly as deep as liberals assumed. But the liberals raised questions about party identity that assumed new importance in the early twenty-first century. Republican trou-bles in wooing nonwhites in the early twenty-first century are not surprising given policy and political decisions made by the party in an earlier era. The weight of his-tory looms large; political parties face a difficult challenge when trying to transform voters' perceptions. As political scientist Thomas Schaller has noted, Romney and Rockefeller would not be surprised by this turn of events. Indeed, in some respects the contemporary challenges facing the GOP are precisely what they feared.[39]

NOTES

1.   Merle Black and Earl Black, *The Rise of Southern Republicans* (Cambridge, MA: Harvard University Press, 2002); David Lublin, *The Republican South: Democratization and Partisan Change* (Princeton, NJ: Princeton University Press, 2004); Byron E. Shafer and Richard Johnston, *The End of Southern Exceptionalism: Class, Race, and Partisan Change in the Postwar South* (Cambridge, MA: Harvard University Press, 2006); Joseph E. Lowndes, *From the New Deal to the New Right: Race and the Southern Origins of Modern Conservatism* (New Haven, CT: Yale University Press, 2008); Thomas Schaller, "What Ever Happened to Moderate Republicans?," *American Prospect*, November 19, 2007, *www.prospect.org*; Christine Todd Whitman, *It's My Party Too: The Battle for the Heart of the GOP and the Future of America* (New York: Penguin, 2005); and Michael K. Fauntroy, *Republicans and the Black Vote* (Boulder, CO: Lynne Rienner Publications, 2007), 56.

2. Rick Perlstein, *Before the Storm: Barry Goldwater and the Unmaking of the American Consensus* (New York: Hill and Wang, 2001); Mary C. Brennan, *Turning Right in the Sixties: The Conservative Capture of the GOP* (Chapel Hill: University of North Carolina Press, 1995); and Robert Alan Goldberg, *Barry Goldwater* (New Haven, CT: Yale University Press, 1995).

3. Samuel Lubell, *The Future of American Politics*, 2nd ed. (New York: Doubleday, 1956), 210–17.

4. See, for example, Thomas J. Sugrue, *Sweet Land of Liberty: The Forgotten Struggle for Civil Rights in the North* (New York: Random House, 2008); Patricia Sullivan, *Days of Hope: Race and Democracy in the New Deal Era* (Chapel Hill: University of North Carolina Press, 1996); Martha Biondi, *To Stand and Fight: The Struggle for Civil Rights in Postwar New York City* (Cambridge, MA: Harvard University Press, 2003); Jeanne Theoharis and Komozi Woodard, eds., *Freedom North: Black Freedom Struggles outside the South, 1940–1980* (New York: Palgrave, 2003); Glenda Elizabeth Gilmore, *Defying Dixie: The Radical Roots of the Civil Rights Movement* (New York: Norton, 2008); Risa L. Goluboff, *The Lost Promise of Civil Rights* (Cambridge, MA: Harvard University Press, 2007); Kevin Schultz, "The FEPC and the Legacy of the Labor-Based Civil Rights Movement of the 1940s," *Labor History* 49 (2008): 71–92; William E. Leuchtenburg, *The White House Looks South: Franklin D. Roosevelt, Harry S. Truman, and Lyndon B. Johnson* (Baton Rouge: Louisiana State University Press, 2006), 119–43; and Kari Frederickson, *The Dixiecrat Revolt and the End of the Solid South, 1932–1968* (Chapel Hill: University of North Carolina Press, 2001), 11–39.

5. Lewis L. Gould, *Grand Old Party: A History of the Republicans* (New York: Random House, 2003), 315–16; and *Congressional Record*, 79th Congress, 1st Session, 782.

6. Richard Norton Smith, *Thomas E. Dewey and His Times* (New York: Simon and Schuster, 1982), 349, 445–48, 501; Anthony S. Chen, "'The Hitlerian Rule of Quotas': Racial Conservatism and the Politics of Fair Employment Legislation in New York State, 1941–1945," *Journal of American History* 92 (2006): 1254; *Crisis*, January 1948; Simon Topping, "'Never Argue with the Gallup Poll': Thomas Dewey, Civil Rights, and the Election of 1948," *Journal of American Studies* 38 (2004): 179–90; Barry K. Beyer, *Thomas E. Dewey, 1937–1947: A Study in Political Leadership* (New York: Garland, 1979), 40–44, 65–67; Alonzo L. Hamby, *Man of the People: A Life of Harry S. Truman* (New York: Oxford University Press, 1995), 458; *Negro Statesman*, July 1948, Box 30, Additional Files, Herbert Brownell Papers, Dwight D. Eisenhower Library (DDEL), Abilene, KS; press release, March 4, 1948, Box 34, Roy Wilkins Papers, Library of Congress, Washington, DC; *New York Herald Tribune*, March 27, 1944; *New York Herald Tribune*, May 12, 1944; DNC Research Division, Files of the Facts, Thomas Dewey, n.d., Box 84, Democratic National Committee Papers, Harry S. Truman Library, Independence, MO; *New York Herald Tribune*, March 2, 1948; and Donald R. McCoy and Richard T. Ruetten, *Quest and Response: Minority Rights and the Truman Administration* (Lawrence: University Press of Kansas, 1973), 122.

7. R. R. Church to Republican National Committee, August 2, 1949, Box 7, Hugh Scott Papers, University of Virginia, Charlottesville, VA; "GOP Groundswell to Left Charted to Pick Up Ballots," December 9, 1949, Box 52, William Workman Papers, University of South Carolina, Columbia, SC.

8. Minutes of meeting of the Republican National Committee, May 2, 1949, and minutes of meeting of the Republican National Committee, August 4, 1949, both in *Papers of the Republican Party*, part 1: *Meetings of the Republican National Committee, 1911–1980*; Series A, *1911–1960*, ed. Paul L. Kesaris (Frederick, MD: University Publications

of America, 1986; hereafter *Papers of the Republican Party* 1A), Reel 9; "Statement of Republican Principles and Objectives," February 6, 1950, Box 125, Herbert Brownell Papers, DDEL; Roy Wilkins to Irving Ives, February 9, 1950, Series 2, Box A205, NAACP Records, Library of Congress, Washington, DC; *Crisis*, April 1950; "Report of the Acting Secretary for the March 1950 Meeting of the Board," n.d., Series 2, Box A509, NAACP Records; and McCoy and Ruetten, *Quest and Response*, 194.

9. *Congressional Record*, 81st Congress, 1st Session, 10, 102; Lubell, *Future*, 101; McCoy and Ruetten, *Quest and Response*, 282–83; minutes of meeting of the Executive Committee of the Republican National Committee, December 8, 1950, and minutes of meeting of the Republican National Committee, January 26, 1951, both in *Papers of the Republican Party* 1A, Reel 10.

10. *Collier's*, July 28, 1951. On the 1930s alliance between southern Democrats and Republicans, see James T. Patterson, *Congressional Conservatism and the New Deal: The Growth of the Conservative Coalition in Congress, 1933–1939* (Lexington: University of Kentucky Press, 1967); and Clyde P. Weed, *The Nemesis of Reform: The Republican Party During the New Deal* (New York: Columbia University Press, 1994).

11. *Collier's*, July 28, 1951; and *Freeman*, August 13, 1951.

12. *Collier's*, July 28, 1951. On the idea of southern exceptionalism during the post–World War II era, see the essays in *The Myth of Southern Exceptionalism*, ed. Matthew D. Lassiter and Joseph Crespino (New York: Oxford University Press, 2010).

13. Frederickson, *Dixiecrat Revolt*, 230; Donald S. Strong, *The 1952 Presidential Election in the South* (Tuscaloosa: University of Alabama Press, 1955), 381; Numan V. Bartley, *The Rise of Massive Resistance: Race and Politics in the South during the 1950s* (Baton Rouge: Louisiana State University Press, 1969), 47–50; Bruce H. Kalk, *The Origins of the Southern Strategy: Two-Party Competition in South Carolina, 1950–1972* (Lanham, MD: Lexington Books, 2001), 8–9; Samuel Lubell, *Revolt of the Moderates* (New York: Harper, 1956), 182–202, 217; Hugh Douglas Price, "The Negro and Florida Politics, 1944–1954," *Journal of Politics* 17 (1955): 198–220; Black and Black, *Rise*, 61–62; Shafer and Johnston, *End*, 30–32, 166–68; Donald S. Strong, "Further Reflections on Southern Politics," *Journal of Politics* 33 (1971): 240–41; and Donald S. Strong, "The Presidential Election in the South, 1952," *Journal of Politics* 17 (1955): 384–88.

14. Henry Lee Moon, "The Negro Vote in the Presidential Election of 1956," *Journal of Negro Education* 26 (1957): 219–30; Samuel Lubell, *White and Black: Test of a Nation* (New York: Harper, 1966), 74; and Republican National Committee Research Division, "The Negro Vote," August 1957, Box 909, General Files, White House Central Files, DDEL.

15. *New York Herald Tribune*, November 20, 1956; *Cleveland Plain Dealer*, December 2, 1956; *Des Moines Register*, November 11, 1956; *Atlanta Journal and Constitution*, November 11, 1956; William D. Workman Jr. to R. D. Blanding, November 14, 1956, Box 33, Workman Papers; *Washington Post*, November 10, 1956; *New York Times*, November 11, 1956; Robert A. Caro, *The Years of Lyndon Johnson*, vol. 3, *Master of the Senate* (New York: Knopf, 2002), 843–44; *New Republic*, December 3, 1956; *Congressional Quarterly Weekly Report*, June 7, 1957; *New York Times*, November 11, 1956; press release, November 9, 1956, Series 3, Box A246, NAACP Records; *Crisis*, December 1956; *Cleveland Plain Dealer*, December 2, 1956; *New York Times*, June 8, 1960; *Ebony*, April 1961; *Ebony*, December 1962.

16. *Jet*, January 30, 1958; *New York Amsterdam News*, January 30, 1960; *Kansas City Call*, January 7, 1960; *New York Times*, June 20, 1960; Clayborne Carson, ed., *The Papers*

of Martin Luther King, Jr., vol. 4, *Symbol of the Movement* (Berkeley: University of California Press, 2000), 482–83; Simeon Booker, *Black Man's America* (Englewood Cliffs, NJ: Prentice Hall, 1964), 207; and Perlstein, *Before the Storm*, 69–95.

17. *Jet*, August 3, 1961; *Ebony*, April 1962; W. J. Rorabaugh, *The Real Making of the President: Kennedy, Nixon, and the 1960 Election* (Lawrence: University Press of Kansas, 2009), 107–13, 122–39; Committee on Commerce, U.S. Senate, 87th Congress, 1st Session, *The Speeches, Remarks, Press Conferences, and Study Papers of Vice President Richard M. Nixon, August 1 through November 7, 1960* (Washington, DC: U.S. Government Printing Office, 1961), 5–7, 48–51, 266–69, 274–75, 321, 470–72, 970–72; and Anthony Lewis, *Portrait of a Decade: The Second American Revolution* (New York: Random House, 1964), 115.

18. Nick Bryant, *The Bystander: John F. Kennedy and the Struggle for Black Equality* (New York: Basic Books, 2006), 185–87; "Negro Vote Overwhelmingly Democratic in '60 Election," December 8, 1960, Series 1, Box 421, Daniel Patrick Moynihan Papers, Library of Congress, Washington, DC; Bryce Harlow, memorandum, December 28, 1960, Box 55, Dwight D. Eisenhower Diary Series, Ann Whitman Files, Dwight D. Eisenhower Papers, DDEL; and Robert D. Novak, *The Agony of the GOP—1964* (New York: Macmillan, 1965), 11–14.

19. *Jet*, January 26, 1961; *New York Times*, January 13, 1962; *Jet*, February 16, 1961; *Jet*, March 30, 1961; *Jet*, July 19, 1962; *New York Times*, August 24, 1962; Philip A. Klinkner, *The Losing Parties: Out-Party National Committees, 1956–1993* (New Haven, CT: Yale University Press, 1994), 54, 65, 126; and *Jet*, November 14, 1963.

20. Karl A. Lamb, "Under One Roof: Barry Goldwater's Campaign Staff," in *Republican Politics: The 1964 Campaign and Its Aftermath for the Party*, ed. Bernard Cosman and Robert J. Huckshorn (New York: Praeger, 1968), 14–15; Lowndes, *From the New Deal to the New Right*, 47–48; *Jet*, February 16, 1961; Peter Edson, "'Operation Dixie' is Rolling," *Ocala* (FL) *Star-Banner*, September 6, 1962 (available at *news.google.com*); George Gilder and Bruce K. Chapman, *The Party That Lost Its Head* (New York: Knopf, 1966), 61; Ripon Society, *From Disaster to Distinction: A Republican Rebirth* (New York: Pocket Books, 1966), 30; *New York Herald Tribune*, February 28, 1961; *U.S. News and World Report*, December 11, 1961; *Jet*, January 24, 1963; Stephen Hess and David S. Broder, *The Republican Establishment: The Present and Future of the GOP* (New York: Harper, 1967), 337–40; and undated memorandum, Box 1, Graham Molitor Papers, Rockefeller Archive Center, Tarrytown, NY. Potter was not always neutral himself. In 1957, he rebutted attacks from a segregationist Democrat in Richmond, Virginia, by assuring the audience, "Our party is for segregation." *Richmond Times-Dispatch*, October 15, 1957.

21. Barry Goldwater, "The GOP Invades the South," n.d., Box 4, Denison Kitchel Papers, Hoover Institution, Stanford University, Palo Alto, CA.

22. *Washington Post*, December 24, 1962; *National Review*, February 12, 1963; *Harper's*, May 1963; "Who's Afraid of the Big, Bad Rock?," Series J.2, Box 20, George Hinman Files, Record Group 4, Nelson A. Rockefeller Personal Papers, Rockefeller Archive Center; and Glenn Feldman, "Race, Emotion, and the Rise of the Modern Republican Party in Alabama and the South," in *Before Brown: Civil Rights and White Backlash in the Modern South*, ed. Glenn Feldman (Tuscaloosa: University of Alabama Press, 2004), 282; keynote address by William D. Workman Jr. at South Carolina Republican state convention, May 26, 1962, and speech by Workman, December 1,

1961, both in Box 5, Workman Papers; *New York Times*, November 21, 1962; *New York Times*, December 2, 1962.

23. *New York Times*, December 1, 1962; *Jet*, January 3, 1963; *New York Times*, November 26, 1962; *New York Times*, November 8, 1962; and *New York Herald Tribune*, December 1, 1962.

24. *New York Times*, May 23, 1961; *New York Times*, August 1, 1961; press release, August 21, 1961, Box 471, Kenneth Keating Papers, University of Rochester, Rochester, NY; "Civil Rights in the 87th Congress, First Session," December 1961, Box 10, Legislative Files, Americans for Democratic Action Papers, State Historical Society of Wisconsin, Madison, WI; and *Jet*, February 22, 1962.

25. *Congressional Record*, 87th Congress, 2nd Session, 2,348–2,350.

26. *Newsweek*, June 29, 1964; *Congressional Quarterly*, September 20, 1963; *Congressional Quarterly*, June 26, 1964; Barry Goldwater to editor of *Arizona Republic*, November 8, 1962, Box 2, Kitchel Papers; Goldwater civil rights voting record, Box 8, Molitor Papers; Cosman and Huckshorn, *Republican Politics*, 70; "Excerpts of Remarks by Senator Barry Goldwater," September 13, 1963, and Robert MacNeil to William McAndrew, October 14, 1963, both in Box 11, Robert MacNeil Papers, State Historical Society of Wisconsin, Madison, WI; *Congressional Quarterly*, November 15, 1963; *New Republic*, November 23, 1963; and *National Review*, April 9, 1963.

27. Press release, July 12, 1964, Box 26, Scott Papers; statement by Governor George Romney, July 15, 1964, Box A15, Gerald Ford Congressional Papers, Gerald R. Ford Presidential Library (GRFPL), Ann Arbor, MI; "Statement by Senator Jacob K. Javits Regarding the National Republican Ticket," July 21, 1964, Series 5, Subseries 2, Box 36, Jacob K. Javits Collection, Special Collections Department, Frank Melville Jr. Memorial Library, State University of New York at Stony Brook, Stony Brook, NY; *Jet*, July 30, 1964; *Jet*, November 4, 1965; *New York Herald Tribune*, July 19, 1964; *Des Moines Register*, July 17, 1964; and *New York Times*, September 7, 1964.

28. *Jet*, March 26, 1964; *Jet*, April 2, 1964; *Newsweek*, July 13, 1964; "Confidential Proceedings of Closed Session of Republican Unity Conference," August 12, 1964, WHCF, EX PL 3, Box 117, Lyndon B. Johnson Presidential Library, Austin, TX; David A. Nichols, *A Matter of Justice: Eisenhower and the Beginning of the Civil Rights Revolution* (New York: Simon and Schuster, 2007), 269; David W. Reinhard, *The Republican Right since 1945* (Lexington: University of Kentucky Press, 1983), 199; and *Wall Street Journal*, July 24, 1964.

29. Ripon Society, *Election '64: A Ripon Society Report* (Cambridge, MA: Ripon Society, 1965) and Ripon Society, "The 1964 Elections: A Summary Report with Supporting Tables," October 1965, both in Box 7, Workman Papers; Ripon Society, *From Disaster to Distinction* (Cambridge, MA: Ripon Society, 1964), 12, 33–46; Hess and Broder, *Republican Establishment*, 2; Gary Donaldson, *Liberalism's Last Hurrah: The Presidential Campaign of 1964* (Armonk, NY: M. E. Sharpe, 2003), 309; memorandum to Thomas Kuchel, n.d., and "Southern Republicanism: An Overview," both in Box 79B, Thomas Kuchel Papers, University of California, Berkeley, CA; and Mark R. Levy and Michael S. Kramer, *The Ethnic Factor: How America's Minorities Decide Elections* (New York: Simon and Schuster, 1972), 45–46.

30. *Crisis*, January 1965; Bernard Cosman, *Five States for Goldwater* (Tuscaloosa: University of Alabama Press, 1966), 42–51; chairman's report, February 1965, Box 55, Group 4, Hinman Files; "Southern Republicanism: An Overview"; Ripon Society, *From Disaster*

to Distinction, 32–33; Frederickson, *Dixiecrat Revolt*, 236; and Ripon Society, *Election '64*.

31. *New York Times Magazine*, November 15, 1964; *Congressional Quarterly*, December 2, 1966; *Congressional Quarterly*, January 29, 1965; *Baltimore Sun*, December 5, 1964; "Southern Republicanism: An Overview"; Ripon Society, *Election '64*, 21; press release, February 11, 1965, Series 1.1, Box 36, Charles McC. Mathias Papers, Johns Hopkins University, Baltimore, MD; *New York Times*, February 19, 1965; Hess and Broder, *Republican Establishment*, 216–21; Edward W. Brooke, *The Challenge of Change: Crisis in Our Two-Party System* (Boston: Little, Brown, 1966), 15; *U.S. News and World Report*, February 1, 1965; *Pittsburgh Courier*, March 6, 1965; *New York Times*, February 21, 1965; *New York Times*, March 14, 1965; and *New York Times*, February 19, 1965.

32. Minutes of meeting, Republican National Committee, January 22, 1965, in *Papers of the Republican Party*, part 1: *Meetings of the Republican National Committee, 1911–1980*; Series B, *1960–1980*, ed. Paul L. Kesaris (Frederick, MD: University Publications of America, 1986), Reel 4; and *New York Times*, February 18, 1965.

33. *Congressional Quarterly*, February 26, 1965; Ripon Society, "Southern Republicanism and the New South," 10, 60, 85; "Southern Republicanism, An Overview"; and "Southern Project Report," April 13, 1966, Box 217, Charles P. Taft Papers, Library of Congress, Washington, DC. The Ripon Society's prediction about a swelling black vote in the South was made before the 1965 Voting Rights Act. In many parts of Dixie, but especially in upper-South states such as Virginia and Tennessee, the black vote steadily grew in the 1960s. Mississippi and other Deep South states, however, saw little or no growth and even experienced a decline in the black electorate in some counties.

34. Interview with James Martin, April 9, 1965, Box 1, Robert Peabody Interviews, GRFPL; "Watson Says GOP Should Avoid Wooing Negro Vote in Dixie Buildup," June 17, 1965, Box 52, Workman Papers; "Southern Republicanism and the New South," 33–34; *New York Times*, February 26, 1965; *New York Times*, April 13, 1966; and Hess and Broder, *Republican Establishment*, 180.

35. Clarence Mitchell to William McCulloch, August 2, 1966, Box 15, William McCulloch Papers, Ohio Northern University, Ada, OH; Rick Perlstein, *Nixonland: The Rise of a President and the Fracturing of America* (New York: Simon and Schuster, 2008), 122; *Congressional Quarterly*, August 12, 1966; *Washington Post*, August 12, 1966; *Philadelphia Evening Bulletin*, September 11, 1966; *Congressional Record*, 89th Congress, 2nd Session, 22,610–22,612; *Congressional Quarterly*, September 16, 1966; *New York Times*, May 3, 1967; George Romney to Charles McC. Mathias, May 23, 1967, Series 4.1, Box 3, Mathias Papers; *New York Times*, July 26, 1967; press release, July 24, 1967, Box 51, Edward Hutchinson Papers, GRFPL; *Congressional Record*, 90th Congress, 1st Session, 19,816, 19,830, 19,957, 19,961; *Congressional Quarterly*, September 8, 1967; *1967 Congressional Quarterly Almanac*, 789–90; *Congressional Quarterly*, September 8, 1967; and *Congressional Quarterly*, October 13, 1967.

36. *Washington Post*, October 28, 1966; report to the chairman, RNC, January 23–24, 1967, Box 55, Series 3, Hinman Files; *New York Times*, November 9, 1966; *New York Times*, November 11, 1966; *Ripon Forum*, November 1966, Box 217, Taft Papers; Levy and Kramer, *Ethnic Factor*, 56–63; Perlstein, *Nixonland*, 150, 164–66; "The 1966 Elections—a Summary Report with Supporting Tables," September 1, 1967, in *Papers of the Republican Party*, part 2: *Reports and Memoranda of the Research Division of the Headquarters of the Republican National Committee, 1938–1980*, ed. Paul L.

Kesaris (Frederick, MD: University Publications of America, 1986), Reel 5; Hess and Broder, *Republican Establishment*, 341–42; Gary Orfield, *The Reconstruction of Southern Education: The Schools and the 1964 Civil Rights Act* (New York: Wiley-Interscience, 1969), 325; and *New York Times*, October 3, 1967; *Reporter*, August 10, 1967.

37. *New York Times*, December 20, 1967; *Congressional Quarterly*, January 19, 1968; "Bridges to Human Dignity," PPS 208 (1968): 23–24, Richard Nixon Presidential Library, Yorba Linda, CA; Perlstein, *Nixonland*, 283–85; *New York Times*, August 12, 1968; *Congressional Quarterly*, September 20, 1968.

38. *Wall Street Journal*, March 13, 1968; *Congressional Quarterly*, March 22, 1968; *Congressional Quarterly*, April 12, 1968; Hugh Davis Graham, "The Surprising Career of Federal Fair Housing Law," *Journal of Policy History* 12 (2000): 217; *1970 Congressional Quarterly Almanac*; Rowland Evans Jr. and Robert D. Novak, *Nixon in the White House: The Frustration of Power* (New York: Random House, 1971), 128–31; Hugh Davis Graham, *The Civil Rights Era: Origins and Development of National Policy, 1960–1972* (New York: Oxford University Press, 1990), 440–43; quarterly report of the Washington bureau, April 5, 1972, Series 4, Box A90, NAACP Records; and Dean J. Kotlowski, *Nixon's Civil Rights: Politics, Principle, and Policy* (Cambridge, MA: Harvard University Press, 2001).

39. Alan Abramowitz, "The Incredible Shrinking Republican Base," *Real Clear Politics*, May 2, 2008, *www.realclearpolitics.com*; Alan Abramowitz, "Diverging Coalitions: The Transformation of the American Electorate," *Rasmussen Reports*, April 6, 2009, *www.rasmussenreports.com*; Frank Newport, "Republican Base Heavily White, Conservative, Religious," *Gallup Politics*, June 1, 2009, *www.gallup.com*; Alexis Karteron, "Race Still Mattered in the 2008 Election," *Defenders*, December 23, 2008, *www.thedefenderson-line.com*; Timothy Noah, "What We Didn't Overcome," *Slate*, November 10, 2008, *slate.com*; William Voegeli, "The Wilderness Years Begin," *Claremont Review of Books*, June 5, 2009, *www.claremont.org*; Thomas Schaller, "Five Questions about the New Electorate," *American Prospect*, September 19, 2008, *www.prospect.org*; Tasha S. Philpot, *Race, Republicans, and the Return of the Party of Lincoln* (Ann Arbor: University of Michigan Press, 2007); and Thomas Schaller, "Gettysburg, Again," *American Prospect*, November 19, 2006, *www.prospect.org*.

CHAPTER 3

"The Republican Party Is Truly the Party of the 'Open Door'"

Ethnic Americans and the Republican Party in the 1970s

Joe Merton

The year 1965 was not a happy time for Republicans. Barry Goldwater's landslide defeat in the previous year's presidential election had left behind only disunity, bitterness, and disillusionment. Public identification with the Republican Party was a meager 24 percent, less than half that of the Democrats.[1] Political scientist Walter Dean Burnham declared, "The GOP is becoming less and less relevant to the central issues and concerns of American politics."[2] Writing in *Time* magazine, former national chairman Leonard Hall blamed his party's shortcomings on its ethnoracial exclusivity. "What's wrong with us?" Hall asked. "We have permitted our party to become too exclusive. . . . Our party gives the appearance of being an organization of white Anglo-Saxon Protestants." Hall recalled a recent meeting at which he noted not a single Jewish, Polish, Italian, or African American representative. "We have been trying to elect candidates with the descendants of the people who came over on the Mayflower," he reflected, "and that boat just wasn't big enough."[3]

Republicans had long struggled to win the votes of southern and eastern European immigrants and their descendants. Ethnic Americans, based largely in the urban North and numbering up to forty million voters, were central to the new "big-city generation" identified by Samuel Lubell as decisive to the dominant New Deal Democratic coalition. Republicans seemed largely resigned to their loss. At a Republican National Committee (RNC) meeting in 1936, Representative John Sosnowski of Michigan attacked Republican "discrimination" toward the foreign-born, but this elicited little change in party policy over the next two decades. The RNC abolished its Nationalities Division in 1955 at the behest of President Dwight D. Eisenhower, showing further disregard for the ethnic vote, even though the Democrats were now intensifying their operations to court it. Without a mechanism to build support in the long term, the GOP relied on preelection activities to gain votes from this constituency. In 1962, Congressman Edward Derwinski of Illinois, a Polish American representing a suburban Chicago district, derided this approach as a "frantic, haphazard three-month gyration doomed to defeat in advance."[4]

Within fifteen years, however, much had changed. The Republican Party entered the 1980s as a united, emboldened, and seemingly inclusive institution. During the 1980 election campaign, Stephen Aiello, an ethnic affairs adviser to the Carter White House, described the GOP ethnic campaign—its $700,000 budget dwarfing that of his party—as the "Goliath" to the Democratic "David." He warned, "The Republicans are making the ethnics their prime campaign target." Millions of ethnic voters consequently switched to the GOP, thereby helping to elect Ronald Reagan president. In Aiello's estimate, the old ethnic Democratic regulars had become "irregular."[5] So how does one explain this incredible shift in Republican fortunes? How did a party once condemned for its ethnic exclusivity, unable to relate to a largely working-class ethnic constituency, and historically associated with nativism and anti-Catholicism come to have such strong appeal to ethnic Americans by 1980?

Recent historical scholarship has done much to place the 1970s at the center of the late twentieth-century conservative counterrevolution. Developments specific to the decade, from the tax revolt to the political mobilization of evangelical Christians, proved critical to the resurgence of conservatism and the Republican Party.[6] Strategist Kevin Phillips outlined the "emerging Republican majority" during the late 1960s; since then, scholars such as Robert Mason have also pointed to the opportunity presented to the Republicans by the declining appeal of liberalism and a divided Democratic Party during this period.[7]

This study similarly argues that a development intrinsic to the 1970s—the emergence of a "white ethnic" identity politics, the "New Ethnicity"—played an invaluable role in the revival of the Republican Party by the 1980s. GOP interest in ethnicity and ethnic politics, previously limited to a rhetorical commitment to the liberation of the Eastern European "captive nations," expanded dramatically from the late 1960s onwards. Attracted to the contemporary debate over white ethnicity during the decade, and cognizant of a palpable political opportunity among ethnic voters, Republicans used an apparently resurgent white, European ethnicity and its various related meanings and identities as a means of organization and mobilization, politics and policy. The story of the party's ethnic strategy is a major element in its revitalization, but is often overlooked in the literature.

Without doubt, one reason for this oversight was the effective disappearance of ethnic identity politics—at least in its white, European form—by the close of the twentieth century. In marked contrast to the continuing influence of race, religion, and gender in identity politics, distinctions of ethnicity and national origin have receded from the political discourse and discussions of early twenty-first-century America. Sociological research has revealed that Americans of European ethnic origin rarely identify with these identities in a political context.[8]

Historiographical neglect of ethnic influences in the 1970s may also be explained by the evident difficulty of defining "white ethnic." Identities of class, religion, and national origin often intertwined with one another in discussions of the white ethnic constituency. At various times, white ethnics were also seen as Catholics, union members, blue-collar workers, or simply whites.[9] In the late 1960s and 1970s, they were identified not only as something uniquely different and diverse—a sharp break from the post-1945 orthodoxy that European ethnic groups had assimilated into a homogenous white American mass—but also an element of "Middle America," a major target for Republicans in this period. And although conventional notions of ethnicity based on religion or national origin continued to possess political power in the 1970s, the "white ethnic" label also reflected more intangible, contemporary concerns. As ethnic activist and intellectual Michael Novak declared, the New Ethnicity "grows out of personal experience . . . a growing self-confidence and social power; a sense of being discriminated against . . . a sense of injustice."[10] These shifting, multiple identities meant that an ethnic appeal could take several forms—targeted at class interests, religious loyalties, national identities, social grievances, or desires—and conversely, as the case of Ronald Reagan reveals, could contain little that was conventionally "ethnic" whatsoever.

This problem of definition, however, also underlines the importance of the white ethnics to the quest for a new Republican majority amid the collapse of the class-based New Deal order and the brief predominance of cultural concerns over distributional politics. The ethnic strategy provided one of many avenues used by the GOP to connect with an increasingly independent white working-class and lower-middle-class electorate. It overlapped with many other areas of Republican strategizing in the wake of liberalism's decline, from appeals to conservative Catholics over new social issues to the targeting of union members on either foreign policy and patriotism or perceptions of their declining socioeconomic mobility and black advancement. At different times and in different hands, ethnicity could mean different things: sometimes religion, culture, and heritage, but also rather more ethereal values, resentments, and aspirations. In truth, in the volatile, uncertain 1970s, many factors influenced ethnic voting, underlining the competing themes and identities huddled under the "white ethnic" umbrella, and the Republicans used ethnicity to tap into those various strands. The ethnic strategy therefore stands as a valuable conduit to explaining the Republican revival of the late twentieth century, and in particular the party's growing appeal to traditionally Democratic voter groups disenchanted by liberalism.

This chapter will challenge existing assumptions about the 1970s in three ways. First, it disputes the conventional portrayal of the era as one of partisan retrenchment. Increasingly personalized, candidate-centered campaigns, an overly powerful executive, decreasing public identification with the political parties (especially the Democrats), and a wider post-Watergate public disillusionment with politics have all been cited as decisive factors in the deterioration of the political party organization during the decade.[11] Nevertheless, there are also grounds for regarding the 1970s as a period of Republican innovation. To paraphrase David S. Broder, the party was not over. Instead, GOP organizational initiatives often complemented executive action in seeking to broaden the base of the Republican Party and open its doors to new voters.

Second, this chapter broadens the story of the Republican revival of the era beyond the Sunbelt. The shift of other elements of the disintegrating New Deal coalition, particularly white southerners, into the Republican Party has generated greater historiographical attention, and with good reason. Ronald Reagan ran exceptionally well in the South in 1980 against a regional opponent, and both the West and the South have remained reliably Republican since the 1960s. The transition of southern whites into the GOP has been smoother and seemingly permanent in comparison to the greater volatility of their ethnic equivalents in the urban and suburban Northeast and Midwest. Yet Republicans also made impressive gains in these regions during the late twentieth century, and ethnic voters proved as important an element—if not always as loyal—in the party's success.[12]

Finally, the chapter takes issue with the rare examples of scholarship that *have* addressed the Republican engagement with white ethnic politics in this period. The GOP ethnic strategy was by no means purely a form of cultural populism targeted mainly at racial resentments.[13] More complex than usually supposed, it was sensitive to the various themes and meanings behind the "white ethnic" identity and adopted strategies to match them. As I will reveal, Richard Nixon largely identified white ethnic assertion as a defense of values, traditions, and even privilege, and appealed to ethnic social grievances. He also pursued initiatives, however, that affirmed the value of ethnic heritage and catered to ethnic activists' concerns about ethnic cultural inferiority. Alternatively, against the backdrop of a difficult economic climate and intensified group conflict, Gerald Ford identified white ethnics as a disadvantaged group (as Nixon had initially done), and appealed more to pressing social needs and aspirations that might bridge group divisions. Whereas party-level ethnic initiatives tended to address issues of heritage and national origin, using Old World identities as an organizing principle for party building, executive actions were rather more interested in white ethnicity's class-oriented components. Even when the New Ethnicity fizzled out in the early 1980s as broader socioeconomic trends undermined traditional indicators of ethnic identity, Republicans—with Ronald Reagan in the lead—articulated a reconfigured vision of white, European ethnicity. Almost postethnic in content, their new approach emphasized universalistic values rather than distinctive ethnic traits and welcomed ethnic Americans into a wider national community.

During the 1970s, the *New York Times* observed, "politically . . . ethnicity became chic." The collapse of the postwar liberal consensus, and its values of universalism and assimilation, toward the end of the 1960s left behind a cultural and political vacuum in ethnic communities. In response, GOP activists, intellectuals, politicians, and policymakers propagated a new "white ethnic" identity politics that would transcend old European ethnic distinctions based on nationality, language, or religion. Party strategists from the White House down to the local level opened their eyes to the electoral potential of the "ethnic vote"—thought to number as many as forty or fifty million Americans in the key industrial states of the Northeast and Midwest. The New Ethnicity gave voice to ethnics' sense of isolation, grievance, and minority status. "I am born of PIGS: Poles, Italians, Greeks and Slavs," Michael Novak declared in *The Rise of the Unmeltable Ethnics*, "born into a history not white Anglo-Saxon and not Jewish" and thus "privy to neither power nor status nor intellectual voice." Novak and many other ethnic advocates encouraged white, European ethnic groups to organize politically in the name of a new, distinct, "white ethnic" group identity, countering the perceived socioeconomic progress of blacks and the establishment liberals who championed their cause. Their initial impact was impressive. "White, middle America ethnics will set the agenda for the 1970s," one ethnic activist confidently proclaimed in 1972. "We are all ethnics now," concluded the *Italo-American Times* in the same year.[14]

The emergence of the New Ethnicity was a largely unexpected development.[15] In the post–World War II era, traditional European ethnic distinctions were presumed to have diminished and European immigrants and their progeny assimilated into a homogenous, affluent national community. Despite its many cultural expressions, however, from Hollywood films such as *Rocky* (1976) to "It's Great to Be Greek" license plates, the New Ethnicity did not simply represent a spirit of Old World ethnic revivalism, or an antidote to the perceived homogeneity of postwar society. Instead, its political edge reflected a fundamentally new definition of ethnicity, much of which had little to do with national origins or heritage. As the pollster Richard Scammon perceptively outlined at a National Center for Urban Ethnic Affairs seminar in 1971:

> We all recognize a new kind of ethnicity in America today . . . a concern over present situations and values . . . [and] much of the voting of so-called white ethnic Americans concerns itself now not with voting for the ". . . ski," or the Irisher, or the Italian, but for something else, for a value system, which the ethnic may feel to be under attack. . . . It is often in the defense of these values . . . that a good deal of this new ethnic political vitality may be sensed.[16]

As Scammon's words suggest, a distinctly conservative motif ran through much of the ethnic revival, which gave it considerable appeal to Republicans searching for ways to connect with disaffected Democratic constituencies. The New Ethnicity rejected the assimilationist impulse rooted in the ideals of postwar liberalism. It manifested, in Michael Novak's words, a "discomfort with the sense of identity one is *supposed* to have—universalist, melted, 'like everyone else.'" Sensitive to this mood, Nixon's 1972 campaign distributed buttons for twenty-seven individual ethnic groups. Taras Szmagala, head of its ethnic operations, recalled, "That was just a recognition that 'I'm a Polish-American,' but that recognition was huge . . . counter-melting-pot, counter-liberal." For some, conservatives regarded white ethnicity as a value system that emphasized defending "tradition"—traditional values that rejected federal assistance in favor of self-reliance, traditional cultures that reinforced long-standing gender roles, traditional neighborhoods resistant to liberal social initiatives or black advancement.[17] As Scammon revealed, the new wave of white ethnic political activism often manifested itself as an attempt to defend these time-honored, traditional values in a modern and sometimes threatening or alienating society and polity. The presence of these conservative symbols in the new white ethnic politics made it an attractive proposition for Republicans during the 1970s.

Republicans perceived the opportunity to turn this ideological affinity into electoral benefit. The 1968 election had already demonstrated the decreasing fidelity of many ethnic groups to the Democrats: 40 percent of Italians voted for Nixon, compared to 25 percent eight years previously, and in New York City, all of Nixon's top eighteen assembly districts were heavily Catholic. These figures provided a stark contrast with the results of 1964, when such districts had gone for Democrat Lyndon B. Johnson over Barry Goldwater. "The cracks in the Democratic wall are apparent," a Republican report on the election stated excitedly. "Traditional Democratic voting blocs once considered 'off limits' by GOP strategists now suddenly appear as likely target groups . . . in the years ahead."[18]

These trends, repeated in the off-year elections of 1969, did not go unnoticed in the Nixon White House. Commenting on the New York mayoral election, Secretary of Labor George Shultz alerted the new president to the "Italian, Irish and other Roman Catholic voters . . . lined up heavily against the candidates who were identified as sympathetic to minority group problems." In a similar vein, political adviser Harry Dent counseled: "We must realize that old [ethnic] political loyalties have been dissolved. We have an unprecedented opportunity to garner votes in large blocks."[19] Politicians and political strategists, both Republican and Democratic, forecast an impending Republican majority among the "ethnic vote."[20]

Of course, not all the political manifestations of the New Ethnicity were conservatively inclined. Some liberal activists and organizations—from the Ford Foundation to the American Jewish Committee—viewed it as a means of defusing racial tension in urban centers and rebuilding support for the black cause. Geno Baroni of the U.S. Catholic Conference, a veteran of civil rights causes, sought to organize ethnic communities under the "white ethnic" label to push for social reform and access to government programs. He demanded a "new urban populism" to bring "urban ethnics"—including racial minorities—together on policy issues.[21] Others (including Michael Novak and many ethnic congressmen) used white ethnicity to address a perceived ethnic cultural inferiority, or offered a new vision of national identity and community defined by ethnic group difference and diversity. In doing so, they formulated an early model of multiculturalism, albeit mainly white and European, reflected in the ethnic heritage studies centers established by Congress in 1972 and the loving portrayal of American diversity in the 1976 Bicentennial celebrations.[22]

The New Ethnicity, however, largely reflected an ethnic disaffection with liberalism. "White ethnic" was as much a political label as a cultural one. For one to be "white ethnic," one might have been the "victim" of the "reverse discrimination" of programs such as school busing or racial quotas; or the forgotten inhabitant of a decaying, transitional urban neighborhood; or a casualty of an American Dream turned sour by an inflationary economy. Rightly or wrongly, many working- and lower-middle-class ethnics blamed Democratic liberalism for their predicament and decried its prioritization of racial minority interests at their expense. As one ethnic activist told sociologists, "What has driven us to our ethnicity is rejection."[23] The New Ethnicity was constructed on such logic, and such sentiments offered significant potential for the Republican Party.

Much of the Republican engagement with white ethnic politics took place within the White House. Influenced by aides such as Dent and Phillips, Richard Nixon made white ethnics an integral part of his plans for a "New Majority" and overtly sought to align them with the Republicans. Responding to the entreaties of ethnic activists such as Baroni, with whom he met at the White House in mid-1970, and urban policy advisers, notably Daniel Patrick Moynihan, Nixon initially based his ethnic agenda on appealing to the class interests of disadvantaged blue-collar workers, considered synonymous with white ethnics.[24] Accordingly, the Department of Labor's "Rosow Report" advocated substantive policies—such as child-care assistance, tax reform, college education grants, and urban renewal—to extend the Great Society impulse to marginalized blue-collar groups and large swathes of what the administration defined as "Middle America." Following its publication in May 1970, an internal White House report on "the ethnic vote" recommended "*positive programming*: a steady flow of Rosow Report–type blue-collar items" and "*positive* Middle American–type programs" in pursuit of this constituency.[25]

The Nixon administration, however, also played directly to other elements of the white ethnic identity. The administration systematically appointed ethnic Americans to executive positions on the basis of their ethnic and national origin. White House aides promoted ethnic studies legislation that gave grade school and college students the opportunity to learn about their ethnic heritage and sought to correct a perceived cultural inferiority among ethnic youth. Other proposals, such as Nixon's rhetorical support for federal aid to Catholic parochial schools, appealed to ethnics' religious affiliation. Despite their undoubted symbolism, such initiatives recognized the new white ethnic identity and underlined ethnicity's renewed salience and political power. But in placing the presidential seal on the politics of white ethnic difference, reelection politics were never far from Nixon's calculations. Ethnics were, as one aide put it, "where the ducks are," and Nixon instructed do-

mestic policy chief John Ehrlichman in late 1970 to launch "a massive all-out effort
. . . far beyond what we've done over the past two years" with ethnic voters. Nixon's
Committee for the Re-election of the President poured millions of dollars into its
1972 ethnic campaign. As Taras Szmagala recalled: "I was very well-funded. . . . No
request that I turned in was turned down."[26]

In Nixon's hands, however, ethnicity often became little more than a wedge to
pry voters away from the Democratic coalition. He jettisoned the idea of substantive reform, which could have solidified ethnic support by easing socioeconomic
needs and concerns, in favor of symbolic, ephemeral gestures to ethnic voters. Admittedly, expensive social initiatives such as those mooted in the Rosow Report
were rendered unlikely by other fiscal priorities, notably the cost of ongoing military commitments in Southeast Asia and Nixon's focus on boosting aggregate demand to strengthen recovery from the 1970 recession in readiness for his reelection. But the new approach also reflected the changing locus of power in the White
House, with advisers such as Moynihan largely marginalized in favor of more
partisan, politically oriented aides, and a wider shift in administration strategy in
the run-up to the 1972 campaign. As an increasingly election-oriented Nixon instructed chief of staff Bob Haldeman, "Get some symbolic things for Poles, Italians . . . no more." Beyond that, he relied on divisive issues such as school busing
and scatter-site housing that served to "drive a wedge right down the middle of the
Democratic Party," as aide Patrick J. Buchanan gleefully declared. This reliance on a
negative politics of white ethnic *ressentiment* intensified group tensions, but the absence of tangible programs to benefit ethnics did little to promote their realignment
with the GOP in the long term.[27]

Despite their short-termism, Nixon's efforts undoubtedly helped restructure
the Republicans' image among ethnic groups. As Ewa Matuszewski, a Polish American running the Nixon campaign in Hamtramck, Michigan, affirmed: "I worked
for [Democratic presidential candidate] Humphrey in . . . 1968. . . . [But] I realized that it was under a Republican administration that the ethnics had made some
leeway in public life."[28] In this recognition of ethnicity and placement of ethnic
Americans both in White House posts and at the 1972 Republican convention, the
Nixon administration redefined the GOP as a broader, more inclusive institution
for white ethnics and other working-class groups. This drew a sharp contrast with
the postreform Democratic Party, which appeared to be traveling in the opposite
direction.[29]

Thanks to Nixon, Republican leaders no longer balked at the prospect of appearing at Cadillac Square in Detroit, the Pulaski Day parade, or an Italian picnic.
Benefiting from this new GOP attentiveness to ethnicity—as well as the wider issues of Vietnam and the economy, which hurt the Democrats and their candidate,
George McGovern—the president was rewarded with a landslide reelection victory.
In winning the votes of 53 percent of Polish Americans and 58 percent of Italian Americans, he set a Republican record that hinted at a potentially permanent

ethnic realignment. "Our future," Buchanan proclaimed after the election, "is the Democratic working man . . . Northern, Catholic—and ethnic."[30]

Nixon's success created an alluring template for his Republican successors to follow. After concerted lobbying from ethnic activists and congressmen, Gerald Ford appointed the first ever White House special assistant for ethnic affairs, Myron Kuropas, replicating similar innovations for African Americans and Hispanics. His administration's most significant gesture came with four White House conferences on ethnicity, which emphasized themes of white ethnic difference and entitlement in major public policy areas. These events brought together activists, intellectuals, politicians, and neighborhood organizers from across the white ethnic movement, and the initial impact was impressive. "This day," Baroni declared at one conference, "will provide the impetus for promoting the special programs so important to ethnic America." "The White House has discovered ethnics," proclaimed one ethnic weekly.[31]

Ford was responding to a new and thriving network of "white ethnic" advocates, organizations, and interest groups. Tokenism could no longer quench the thirst of increasingly vocal ethnic lobbies for recognition and recompense. Ford thus approached ethnic identity politics in a very different fashion from that of his predecessor. Against the backdrop of a worsening economic climate and incidents of intense ethnoracial group conflict (especially over school busing in Boston and the promotion of minority police officers in Detroit), officials focused on aspirations, not resentments; Kuropas recalled that they embraced cultural pluralism as a means of "bringing groups together, mutual understanding." The White House conferences sought to build multiethnic coalitions around policy issues of mutual interest and stressed unity through the recognition of group difference. In contrast to Nixon, Ford refused to intervene in wedge issues threatening to tear the Democratic coalition apart—notably Boston's school busing crisis. When ethnic leaders visited the White House, the agenda featured neither traditional "ethnic issues," such as the captive nations, nor "social issues," like busing and welfare. Instead, delegates explored the possibility of adopting a Canadian "mosaic" approach to ethnic diversity, a presidential commission on the status of American pluralism, and a federal training program that would "sensitize officials to multiethnic factors." Such a development clearly reflected the growing political significance of the New Ethnicity.[32]

All this did not overshadow electoral calculation in Ford's dealings with ethnic voters. Nixon holdovers remained on his staff, including Office of Public Liaison (OPL) chief William Baroody. Baroody saw the OPL and the special assistant for ethnic affairs as a means of "reviving and even expanding the New Majority coalition," a point he emphasized repeatedly during his first meeting with Ford in August 1974. "The ultimate goal," he declared, was "to recreate the New Majority and expand it." A 1975 Baroody presentation urged a renewed focus on "the New Majority," especially "the 'peripheral urban ethnic' . . . containing many blue collar ethnic and Roman Catholic working-class elements." "They can be won back," he concluded in the wake of the Republican disaster in the Watergate- and recession-affected midterm elections of 1974. "This block . . . must receive our careful attention."[33] By underlining the possibility of repeating the New Majority effort of 1972, Nixon veterans such as Baroody played a key role in encouraging Ford to embrace white ethnicity.

Ford eventually lost a tight election to the Democratic candidate Jimmy Carter. But while the presence of a regional candidate on the ticket convinced many southerners to return to the Democratic fold, the results showed continuing Republican strength among Italian, Polish, and Catholic voters. In its final report, Ford's Ethnic Desk optimistically concluded, "Prior to the 1972 campaign, there existed an inability by the Republican Party to expand its base in the ethnic voter bloc. It is evident progress is now being made."[34]

Republican presidential aspirants for 1980 were not slow to pick up the ethnic baton. Representative Philip Crane of Illinois and Senator Robert J. Dole of Kansas built liaisons with the ethnic community, but no one did so as assiduously as Ronald Reagan. His appeal to other elements of the New Majority has been well documented, but Reagan had also picked up strong ethnic support in the 1976 presidential primaries (over half of his New York delegates were Italian Americans). Testifying to the former California governor's courting of the ethnic vote as GOP frontrunner in 1980, *Newsweek* quipped that he took care "to drop more Polish names than a social climber in Krakow."[35]

Reagan's success with ethnic voters, however, also reflected the transformed political environment of 1980 and the transformed content of the GOP ethnic strategy. The New Ethnicity had petered out, its image of the nation as a disparate collection of competing ethnic interest groups increasingly unpopular. Attempts to build a racialized white ethnic identity foundered on the entrenched whiteness of ethnic Americans. Economic crisis pushed ethnocultural concerns underground, while growing antigovernment sentiment rendered pro-ethnic federal programs untenable. And in truth, the 1970s had been kind to the majority of the white ethnics: the 1980 census and other federal studies revealed that many had made impressive educational and economic gains during the decade, debunking notions of white ethnic disadvantage. Such progress led to a shift in socioeconomic interests and an increased receptiveness toward the Republican credo of lower taxes and reduced federal programs. As historian John Bukowczyk has written, for Polish Americans, "voting Republican was . . . another aspect of upward mobility and assimilation, of 'having arrived.'"[36]

However, the Reagan team by no means abandoned the ethnic strategy. Instead, more cognizant than ever of the political opportunities among ethnic voters, it reconfigured the use of white, European ethnicity to reflect the transformed exogenous environment and an increasingly suburban, affluent, homogeneous ethnic constituency, concerned about nonethnic issues such as inflation, unemployment, and declining national prestige. "Let's not fall into the same old trap of prais-ing 'ethnics' as ethnics—we are praising their values," proclaimed Reagan aide Bill Gavin, a Nixon administration veteran and author of *Street Corner Conservative*, a 1975 call to arms for working-class urban whites. "Ethnicity means something more than ritual speeches about Captive Nations or election-year indulging in ex-otic foods," he declared in 1980. "It means *caring about the way people are, the way they want to lead their lives, the great pressures . . .* [of] *a society that often neglects and even ridicules traditional values.*"[37]

Reagan thus subsumed ethnicity into a vision of a resurgent national whole, one that placed the white ethnics' historical experience—immigration, self-reliance, upward mobility—at the heart of the American narrative. In doing so, he gave them a sense of inclusion and recognition that neither Nixon nor Ford had consis-tently provided. During the 1980 Republican campaign, a multiethnic Labor Day picnic in the shadow of the Statue of Liberty—a symbolic site for ethnic Ameri-cans—was the occasion for a heartily patriotic rendition of "God Bless America" and harsh criticism of Carter's economic record and unpopular liberal social pro-grams. Reagan also spoke of the nation's economic woes at a Polish barbecue in Detroit. Both Nixon and Ford had mainly affirmed notions of white ethnic identity and group difference in their public policy initiatives and compartmentalized po-litical strategies. The universalistic Reagan transcended white ethnic identity poli-tics to envision an inclusive "coalition of shared values." He idealized a national community that united ethnic voters with white southerners, union members, re-ligious conservatives, and big business around ethnic (and thus, in Reagan's inter-pretation, quintessentially American) values such as work, family, neighborhood, and patriotism, and collective, nonethnic themes of national renewal, traditional values, and antigovernment sentiment. This enabled Reagan to defend the values articulated by Scammon and Novak, while also speaking to wider concerns over the economy and the Cold War. Measured by electoral outcome, this was a highly effective strategy. Reagan won impressive majorities among the "white ethnics," a term that spanned national origin groups such as Irish Americans, Slavic Ameri-cans, and Italian Americans, as well as blue-collar workers and Catholics.[38]

Although the White House served as the main agent of this new GOP ethnic orientation, the national party was also instrumental in converting ethnic voters to its cause. Complementing (and sometimes conflicting with) executive initiatives, Republican operatives at both the national and grassroots levels answered Leonard Hall's call in the wake of the disastrous 1964 election campaign to expand the par-ty's base. In doing so, individuals such as Ray Bliss and William Brock provided the institutional foundations for an assault on traditionally Democratic ethnic constituencies. They succeeded in building a GOP infrastructure in ethnic com-munities across the urban North that catered to these groups, provided them with a sense of recognition and inclusion and, aided by national trends, facilitated their pro-Republican transition.[39]

The election of Ray Bliss as RNC chairman in 1965 was a first step. One analysis credits him with turning the committee from "a second-rate answering machine" into an organization capable of achieving majority status for the party. Bliss sought to broaden the Republican base in order to make it "the party of all the people." Having taken initial steps to enhance its reach in urban constituencies, the party established a full-time ethnic division in 1968, devoting substantial backing to the Nixon campaign.[40] "1968 was a key year," Republican ethnic activist Jack Burgess recalled. "It was the first time we had a full-time working operation with hundreds of names, contacts, indexes, newsletters . . . [and] we formed groups like Polish-Americans for Nixon-Agnew . . . organizing them, gathering mailing lists, making contact with key members in each community. By '72 . . . we were able to deluge all these communities."[41]

In the aftermath of Nixon's victory, Bliss made the ethnic division permanent for the first time in Republican history. "We have a tremendous reservoir there of leadership," he declared, "if only we develop it." That the party did; by 1972, there were over one thousand ethnic Republican clubs operating in twenty states. "Quietly, almost invisibly, the Republican Party has been developing a presence and a voice in ethnic neighborhoods," the *New York Times* observed, outlining the growth of such clubs across the Northeast and Midwest. The GOP's institutional expansion provided a welcome contrast for ethnic voters with the Democrats' McGovern-Fraser reforms. "This year more than ever, ethnics are joining the Republican Party in increasing number," activist Laszlo Pasztor excitedly informed the 1972 GOP convention. The conversion of Pasztor, previously active in Republican appeals to the captive nations, to the New Ethnicity reflected the shifting tone—and growing power—of ethnic politics by the 1970s. "The Republican Party is truly the party of the 'open door,'" he proclaimed.[42]

Further attempts to broaden the GOP's ethnic base continued apace. "[My aim is] to strengthen and expand what we have now . . . [and] to broaden our Heritage effort to mobilize more of the New Majority," wrote new RNC chair George H. W. Bush to the Polish American Congress in mid-1973. Responding to pressure from grassroots ethnic party activists, as well as the White House, Bush oversaw the introduction of further ethnic auxiliaries within the party. By 1976, therefore, National Republican Heritage Groups Councils were operational in twenty-four states, and local Republican ethnic federations in thirty. A substantial political organization had been established that could elect Republican candidates from traditional Democratic strongholds, develop a Republican presence in ethnic communities, and act as a springboard for further ethnic participation. Taras Szmagala, now working for the RNC, recalled: "The structure we established, with an ethnic operation in each state . . . ensured that more and more people were openly Republican. They got involved in local politics. . . . People were now active . . . at the local level."[43]

Beyond creating these new organizational structures, the Republicans began to pick up impressive victories in constituencies previously considered staunchly Democratic. Ethnic Republican mayors were elected in Detroit (Roman Gribbs, 1969), Cleveland (Ralph Perk, 1971), and Providence (Vincent Cianci, 1974). In Cleveland, Perk established the American Nationalities Movement, which acted as a conduit to increase ethnics' role in local decision making, cut significantly into Democratic registration in the city, and encouraged ethnic Democrats to cross party lines. His success also underlined the potential power of white ethnic politics as a means of organization and mobilization. "There's a new sense of ethnicity," underlined Perk's assistant for nationality affairs. "We want to show everybody that the ethnics can run the city as well as anybody else." Ethnic Republican candidates were elected to the Board of Education and other decision-making bodies, laying the foundations for future Republican—and ethnic—success in Cleveland.[44]

During the late 1970s, RNC chairman William Brock continued this work and integrated it with a renewed drive toward Nixon's New Majority. Determined to change the image of the Republican Party, he called on members "to change, not our principles . . . but, rather, change ourselves and the way in which we are perceived." Free from executive interference, Brock sponsored outreach programs for groups previously underrepresented in the party, including ethnics. The party directed its attention toward the grass roots, particularly local races for courthouses, state legislatures, and small-town mayorships. It sought out candidates who reflected their communities—from Asian Americans in California to a Polish volunteer firefighter who became the first Republican elected in a habitually Democratic district of Wilmington, Delaware. Using direct mail, Brock increased the number of party contributors from 350,000 in 1977, raising $7.3 million, to 550,000 contributors, raising $12 million in funds by 1979. As testament to the wider economic base of the party, the average individual contribution was just $26. Confident the GOP had built a new constituency, Brock publicly proclaimed in 1980 that "the Republicans are becoming the party of the people." During the national convention, which was held in Detroit to symbolize the new inclusiveness, he told the RNC that the party was in its "strongest position . . . possibly . . . since 1928," a development reflecting its "new and much broader . . . foundation."[45]

Brock's confident proclamations marked the culmination of a concerted attempt to broaden the party base during the 1970s. Aided by an unpopular incumbent Democratic president, fears of national decline, the grievous state of the economy by the close of the decade, and broader socioeconomic trends, the ethnic strategy played its part in the Republican capture of the Senate and the presidency in 1980. Despite its uncertain and contested meanings, white ethnicity was a major component of the national political conversation during the 1970s. Local ethnic clubs and auxiliaries joined the national party and the White House in attempting to use it as a means of voter organization and mobilization, providing a sense of political place to millions of ethnic voters in an era of considerable partisan flux. By refashioning itself as the "party of the open door" to ethnic voters, a once predominantly WASP-establishment party became receptive to the millions of independent, working- and middle-class voters identified by pollster Stan Greenberg in the 1980s as one of the major swing groups in American politics—the "Reagan Democrats."[46]

Of course, one must not apply too much agency to the Republican ethnic strategy in tracing the GOP revival of the 1970s. As stated above, even in the "Ethnic Seventies," many other factors besides ethnicity dictated ethnic voting.[47] Concerns over the economy, Vietnam, race, and the changing composition of the political parties were arguably more influential in guiding ethnic political behavior. The interests of class, race, and religion often transcended those of ethnic or national origin in influencing ethnic voters' ballot choices. Wider socioeconomic trends undermined the politics of white ethnicity and played as significant a role in shaping nascent Republican identification among ethnic Americans. Contrary to the claims of the New Ethnicity, the white ethnics proved little different politically from the majority of white Americans, and by the early 1980s the GOP's ethnic auxiliaries had largely dwindled away.

But that does not render irrelevant the narrative of the Republican ethnic campaigns. By no means just an offbeat footnote in the history of the 1970s, or a dated relic of a redundant political moment, the ethnic strategy remains a story of considerable significance. First, it highlights the great salience of white, European ethnicity to the politics of the late 1960s and 1970s. This was a time when ethnicity was a subject of considerable contemporary debate; when white ethnic identity politics was new, exciting, and above all different; and when white, European ethnics could still be considered "ethnic." White ethnicity was reified in this period as a potent means not only of cultural expression but also of political assertion, organization, and mobilization. In its discovery of white ethnicity, the GOP recognized an electoral opportunity that it embraced to great effect.

Second, the GOP ethnic strategy underlines the palpable sense of political vacuum and flux during the 1970s, an era in which such unlikely practitioners of ethnic politics as Sunbelt conservative Richard Nixon, small-town midwesterner Gerald Ford, and Tennessee's William Brock were willing political innovators. These Republican leaders reached out to newly available yet increasingly diffuse ethnic blocs. Such gestures contrasted with the universalistic appeals, far removed from ethnic bloc politics, made by Presidents Kennedy, Johnson, and even Reagan on either side of the 1970s. The volatile political environment of this decade, combined with the powerful recent impact of the black civil rights movement, gave the politics of white ethnicity great traction and influence in political circles. Indeed, considering its lack of a genuine grassroots following and remarkably brief existence, it arguably enjoyed far greater agency than it otherwise deserved.

Finally, the Republican ethnic strategy played an important role in providing ethnic voters with a sense of recognition and political belonging in this era of flux and uncertainty. The party's attempts to broaden its base and appeal to ethnic voters, as Catholics, blue-collar workers, union members, or indeed "white ethnics," contrasted favorably with the Democrats, whose party reforms and quotas only exacerbated the drift of these traditional constituent groups away from the party. Outreach mechanisms established during the 1970s, although now largely defunct, provided important initial conduits to ethnic participation in the party, and established bases in communities across the urban North previously considered off-limits for Republicans. Moreover, the GOP's utilization of Novak's definition of ethnicity, rather than more conventional meanings, gave it appeal to large swaths of voters and bestowed additional impact and longevity on the ethnic strategy. The party's attentiveness to ethnic values, rather than ethnicity per se, allowed it to place ethnic Americans at the heart of a universalistic "nation of community" (albeit one that often required the exclusion of others) that cherished such shared ideals. As a consequence, Republican politicians retained ethnic appeal well beyond the abolition of the Office of Ethnic Affairs and the "twilight of ethnicity" in the 1980s. In this sense, the Republican ethnic strategy lived on even after the nation's Poles, Greeks, and Italians were no longer regarded as "ethnic"—the ultimate tribute to its success.

NOTES

1. Gallup Organization, survey on partisan identification, January 7–12, 1965, iPOLL Databank, Roper Center for Public Opinion Research, University of Connecticut, Storrs, CT, *www.ropercenter.uconn.edu.*

2. *Commonweal*, March 19, 1965, 718.

3. *Time*, April 2, 1965.

4. Samuel Lubell, *The Future of American Politics* (New York: Harper, 1952), 29–35; remarks by Representative John Sosnowski to RNC executive session, Chicago, December 17, 1936, in *Papers of the Republican Party*, part 1: *Meetings of the Republican National Committee, 1911–1980*; Series A, *1911–1960*, ed. Paul L. Kesaris (Frederick, MD: University Press of America, 1986), Reel 5; Perry L. Weed, *The White Ethnic Movement and Ethnic Politics* (New York: Praeger, 1973), 140–44; and "Report of Subcommittee on Nationalities and Minority Groups by Rep. Edward Derwinski," Oklahoma City, January 12, 1962, in *Papers of the Republican Party*, part 1: *Meetings of the Republican National Committee, 1911–1980*; Series B, *1960–1980*, ed. Paul L. Kesaris (Frederick, MD: University Press of America, 1986), Reel 1.

5. Stephen Aiello, memorandum to Landon Butler, October 16, 1980, Box 48, Stephen Aiello Files, Jimmy Carter Presidential Library, Atlanta, GA; Aiello, memorandum to Hamilton Jordan, n.d., Box 49, Aiello Files; and Gerald M. Pomper et al., *The Election of 1980: Reports and Interpretations* (Chatham, NJ: Chatham House, 1981), 179.

6. For examples of such scholarship, see Bruce J. Schulman and Julian E. Zelizer, eds., *Rightward Bound: Making America Conservative in the 1970s* (Cambridge, MA: Harvard University Press, 2008); Godfrey Hodgson, *The World Turned Right Side Up: A History of the Conservative Ascendancy in America* (Boston: Houghton Mifflin, 1996); and Thomas Byrne Edsall with Mary D. Edsall, *Chain Reaction: The Impact of Race, Rights, and Taxes on American Politics* (New York: Norton, 1992), 99–136.

7. Kevin P. Phillips, *The Emerging Republican Majority* (New Rochelle, NY: Arlington House, 1970), and Robert Mason, *Richard Nixon and the Quest for a New Majority* (Chapel Hill: University of North Carolina Press, 2004). For more on the trials of

liberalism during the 1970s, see Iwan Morgan, *Beyond the Liberal Consensus: A Political History of the United States since 1965* (London: Hurst, 1994), 124–30, 157–70; Bruce J. Schulman, *The Seventies: The Great Shift in American Culture, Society, and Politics* (New York: Free Press, 2001), 121–43; Steven M. Gillon, *The Democrats' Dilemma: Walter F. Mondale and the Liberal Legacy* (New York: Columbia University Press, 1992), 187–213, 251–99; and Bruce Miroff, *The Liberals' Moment: The McGovern Insurgency and the Identity Crisis of the Democratic Party* (Lawrence: University Press of Kansas, 2007), 247–78.

8. For examples of such research, see Herbert J. Gans, "Symbolic Ethnicity: The Future of Ethnic Groups and Cultures in America," *Ethnic and Racial Studies* 2 (January 1979): 1–19; Richard D. Alba, *Ethnic Identity: The Transformation of White America* (New Haven, CT: Yale University Press, 1990), 150–57; and Mary C. Waters, *Ethnic Options: Choosing Identities in America* (Berkeley: University of California Press, 1990).

9. As Nixon aide Charles Colson wrote, relating the administration's efforts to appeal to Eastern European ethnics to its work with union members, "By and large we are talking about many of the same people." Charles Colson, memorandum to H. R. Haldeman, September 14, 1970, Box 38, Charles W. Colson Files, White House Special Files (WHSF), Staff Member and Office Files (SMOF), Nixon Presidential Materials Project (NPMP), National Archives, College Park, MD.

10. Michael Novak, "The New Ethnicity," *Center* 7 (July–Aug 1974): 18–25.

11. David S. Broder, *The Party's Over: The Failure of Politics in America* (New York: Harper and Row, 1972), xx–xv, 171; Ripon Society with Clifford W. Brown Jr., *Jaws of Victory: The Game-Plan Politics of 1972, the Crisis of the Republican Party, and the Future of the Constitution* (Boston: Little, Brown, 1974), 20–23, 187–93; Austin Ranney, "The Political Parties," in *The New American Political System*, ed. Anthony King (Washington, DC: American Enterprise Institute, 1978), 213–47; and John R. Petrocik, *Party Coalitions: Realignment and the Decline of the New Deal Party System* (Chicago: University of Chicago Press, 1981). For a convincing rebuttal of this orthodoxy, at least on the GOP side, see Daniel J. Galvin, *Presidential Party Building: Dwight D. Eisenhower to George W. Bush* (Princeton, NJ: Princeton University Press, 2010), 70–119.

12. Much excellent work has been produced on the Republican takeover of the Sunbelt. For example, see Lisa McGirr, *Suburban Warriors: The Origins of the New American Right* (Princeton, NJ: Princeton University Press, 2001); Matthew D. Lassiter, *The Silent Majority: Suburban Politics in the Sunbelt South* (Princeton, NJ: Princeton University Press, 2006); Earl Black and Merle Black, *The Rise of Southern Republicans* (Cambridge, MA: Harvard University Press, 2002); and Joseph Crespino, *In Search of Another Country: Mississippi and the Conservative Counterrevolution* (Princeton, NJ: Princeton University Press, 2007).

13. For work that ties the Republican ethnic strategy to racial conservatism, see Thomas J. Sugrue and John D. Skrentny, "The White Ethnic Strategy," in Schulman and Zelizer, *Rightward Bound*, 171–92; Matthew Frye Jacobson, *Roots Too: White Ethnic Revival in Post–Civil Rights America* (Cambridge, MA: Harvard University Press, 2006), 177–205; and Orlando Patterson, *Ethnic Chauvinism: The Reactionary Impulse* (New York: Stein and Day, 1977), 158–85.

14. *New York Times*, December 30, 1979, D6; Michael Novak, *The Rise of the Unmeltable Ethnics: Politics and Culture in the Seventies* (New York: Macmillan, 1972); *Harper's*, September 1971, 44–50; *New York Times*, March 16, 1972, 49; and *Italo-American*

Times, July 1972, Italian-American Periodicals Collection, Immigration History Research Center (IHRC), University of Minnesota, Minneapolis.

15. The emergence of the "New Ethnicity" is explored most recently in John D. Skrentny, *The Minority Rights Revolution* (Cambridge, MA: Harvard University Press, 2002), 277–81; Jacobson, *Roots Too*; and David R. Colburn and George E. Pozzetta, "Race, Ethnicity, and the Evolution of Political Legitimacy," in *The Sixties: From Memory to History*, ed. David Farber (Chapel Hill: University of North Carolina Press, 1994), 119–48. A sociological and current affairs literature on the white ethnics existed during the 1970s, but died out by the following decade. Examples include Novak, *Unmeltable Ethnics*; Andrew Greeley, *Why Can't They Be Like Us? America's White Ethnic Groups* (New York: Dutton, 1971); Mark R. Levy and Michael S. Kramer, *The Ethnic Factor: How America's Minorities Decide Elections* (New York: Simon and Schuster, 1973); Joseph Ryan, ed., *White Ethnics: Their Life in Working Class America* (Englewood Cliffs, NJ: Prentice Hall, 1973); Richard Krickus, *Pursuing the American Dream: White Ethnics and the New Populism* (Garden City, NY: Doubleday, 1976); and Michael Wenk, S. M. Tomasi, and Geno Baroni, eds., *Pieces of a Dream: The Ethnic Worker's Crisis with America* (New York: Center for Migration Studies, 1972).

16. Scammon quoted in Weed, *White Ethnic Movement*, 217.

17. Novak, "New Ethnicity," 18–25; author's interview with Taras Szmagala, Washington, DC, March 11, 2007; Sugrue and Skrentny, "White Ethnic Strategy," 175.

18. Levy and Kramer, *Ethnic Factor*, 18–19; *Congressional Quarterly Weekly Report*, March 11, 1972, 534; Phillips, *Emerging*, 172; and RNC research report, "Key Sub-Population Groups in the 1968 Elections," January 1970, in *Papers of the Republican Party*, part 2: *Reports and Memoranda of the Research Division of the Headquarters of the Republican National Committee, 1938–1980*, ed. Paul L. Kesaris (Frederick, MD: University Publications of America, 1986), Reel 8.

19. Shultz, memorandum to Nixon, June 26, 1969, Box 23, Records of the Secretary of Labor, George P. Shultz, Office of Records Services, National Archives, College Park, MD; and Dent, memorandum to Nixon, October 13, 1969, Box 2, Harry S. Dent Files, WHSF, SMOF, NPMP.

20. Andrew Hacker, "Is There a Republican Majority?," in *The White Majority: Between Poverty and Affluence*, ed. Louise Kapp Howe (New York: Vantage Press, 1970), 263–78; *Newsweek*, October 6, 1969, 38–43; and Richard M. Scammon and Ben J. Wattenberg, *The Real Majority* (New York: Coward-McCann, 1970), 59–71.

21. Weed, *White Ethnic Movement*, 18–41; and Geno Baroni, "Ethnicity and Public Policy," in Wenk, Tomasi, and Baroni, *Pieces of a Dream*, 8–11.

22. For more on ethnic diversity and the Bicentennial celebrations, see Natasha Zaretsky, *No Direction Home: The American Family and the Fear of National Decline, 1968–1980* (Chapel Hill: University of North Carolina Press, 2007), 146–52.

23. Howard F. Stein and Robert F. Hill, *The Ethnic Imperative* (University Park: Pennsylvania State University Press, 1977), 216. These sentiments were best encapsulated in a 1969 article by Pete Hamill in *New York* magazine, which gained great currency within the Nixon administration. See Hamill, "The Revolt of the White Lower-Middle Class," in Howe, *White Majority*, 10–22, and also "The Forgotten American," *Harper's*, August 1969, 27–34; and "The Troubled American," *Newsweek*, October 6, 1969, 20–38.

24. Like many liberal ethnic activists, advisers such as Moynihan and Secretary of Labor George Shultz identified ethnics as part of a wider blue-collar constituency suffering from a perceived socioeconomic "squeeze" in the early 1970s. They believed that

substantive policy could ease these groups' alienation and disadvantage and improve race relations in American cities: Moynihan called for an expansion of Great Society programs to allow the white working class "to regain a sense of positive action from the operation of American government." See Council for Urban Affairs meeting minutes, February 12, 1969, Container 1:264, and Moynihan, memorandum to Nixon, May 17, 1969, Container 1:243, both in Daniel P. Moynihan Papers, Manuscript Division, Library of Congress, Washington, DC.

25. "The Ethnic Vote in the 1970 and 1972 Elections," n.d., Box 9, Dent Files. For discussion of the "Rosow Report," see Jefferson Cowie, "Nixon's 'Class Struggle': Romancing the New Right Worker, 1969–1973," *Labor History* 43 (2002): 257–83; and Joe Merton, "The Politics of Symbolism: Richard Nixon's Appeal to White Ethnics and the Frustration of Realignment, 1969–72," *European Journal of American Culture* 26 (2008): 181–98.

26. *Italo-American Times*, November 1972, Italian-American Periodicals Collection; Huston, memorandum to the Middle America Group, January 20, 1971, Box 3, Patrick J. Buchanan Files, WHSF, SMOF, NPMP; Nixon, memorandum to Ehrlichman, November 30, 1970, Box 154, H.R. Haldeman Files, WHSF, SMOF, NPMP; and author's interview with Szmagala.

27. Nixon quoted in Dean J. Kotlowski, *Nixon's Civil Rights: Politics, Principle, and Policy* (Cambridge, MA: Harvard University Press, 2001), 20; and Buchanan, memorandum to Ehrlichman, Haldeman, and Colson, September 23, 1971, Box 3, Buchanan Files.

28. *Baltimore Sun*, November 5, 1972, 2.

29. Indeed, the Democratic Party reforms of the early 1970s increased the influence of liberal activists and expanded participation through quotas for women, minorities and younger voters, but diminished the influence of the old ethnic party regulars, and 1972 Democratic candidate George McGovern displayed little sensitivity to ethnic votes. As journalist Mike Royko angrily proclaimed upon the expulsion of Mayor Richard J. Daley's Illinois delegation from the 1972 party convention, "[The] reforms have disenfranchised Chicago's white ethnic Democrats." *Chicago Daily News*, July 6, 1972, Box 21, Mike Royko Papers, Newberry Library, Chicago, IL. For more, see Miroff, *Liberals' Moment*, 1–7, 189–94; and Krickus, *Pursuing the American Dream*, 242–50.

30. Dent, memorandum to Haldeman, July 21, 1972, Box 399, Haldeman Files; Levy and Kramer, *Ethnic Factor*, 226; Krickus, *Pursuing*, 280; and Buchanan, memorandum to Nixon, November 10, 1972, Box 2, Buchanan Files.

31. Ethnicity meeting schedules, Box 55, William S. Baroody Papers, Gerald R. Ford Presidential Library (hereafter GRFPL), Ann Arbor, MI; "Ethnicity and Neighborhood Revitalization Conference Proceedings," May 5, 1976, Baroody Papers; and *Jednota*, May 19, 1976.

32. Author's interview with Myron Kuropas, Chicago, September 27, 2008; Ralph Jalkanen to Marrs, January 31, 1975, Box 68, Theodore S. Marrs Files, GRFPL; and Mayor Ralph Perk et al. to President Ford, January 28, 1975, Marrs Files.

33. "Talking Points for Meeting with President Ford," August 12, 1974, Box 63, Baroody Papers; and presentation for Baroody, "Constituency Groups," October 27, 1975, Box 48,Baroody Papers.

34. Petrocik, *Party Coalitions*, 95–96; *New Republic*, October 2, 1976, 10–11; and "Final Report—Ethnic Desk," n.d., Box 15, Robert P. Visser Papers, GRFPL.

35. "Proposed Actions," n.d., Box 49, Baroody Papers; and *Newsweek*, October 20, 1980, 35.

36. United States Commission on Civil Rights, *The Economic Status of Americans of*

Southern and Eastern European Ancestry (Washington, DC: U.S. Government Printing Office, 1986), 1–5; HEW Office of Research and Statistics, "The Status of Italian-American Families" (report), 1977, Box 124, National Italian-American Foundation (NIAF) Records, IHRC; and John J. Bukowczyk, *And My Children Did Not Know Me: A History of the Polish-Americans* (Bloomington: Indiana University Press, 1987), 136.

37. Bill Gavin, memorandum to Peter Hannaford and Martin Anderson, April 10, 1979, and Gavin, memorandum to Anderson, n.d., Box 3, Deaver and Hannaford Inc. Records, Hoover Institution, Stanford University, Palo Alto, CA, emphases in the original.

38. *New York Times*, September 2, 1980, 1; *New York Times*, April 12, 1980, 10; Pomper, *Election of 1980*, 71–73; and Theodore H. White, *America In Search of Itself: The Making of the President, 1956–1980* (New York: Harper, 1982), 414.

39. Indeed, voter independence was on the increase among ethnic voters during the 1970s, reflecting a wider pattern of partisan dealignment among the electorate. Thirty-three percent of Polish Catholics regarded themselves as independents by the end of the 1970s (compared with 28 percent in the 1950s). Among higher-status Catholics the shift was even more pronounced; 43 percent were self-identified independents, compared to 29 percent twenty years earlier. By 1981, polls demonstrated that these independents were leaning toward the resurgent Republicans ahead of the Democrats. See Petrocik, *Party Coalitions*, 82–83; *New York Times*, June 14, 1981, 110.

40. Tim Hames, "Power without Politics: The Republican National Committee in Political Life and the Debate over Party Renewal," University of Oxford DPhil thesis (1990), 70, 73; *Time*, November 18, 1966; and Weed, *White Ethnic Movement*, 134.

41. Author's interview with Jack Burgess, Washington, DC, January 28, 2008.

42. Ray Bliss, report on the 1968 elections to RNC meeting, Washington, DC, January 17, 1969, in *Papers of the Republican Party*, Part 1, Series B, Reel 7; *Congressional Quarterly Weekly Report*, March 11, 1972, 534; *New York Times*, September 24, 1972, 46; and Laszlo Pasztor, remarks to RNC Committee on Rules, Miami Beach, August 14, 1972, in *Papers of the Republican Party*, Part 1, Series B, Reel 9.

43. Bush to Mazewski, July 2, 1973, Box 98, Aloysius Mazewski Papers, IHRC; remarks by Derwinski to RNC meeting, Arlington, VA. February 27, 1976, in *Papers of the Republican Party*, Part 1, Series B, Reel 13; and author's interview with Szmagala.

44. *Washington Post*, August 13, 1973, A1; and *Cleveland Plain Dealer*, February 7, 1972.

45. Hames, "Power without Politics," 77–90; *New York Times*, June 27, 1979, 14; author's interview with Bill Brock, Washington, DC, January 24, 2008; *National Journal*, September 27, 1980, 1617–1621; Bill Brock, remarks to RNC meeting, Detroit, July 9, 1980, in *Papers of the Republican Party*, Part 1, Series B, Reel 18.

46. Stanley B. Greenberg, *Middle Class Dreams: The Politics and Power of the New American Majority* (New Haven, CT: Yale University Press, 1996).

47. I take the phrase "Ethnic Seventies" from a 1971 interview with Norman Podhoretz. See *Washington Post*, April 11, 1971, G1. It can also be found as "The Seventies: Decade of the Ethnics," in Novak, *Unmeltable Ethnics*, 3–48.

CHAPTER 4

The Republican Party and the Problem of Diversity, 1968–1975

Catherine E. Rymph

In July 2005, Republican National Committee (RNC) chair Ken Mehlman delivered a widely covered address to the National Association for the Advancement of Colored People (NAACP) convention in Milwaukee. In it, he apologized for his party's electoral strategy on race. Over the last three decades, Mehlman noted, "some Republicans gave up on winning the African American vote, looking the other way or trying to benefit politically from racial polarization. I am here today as the Republican chairman to tell you we were wrong."[1] This statement of regret referred to GOP efforts from the late sixties onward to woo traditionally Democratic voters through promising to slow the pace of black civil rights advancements and appealing to white southerners in particular through use of coded (rather than explicit) racial appeals.[2] Historians disagree in their assessment of how important this "Southern Strategy" was to Richard Nixon's election as president in 1968 and to Republican resurgence thereafter.[3] Yet the charge remains that over a period of some forty years the GOP benefited from unsavory racial politics that eschewed any credible appeal to black voters.

Mehlman's disavowal of the Southern Strategy undoubtedly reflected concern about the GOP's lack of support among black voters and the political benefits of "racial polarization" in a demographically changing United States. The apparent dangers for the party were underlined by its defeat in the 2008 presidential election. The McCain/Palin presidential ticket attracted less support than its Democratic counterpart from virtually every demographic group other than older white voters.[4] This outcome resurrected intraparty debate about how to craft a new winning strategy. For Republicans of similar outlook to Mehlman, distancing their party from the Southern Strategy that had once been seen as the way forward was essential to its renewal.

Mehlman, of course, was not the first Republican to see racial homogeneity as a potential liability. There were those who recognized such pragmatic concerns in the late sixties and early seventies—when the demographic transformation of the next forty years was hard to foresee. The origins of the Southern Strategy are conventionally associated with Nixon's 1968 campaign. Yet the GOP in the Nixon years was by no means unanimous in its support for this approach to party building. Some Republicans preferred to reach out to African Americans and other groups that were underrepresented in the party. Nixon himself had declared in a 1971 speech that the GOP should be the "Party of the Open Door." His use of this slogan was targeted at voters of different political loyalties, but some Republicans interpreted it as reinforcement of their efforts to attract more racial minorities.[5] One obvious target for reform—both symbolic and substantive—was the "face" of the GOP: that is, its official organizations. The ultimate failure of efforts to transform the party's makeup, however, illuminated the difficulties of diversifying an institution rooted in the very ideology of individualism.

In August 1972, during the Republican National Convention, black Republican Wilbur Colom of Washington, DC, testified before the Committee on Contests as it considered the merits of delegate challenges based on the homogeneity of state delegations to the convention. He was asked whether he, as an African American, felt unwelcome in the Republican Party. "Very much so," he replied, surely to the dismay of the committee. "The Democrats are constantly knocking on your door with stuff trying to get you to do something for them, right. Trying to get you to vote. You feel welcome plus you see people that you identify with. I see young people, I see Black people and I see other people I feel who speak for me in the Democrat Party where I don't see that here." Frustrated as he may have been with the Republicans, Colom nonetheless believed working within the GOP made sense because, as he saw it, African Americans could not be well served by a Democratic Party that had come to take them for granted. "We [African Americans] have to have an alternative," Colom insisted. "I think the Republican Party can become that alternative if it makes that substantial effort."[6]

Colom presented his concerns in terms of what was best politically for African Americans. Meanwhile, there were plenty of Republicans in the early seventies who also insisted that reaching out to African Americans would be good for the GOP. They believed that the GOP's future strength depended on its diversity (to use a more current term), at the very least in its governing bodies. At stake here was Republican appeal not only to black voters like Colom, but also to moderate white voters who were uncomfortable being associated with a party that was so "lily-white." As one young white Republican put it, "I personally don't want to see the television cameras scan across [my district's delegation] and see no Blacks, women, or youth."[7] This young man spoke in the context of contentious debates over the wisdom of attempts to broaden the party, particularly in terms of race. Paradoxically, such efforts ultimately did more to politicize white women as a force within the GOP than any other group, despite a lack of concern about their underrepresentation in its affairs.

These deliberations were the latest stage in a debate prompted by Barry Goldwater's landslide defeat in the 1964 presidential election. The Arizona senator had voted against the Civil Rights Act of 1964 in line with his long-standing support of states' rights. While this helped him in the Deep South, it did nothing to prevent his candidacy being an electoral disaster elsewhere. In its postmortem on the debacle, the Ripon Society, an organization of moderate and liberal Republicans, denounced Goldwater's campaign strategy as "weird and frightening" for its efforts to capitalize on resentment against the 1964 Civil Rights Act. Not only had this failed to maximize support among whites outside the South, but it had also reduced black support to insignificance. In 1960, the Republican presidential ticket headed by Richard Nixon had captured 32 percent of the black vote—a drop from Eisenhower's performance in 1956, but nonetheless substantial; in 1964, by contrast, Goldwater had won only 6 percent of African Americans' ballots.[8]

If the GOP was going to earn back a respectable level of black support, it had much work to do. In 1967, in response to the wave of urban upheavals, the Republican National Committee began setting up action centers in urban areas as a way to reach out to "ghetto" voters and to pointedly counter those advocating that the party "[write] off the Negro vote." The centers investigated discrimination complaints, sponsored Little League teams, and, in general, tried to connect community service to the GOP.[9] But the problem of black skepticism toward the GOP was significant and multifaceted, and it was resistant to simple solutions of this kind. Historians have recently begun paying more attention to the efforts of some Republicans to attract black support through delivering targeted appeals, working with black churches, registering voters, and changing the wording of party platforms.[10] GOP leaders were themselves divided as to whether or not active outreach to minority voters was actually the best approach. For supporters of this strategy, an obvious area in which to practice inclusion was the party itself, whose official organizations were overwhelmingly white.

In 1968, after a summer marked by minority and youth unrest nationwide, the Republican National Convention made two decisions that intensified debate about party reform. First, it adopted changes to the party's nondiscrimination clause (Rule 32), instructing state Republican parties to "take positive action to achieve the broadest possible participation in party affairs." Second, it appointed a Delegates and Organization (DO) Committee to draft changes to the party's rules that would help open participation at future conventions to hitherto underrepresented demographic groups. According to the *Miami Herald*, the move for reform indicated that the GOP "had become sensitive to the charge that there were too few Negroes and other minority groups represented at its conventions."[11] In other words, the party seemingly recognized that a lack of diversity was bad for its public image. And indeed, although some Republicans were sincerely committed to diversification as a matter of justice, the most effective proponents of reform framed the issue in terms of party competitiveness. In their assessment, reform was necessary to show Americans that the GOP was the Party of the Open Door and would respond to new political realities that the Democrats appeared to be facing more forcefully.

It was certainly not difficult to make the case that the Republican Party as an organization needed to embark on special efforts to diversify. African Americans had constituted about 3 percent of Republican delegates in 1968. As one newspaper account observed, there were more African Americans serving on the Democratic Party's Michigan delegation *alone* than there were from all fifty states at the Republican convention.[12] Furthermore, Richard Nixon gained the support of only 12 percent of black voters in the presidential election (an improvement over Goldwater's dismal performance in 1964, but less than half of what he had previously received in 1960). In a period associated with the politicization of youth, persons under thirty made up less than 1 percent of GOP convention delegates. Women seemingly fared much better in constituting about 17 percent of delegates, but in reality this was a meager showing, since their presence had been institutionalized on the RNC since the 1920s and on convention committees since the 1940s.[13]

The DO Committee, under the leadership of Rosemary Ginn of Missouri, worked between 1968 and 1972 to hammer out a series of proposals intended to broaden participation. Many of its initial ideas were welcomed by RNC members as sensible and necessary. These included recommendations that party officials no longer be given "automatic" delegate positions and that delegate fees be eliminated. Similar rules were implemented with little controversy by the Democratic Party.[14] Such reforms promised to democratize the process of delegate selection by ending elite control of conventions. These were the changes that arguably had greatest impact on the Republican Party, especially when combined with amendments in state laws that shifted the presidential nomination process to primaries and caucuses. Giving more voice to people at the grass roots ultimately facilitated the rise of the New Right within the GOP in the 1970s. Party professionals, who were more likely than grassroots activists to be moderates, lost much of their influence over the nomination process.

At the time, controversy centered (as it did in the Democratic Party) on those recommendations that sought explicitly to increase the convention participation of specific groups. In the Republican Party, these recommendations came to be known as DO 7, DO 8, and DO 9.[15] The party rules in place at the time already provided for equal representation of men and women on all four major convention committees (Resolutions, Rules, Credentials, and Party Organization). DO 7 proposed that the size of each convention committee be increased to add a member of a "minority ethnic group" and a person under the age of twenty-five from each state (each committee, under such a system, would receive 100 additional members); DO 8 addressed the persistently low number of women serving as convention delegates, suggesting that the states "endeavor to have" equal numbers of male and female delegates at the conventions.[16] DO 9 further spoke to the problem of low youth participation, recommending that states send a number of delegates under age twenty-five proportional to the population of young voters in the state.

These proposals could not escape comparison with what the opposition was doing in this area. In the wake of their highly contentious 1968 Chicago convention, the Democrats had appointed their own commission to study party rules. The findings of the so-called McGovern-Fraser Commission led to adoption of significant reforms governing delegate selection for the 1972 convention. In particular, state Democratic parties were required to include youth, minorities, and women as delegates "in reasonable relationship to their presence in the population of the state."[17] The Republican debates over DO 7, DO 8, and DO 9, along with the parallel Democratic discussion of similar proposals from the McGovern-Fraser Commission, occurred in the broader context of a "minority rights revolution." Another element in this was the Nixon administration's development of policies to increase opportunities for the nation's "official minorities" in education, business, and employment.[18] Thus the proposals for GOP reform would borrow some of the language and logic of the minority rights discourse, as well as from understandings of the party's own history and needs. And while Republican reformers were well aware of the McGovern-Fraser rule changes, they sought to distinguish their own efforts from these.

At the 1972 convention, RNC members and convention delegates worked to address the implications of the reform process begun in 1968. Instead of being quietly shelved, as some Republicans had hoped, the rules changes became the subject of efforts to test their meaning. On the one hand, the Credentials Committee was presented with two delegate challenges that were motivated specifically by the new "take positive action" language. Meanwhile, a group of about fifty members of Congress as well as representatives from the recently formed feminist organization the National Women's Political Caucus arrived in Miami bent on pushing for some of the more controversial proposals to be accepted.

Despite its vagueness, the "take positive action" requirement adopted at the 1968 convention (directing state parties to "take positive action to achieve the broadest possible participation in party affairs") appeared to have had some effect on delegate selection. Comparing the makeup of 1972 convention delegates in percentage terms with 1968, female participation had almost doubled, that of under-thirties had increased tenfold, and black participation had doubled.[19] Judged on this basis, the new requirement could be seen as a success, but it also opened a door for delegate challenges. What did "positive action" mean? Did it mean doing a little publicity and recruitment? Did it mean trying really hard? Or did it mean, as one challenger from Virginia put it, that the state parties now had a "responsibility to institute and monitor a program"? For this challenger, the fact that his district's delegation contained no youth, female, or African American delegates was evidence in itself that the State of Virginia was not in compliance with Rule 32.[20]

The Republican delegate challenges of 1972 were ultimately unsuccessful. Accordingly, they did not become the stuff of national drama, as had been the case when the GOP nomination battle between Dwight D. Eisenhower and Robert Taft came to hinge on their outcome in 1952, or when the Mississippi Freedom Democratic Party used delegate challenges to undermine the legitimacy of the all-white delegations from Deep South states at the Democratic convention in 1964. Nevertheless, the 1972 delegate challenges still raised important questions about what the party was trying to achieve with the "positive action" language. Was the directive merely a feel-good statement designed to give the impression that the party was taking action? Or was Rule 32 going to have real teeth? How could a state demonstrate that it had indeed taken "positive action"?

Such questions reverberated through the subsequent debates over the rules changes proposed by the DO Committee. Reformers argued that the party badly needed to find a way to broaden itself, while horrified opponents warned of a dangerous effort to "quota-ize" (or "McGovernize") the party. As one DO opponent put it, attaching a different meaning to Nixon's phrase than did supporters, "We will be the Party of the open door, not the Party of pigeon holes.[21]" Part of the problem with requiring that additional seats on committees go to African Americans or that states increase their numbers of minority delegates pertained to recruitment. Meeting such obligations meant selection from a very small pool of candidates or bringing in and elevating to leadership individuals who were not party activists and perhaps not even party supporters. Indeed, the very committee that proposed the DO reforms, unlike its Democratic counterpart, contained no youth or minority members—representatives of these groups simply were too scarce within the GOP structure.[22]

How to get around this impasse over quotas? A way forward suggested by Laszlo Pasztor, a Hungarian American who headed the National Republican Heritage Council (NRHC), was to demonstrate that the party was already diverse. Formed in 1970, Pasztor's organization was something of a thorn in the side of the Nixon administration because its fierce anticommunism was out of step with the administration's promotion of détente. It included members of a number of ethnic groups, including Cubans, Serbians, Estonians, Czechs, Slovaks, Poles, Mexicans, and Native Americans.[23] Pasztor contrasted NHRC's self-generated clubs with "black operations" whose establishment had only been effected with "outside money."[24] Seeing his organization as the true exemplar of diversity, he proposed to the Rules Committee that it be given an ex officio seat on the RNC Executive Committee as a means of attracting larger numbers of ethnic Americans to the party. Initially his testimony was misunderstood as a request for a "heritage" representative from each state on each convention committee (along the lines of DO 7). This raised alarm that accommodation of his proposal would open the floodgates for demands from Greeks, Jews, senior citizens, and "everything in the world."[25]

An undaunted Pasztor personally reassured the Rules Committee that the Heritage group was merely asking for one seat on the Executive Committee rather than for the dreaded quotas. The goal was not to "segregate [ethnics] off" but to bring more into the party by showing other ethnics that they were recognized.[26] This clarification paved the way for adoption of the proposal, but it was a short-lived victory. The ex officio position ended up being eliminated as a result of vote trading at the 1976 convention.[27]

In 1972, Pasztor astutely made his case in terms of what Heritage groups could do to help the Republican Party make a convincing case that it was "really the party of the open door."[28] The GOP, he argued, had "a fantastic opportunity to prove to all citizens in the US that the allegation that we are the party only of the White Anglo Saxon Protestant is just humbug that the Democrats are trying to smear us with."[29] The implication of his message was twofold: the GOP had limited prospects for achieving diversity through attraction of black votes, but it could do so with relative ease through reaching out to Heritage groups. Pasztor and other ethnic leaders were, at this time, in the midst of making their case to Nixon administration officials that ethnic groups deserved to be recognized as designated minorities, thereby making them eligible for government affirmative action programs. Although ethnic leaders would eventually lose that battle, the definition of what constituted a "minority" was very much in flux as Pasztor brought his case to the RNC Rules Committee.[30]

Although not embraced by all Republicans, Pasztor certainly helped his case by his firm disavowal of quotas, which were associated with the McGovern-Fraser Commission and generated intense discomfort within the GOP. Although other reasons were occasionally given for opposing reforms—such as the prospect of unwieldy convention committees of up to 200 members if DO 7 passed—the specter of quotas was *the* prevailing negative buzzword. "No matter how well they are disguised," Conservative Party senator James Buckley of New York declared, "no matter from what wellsprings of human compassion they may arise, these calls for quotas are the most reactionary proposals being made today."[31]

And yet the term "quota" was an unstable one. For all their hostility to quotas in general, some Republican opponents of DO 7 and DO 9 twisted themselves in rhetorical knots to find ways nonetheless to support quotas for another group—women. This was somewhat ironic given that women had *not* been the focus of the DO Committee when it was set up in 1968. This body was primarily interested in broadening the party in terms of age and race. It was unease about the lack of African American and young voters, both newly conscious political groups, that had inspired the drive for reform in the first place. The women's movement had only begun to coalesce at the time the Republicans began addressing the issue of diversity. Although the DO Committee adopted DO 8—that states should "endeavor to have" delegations made up of equal numbers of men and women—addressing women's representation was an afterthought. Surveys that the DO Committee sent to GOP leaders in 1970 generated little discussion about women's representation in the party. Even female advocates of DO 8 recognized that women were not intended as the focus of the DO Committee.[32]

Yet, in contrast to the DO 7 and DO 9 recommendations, which specifically dealt with youth and minority participation, DO 8 made it into the new rules. To explain why this was the case, it is useful to look more closely at the philosophical rejection of "quotas" that was at the heart of objections to the proposed reforms. That Republicans opposed reform because they were concerned about quotas may not seem surprising (Democratic opponents of the McGovern-Fraser reforms raised similar objections). This line of objection, though, was not as consistent or "principled" as it seemed. Dating back to the twenties, "quotas" for women had been an uncontroversial component of party policy. In 1924, in response to a similar measure instituted by Democrats four years earlier, the GOP had doubled the size of the RNC by adding a committeewoman from each state. In the 1940s and again in the 1960s, it expanded the convention committees to include equal numbers of men and women.

Those in 1972 who were against any new quotas suggested by the DO recommendations certainly did not propose eliminating existing seats for women, which were established and unassailable. The chairman of one of the Rules subcommittees, for example, who was "unalterably opposed" to adding a young person and a minority member to each convention committee, noted that "the one man and one woman could certainly represent ethnic minorities, represent youth."[33] And although its "endeavor to have" language seemingly implied additional quotas for female delegates, DO 8 actually earned support from some who otherwise were firm in denouncing quotas.

A group of fifty House members sought compromise measures to bring more youth and minorities into the party, but rejected the "arbitrary and imposed quotas" of DO 7 and DO 9. Its leader, Tom Railsback of Illinois, dismissed quotas as a means of expanding the party because to "single out any group" would discriminate against groups not singled out and would interfere with the autonomy of the state organizations; nevertheless, he accepted that "women deserve special attention." Acknowledging the contradiction between his support for DO 8 but not DO 7 and DO 9, he justified it through appeal to precedent—in the form of existing rules—and practicality; namely, recognition for the role long played by women as the "the backbone of the Republican effort at the grassroots." Moreover, Railsback insisted that DO 8 was not a quota, as it merely required states to make a "good-faith effort."[34] Basically, Republican women had, decades earlier, institutionalized a presence both on the RNC and at the conventions. Women had normalized their "quota" so that the idea of extending it in 1972 was acceptable to those like Railsback, who were otherwise dubious of "singl[ing] out any group."

Not mentioned by Railsback but equally important was the fact that many Republican insiders simply did not fear an increase in female delegates as they did an increase in youth and minority delegates, who they assumed would be dedicated to overthrow of the status quo. One critic of the DO proposal cautioned that the Democrats had been taken over by "bare-footed hoodlums" as the result of the McGovern-Fraser reforms.[35] Another warned that if Republican reformers were successful, they would set the party off on a "leftward lunge" that could leave us with "two liberal parties in American with no place for the majority."[36]

In other words, opponents feared the DO reforms would lead to a takeover of the party by outsiders who might be both unpredictable and "leftward" leaning. Thus, they fought proportional or designated representation for youth and minorities, whom they associated with left-wing politics. Many also opposed such representation for women, even mocking the idea of their playing a greater role in the party. Yet some opponents of DO 7 and DO 9 found DO 8—for women—more acceptable.[37] Unlike youth and racial minorities, women were already in the party in large numbers. They were a familiar presence in the party, they were loyal workers, and they were certainly not viewed as a potentially disruptive left-wing force. Despite the work that organized feminists did on behalf of DO 8 at the convention, Republican women were still viewed as safe. They were regarded as a known quantity, unlike the original targets of reform—blacks and the young.

In fact, Republican women were not quite as safe or reliable as was assumed. Before Miami, there was nothing that could have been called an organized feminist presence in the GOP. After Miami, there was. At the 1972 convention, a number of prominent female Republican stalwarts observed with frustration the debates over Rule 32, in which witnesses stood before the "all-white, almost all middle-aged and almost all WASP" Rules Committee to testify that their party was not in need of reform.[38] The extent of that opposition, especially to DO 8, helped bring these women together, across party factions, into a feminist movement within the Republican Party. This development would actually prove quite disruptive. The nascent Republican feminist coalition formed at the convention went on to pressure the party not only to continue to bring more women into positions of leadership, but also to support the Equal Rights Amendment, abortion rights, and affirmative action—issues that would prove highly divisive within GOP ranks in the 1970s and 1980s. In 1975, some of its supporters formed the Republican Women's Task Force, as part of the National Women's Political Caucus, to keep the feminist agenda on the Republican table.

Ultimately, efforts to bring more women into the party organizations would fare better than efforts to bring about racial diversity. Like so many other movements for women's rights in U.S. history, Republican feminism owed its advance to the drive for race-based reforms. It emerged—at least indirectly—out of the conflicts within the GOP over how to adjust to the racial landscape of the late 1960s. In essence, attention to women's issues developed somewhat accidentally as a by-product of this infighting when a small group of emerging Republican feminists enthusiastically seized on the equity principles at stake to promote their cause in tandem with that of racial minorities.

While race was never central to their agenda, Republican feminists supported affirmative action for minorities as well as women—a position that would, by the 1980s, put them at odds with party leadership. By then, the party was moving rightward under Ronald Reagan, and economic and social conservatives exerted increasing influence within it. Reagan's advocacy of "color-blind" equal opportunity resonated with a society growing skeptical of some of the directions that the minority rights revolution was taking. Republicans who continued to emphasize women's rights and group rights for minorities increasingly fell out of favor. Mary Louise Smith, for example, who was elevated to RNC chair in 1974 under President Ford, was later appointed by Reagan to the U.S. Commission on Civil Rights as a gesture to Republican feminists who had campaigned for him in 1980 despite his opposition to the women's rights positions they held dear. She was later removed from this post, however, owing to her repeated clashes with the administration over busing and affirmative action.[39] By this point, whatever influence Republican feminists may have briefly had within the GOP had been lost to a new constituency of female conservative operatives.[40]

In the end, the Republican convention in 1972 accepted the Rules Committee's proposals, which included DO 8, an expanded "take positive action" statement, and the addition of sex and age to the party's nondiscrimination statement. DO 7 and DO 9 were rejected. Although DO 8 ("endeavor to have equal numbers of men and women as delegates") never had the teeth that feminists wanted, its adoption ultimately signified that the reform process begun by the Delegates and Organization Committee in 1968 had done more to politicize Republican women than to diversify the makeup of the party in terms of race and age. The party's right turn in the late 1970s and 1980s effectively ensured that the latter elements of the early 1970s participation agenda remained unfulfilled. The realignment of large numbers of white male Democratic identifiers to the GOP in the Reagan era further inhibited efforts to broaden the party's demographic makeup.

The DO Committee's original goal was to attract more African Americans to the party. The attempt to do so by opening up the party's official organizations failed. Whether or not DO 7 would have made much difference had it been passed in 1972, it is certainly true that the path the GOP *did* pursue (of emphasizing individualism and downplaying group identity and group concerns) has not produced a racially diverse party. The selection in late 2008 of Michael Steele as the first African American RNC chair was in part an attempt to redress the GOP's demographic image that looked increasingly at odds with the nature of contemporary America. At the 2008 Republican National Convention, just 2 percent of the delegates were black (a smaller percentage than even in 1968 when the reform process was initiated).[41] When the television cameras scanned the crowds at the convention, the absence of African Americans was noteworthy, especially during a year in which the Democratic candidate was Barack Obama and about 25 percent of Democratic convention delegates were African American. Who serves as delegates to the conventions may appear now to be a mostly symbolic issue. Although delegates do help write platforms, they do not choose the candidates as they once did. But symbolism is an important element of the party's image.[42] And the lack of African American delegates at party conventions is echoed in other measures of black influence in the party: in 2011, two African American Republicans were serving in Congress, compared with thirty-nine Democrats. (Latino Republican representation in Congress was somewhat higher, although still lagging well behind that of Latino Democrats.) Herman Cain's brief stint as a frontrunner in the campaign for the 2012 Republican presidential nomination seems to have done little to diversify the party as a whole.

The position of women in the GOP is a little more difficult to evaluate. Although Republican feminism is no longer a going concern, women remain very involved with the party as voters and as activists. Middle-class white women in particular are recognized as a critical constituency; in recent elections, voters from this group have split their ballots rather evenly, rendering them a sought-after prize for both parties. As officeholders, Republican women are not faring so well, at least not when compared with Democrats. Republicans made up a greater number of the women serving in Congress in the 1940s and were about evenly matched with Democrats in the 1950s and 1960s. But since the mid-1970s, Democratic women have far outnumbered their Republican counterparts in the House, and the same has been true in the Senate since 1992. Despite the attention given to high-profile Republican women running for office in 2010, they still lag behind their Democratic counterparts. When the 112th Congress met at the start of 2011, five of the seventeen women in the Senate were Republican; twenty-four of seventy-one in the House. Republican women governors, however, outnumbered their Democratic counterparts four to two. And there were two women—former Alaska governor Sarah Palin and Minnesota congresswoman Michelle Bachman—among the possible contenders for the 2012 Republican presidential nomination, although Palin ultimately did not run and Bachmann dropped out of the race after the Iowa caucuses.

The response to Palin's 2008 nomination as vice president among her female supporters suggests that there is a real hunger among female conservatives to see other women in positions of leadership—as long as those leaders share their values. But how much room is there in the party for Republican women (or African Americans, for example) who are not as conservative as the "base"? In May 2009, moderate Republican senator Olympia Snowe of Maine called for a "re-evaluation of our inclusiveness as a party" and of "diversity within the party."[43] Her plea on this score referred not to gender, race, ethnicity, or age, but to intellectual and political diversity. In the wake of the recent defection of Pennsylvania senator Arlen Specter to the Democrats, Snowe's words were a warning against the dangers of driving moderates out of the party.

The GOP's diminishing ideological diversity in the late twentieth and early twenty-first centuries arguably contributes to the ongoing difficulties of achieving other forms of party diversity. The overall effect has been to restrict Republican appeal to increasingly significant demographic constituencies.

Studies indicate that many black voters are culturally conservative and support

Republican positions on gay rights, abortion, school vouchers, and other issues. Yet the popular perception remains that the GOP is unreceptive to African Americans and opposed to the other issues that many blacks support. Those early 1970s Republicans who believed that winning elections required building a diverse party through the targeted, affirmative strategies of DO 7, DO 8, and DO 9 lost that battle. Their opponents expressed (although not always consistently) an ideological opposition to mandating formulas for delegate selection to the states that for a time played well to the public and even attracted some prominent minority supporters.

Despite its revival in the 1970s and substantial electoral success thereafter, the Republican Party may well have paid a heavy price for its lack of diversity. This can arguably be seen as a factor in its ultimate failure to build a new majority that would have made it the dominant party of government in the manner of the Democrats during the New Deal order. Moreover, the GOP's lack of diversity in an increasingly diverse America may well limit its electoral prospects as the twenty-first century progresses.

Ken Mehlman's 2005 address to the NAACP signified that the contemporary Republican Party welcomed African Americans. In reality, however, their inclusion was still predicated on adherence to an individualist ethos that makes no claims about group rights or group grievances. The same is true of the party's attitude toward the increasingly significant Latino constituency that has become the nation's largest minority. The views and experiences of "multicultural conservatives" who insist they "want to speak only as Americans, as individuals," are touted as proof of the relevance of Republican individualist rhetoric.[44] Whether one agrees in principle with that individualism or not, this approach has not been effective in addressing the problems that the DO Committee set out to tackle in 1968: the party remains overwhelmingly white, is widely seen as indifferent or hostile to the concerns of minorities, and has been unable to address even the symbolic issue of boosting minority presence among the delegates cheering for the GOP and its candidates at the national conventions.

NOTES

1. "RNC Chief to Say It Was 'Wrong' to Exploit Racial Conflict for Votes," *Washington Post*, July 14, 2005.

2. Dan T. Carter, *The Politics of Rage: George Wallace, the Origins of the New Conservatism, and the Transformation of American Politics*; (Baton Rouge: Louisiana State University Press, 2000), 326–31.

3. See, for example, Kevin M. Kruse, *White Flight: Atlanta and the Making of Modern Conservatism* (Princeton, NJ: Princeton University Press, 2005); Matthew D. Lassiter, *The Silent Majority: Suburban Politics in the Sunbelt South* (Princeton, NJ: Princeton University Press, 2006); and Joseph Crespino, *In Search of Another Country: Mississippi and the Conservative Counterrevolution* (Princeton, NJ: Princeton University Press, 2007).

4. "Exit Polls," *New York Times*, November 5, 2008, *elections.nytimes.com*.

5. See, for example, press release, Republican National Convention, August 17, 1972, Folder 62, Rosemary Ginn Papers, Western Historical Manuscripts Collection, State Historical Society of Missouri, Columbia, MO.

6. Transcript of Committee on Contests, August 1972, *Papers of the Republican Party*, part 1: *Meetings of the Republican National Committee, 1911–1980*; Series A: *1960–1980* (Frederick, MD: University Publications of America, 1986; hereafter *Papers of the Republican Party* 1A), Reel 9, Frames 48–49.

7. Transcript of Committee on Contests, August 1972, *Papers of the Republican Party* 1A, Reel 10, Frame 31.

8. Nicol C. Rae, *The Decline and Fall of the Liberal Republicans: From 1952 to the Present* (New York: Oxford University Press, 1989), 75; and Ripon Society, *Election '64: A Ripon Society Report* (Cambridge, MA: Ripon Society, 1965), 19.

9. "Elly Peterson Builds Urban GOP," *Washington Evening Star*, September 15, 1969.

10. See, for example, Timothy N. Thurber, "Goldwaterism Triumphant? Race and the Republican Party, 1965–1968," *Journal of the Historical Society* 7 (2007): 349–84.

11. "GOP Wars Quietly on Convention Disorders, Discrimination," *Miami Herald*, August 24, 1970.

12. "Half of Republican Delegates in '72 May Be Women," *New York Times*, July 23, 1971; and "GOP Reform Committee Holds Closed Session" (undated clipping), c. 1970, Folder 39, Ginn Papers.

13. Rae, *Decline and Fall*, 99; and Ripon Society, *Election '64*.

14. Bruce Miroff, *The Liberals' Moment: The McGovern Insurgency and the Identity Crisis of the Democratic Party* (Lawrence: University Press of Kansas, 2007), 21.

15. Although the exact wording changed, the basic thrust of these proposals remained the same. I will refer to them generally as DO 7, DO 8, and DO 9.

16. National Women's Political Caucus, "D.O. 8," 1972, 10, Folder 406; DO Committee recommendations, c. 1970, Folder 110, Ginn Papers.

17. Austin Ranney, *Curing the Mischiefs of Faction: Party Reform in America* (Berkeley: University of California Press, 1975), 113.

18. See John D. Skrentny, *The Minority Rights Revolution* (Cambridge, MA: Harvard University Press, 2002).

19. Ripon Society, *Election '64*; "Half of Republican Delegates in '72 May Be Women," *New York Times*, July 23, 1971. According to the Republican Party's figures, two states, Minnesota and Arkansas, had sent delegations to the 1972 convention that were 50 percent women; the delegations of seven other states were over 40 percent women. Six states sent delegations that were more than 10 percent nonwhite. Six states sent delegations that were over 12 percent "youth." "Answerdesk '72," August 11, 1972, Folder 173, Ginn Papers.

20. Transcripts of Credentials Committee, August 15, 1972, *Papers of the Republican Party* 1A, Reel 7, Frame 36.

21. Senator Bill Brock, press release, August 9, 1972, Folder 57, Ginn Papers.

22. "GOP Reform Committee Holds Closed Session" (undated clipping), c. 1970, Folder 39, Ginn Papers.

23. Transcripts of RNC Subcommittee on Rules 19–29, August 15, 1972, *Papers of the Republican Party* 1A, Reel 10, Frames 342–43 and 346. Pasztor (and his connections to the GOP) would later come under fire when he was revealed to have been a Nazi collaborator during World War II.

24. Transcripts of RNC Subcommittee on Rules 19–29, August 15, 1972, *Papers of the Republican Party* 1A, Reel 10, Frame 331.

25. Transcripts of RNC Subcommittee on Rules 19–29, August 15, 1972, *Papers of the Republican Party* 1A, Reel 10, Frame 298.

26. Transcripts of RNC Subcommittee on Rules 19–29, August 15, 1972, *Papers of the Republican Party* 1A, Reel 10, Frame 335.

27. Republican Women's Task Force newsletter, August–September 1976, Republican Women's Task Force, Box 37, Patricia Lindh and Jeanne Holme Files, Gerald R. Ford Presidential Library, Ann Arbor, MI.

28. Transcripts of RNC Subcommittee on Rules 19–29, August 15, 1972, *Papers of the Republican Party* 1A, Reel 10, Frames 331 and 33.

29. Transcripts of RNC Subcommittee on Rules 19–29, August 15, 1972, *Papers of the Republican Party* 1A, Reel 10, Frame 331.

30. See Skrentny, *Minority Rights Revolution*, 275–314.

31. "Statement of Senator James L. Buckley before the Committee on Rules," August 14, 1972, Folder 185, Ginn Papers.

32. Surveys and questionnaires sent to Republican activists by the DO Committee are found in Folders 111–53, Ginn Papers; Wilma Rogalin to Rosemary Ginn, July 26, 1972, Folder 175, Ginn Papers.

33. Transcripts of RNC Subcommittee on Rules 1–18, August 15, 1972, *Papers of the Republican Party* 1A, Reel 10, Frame 169.

34. Recommendations of the Republican Ad Hoc Committee on Delegate Selection Reform, Folder 177, Ginn Papers.

35. Florence [surname unknown] to Rosemary Ginn, memorandum on press conference by Republicans For an Open Party, August 8, 1972, Folder 51, Ginn Papers.

36. Lawrence D. Pratt, "Dear Delegate," August 7, 1972, Folder 32, Ginn Papers.

37. Bobbie Greene Kilberg, "A Republican Woman Looks at Her Party," *Washington Post*, August 15, 1972.

38. Bobbie Greene Kilberg, "Republican Women Assessing Their Gains and Losses," *Washington Post*, September 2, 1972.

39. Catherine E. Rymph, *Republican Women: Feminism and Conservatism from Suffrage through the Rise of the New Right* (Chapel Hill: University of North Carolina Press, 2006), 234.

40. For more on this point, see Rymph, *Republican Women*, 212–38.

41. "African Americans Lacking in Republican Delegation," *Guardian*, September 4, 2008, *www.guardian.co.uk*.

42. The GOP has a similar problem with young people, who continue to lean Democratic. While I was unable to find figures on the number of young people serving as delegates to the Republican National Convention, two-thirds of voters aged 18–29 voted in 2008 for Barack Obama. And young people were around 16 percent of delegates to the Democratic National Convention, according to the *New York Times*. Michael Falcone, "Political Realities May Pose Test to Obama's Appeal to Young Voters," *New York Times*, August 30, 2008.

43. Olympia Snowe, "We Didn't Have to Lose Arlen Specter," *New York Times*, April 29, 2009.

44. Angela Dillard, *Guess Who's Coming to Dinner* Now?: *Multicultural Conservatism in America* (New York: New York University Press, 1994), 14.

CHAPTER 5

Republican Populism in the Quest for a New Majority

Pat Buchanan in the White House

Timothy Stanley

This chapter examines the role that conservative populism played in the post–Barry Goldwater revitalization of the Republican Party. Although antiestablishment themes were present in Richard Nixon's administration and Ronald Reagan's presidential campaigns, some populists felt that the GOP failed to appreciate their potency. One such critic was Patrick J. Buchanan, who served as speechwriter and political adviser to President Nixon. The conservative populism espoused by Buchanan exerted some influence on his boss's strategy for the construction of the so-called New Majority (comprising the Republican core and crossover Democrats, particularly white southerners, lower-middle-class sub-urbanites, and urban Catholics). The president and his aide, however, had quite different interpretations of electoral politics.[1] This chapter asks what Buchanan wanted Nixon to do in office, and how he thought adoption of his agenda would help Nixon's reelection and build a permanent Republican majority. His abject failure to promote that agenda is illustrative of a recurring conflict between governing moderates and activist populists within the GOP in the post-Goldwater era. The cultivation of the middle ground has militated against a nakedly populist electoral strategy, even during the ideologically conservative administration of Ronald Reagan.[2] This forced Buchanan into open rebellion in the 1990s, when he ran for the Republican nomination against incumbent president George H. W. Bush.

Populists divide the world between unscrupulous elites and virtuous citizens. In historian Michael Kazin's words, they "conceive of ordinary people as a noble as-semblage not bounded narrowly by class, view their elite opponents as self-serving and undemocratic, and seek to mobilize the former against the latter." In the 1970s, American conservatives used new populist rhetoric to repackage old ideas. Praising the faith, values, labor, and ethnicity of Middle America, they made fresh appeals to the wallet and the soul.[3] Economic conservatives argued that big government stole money from hardworking Americans in excessive taxes and redistributed it to fashionable minorities in welfare handouts. Social conservatives charged that same state apparatus with forcing secular humanism on a virtuous population. Both groups sought to make the Republican Party the agency of their particular message. They argued that their politics was principled and, potentially, popular. Trying to make the GOP look more like the choice of ordinary, hardworking, God-fearing Americans, they hoped to attract Democrats outraged by their party's cultural, economic, and racial liberalism.[4] At various moments since the 1960s, the GOP's presidential nominees and congressional leadership have adopted parts of the populist strategy to win office—painting their opponents as elitist liberals and offering a reassertion of popular cultural values. But populist conservatives have still expressed frustration with the Republican Party, sometimes threatening to bolt from it altogether.[5]

A speechwriter, pundit, and three-time presidential candidate, Pat Buchanan's name is synonymous with populist conservatism. In the Nixon White House, Buchanan was favored for producing "cutting-edge" conservative speeches and catchphrases that rattled the liberal critics and brought the Archie Bunkers watching at home to their feet.[6] Speeches were produced collaboratively and via a lengthy process of consultation, so few were definitively Buchananite.[7] Buchanan's vim, however, was evident in Nixon's defiant defenses of his Vietnam policy, and he enjoyed comparatively free rein in writing for the hatchet man of the administration, Vice President Spiro Agnew. Buchanan was responsible for Agnew's famous attack on the unfriendly coverage the administration had received from the national media, delivered at Des Moines, Iowa, in November 1969.[8] The speech was important, in the view of many conservatives, as the first to popularly associate the media with elite interests. It helped excuse the administration's declining poll ratings as a conspiracy against a basically decent but insufficiently liberal president.[9]

Pat Buchanan also worked as an editor or author of daily news summaries. These condensed media coverage of the administration and were often the president's first source of information as to how his policies were perceived. After Watergate, the summaries were blamed by some journalists for convincing the president that he was besieged by snobbish liberal critics and that his more progressive campaigns were a waste of time and money.[10] To be sure, Buchanan capitalized on his boss's dislike of watching TV news to try to shape his reaction to events. Buchanan coordinated with friends in the media the placing of articles that made a case for conservatism, to give the impression of an emerging intellectual consensus.[11] Liberal critiques were quoted selectively to confirm the conspiracy that Agnew had identified in Des Moines. But the summaries illustrated the limits of Buchanan's influence as well as its potential. If in the mood, Nixon pored through the reports, praised them, and wrote reams of notes on them. Some, however, were ignored.[12] When the Watergate transcripts were released, they revealed that Nixon privately read for himself almost every single article that Buchanan had meticulously paraphrased anyway. The speechwriter did not shape the president's view of the media; he merely confirmed it.[13]

Also a canny political strategist, Buchanan played a small role in the "dirty tricks" campaign during the Democratic primaries of 1972.[14] From his perspective, the necessity of such tactics was a further example of the elites' domination of U.S. politics. Buchanan, like Nixon, felt that so many public institutions were dominated by liberals that the White House was a veritable oasis of legitimate, popular government. In his rationale, fighting dirty in these circumstances was an act of populist resistance—even if the people did not realize it.[15]

Finally, Buchanan acted as the key administration go-between with conservatives, wrote op-eds in right-wing journals that gave White House policy intellectual bona fides, and met personally with politicians and activists like Governor Ronald Reagan of California, Congressman John Ashbrook of Ohio, and *National Review*'s William F. Buckley Jr. to convince them of the president's goodwill.[16] Buchanan—a devout Catholic—was occasionally used as a private point man between Nixon and the Catholic Church. In this regard, his ethnicity and religiosity put him in good stead among the largely Protestant White House staff. In April 1969, Buchanan negotiated a deal with Cardinal Terrence Cooke whereby the Vatican would hold off from attacking administration policy in Vietnam in return for increased federal aid to the collapsing parochial schools system.[17]

Pat Buchanan admired Richard Nixon as a Republican statesman. There was a generational difference, however, between the two men. Nixon's politics was shaped by internationalist anticommunism and the New Deal. He disliked the bureaucracy of the New Deal and its Great Society successor, but appreciated the enduring popularity of social welfare. He was also envious—if profoundly skeptical—of the Camelot mystique of John F. Kennedy's presidency, which romanticized government activism and the power elites that practiced it.[18] Richard Nixon was a political pragmatist whose message shifted according to the context in which it was delivered. In the view of Howard Phillips—a movement conservative and later a supporter of Buchanan's presidential campaigns—Nixon was not an "active liberal," but the "combination of his not giving a damn, on the one hand, and his desire to win the approbation of the American establishment on the other" made him resistant to ideological conservatism and wary about being anything other than statesmanlike in public.[19]

Buchanan was closer in instinct to the New Right of the 1970s—a movement that protested secular humanism and cultural change, and which attracted activists from outside the GOP establishment.[20] From an urban, Democratic household, he was raised with a strict Catholic faith that inculcated in him the conviction that a nation's culture reflected its relationship with God. In Buchanan's eyes, an America that was not respectful of authority, patriotic, and self-reliant had broken its covenant with the Almighty. For him, therefore, politics was not a profession but a crusade.[21] Buchanan tended to prioritize social traditionalism over economic Darwinism. His philosophy was spiritual rather than materialistic, making him as disdainful of those who said that society could be saved by cutting taxes as he was of those who claimed salvation lay in raising them.[22] He prioritized saving souls, including his own, before increasing the GNP. This made him sensitive to religious constituencies and contemptuous of moneyed lobbies on both the Left and the Right.[23]

Like the New Right, Pat Buchanan was also a populist. His contempt for entrenched sources of power, snobbery, and Episcopalian do-goodery encouraged his advocacy of conservatism's reorientation toward the politics of the "little man." He argued that the president should mimic the style and some of the policies of the segregationist Democrat George C. Wallace, adopting the mantle of a "fighter" against entrenched special interests.[24] He appreciated the values of blue-collar workers and family farmers better than most Republicans. In particular, he understood that while working-class Democrats might have looked to their party for social benefits, many increasingly resented its association with hippies, yippies, and all other parts of the 1960s counterculture that scorned the values and traditions in which they had been raised. Believing that material interests were easily eclipsed by the demands of faith, flag, and family, Buchanan argued that a populist social conservatism could capture key constituencies from libertine Democrats. This could be accomplished through both the substance of administration policy and the style of selling it to the people, painting the opposition as decadent elites.[25]

What then did Buchanan want the Nixon administration to do and what electoral appeal did he think it would have? In many regards, he wanted a return to Goldwaterism: cut taxes, roll back welfare, and shrink the state. But it was about social issues—law and order, patriotism, religious values, race—that he felt most passionate and saw the greatest political ground to be gained. Buchanan looked at the 1968 presidential election returns and deduced that the Republicans remained a minority party. The racially conservative and populist campaign of George C. Wallace had split the Democratic majority early on in the campaign, peeling away southerners and northern blue-collar ethnics. Yet the Democratic candidate, Hubert Humphrey, was able to dramatically reduce Nixon's margin of victory (43.4 to 42.7 percent) in the last few weeks of the election by winning back northern conservatives from Wallace with an appeal to New Deal economic liberalism. The best way to construct a new Republican majority, Buchanan concluded, was to graft the Wallace votes onto the existing Republican minority—a stratagem similar to that advocated by former Nixon campaign aide Kevin P. Phillips in his book *The Emerging Republican Majority*. Given the lingering appeal of liberal economics, this could only be done by appropriating Wallace's position on social issues.[26]

Of course, some of these social issues had a racial dimension. Buchanan argued that conservatives should turn white backlash against legal and welfare-oriented efforts to erase segregation to their advantage. A case in point was his opposition to court-ordered busing to desegregate public schools. In a 1970 memo to the president, he pointed to the unpopularity of busing to argue that "the ship of integration is going down; it is not our ship: it belongs to national liberalism—and we cannot salvage it; and we ought not be aboard." The administration's opposition could drain support from Wallace Democrats, he argued.[27] Nixon's policies suggest that he agreed. In 1968, candidate Nixon argued that it was hypocritical to use federal authority to integrate the South while the North remained equally—though unofficially—just as segregated. For a while, President Nixon hedged his bets on busing, showing "minimal compliance" by walking a tightrope between convincing liberals that the administration was obeying the law and conservatives that it was doing no more (and reluctantly so). But in the summer of 1971, he started to speak out and, as George Wallace won surprise victories in the Michigan and Maryland 1972 Democratic presidential primaries, he finally called for a congressional moratorium on court-ordered busing.[28] Many pundits dubbed the administration's position on racial matters "the Southern Strategy," the goal of which was to "appease Southern whites, completely undercutting the Wallace base and grafting the Dixie states into a conservative coalition with the Republican base in the West and Midwest," according to a contemporary journalist.[29]

Buchanan's advocacy of social issue prioritization reflected conviction and political savvy. Buchanan recognized that the Democrats enjoyed a monopoly on economic issues.[30] While he favored cutting taxes and regulation, he acknowledged that the bare bones of the welfare system could never be removed altogether. In 1970, he wrote an interpretive essay on Richard Scammon and Ben Wattenberg's controversial book, *The Real Majority*. This study of electoral data suggested, according to Buchanan, that the administration's target constituency should be

> law and order Democrats, conservatives on the Social Issue but progressive on domestic issues. . . . We should win these Democrats to the Presidential banner by contending that RN is a progressive on domestic policy blocked by obstructionists in the left-wing leadership of the Democratic Party; that RN is a hard liner on crime, drugs and pornography, whose legislation is blocked by ultra liberals in the Senate. . . ; that the president is a man trying with veto after veto to hold down the cost of living but is being thwarted by radicals and wild spenders. . . . These would be the ways we would best appeal to the patriotic, hardline pro-Medicare Democrats who are the missing element in the Grand New Party.[31]

Buchanan could not go too far in using *The Real Majority* to demand an overhaul of administration policy, but he did insist that it confirmed the virtues of a new "style" of political presentation that he called "hardball."[32] Within Buchanan's politics, populist *style* was as important as conservative *substance*. In his mind they were one and the same thing. Taking as his basic premise that the real America was conservative, he reasoned that to act like a conservative was to act like a real American. In line with this, Buchanan urged the president to reject all aspects of the Kennedy style: dress down, act up, speak his mind, and confront opponents head on.[33]

Beyond his views on *The Real Majority*, Buchanan did not want the president to sacrifice his innate conservatism on economic issues but, conceding that he had, he advised Nixon to avoid talking about issues pioneered by liberals. Nixon should focus instead on "crime, drugs, juvenile delinquency, and high taxes. . . . We should use these as our cutting edge issues, not theirs, and let them do the housing, education, unemployment routine."[34]

In a refrain that would recur throughout his career, Buchanan argued that social and racial issues offered an opportunity to take a stance that was both conservative and popular.[35] He promoted the ideas of Kevin P. Phillips, especially Phillips's assertion that an opportunity beckoned to mobilize new conservative constituencies mostly found in the West, the border South, and the ethnic urban North. What was so liberating about Phillips's work was that it argued that Republicans need not negotiate with eastern elites, and that they would actually gain votes in other parts of the country by actively ignoring them.[36] Demographically, the so-called Sunbelt was growing (fueled by retirements, flight from urbanization, defense dollars, smaller taxes, and a low regulatory burden) while the industrial Northeast was ossifying, its state governments crippled by crime, unemployment, and ballooning welfare budgets. Phillips argued that Nixon should embrace a populist strategy to solidify the "emerging Republican majority" of the Sunbelt and suburbs—stressing opposition to elitism and the cultural values of the Northeast that would run particularly well in the South. Again, this approach was controversial because critics presumed that it manipulated racial conflict—especially white anger at enforced desegregation and competition between the races over national resources. Liberal op-ed writers also inferred a malign neglect of the needs of the North. As such, the administration chose to publicly deny that Phillips had ever met the president or even visited the White House.[37] Yet Phillips held several electoral strategy meetings that both the president and Buchanan were present at and Nixon showered praise on his contributions.[38]

But how much influence did conservative populism have on Nixon's electoral strategy? Like many people on Nixon's staff, Pat Buchanan complemented some aspect of his boss's complex personality. Nixon, like Buchanan, came from a humble background and was a conservative by instinct. He had fashioned an image for himself that was ordinary and antiestablishment—a spokesman for the "forgotten American."[39] Sources confirm that Nixon, more than capable of class envy and paranoia, was indeed attracted to Buchanan's chutzpah and confrontational conservatism, and his "eccentricity and encyclopedic knowledge."[40] Both felt, given the weight of power and influence stacked against them, that they had to play tough to get what they wanted. They were at one in their loathing for the national media.[41]

Richard Nixon operated within a political climate that increasingly favored appeals based on patriotism and social conservatism—a climate that he helped foster with his 1968 campaign's use of "law and order" issues. But while the country was more conservative, Nixon, like Buchanan, conceded that the majority was still

Democratic. Unlike Buchanan, Nixon concluded that this necessitated a centrist rather than a populist strategy. The president certainly perceived the need to move beyond classic party-led voting patterns—to fashion a New Majority by stressing themes that appealed to disaffected Democrats. That often involved manipulating social and racial reaction.[42] But two caveats prevented an embrace of Buchanan-style populism. First, the civil rights movement had raised an expectation of racial progress that had become political orthodoxy. Thus, it was during the Nixon administration that quotas were first used in federal hiring, and the president could never be seen to be race-baiting.[43] Second, most Americans still wanted the government to supervise a "full-employment" economy and provide basic welfare support. Buchanan regarded the Great Society as a liberal, bureaucratic assault on the American family. It replaced patriarchal order with welfare and stole money from the not-so-affluent to give to the indigent poor. By turning people into "wards of the state," he argued, liberal technocrats could culturally indoctrinate them and reap their votes.[44] But the entitlement programs of the New Deal and the Great Society had (liberal) populist appeal for middle-class taxpayers. Voters would not accept an outright jettisoning of economic matters in favor of posturing on race and cultural change. These issues were too important to them to ignore.[45]

It was also evident that populism had its electoral limits. Nixon threw himself into the 1970 midterm congressional races to attack with gusto so-called radical liberal elites and their Democratic allies, but with mixed results. His aggressive campaigning style made him look less than presidential and twelve seats were lost in the House (although one Republican and two independent seats were gained in the Senate).[46] The experiment in populism (with a focus on social issues at the expense of economics) was deemed a failure and, as Phillips later noted, "cast a long midterm shadow" over future electoral strategy in the Nixon White House.[47]

In recognition of the failures of the 1970 campaign, the 1971 State of the Union put the administration back onto an orthodox public policy course. Buchanan did not approve. Nixon offered a six-part plan that included welfare reform through the enactment of a guaranteed income, an "expansionary budget" to attain full employment, better protection of the environment, more healthcare benefits, bureaucratic reform, and revenue sharing. The first four offended Buchanan's anti–big government philosophy, but also his sense of political priorities. The future lay, he argued, in stressing the social issues—not trying to compete with the liberals in largesse. He was ambivalent about bureaucratic reform and revenue sharing, which became grouped together under the umbrella idea of "the New Federalism" (a term coined by Buchanan).[48] Cutting waste and delegating tax money and operational responsibility to a local level smacked of a return to a "states' rights" sensibility. It defunded the Great Society and, most attractively, began the process of "bypassing the bureaucracy."[49]

But conservatives also understood that this represented a reform of federal management rather than an attempt to reduce the size of government itself—indeed, the White House increased support for local government activism where it was perceived to be more effective than federal efforts. The New Federalism did not dispute the positive role of government in people's lives; it simply reformed the method of government, with a preference for decentralization.[50] The New Majority conservatism did not preclude government-funded welfare or social support. The New Federalism was an example of how government could be stripped of waste and, by making local officials responsible for it, hopefully be more focused on the genuinely needy.[51]

In early 1971, Buchanan wrote a couple of brutal memos to Nixon that outlined the view of the administration among its conservative critics. "We suffer," he warned, "from the widely held belief that the President has no Grand Vision that inspires him. . . . Left and right, both now argue that the President, and his Administration, do not take decisions on the basis of political principle—but on the basis of expediency."[52] "The President," it seemed to the Right, "is adopting a liberal Democratic program . . . and the President's ability to drag the GOP along behind his proposals makes him a more effective 'President Liberal' than any Democrat could ever be." In consequence, not only might conservative voters sit out the 1972 elections or switch to a Wallace third-party campaign, but Nixon could also face an internal challenge for the GOP presidential nomination. This incarnation of Richard Nixon was "no longer a credible custodian of the conservative political tradition of the GOP."[53]

White House chief of staff H. R. Haldeman once wrote of Buchanan that his services as a speechwriter were invaluable and that the president felt that on most policy issues he was "probably right." But the "silent majority" was not as conservative as he seemed to presume. They might loathe criminals, kooks, and draft dodgers, but Americans still liked the thought of global peace, Social Security, and healthcare reform—if balanced by fiscal prudence and responsibility. Thus, the New Majority that Nixon wanted to build was grounded in centrism.[54] Fellow speechwriter Bill Safire wrote in response to Buchanan's memoranda on the State of the Union, "Aside from his desire to turn the next election into a Viking's funeral, what is the writer's biggest misconception? Old fashioned purism. The left is the left, the right is the right, and never the twain shall meet. A choice not an echo. I disagree. . . . In this transitional era, with liberals and conservatives joining to praise ecology and decentralization, the political center is the place to be."[55]

There was no finer example of tactical centrism than Nixon's wildly popular trip to China, which outraged Buchanan and his conservative friends.[56] American anticommunism was an important aspect of conservative populism, with its critique of conspiracy and liberal betrayal. Religious conservatives were particularly aggrieved at the loss of China, as it had been the focus of much Christian missionary activity.[57] But the American public welcomed any move that lessened Cold War

tensions and reduced the likelihood of nuclear war. Buchanan accompanied Nixon
on the visit and was brusque with his hosts. He complained to Henry Kissinger
that some of the president's rhetoric there bordered on the fawning.[58] Nixon was
furious and wanted Buchanan to leave the administration. Buchanan backed down
and he kept his job, but the incident contributed to him being denied a management role in the 1972 campaign. Fortunately for Buchanan, this helped to spare
him from involvement in the Watergate scandal. But it reflected the difficult relationship conservatives had with an administration that drew their plaudits for its
position on Vietnam but criticism for much else. As an ideologue, Buchanan was
a helpful bridge to the Right and a passionate wordsmith. But he was politically
dispensable.[59]

Nixon adopted a rose-garden strategy for reelection in 1972. He was helped by
an implosion on the Democratic side, which the administration exploited. During
its primaries, the Democratic Party welcomed into its ranks the cultural vanguard
of the 1960s (including antiwar protestors, feminists, gays, and civil rights activists)
and flirted with policies that were summed up as "amnesty, acid, and abortion." Arguably, Nixon was reelected by default—confirming the wisdom of monopolizing
the center ground and rendering conservative populism unnecessary. But Buchanan
had cause for cheer. For one, much of the administration agreed that it was important to reach out to urban ethnics, including Catholics, through cultural appeals.
While middle-class southerners were crucial to the emerging New Majority, capturing the Polish, Irish, and Italian votes in the cities would deliver a fatal blow to the
Democratic coalition.[60] This could be done institutionally through appointments,
Buchanan thought; he lobbied hard for an Italian American Supreme Court nominee.[61] It could also be done by adopting policies that appealed to ethnic groups.
Hence, Catholics were wooed with aid to parochial schools and presidential support for nascent efforts to curtail liberal abortion laws.[62] Nixon took the point that
the only way to stop ethnics from drifting back to the Democrats out of loyalty to
the New Deal was "by hammering hard on those issues that annoy these people
about McGovern. In other words, the blue collar issues, and the Catholic issues,
where McGovern simply cannot be as appealing to them as we are." This signaled
the beginning of a long-term GOP commitment to a pro-life, religiously conservative movement that would falter under Ford but return under Reagan.[63]

This "ethnic" strategy involved populist rhetoric and rested on the populist assumption that people's values can be determined by their faith and origin. But it
was not ideologically conservative. In one debate on election strategy, Nixon agreed
with veteran political consultant Murray Chotiner on the need to "go for Poles,
Italians, Irish" and to give up on "blacks and Jews." But while the administration
should "go gung-ho on Catholic issues," it should avoid a "hard right reactionary
philosophy" (particularly in economics) lest it be accused of extremism. Nixon
thought that ethnics were not drifting toward the president because they were

born-again Republicans or self-consciously conservative. Rather, they were reacting against the "demonstrations of intellectual snobs."[64]

Despite his president's pragmatism on economics and even foreign policy, Buchanan could nevertheless rejoice in the widely held view that the 1972 result confirmed that, first, social liberalism was unpopular and, second, Republicans should go after southerners and blue-collar ethnics with cultural appeals. The president swept not only the South (taking an astonishing 78 percent in Mississippi) but also the North, in part by breaking into the blue-collar constituency that ordinarily belonged to the Democrats. Nationwide, Nixon took 54 percent of the votes of union members and 52 percent of Catholic votes (compared to just 33 percent in 1968). "While the Nixon landslide was a victory of the man over McGovern," wrote Buchanan, "it was also a victory of the New American Majority over the New Politics, a victory of traditional American values and beliefs over the claims of the counter-culture." There was no greater testament to Richard Nixon's success than the "benevolent neutrality" of the AFL-CIO in the 1972 election. Admittedly, this had been made possible by the administration's embrace of "liberal economics," but it was mostly built on patriotism and outrage at the leftward drift of the Democrats, as well as a desire to recover labor's influence within the party.[65]

While he lobbied for the Southern Strategy, Buchanan's memos and news summaries suggest that winning the South did not thrill him nearly as much as winning the states often associated with the counterculture. The politics of class and culture had intersected, giving the Republicans an opportunity to build a coalition "between the lower and middle class Democratic center and right" against the "upper middle class elite and left." Buchanan's formulation was populist in the way it divided the country into economic and cultural interest groups. Arguably, George McGovern's candidacy posed a challenge to business elites and the so-called military-industrial complex. But Buchanan saw McGovern as the elitist. To him, Nixon's victory was that of one social group (Middle America) over another (wealthy liberals).[66]

The New Majority revolution was stillborn. Just seven months after Nixon's remarkable reelection victory, a Senate committee began televised hearings into the administration's role in a break-in at the Watergate complex. This was a tragedy for conservatives like Pat Buchanan, because the second administration had begun by unveiling a fresh commitment to conservative ideas that were far more to his liking. Nixon had promised a conservative revolution, including an expansion of revenue sharing, budget slashing, and tax cutting.[67] For instance, on the environment, the president had signaled that he was tired with overregulation and overspending on protection and cleanup. Not only was it damaging to the needs of producers during a period of economic slowdown, but it gave liberals too much airtime. Whatever the White House did was never enough to satisfy the liberals. To quote one administration official's advice to the president, "You can't win on the environment, but they [the Left] can beat you up with it." Buchanan was overjoyed with the emergence of a new discourse in American conservatism that pitted industrialists and working-class voters against middle-class conservationists.[68]

But while Buchanan was pleased with the new direction in substantive policy, he was disappointed at Nixon's inability to bring the public with him—long before Watergate destroyed his credibility.[69] The problem was that Nixon's fall strategy of appealing to the voters' innate social conservatism while keeping the money flowing for popular Social Security entitlements and bolstering up the economy did not prepare the country well for the radical reforms of the spring. Matched against his earlier image of statesmanship, the retrenchment made Nixon seem calculating. Worse still, he was reaping the failure of the first administration to establish a clear conservative rationale. Without having argued the philosophical case for winding down the Great Society, Nixon risked appearing not only manipulative but also cruel. The administration seemed "heartless, evasive, aloof, condescending, sinister, power hungry, petty, and paranoid. . . . We have not used to our full advantage the dichotomy between the American public's theoretical approval of Federal spending programs and its practical opposition to increased Federal spending or taxes," according to aide Frank Gannon.[70] There was an important lesson to be taken from the first few months of Nixon's new administration. Without understanding the benefits of conservative policies, voters would reject a conservative candidate. Buchanan would make similar criticisms of Gerald Ford and George H. W. Bush, neither of whom was a populist and both of whom used a puzzling mix of moderation and appeals to the party base that undermined a consistent, conservative message.[71]

Buchanan's frustration with the Republican establishment under Nixon turned to outright hostility under Ford. He was denied his dream job of ambassador to South Africa and quit politics to pursue a career as a columnist and talk-show host.[72] In 1975 he wrote, "The right should make it clear that the [policies] being pursued in Washington, by the Administration and the Congress, is done against the protest of the right. Conservatives should behave politically as what they are— strangers to the corridors of power, dissenters outside the councils of government, men without power and without responsibility for what is happening." The Republicans had "not yet decided irrevocably where they stand on the issues of the new era," he complained. "The party wishes to be thought of as both principled and progressive. It prefers the comfortable, less bitter conflicts of an earlier age." Its leadership belonged "to the fifties . . . the age of Eisenhower and Kennedy . . . where there was bipartisan cooperation between liberals and conservatives when we reached the water's edge."[73] That year he, along with several other conservative populists, tried to convince Ronald Reagan, John Connally, or George Wallace to run against Ford.[74]

He was impressed with Ronald Reagan's 1976 candidacy, which expressed a more populist approach to politics. Buchanan then offered Reagan support in

1980, and his sister, Bay, was campaign treasurer. With his ideological appeals for increased defense expenditure, tax cuts, and the protection of the unborn, President Reagan appeared to demonstrate that conservative ideas, well sold, could appeal to white southerners, suburbanites, urbanites, and the lower middle class. The growing conservatism of the congressional GOP, religious revival, and the triumph of supply-side economics suggested that the populist hour had come. But it did not last.[75]

Even the Reagan administration was sensitive to charges of bellicosity or a lack of compassion. Contrary to popular myth, White House staff often dodged controversial issues and some historians have reevaluated Reagan as either a dove or a sophisticated, socially tolerant libertarian. Unlike Nixon's, Reagan's conservatism was ideological. But he shared his predecessor's pragmatism and courted favorable public opinion.[76] When he entered the administration as director of communications in 1985, Buchanan still remained a critic of the influence of moderates.[77] By 1988, the ban on prayer in public schools remained in place, abortion was still legal, and affirmative action still practiced in federal hiring. Buchanan was even more critical of the administration of George H. W. Bush, especially after he signed a budget deal with the Democratic Congress that raised taxes. Buchanan entered the 1992 presidential primaries to challenge the incumbent president and to call for the party to return to its core principles of low taxes and cultural traditionalism. The campaign was idiosyncratic, but the support Buchanan enjoyed among movement conservatives, and his capture of between one-quarter and one-third of the vote in every primary he entered, pointed to a constituency of disaffected populist conservatives.[78] Buchanan argued that Bush's defeat in the general election of 1992 reflected his failure to manipulate the social issues that were the Republican Party's trump card in an era of recession.

By the end of the Cold War, Buchanan's politics had changed. He now advocated isolationism in foreign affairs and protectionism in economics. To some Republicans and commentators, this reflected a shift to the left. Buchanan argued that he was in fact returning to pre–Cold War conservative values, steeped in economic nationalism. Few other conservative Republicans reached the same conclusions as Buchanan, but his politics was at least consistent in its populism. To the list of elite groups who threatened the republic, Buchanan now added Israeli lobbyists and global corporations.[79] His ongoing mission—to integrate disaffected Democrats into a populist New Majority—gained some ground. When he ran again for the Republican nomination in 1996, one postelection analysis found that his Republican presidential primary voters were the poorest, the youngest, the least well educated, the least fiscally conservative, the most pro-life, and, crucially, the most likely to be registered as a Democrat.[80]

Buchanan argued that his frustration with President Nixon was but one example of the failure of the GOP to capitalize on populism. He used his presidential campaigns in part to try to do what Nixon did not—to build a long-term alliance of social conservatives and the economically distressed.[81] Kevin P. Phillips concurred that Republicans had failed to maximize the appeal of populism and detected a refreshing "middle-class radicalism" in Buchanan's campaigns that sought to both streamline the state and force it to serve the economic needs of a troubled middle America. He compared it with the insurgent candidacies of liberal Democrat Jerry Brown, racial conservative David Duke, and tycoon Ross Perot. Democratic strategist Stanley B. Greenberg disagreed strongly, pointing out that these four men "offered radically different programs, attacked different villains and appealed to fundamentally different groups in society." To his liberal critics, there was no universal theme in American populism and Buchanan's greatest achievement was helping to give an everyman gloss to reactionary ideas.[82]

Arguably, Buchanan's political strategy was flawed. Its economic appeal was limited to a declining class of conservative blue-collar workers. His failure to move beyond a third of the vote in any primary reflected fears that he was too extreme to be elected, as well as the moderation of the bulk of registered Republicans. In this regard, populism did not command majority support in a country seeking sophisticated answers to complex questions. Americans have rarely voted for partisanship and, in 1996, chose President Bill Clinton for his comparative centrism over Republican nominee Bob Dole (who was associated with the federal government shutdown of 1995). Populism seems to remain a way of communicating frustration by marginalized voters rather than a strategy for government.

Thus, Nixon's centrist strategy was probably more appropriate than Buchanan's to the troubled era of the early 1970s, although it undoubtedly depended on the implosion of the Democrats. That the initiative Buchanan hated the most—the trip to China—remains Nixon's most iconic and enduring is instructive. Despite his reputation, President Nixon was reelected because he was perceived as a moderate and capable administrator at home and a peacemaker overseas. Nevertheless, Buchanan's critique of his boss and his later campaigns highlight an ongoing debate over political strategy within the GOP. The party has undoubtedly moved to the right since the Nixon era, but its leadership remains wary of sacrificing the center ground or alienating moderate voters. Buchanan's candidacies communicated anger from the party base and a warning that populism remains a potent, polarizing force in U.S. politics.[83]

NOTES

1. For discussion of the New Majority, see Thomas J. Sugrue and John D. Skrentny, "The White Ethnic Strategy," in *Rightward Bound: Making America Conservative in the 1970s*, ed. Bruce J. Schulman and Julian E. Zelizer (Cambridge, MA: Harvard University Press, 2008), 29–51.
2. Ronald Reagan's staff did their best to soften his conservative image. Robert Dallek,

Ronald Reagan: The Politics of Symbolism (1984; Cambridge, MA: Harvard University Press, 1999), 58–59.

3.   Michael Kazin, *The Populist Persuasion: An American History* (New York: Basic Books, 1995), 1, 245–68.

4.   Donald T. Critchlow, *The Conservative Ascendancy: How the GOP Right Made Political History* (Cambridge, MA: Harvard University Press, 2007), 128–37.

5.   A good example of a populist strategy was the 1994 "Contract with America." Kazin, *Populist Persuasion*, 274. In 1976, several prominent populist conservatives (including Pat Buchanan, Richard Viguerie, and Kevin Phillips) tried to engineer a third-party Wallace-Reagan ticket. William C. Berman, *America's Right Turn: From Nixon to Bush* (Baltimore: Johns Hopkins University Press, 1994), 28.

6.   Notes on meeting with Nixon, October 16, 1970, File 5-33-85, *Papers of the Nixon White House*, part 5: *H. R. Haldeman: Notes of White House Meetings, 1969–1973* (Frederick, MD: University Publications of America, 1989; hereafter *Haldeman Minutes*).

7.   The debate over the wording of Nixon's call for a moratorium on court-ordered busing was a case in point: William Safire, memorandum to Nixon, March 14, 1972, File 7-368-003, *Papers of the Nixon White House*, part 7: *President's Personal Files, 1969–1974* (Frederick, MD: University Publications of America, 1991; hereafter *Personal Papers*).

8.   Notes on meeting with Nixon, November 1, 1969, File 5-13-09, *Haldeman Minutes*.

9.   Author's interview with David Keene, February 22, 2010.

10. "Nixon's Presidency Is a Very Private Affair," *New York Times*, November 2, 1969, SM28; Stephen E. Ambrose, *Nixon*, vol. 2: *The Triumph of a Politician, 1962–1972* (New York: Simon and Schuster, 1989), 248–49, 409.

11. Author's interview with David Keene, February 22, 2010.

12. Author's interview with Patrick J. Buchanan, February 21, 2010.

13. "Richard Nixon's Collapsing Presidency," *Time*, May 20, 1974, 15.

14. "Buchanan Sought to Block Muskie," *New York Times*, September 27, 1973, 1.

15. "The Legend of Saint George McGovern," *New York Times*, November 24, 1972, 37.

16. Buchanan, memorandum to Haldeman, January 14, 1971, File 6A-116-04, *Papers of the Nixon White House*, part 6, series A: *The President's Office Files: Documents Annotated by the President, 1969–1974* (Frederick, MD: University Publications of America, 1990; hereafter *Annotated Nixon Papers*).

17. Buchanan, memorandum to Nixon, April 11, 1969, File 6A-12-43 B, *Annotated Nixon Papers*.

18. William E. Leuchtenberg, *In the Shadow of FDR: From Harry Truman to George W. Bush* (Ithaca, NY: Cornell University Press, 2001), 164; and Paul R. Hengeller, *The Kennedy Persuasion: The Politics of Style since JFK* (Chicago: Ivan R. Dee, 1995), 93.

19. Deborah Hart Strober and Gerald S. Strober, *The Nixon Presidency: An Oral History of the Era* (Washington, DC: Brassey's, 2003), 108.

20. Berman, *Right Turn*, 29.

21. "Buchanan's Alternative: Not Kinder Nor Gentler," *New York Times*, January 15, 1992, A1.

22. Patrick J. Buchanan, *The Great Betrayal: How American Sovereignty and Social Justice Are Being Sacrificed to the Gods of the Global Economy* (Boston: Little, Brown, 1998), 289.

23. Buchanan, *Right from the Beginning*, 6–14.

24. H. R. Haldeman, *The Haldeman Diaries: Inside the Nixon White House* (New York: Putnam, 1994), 397. For Buchanan's relationship to Wallace, see Dan T. Carter, *From George Wallace to Newt Gingrich: Race in the Conservative Counterrevolution, 1963–1994* (Baton Rouge: Louisiana State University Press, 2000), 93–94.

25. Robert Mason, *Richard Nixon and the Quest for a New Majority* (Chapel Hill: University of North Carolina Press, 2004), 39.

26. Author's interview with Patrick J. Buchanan, April 21, 2010.

27. Patrick J. Buchanan, "The Ship of Integration Is Going Down," *Harper's*, June 1972, 66.

28. Kevin L. Yuill, *Richard Nixon and the Rise of Affirmative Action: The Pursuit of Racial Equity in an Era of Limits* (Lanham, MD: Rowman and Littlefield, 2006), 225–27.

29. "Is Mr. Nixon Pursuing a Southern Strategy?," *National Observer*, December 15, 1969, 21; for an excellent, recent review on this subject, see Matthew D. Lassiter, *The Silent Majority: Suburban Politics in the Sunbelt South* (Princeton, NJ: Princeton University Press, 2005).

30. Mason, *New Majority*, 180.

31. Ibid., 84.

32. "Reagan May Recall Columnist," *New York Times*, February 5, 1985, B20.

33. Buchanan, memorandum to Nixon, September 2, 1969, File 6A-32-05, *Annotated Nixon Papers*.

34. Buchanan, memorandum to Nixon, March 9, 1973, File 6A-275-10, *Annotated Nixon Papers*.

35. Buchanan, memorandum to Nixon, August 4, 1970, File 6A-88-13, *Annotated Nixon Papers*.

36. Buchanan, memorandum to Nixon, February 25, 1970, File 6A-73-05, *Annotated Nixon Papers*.

37. "The Middle American Who Edits Ideas for Nixon," *New York Times*, April 12, 1970, SM117.

38. Notes on meeting with Nixon, July 10, 1970, File 5-27-49, *Haldeman Minutes*.

39. Herbert S. Parmet, *Richard Nixon and His America* (Boston: Little Brown, 1990), ix, 528.

40. Ambrose, *Triumph of a Politician*, 67.

41. Long before Watergate, Buchanan called for antitrust legislation to break up the television news networks. "Nixon Aide Scores TV News Practice," *New York Times*, May 6, 1972, 1.

42. Mason, *New Majority*, 161–91.

43. Dean J. Kotlowski, *Nixon's Civil Rights: Politics, Principle, and Policy* (Cambridge, MA: Harvard University Press, 2001), 97–124.

44. Justin Raimondo, *Reclaiming the American Right: The Lost Legacy of the Conservative Movement* (Wilmington, DE: Intercollegiate Studies Institute, 2008), 278.

45. Notes on meeting with Nixon, December 16, 1969, File 5-13-64, *Haldeman Minutes*.

46. "Pattern Unclear: Vote Is Kaleidoscopic, But President Fails in Primary Goals," *New York Times*, November 5, 1970, 1.

47. Kevin P. Phillips, *Post-Conservative America: People, Politics, and Ideology in a Time of Crisis* (New York: Random House, 1983), 56.

48. William Safire, *Before the Fall: An Inside View of the Pre-Watergate White House* (1975; New Brunswick, NJ: Transaction Publishers, 2005), 220.

49. J. Brooks Flippen, *Nixon and the Environment* (Albuquerque: University of New Mexico Press, 2000), 76.

50. Timothy J. Conlan, *From New Federalism to Devolution: Twenty-Five Years of Intergovernmental Reform* (Washington, DC: Brookings Institution, 1998), 77–78.

51. Briefing on Nixon's meeting with state legislators, James H. Falk, March 29, 1973, File 7-463-0043, *Personal Papers*.

52. Buchanan, memorandum to Haldeman, January 14, 1971, File 6A-116-04, *Annotated Nixon Papers*.

53. Buchanan, memorandum to Nixon, January 6, 1971, File 6A-114-16, *Annotated Nixon Papers*.

54. Notes on meeting with Nixon, January 3, 1969, File 5-11-77, *Haldeman Minutes*; notes on meeting with Nixon, June 12, 1970, File 5-80-74, *Haldeman Minutes*.

55. Safire, *Before the Fall*, 547.

56. Notes on meeting with Nixon, July 16, 1971, File 5-54-30, *Haldeman Minutes*.

57. Kazin, *Populist Persuasion*, 183.

58. Haldeman, *Diaries*, 423.

59. Notes on meeting with Nixon, March 6, 1972, File 5-71-48, *Haldeman Minutes*; "Last Days in the Bunker," *New York Times*, August 18, 1974, SM202.

60. Haldeman, *Diaries*, 177.

61. Buchanan, memorandum to Nixon, May 26, 1969, File 6A-18-52, *Annotated Nixon Papers*.

62. "Nixon Aides Explain Aims of Letter on Abortion Law," *New York Times*, May 11, 1972, 1.

63. Nixon, memorandum to Carlson, Haldeman, August 9, 1972, File 7-19-0057, *Personal Papers*.

64. Memorandum, September 8, 1970, File 5-14-15, *Haldeman Minutes*.

65. "McGovern, Meany and Labor's Rank and File," *New York Times*, June 24, 1972, 26.

66. Patrick J. Buchanan, *The New Majority: President Nixon at Mid-Passage* ([Philadelphia:] Girard Company, 1973), 55–68.

67. Bruce J. Schulman, *The Seventies: The Great Shift in American Culture, Society and Politics* (2001; Cambridge, MA: Da Capo, 2002), 41.

68. Flippen, *Nixon and the Environment*, 134–35.

69. Notes on meeting with Nixon, January 18, 1973, File 5-88-94, *Haldeman Minutes*.

70. Frank Gannon, memorandum to Ehrlichman, March 30, 1973, File 6A-281-22, *Annotated Nixon Papers*.

71. Mason, *New Majority*, 193.

72. "Ringside With Braden and Buchanan," *Washington Post*, July 2, 1981, C1.

73. Patrick J. Buchanan, *Conservative Votes, Liberal Victories: Why the Right Has Failed* (New York: Quadrangle, 1975), 168–69.

74. Author's interview with Richard Viguerie, March 21, 2010.

75. On the swing to the right in a populist context, see Chip Berlet and Matthew N. Lyons, *Right-Wing Populism in America: Too Close for Comfort* (New York: Guilford Press, 2000), 199–227.

76. Fine examples of historical revision are Paul Lettow, *Ronald Reagan and his Quest to Abolish Nuclear Weapons* (New York: Random House, 2005), and John Patrick Diggins, *Ronald Reagan: Fate, Freedom, and the Making of History* (New York: Norton, 2006). For the charge of pragmatism, see Paul Kengor and Peter Schweizer, eds., *The Reagan Presidency: Assessing the Man and His Legacy* (Lanham, MD: Rowman and Littlefield, 2005), 18.

77. Buchanan clashed with moderates and pragmatists like Donald Regan and Robert McFarlane over taxes and foreign policy, sometimes allowing his anger to leak to the

press. "Buchanan, a Tough Conservative, Is Leaving Post at White House," *New York Times*, February 4, 1987, A19.

78. For the best discussion of Buchanan's presidential ambitions, see Martin Durham, *The Christian Right, the Far Right and the Boundaries of American Conservatism* (Manchester, UK: Manchester University Press, 2000), 147–67.

79. "The Jew World Order," *New York Times*, March 9, 1995, A25.

80. "How 'Front Runner' in GOP Race Had a Flat Tire in New Hampshire," *New York Times*, February 22, 1996, B7.

81. Irwin M. Stelzer, "Buchanan's Surprisingly Respectable Economics," *Weekly Standard*, March 11, 1996, 24.

82. Stanley B. Greenberg, *Middle Class Dreams: The Politics and Power of the New American Majority* (New Haven, CT: Yale University Press, 1996), 237.

83. Patrick J. Buchanan, *Where the Right Went Wrong: How Neoconservatives Subverted the Reagan Revolution and Hijacked the Bush Presidency* (New York: Thomas Dunne, 2004), 175–94.

CHAPTER 6

John Tower, Texas, and the Rise of the Republican South

Sean P. Cunningham

In 1961, a short, unimposing, former college professor named John Tower shocked political observers nationwide by winning a seat in the United States Senate. The main cause of surprise was that a Republican had won—in Texas. Texas was a Democratic state, had always been a Democratic state, and seemed as reliably Democratic as any state of the "solid South." Tower's election, albeit under special circumstances, was the first statewide victory for a Republican in Texas since Reconstruction. It represented a key turning point in the complicated narrative that is the South's partisan realignment.

This chapter examines how the electoral career of John Tower embodied the South's post-1945 political realignment, with all its starts, stops, acceleration points, factional tensions, and surprises. Tower's rise to political prominence, along with his indispensable role in building a two-party Texas, was fraught with paradoxes. A darling of the conservative, anticommunist, libertarian Right, he won his Senate seat in 1961 primarily by carrying the protest votes of liberal Democrats disillusioned with the conservative establishment of their own party. Reelected in 1966 for much the same reason, Tower finally faced a Democrat the liberals could support in his bid for a third term in 1972. Adapting to this new situation, he achieved victory with a virulently antiliberal campaign, while simultaneously becoming the first Texas Republican to win a plurality of Mexican American voters in a statewide election. An even greater irony marked his run for a fourth term in 1978. Having done much to build the Lone Star state's GOP, Tower found himself all but abandoned by Texas conservatives because of his refusal to support Ronald Reagan's challenge to Gerald Ford for the 1976 Republican presidential nomination.

When John Tower finally retired from the United States Senate in 1985, Texas ranked among the strongest Republican states in terms of national politics. As such, it typified the transformation of the Democratic solid South into a Republican stronghold. This was a remarkable shift for a state whose political culture was based on tradition and loyalty. Tower's political career, therefore, serves as a window into the origins of partisan realignment in the old Confederacy. It also offers a valuable state-based case study of the tensions between ideology, intraparty factions, and party building in the rise of the southern GOP.

In explaining Tower's vanguard position in the emergence of conservative Texas Republicanism, due acknowledgment should be made of his highly effective political style. During his time on the national stage, Tower helped localize the use of populist conservative rhetoric, stressing—among other things—the monopolistic dominance of establishment Democrats in Texas, while connecting the value of building a strong GOP to notions of local control and autonomy from national liberalism. He adopted and at times perfected the critically important skill of communicating conservative Republican principles on a level accessible to a growing middle class. He made better use of television and public relations than any Texas conservative before him. Although he was never the darling of the Christian Right, with whom he fell out in the 1970s, Tower also used notions of God, family, and patriotism to create a stronger emotional bond between Texans and the Republican Party. In short, he both developed and used most of the techniques critical to the broader success of modern conservatism and the corollary rise of the Republican Party during the 1960s and 1970s.

While most scholars readily acknowledge that these techniques were fundamentally important to the modern conservative ascendancy, historians interested in understanding and explaining the nation's post-1945 political changes have also debated the centrality of race and southern realignment to that shift. Among the simplest and most common explanations for Republican growth in the South holds that Lyndon B. Johnson's promotion of the Civil Rights Act of 1964 so alienated white conservatives in the South as to spark realignment. The electoral map of 1964 seems to bear out this conclusion. Though thoroughly trounced nationally, conservative Republican presidential candidate Barry Goldwater swept the Deep South. With the exception of his home state of Arizona, which he carried by only one point, the sole entries in his column were the five states of this region. Winning just 38.5 percent of the national popular vote, he secured landslide margins of victory in Mississippi (87 percent), Alabama (69 percent), South Carolina (59 percent), Louisiana (57 percent), and Georgia (54 percent). Considering the centrality of race to southern politics, coupled with the immediate evidence of Goldwater's success in the South, it would seem that Johnson may indeed have signed away the region for a generation (or more) through his support for the most sweeping and crucial piece of civil rights legislation in the twentieth century.[1]

Problems with this argument, however, are plentiful. For one thing, the "South" consists of more than simply those states carried by Goldwater in 1964. Other southern states stuck with Johnson, despite having voted Republican for other reasons and at other times throughout the twentieth century. For instance, North Carolina cast its votes for the Republican presidential candidate, Herbert Hoover (and against his Catholic Democratic opponent, Al Smith) in 1928, but would not do so again until 1968, when it went for Richard Nixon. Florida also went GOP in

1928, then voted for Dwight D. Eisenhower twice (1952 and 1956), and for Nixon thrice (1960, 1968, and 1972). In fact, the Sunshine state cast its electoral lot with every Republican presidential candidate between 1952 and 1992, with the solitary exceptions of 1964 and 1976, when it voted for Lyndon B. Johnson and Jimmy Carter, respectively. Tennessee's electoral vote history during this time is identical to Florida's, with the exception of 1992, when it went for Bill Clinton and native son Al Gore. Running for president in 2000, Gore famously lost his home state, where victory—regardless of the controversial outcome in Florida—would have secured him the presidency. In contrast, Mississippi, Alabama, and Georgia had never voted Republican prior to 1964. The white alienation case for the South's realignment to the GOP in 1964 and beyond also ignores the reality that politics is about far more than simply presidential elections. The partisan shift of the region was not evident until much later in regard to the pursuit of other offices. As Earl and Merle Black have pointed out, most southern states did not begin to elect Republicans en masse at the state and local level until at least the 1990s.[2]

Other historians have found the origins of southern Republicanism—and of modern American conservatism—in different places and at different times. In his seminal biography of George Wallace, Dan T. Carter identified the roots of southern (and national) conservatism in the raging rhetoric of Alabama's most notorious promoter of race-baiting, backlash politics. Kevin M. Kruse's study of Atlanta, however, discerned them in the somewhat moderated, though equally race-based, language of property rights, homeownership, and "white flight." According to Kruse, the development of this rhetoric predated both Wallace's rise to national prominence and the Civil Rights Act of 1964. Other scholars working on the South, including Matthew D. Lassiter, Joseph Crespino, and William Link, also see modern conservatism emanating from a sometimes subtler, sometimes less overt, but still always racially charged rhetoric that was born not so much of "massive resistance" to either desegregation or the Civil Rights Act of 1964 specifically, but from the grassroots energy of the region's emerging suburban middle class, which responded to threats like busing with both political hostility and partisan realignment. Former Nixon adviser Kevin P. Phillips may have connected what he famously called the "emerging Republican majority" with the GOP's development of a so-called Southern Strategy. In the estimate of the aforementioned historians, however, it was actually a more rhetorically colorblind "Suburban Strategy" that brought the Republican Party electoral credibility in the old Confederacy.[3]

Regardless of when, why, or how scholars see the postwar genesis of the Republican Party's southern revitalization, it seems clear that, even as historians of the Civil War era now readily acknowledge, there never was such a thing as a truly "solid South." Different southern states began voting Republican at the local, state, and national levels at different times and for somewhat different reasons.[4] It should be noted, for instance, that the rise of a politically motivated evangelical Right—something that did not begin in earnest until the mid-1970s—complicates the reasons for realignment even further. For instance, it was not until the early 1970s, and specifically 1973, that politically mobilized evangelicals, responding in part to a series of Supreme Court decisions, especially *Roe v. Wade*, began to participate more vigorously in national political battles. Still, it is possible to learn about the connections between southern politics and the rise of modern conservatism by studying well-selected isolated moments, individuals, and even states—including John Tower and Texas.

John Tower's first major political splash came in 1960, when he lost his bid for a seat in the United States Senate by only seventeen percentage points. In almost any other context, such a defeat would have been considered a sound thumping, but in Texas, against the incumbent Lyndon B. Johnson (simultaneously running for vice president), this was an impressive showing. In 1954, LBJ had defeated his Republican opponent, Carlos Watson, 85 to 15 percent. At the time a political science professor at Midwestern University in Wichita Falls, Tower's strong run positioned him for another Senate bid in 1961. This was a special election to fill the seat that LBJ had vacated upon assuming the vice presidency. Still, the odds against Tower were long. Texas had not sent a Republican to the United States Senate since the Reconstruction elections of 1870 put James W. Flanagan and Morgan C. Hamilton in office, though neither of those men had actually been favored by most white Texans.[5]

Not surprisingly, Tower's opponent was a representative of the state's long-entrenched conservative Democratic establishment, William Blakely. A conservative businessman from Dallas, Blakely was appointed interim senator by Governor Price Daniel in January 1961 and immediately announced his intent to run for the seat in his own right in the forthcoming special election. The only conservative in a contest that also featured three squabbling liberals, he easily won the Democratic primary, which was usually a guarantee of victory in the general election.[6]

Lulled by history into a complacent expectation that he would overwhelm Tower, Blakely followed the imperious strategy of previous Democratic nominees. Lyndon B. Johnson, in particular, ignored his Republican opponent's presence on the ballot both in 1948 and 1954, choosing instead to stroll to general election victory as if he were in a one-party race. Sharing the habitual Democratic belief that victory was an entitlement for the party's candidate, Blakely did not court disgruntled liberals, many of whom began to talk about "going fishing" when Election Day finally rolled around. Moreover, he barely acknowledged his GOP opponent, despite Tower's strong showing against Johnson in 1960.[7]

Tower, on the other hand, ran an aggressive campaign, not against his Democratic opponent's liberalism—for Blakely was no liberal—but against the dominance of one-party rule and "establishment" politics. In this rather populist fight, Tower found allies on both the Republican Right and the liberal Left. Long a small minority in Texas, Republicans had largely confined their ambitions to organizational survival, depending on federal patronage from Republican administrations to do so. Mounting a competitive statewide campaign was beyond their hopes now.

With Eisenhower's victories in the Lone Star state in 1952 and 1956, as well as Nixon's solid showing in 1960, many in the GOP dared to believe that their time had come.[8]

With that hope in mind, Texas Republicans sought to convince voters that regardless of ideology, it was time they had an actual choice at the ballot box. Liberals wholeheartedly agreed and many supported Tower for that reason. Even the state's leading and famously liberal political periodical, the *Texas Observer*, endorsed Tower as a step toward legitimate two-party politics. Liberals resented the conservative Democratic establishment for long hindering the advancement of many progressive reforms advocated by the national Democratic Party. A Tower victory, many believed, would force conservatives either to embrace the liberal minority within the state party or to leave the party altogether—options they found equally pleasing.[9]

As well as charging that Democratic one-party rule was akin to political life in "Communist Russia," Tower addressed claims that the national GOP was ruled by a moderate northeastern establishment. "As a conservative I often wish that my own party were free of some of its liberal elements and that its policies were more resolutely conservative," he told an audience in Brownwood in 1961. "But I would much rather be a constituent of a large, moderately conservative party that could reasonably expect to always influence public policy and periodically control the government, than a small, more conservative, but politically impotent group." According to Tower's argument, Texans who continually sent conservative Democrats to Washington were disfranchising themselves through their support for the minority wing of a nationally liberal party.[10]

When the Democratic candidate finally took the Tower challenge seriously, his first line of attack painted his Republican opponent as too moderate to represent Texas in the U.S. Senate. Exploiting Tower's credentials as an academic—especially his education at the London School of Economics—Blakely stoked the flames of antiliberalism as a means of separating him from those conservatives who typically voted Democratic but were interested in developing a two-party system in Texas. This strategy, while often effective in Texas politics, did not work so well on this occasion.[11] Tower, meanwhile, continued to embrace all Texans, liberal or conservative, interested in ending, as he put it, the system of "political bosses." He also shaped an image of himself conducive to the traditional values and tenets of Texas conservatism, namely that he was a "family man" and a "church man from a church family," whose father had been a Methodist minister.[12]

In some ways typical and in other ways very atypical, Tower's 1961 run for the Senate reflected both the traditions of Texas conservatism and the undervalued populist issue of distributing more fairly the means of political power. He was among the first southern Republicans to focus significant attention on the notion of a monopolistic and Democratic "good ol' boys" club, thereby helping to pioneer the use of this populist theme in future GOP campaigns. In large part because of this strategy, his campaign attracted scores of volunteers, many of them women, from the growing suburbs of the Dallas area. For many supporters, the Tower campaign—which many called "their" campaign—was a statement of defiance, not only against the liberalism of the national Democratic Party, but also against the entrenched and stale Texas Democratic establishment, however conservative it might have been. Indeed, it was this momentum that carried Tower to his slim but still shocking and groundbreaking victory by a mere 1 percent of the overall vote.[13]

Dismissed as a fluke in 1961, Tower won reelection five years later, once again defeating a representative of the conservative Democratic establishment, state attorney general Waggoner Carr. Liberals once again played a key role in his victory. Flouting bumper stickers such as one that read, "Sometimes Party Loyalty Asks Too Much," they rallied behind Tower, who also made significant inroads with Texas's Mexican American voters. Instead of squeezing home as in 1961, the GOP incumbent achieved reelection with a landslide 57 percent share of the vote, thereby becoming the first Republican in the state's history to serve more than a single term.[14]

Tower's victory over Carr was critically important in the history of modern Texas conservatism—arguably more so even than his defeat of Blakely in 1961. In national terms, it was part of a Republican comeback from the 1964 nadir that saw the party gain forty-seven seats in the House and four in the Senate. This outcome did not represent a conservative sweep—moderates also benefited from the anti-Democratic trend—but it quelled discussion of the GOP's demise, both nationally and in the South. More pertinently for the conservative cause, Tower's victory, together with Ronald Reagan's California gubernatorial victory that many Texans had supported from afar, showed that the GOP Right was not down and out as pundits commonly claimed. These two successes indicated that it was a significant force in the emerging Sunbelt.

Deeply involved with Goldwater's run for president, Tower was expected to be a casualty of its massive failure in Texas, but the seeds of his reelection can be found in the rubble of that campaign. His seconding speech in support of the Arizonan's nomination at the Republican national convention raised his national profile. During appearances in Texas, Tower often presented himself as able to straddle party lines to win cross-party votes. In contrast, his convention speech was unabashedly partisan in its wholehearted identification with the conservative movement. He spoke passionately about the need to defend America against communism and painted a picture of lawlessness and crime that he also connected to permissiveness in Washington. Goldwater's consequent loss in Texas by a margin of 27 percent suggested that Tower was doomed to the same fate two years later.[15] His victory discredited any assumption that the GOP flame had burned out in Lyndon B. Johnson's home state, whose growing population would soon make it a pivotal force in national elections.[16]

Tower was also instrumental in pioneering an image, however questionable its sincerity, of Republican conservatism as colorblind in comparison with the Democratic brand of this philosophy. Despite siding with Goldwater in opposing the 1964 Civil Rights Act as a violation of states' rights, he promoted the Texas GOP as a home for minorities interested in supporting urbanization, economic development, and traditional "American" values, broadly and vaguely defined. Tower's position on this score earned him another endorsement from the liberal *Texas Observer*. The League of United Latin American Citizens (LULAC) and several smaller Mexican American political action groups in South and Central Texas also joined his column. While respectful of Tower's platform, their main purpose in endorsing him was to send a message to state Democratic leaders. Trumpeting the "need for a two-party Texas," Corpus Christi city councilman and LULAC associate M. P. Maldonado chaired the critically important "Amigocrats for Tower Committee."[17] The *Texas Observer* further strengthened the incumbent's support among state minorities, and especially Mexican Americans, by publishing photographs of Waggoner Carr attending a 1957 meeting of a local White Citizens Council. In essence Tower's reelection strategy, which opportunistically hinged on anti-Democratic sentiment, proved highly effective in directly appealing to state minority voters at a crucial time when they were beginning to find fewer obstacles on their way to the ballot box.[18]

Assessment of the historical significance of Tower's 1966 campaign should also recognize its role in advancing Texas politics into a much more media-savvy age. It featured a thirty-minute documentary film about his life and rise to the Senate that included staged and rather disingenuous shots of him riding a horse and wearing a cowboy hat. In reality, Tower was fonder of pinstriped three-piece suits, but these accoutrements and the stuffy offices that went with them made for boring television and hardly undermined lingering perceptions of the GOP as a "corporate" party. Additionally, Tower broke ground by advertising in magazines such as *Texas Football*, which sports fans viewed as a virtual bible for high school, college, and professional gridiron action across the state, as well as *GameDay* programs, sold to thousands of fans attending college football games across Texas each Saturday throughout the fall. Carr was reportedly furious with his staff for being outflanked by Tower's appeal to the "football crowd."[19]

Though always emphasizing the importance of making Texas a legitimate two-party state, Tower focused sharp critiques against "Washington liberals," thereby making his race more of a referendum on national trends than on state or local ones. Like many aspiring populists, Tower routinely invoked the name of Thomas Jefferson in his speeches, connecting Republican ideological principles of free market individualism and liberty with those espoused by the iconic author of the Declaration of Independence. Without actually co-opting the precise language most commonly employed by segregationists, Tower gradually and effectively framed the Texas GOP as the home for colorblind Jeffersonian states' rights, though not necessarily white supremacy. In this sense, like Goldwater before him and very much like

Reagan in later years, he struck an effective chord in connecting conservative Republicanism with Jeffersonian populism—all while "proving" his sincerity by reaffirming his own personal commitments to racial equality and individual freedom.[20]

Another important outcome of the 1966 race, and one that portended a critical element of Texas and southern factionalism and realignment in the coming years, was the discord that losing seemed to breed within the Democratic Party. Carr berated liberals for his loss, as did other conservative Democrats. Liberals willingly accepted the "blame," bragging that conservative Democrats had been taking their support for granted for far too long and that Tower's victories were the outcome of this neglect. GOP partisans, of course, were hesitant to credit liberal Democrats for Tower's success, citing instead the growing number of registered Republicans as evidence that what Texans really wanted was a conservative senator unencumbered by a liberal Democratic Party at the national level.

GOP emphasis on the national Democratic Party's perceived liberalism paid increasing dividends in the latter years of the 1960s. Images of race riots, street violence, antiwar protests, rampant drug use, and flaunted sexuality suggested to many Texans that the nation was sinking into a relativistic and immoral abyss. Factional tensions were exacerbated within the state and national Democratic Party during this time. These tensions helped conservatives to gain strength within the GOP and liberals, including those in Texas, to do so within the Democratic Party. This polarization helped Republicans like Tower in encouraging Texans to sacrifice their long-standing partisan traditions in favor of their more important ideological loyalties—a strategy that the Republicans considered the quickest and surest way to build the state GOP.

By the early 1970s, John Tower's victories in 1961 and 1966, coupled with his compilation of an impressive eleven-year record of service in Washington on behalf of Texas, created a climate in which partisan realignment seemed increasingly possible and even attractive to many state conservatives. Richard Nixon's appointment of former Democratic governor John Connally as treasury secretary in his administration further encouraged their hopes. It is fair to say that without Tower's campaigns in the 1960s, the Texas Republican Party would have continued to languish well into the 1970s. Yet, a funny thing happened on the way to statewide partisan realignment. Just as conservative Republicanism seemingly became more popular in Texas, particularly with the national Democratic Party's leftward drift during the late 1960s and early 1970s, Tower slowly came to be perceived as out of step with Texans' views regarding modern conservatism and establishment politics.

The GOP trailblazer claimed two further reelection victories in 1972 and 1978, but not without facing an entirely different set of obstacles and alienating many conservatives from his own party. In this, scholars of the South's partisan realignment must acknowledge the nonlinear nature of Republican growth in the region, along with the corresponding tension that developed as racial concerns increasingly gave way to other issues, including taxation, abortion, sexuality, economic development, inflation, and a growing momentum for broad antiliberalism. As John Tower began to see Republican viability in Texas as a real possibility, he mistakenly began to "play it safe" and moderated his own political ideology. Even more harmful to his career, Tower allowed that moderation to come under attack from members of his own party.

Two ill-advised decisions caused Tower's first stumbles with Texas's emerging conservative Republican electorate in 1971. The first was his resignation from the advisory board of the conservative national organization Young Americans for Freedom (YAF), a move that earned condemnation from many on the Republican Right—notably Ronald Reagan. A major player in the ideological consolidation of modern conservatism since 1960—even if increasingly marginal in the following decade—YAF had hitherto received Tower's support. Tower's reasons for resigning were his lack of time and availability to help the organization. In response, YAF supporters charged that he was so preoccupied with building the Texas GOP at any cost that his ideological commitment to their cause was in decline. Some even speculated that Tower might sacrifice conservatism altogether in the interests of building a moderate, big-tent Texas GOP.[21]

Tower's second error of judgment was to oppose a suburban Dallas grassroots organization that was campaigning against a joint state-federal construction project to convert the Trinity River into a shipping canal linking the Dallas–Fort Worth metroplex with the Gulf of Mexico. Though long supported by business leaders, conservative Democrats, and Lyndon B. Johnson, the plan encountered growing opposition in 1971–1972 on the grounds that first, canalization would cause significant environmental harm to natural habitats along the river, and second, local residents would face a higher tax burden to pay for it. Tower supported local businessmen who lobbied for the project and acknowledged the need for higher taxes, all the while claiming that the canal would diversify the Dallas economy and make Texas more competitive in a globalizing market. The backlash caught him somewhat off guard and put him at odds with both suburban opponents of higher taxes and local environmentalists, many of whom had been among Tower's liberal supporters in 1961 and 1966.[22]

With these controversies as a backdrop, Tower ran for reelection in 1972 by trying to reestablish credibility with conservatives and sacrificing the support of liberals. To do this, he exploited George McGovern's unpopular and, according to many, "extremist" liberal campaign for the presidency as a primary weapon against his Senate challenger, the earthy and populist judge Harold "Barefoot" Sanders. Sanders had won an upset victory in the Democratic nomination contest over the famously liberal Ralph Yarborough (a former two-term U.S. senator who had lost to Lloyd Bentsen in the 1970 primary) by charging that his opponent's politics were unrepresentative of state values. Ironically, he then made the fatal mistake of endorsing McGovern's presidential candidacy, enabling Tower to vilify him as a national liberal. Although Sanders was merely being loyal to his party's nominee, the refusal of Democratic gubernatorial nominee Dolph Briscoe, as well as dozens of other Democrats both nationally and in Texas, to follow suit only added grist to charges of his ideological unreliability. The McGovern endorsement eventually cost him significant loss of support among conservative Democrats in the November ballot.[23]

Liberals, in contrast, were now far more inclined to support Sanders for this very reason than they had been for either of Tower's previous two opponents. Needing to bridge his growing credibility gap with grassroots conservatives, the incumbent Republican ran a far more aggressively antiliberal campaign in 1972 than had been the case in either 1961 or 1966. Never failing to connect Sanders with McGovern, McGovern with the national Democratic Party, or the national Democratic Party with "extremist" liberalism, Tower exchanged the support he had received from Texas liberals in 1961 and 1966 for the support of many conservative Texas Democrats in 1972. In this sense, Tower's 1972 campaign was more emblematic of the perceived causality of southern political realignment than were either of his previous two contests. Not surprisingly, therefore, the 1972 U.S. Senate race between Tower and Sanders was, in many ways, a state referendum on the liberalization of the national Democratic Party. As such, conservatives in both parties rallied to Tower while most liberals stuck with Sanders.

The poisonous response to McGovern's campaign in Texas may have facilitated ideological polarization, but Tower's victory also owed something to his campaign's state-of-the-art organization, its nontraditional appeal to rural segments of the electorate, and its ability to connect some of the tenets of modern Republican conservatism to the needs of Texas's Mexican American voters. By saturating local radio markets and giving speeches in an array of rural settings, during which he displayed a surprising adroitness with agricultural issues, Tower became the first Texas Republican in history to win a majority of rural voters. After the election, a campaign organizer referred to this accomplishment as "the most significant achievement" of the 1972 race.[24]

Tower's 1972 campaign was even more media-savvy than his 1966 efforts, and added Mexican American markets in South and West Texas to its list of advertising stages. He ran Spanish-language radio spots in Spanish-speaking districts, advocated bilingual education in public schools, and, when speaking before Mexican American audiences, supported healthcare for the poor, public housing, school lunch programs, and community health centers for migrant workers. Counterbalancing this deviation from his antiliberal strategy with the rest of the state, however, the Republican also marketed himself to Mexican American Catholics by criticizing the moral waywardness of American youth, something he actively blamed on the permissive moral relativism coming out of Washington. He was even more forceful in asserting that Mexican American economic hopes were no different than those of other Texans and were best realized through support of the free market, broad-based economic development, and small business.[25] On Election Day, Tower became the first Republican to win a plurality of Mexican American voters in a statewide contest in Texas, winning a previously inconceivable 45 percent of their ballots, an eleven-point improvement over his impressive support from that constituency in 1966.[26]

Tower's focus on the evils of McGovernite liberalism redeemed his standing among conservatives. In truth, however, he remained committed, above all else, to the growth of the Republican Party in Texas, not the advancement of conservative causes. To his mind, these two goals were not complementary. Tower was seared by the experience of the 1964 Goldwater campaign, considering himself lucky to survive the fallout from it. The fate of McGovern's brand of ideological politics reinforced his conviction that working through the established party structure was the safest way to maintain the momentum that he and other southern and western Republicans had built up over the past decade. Accordingly, the now third-term senator made a strategic decision pertaining to the 1976 presidential election that conformed with his politically pragmatic assessment of GOP needs for building a new majority in both the Lone Star state and the nation at large. When Ronald Reagan challenged incumbent Gerald Ford for the party's presidential nomination, Tower not only backed the latter but also chaired his campaign in Texas. Though not a significant break from the standard play among other national Republican senators, this decision almost destroyed Tower's political career in his home state and threatened to undermine his legacy as a father of modern Texas Republicanism.[27]

Backing Ford over Reagan was, for Tower, a poorly calculated initiative based on outdated assumptions about the nature of the Texas conservative electorate. The former California governor ran a successful campaign in Texas by attacking Ford and the "Fifth Avenue" crowd of Republican moderation, a sobriquet that became interchangeable in his election rhetoric with the "liberal northeastern establishment." Tower's vocal opposition to Reagan placed him in the untenable position of defending what most conservative Texans perceived as Ford's quite moderate record. As a result, he found himself increasingly criticized in Reagan's campaign remarks for ideological frailty, stuffiness, and being too middle-of-the-road for Texas. Taking every opportunity to link Ford and Tower, the standard-bearer of the GOP's increasingly influential conservative wing damned both men as weak-willed on national defense, unsupportive of the suburban middle class, and hostile to the Texas oil industry.

On May 1, Reagan easily defeated Ford in the state GOP primary, winning 66 percent of the vote and sweeping every delegate. The loss undermined Tower's credibility, alienated him from a majority of new conservative Republican voters, many of whom Reagan had attracted to the party, and cost him a seat with the Texas delegation to the Republican National Convention in Kansas City that summer (his lone absence from this body between 1956 and 1980). Attending the convention instead as part of the President Ford Committee, he chose not to visit any Texas delegation events. When asked about the apparent snub, Reagan delegate and campaign organizer Ray Barnhart told reporters that Tower would not have been welcomed by his fellow Texas Republicans anyway.[28]

Though embittered by his exclusion from the Texas delegation in 1976, Tower understood that he needed to mend fences with Reagan conservatives in order to win a fourth senatorial term in 1978. He began this rehabilitation effort by attacking the national party for its liberalism and contextualizing state politics as part of the broader national fight for limited government. In using this strategy, Tower was among the first southern Republicans to successfully localize the populist conservative themes that had been evolving in national campaigns for almost two decades. Though Tower often spoke passionately, if vaguely, about federal encroachment, he also used a variety of issues—including busing, high property taxes, and rising energy costs—to rally grassroots support.

Tower also adopted other hot-button conservative issues, notably the controversy over the Panama Canal treaties that Reagan and Jesse Helms had successfully exploited in their respective 1976 presidential and senatorial primary victories in North Carolina. Taking a leaf out of their playbook, Tower began referring to the treaties, which would have essentially relinquished American sovereignty in the Canal Zone to the left-leaning Panamanian government, as a "communist giveaway." Having passively endorsed Ford's support for these treaties in 1976, he aggressively joined Reagan's opposition to their ratification. Bound by his endorsement of the sitting president, Tower had not drawn attention to his previously consistent opposition to the general idea of the treaties since 1966. In the run-up to the 1978 election, however, he took every opportunity to remind Texas conservatives, who were almost uniformly against the treaties, of his longtime resistance to them. Tower also won favor with conservatives in making public a letter to Jimmy Carter that criticized the president's remarks contrasting the Canal Zone with Texas, which the United States had "bought and paid for." In this, he reminded Carter that Texas had won its independence from Mexico because of "blood," not money, and insisted that the Lone Star state had voluntarily surrendered its own sovereignty to the United States rather than being "bought and paid for."[29]

At the same time, Tower also amped up support for Texas oil producers in the wake of Reagan's accusations that he was insufficiently solicitous of their interests. Opposition to Jimmy Carter's push for a new energy policy gave him the opportunity to demonstrate his fealty. It also established him more generally as a strong critic of a Democratic administration that had lost significant support in Texas in the two years since Carter had carried the state over Ford in 1976.[30]

Despite these efforts to reconstruct his popularity among Texas conservatives, Tower still struggled to win support from former Reagan backers. Ultimately, he won his final Senate reelection by a margin of just 1 percent of the vote over Bob Krueger, whose marital status—he was single—and experience as an English professor at Duke University were both used to suggest that not only was the Democratic candidate an ivory tower elitist, but perhaps gay. In fact, rumors suggesting Krueger was a closet homosexual were among several unseemly tactics used by Republican strategists to discredit the Democratic candidate with conservative Texas voters in 1978.[31]

Still, Tower's win in 1978 was his narrowest since 1961. During the lead-up to the midterm contest, several independent conservative groups connected to Reagan's 1976 campaign launched limited media attacks against Tower. These reminded voters that the Republican senator had opposed Reagan not only in 1976 but also in 1968, when the California governor had made his first, albeit embryonic, bid for the White House. Texas social conservatives also slammed Tower for his support of proposed legislation that would have permitted the use of federal funds for abortions, a stance that contrasted with the opposition of the state's Democratic senator, Lloyd Bentsen. One of several issues new to the political culture of the mid-1970s, abortion would bolster conservative Republican efforts to build a new majority for years to come but hampered Tower's relationship with evangelicals, many of whom came to view him as only nominally Methodist and quite socially moderate.[32]

Reagan's decision to endorse Tower and then campaign in Texas on his behalf provided the incumbent with much-needed salvation. Already priming for another White House bid, Tower's former nemesis now used the Lone Star state's Senate election as a staging ground for his own political race in 1980. "Together we can stop Jimmy Carter and his band of fumbling advisors," Reagan told Texas voters in a direct mailing written on behalf of Tower. This support certainly helped Tower but was primarily a means to boost Reagan's own national candidacy and his parallel drive to position the Republicans as a conservative party in their quest for a new majority. Reagan urged Texas voters to oppose Carter by "seeing that conservatives like John Tower are not replaced by liberals." Tower also earned endorsements from other Texas conservatives, including George H. W. Bush and former governor Allan Shivers, who together authorized a direct mailing urging his reelection as necessary to counter "big labor, big government, and the liberal elements" of the "Washington establishment." These plaudits added conservative credibility to Tower's campaign and were a major factor in his reelection.[33]

Tower did not run for a fifth term in office, even though he actively participated in Ronald Reagan's successful 1980 and 1984 campaigns for the presidency. Retiring from the Senate in January 1985, he was succeeded by former conservative Democrat and GOP convert Phil Gramm. The seat remains in Republican hands at the time this chapter was written. As a further sign that Tower's political career ended with the GOP on the rise in his home state, Texas had also elected its first Republican governor since Reconstruction with William Clements's victory in 1978. Moreover, the Lone Star state has not voted for a Democratic presidential candidate since it narrowly swung for Jimmy Carter in 1976. When Texans backed Carter in that election, most did so—and many of them had been Reagan backers during the GOP primary earlier that spring—because he campaigned as a southern populist, born-again Christian, peanut-farming Sunday School teacher who wanted

to throw out the corrupt Washington establishment, most vividly imagined in voters' minds by connecting the GOP to Richard Nixon and Watergate. Far from
representing a momentary break with conservative values, Carter's success actually
mirrored the appeal of Reagan that was ultimately instrumental in making Texas
one of the most reliable of red states. By 2002, Republicans held all twenty-seven
statewide offices in Texas. Meanwhile, the national power of the Texas GOP had
become self-evident in both the presidential and congressional wings of the party.[34]

But Texas's experience is not necessarily the South's experience, if such a thing
actually exists. In John Tower's political career, one can see aspects both common
to and dissimilar from broader experiences both regionally in the South and even
in Texas. For Tower, the ultimate goal was always party building. Tower was certainly interested in forging his own career as well, but he viewed his greatest legacy
as the development of a viable and eventually dominant Texas Republican Party.
In seeking that end, Tower accepted the support of liberals when advantageous to
do so and launched attacks on them when that became the stronger play. He insisted on using the best technology available, made active use of statistics and polls,
studied voter demographics extensively, and extended Texas politics into the age of
broadcast media, using radio and television in ways that no Republican and few,
if any, Democrats previously had. Tower also established himself as a leader of the
national Republican Party and helped convince Texans that what mattered most in
determining which political party to support was not state tradition but national
ideology. He persuaded voters that national politics shaped partisan agendas, even
at the state level, and that conservative Democrats would have to switch parties in
order to have a voice in shaping that national agenda. Despite almost falling victim
to his prioritization of party building over support of Reaganite conservatism in
1976, Tower survived and is still remembered as the father of the modern Texas Republican Party.

Tower's legacy, and that of the Texas Republican Party he helped to build, is
also complicated by the fact that he reaped the benefits of consistently moderat-
ing his politics to appeal to Mexican Americans, while also using social issues like
abortion, school prayer, and sexuality to earn the support of loyal Catholics. At
the same time, however, he never made any serious efforts to win black voters, nor
did he ever have much success with that constituency. This dichotomy partly reflects the reality that there were more Mexican Americans than African Americans
in Texas. It also testified to Tower's conviction, one he came to hold deeply by 1972,
that winning the black vote in Texas was too costly and provided too little reward.
A critic of the Civil Rights Act of 1964 on constitutional grounds, he also opposed
the Civil Rights Act of 1966 and several school desegregation measures in East
Texas. In addition, Tower supported a constitutional amendment to outlaw busing
and appealed very directly to the politics of white flight in and around Texas's major
cities.[35]

Still, Tower never made the politics of race a top priority. While rarely ignoring it, he did not play the race card in the same manner as many contemporary southern politicians. In this sense, his politics reflected Texas politics, which—while certainly not progressive in its response to race—was rarely obsessed with skin color the way that, for instance, Mississippi had been and continued to be. As esteemed political scientist and observer of southern politics V. O. Key explained as early as 1949, race simply was not the same factor in Texas as it was in other parts of the South.[36]

If, therefore, John Tower or Texas can serve as a reasonable mirror of the complexity of southern politics and the rise of modern conservatism, it can be observed that the growth of the Republican Party in the South during the 1960s, 1970s, and 1980s was the product of a multiplicity of forces, acting in concert in different ways and at different times, with often unpredictable effects. Whereas some southerners came to the GOP strictly because of the national Democratic Party's stand on civil rights, others were more attracted to the GOP's call for limited government, lower taxes, law and order, or "family values." And while it is certainly the case that such "code words" may have given many white southerners an easy way around what became an increasingly archaic and unacceptable worldview based on skin color, it is also true that for others, race was not the sole determinant of their decision to abandon the party of secession.[37]

Last, if John Tower's career teaches us anything, it is that the GOP was an active agent in shaping the political future of the South during the last three decades of the twentieth century. Rather than simply the incidental result of actions taken by conservative Democrats, the rise of state Republican parties across the region was the product of their active fight for legitimacy, in addition to their opportunistic utilization of the South's growing anti-Democratic animus. In this sense, to understand the South's partisan realignment is also to understand that in an age of intense social and cultural analysis, the top-down role of leaders in developing party organization and strategy still matters a great deal.

NOTES

1. For more on Goldwater's 1964 campaign, see Rick Perlstein, *Before the Storm: Barry Goldwater and the Unmaking of the American Consensus* (New York: Hill and Wang, 2001).

2. Earl Black and Merle Black, *The Rise of Southern Republicans* (Cambridge, MA: Harvard University Press, 2002).

3. Kevin P. Phillips, *The Emerging Republican Majority* (New Rochelle, NY: Arlington House, 1969); Dan T. Carter, *The Politics of Rage: George Wallace, the Origins of the New Conservatism, and the Transformation of American Politics* (New York: Simon and Schuster, 1995); Joseph Crespino, *In Search of Another Country: Mississippi and the Conservative Counterrevolution* (Princeton, NJ: Princeton University Press, 2007); Kevin M. Kruse, *White Flight: Atlanta and the Making of Modern Conservatism* (Princeton, NJ: Princeton University Press, 2005); Matthew D. Lassiter, *The Silent Majority: Suburban Politics in the Sunbelt South* (Princeton, NJ: Princeton University

Press, 2005); and William A. Link, *Righteous Warrior: Jesse Helms and the Rise of Modern Conservatism* (New York: St. Martin's Press, 2008).

4. Black and Black, *Rise*.

5. Roger M. Olien, *From Token to Triumph: The Texas Republicans since 1920* (Dallas: SMU Press, 1982), 172–76.

6. Randolph Campbell, *Gone to Texas: A History of the Lone Star State* (New York: Oxford University Press, 2003), 433.

7. Olien, *From Token to Triumph*, 173–76.

8. Ibid.

9. Campbell, *Gone to Texas*, 432–34.

10. John Tower, "The Value of the Two-Party System" (speech), Brownwood, TX, 1961, Box 19, John G. Tower Papers (hereafter JTP), John Tower Library, Southwestern University, Georgetown, TX.

11. Olien, *From Token to Triumph*, 173–76.

12. Campbell, *Gone to Texas*, 432–34.

13. Press release, February 15, 1961, Box 438, JTP; general correspondence, Box 437, Box 439, Box 706, JTP; Kenneth Bridges, *Twilight of the Texas Democrats: The 1978 Governor's Race* (College Station: Texas A&M University Press, 2008), 1–22; and Campbell, *Gone to Texas*, 433.

14. *Dallas Morning News*, November 8, 1966.

15. Goldwater's defeat in Texas can be attributed to three main factors: (1) his opponent was a Texan; (2) Kennedy's assassination in Dallas, for which Texans were made to feel partially responsible; and (3) the related paranoia about being perceived as "extreme."

16. "A Declaration of Republican Principle and Policy," n.d., Folder 2, Box 442, Tower Senate Club, 1964 Goldwater Presidential Campaign, JTP; seconding speech to the Goldwater nomination, Box 442, Tower Senate Club, 1964 Goldwater Presidential Campaign, JTP.

17. "How to Canvass and Win the Latin-American Voter of Low Income," El Paso County GOP, Box 2, Citizens for Reagan Papers, Hoover Institution, Stanford University, Palo Alto, CA; James Leonard, memorandum to Tower, April 25, 1966, Box 711, Austin Offices, JTP; M. P. Maldonado, chairman, Amigocrats for Tower Committee, form letter, c. 1966, Box 725, JTP.

18. Marvin Collins to O'Donnell, October 10, 1966, Austin Office, Box 711, JTP; James Reston, *The Lone Star: The Life of John Connally* (New York: Harper and Row, 1989), 301–2, 314.

19. Jerry Kamprath, memorandum to Tower chairmen, July 27, 1966, Folder 21, Box 711, Austin Office, JTP; "Tower Topics," October 8, 1966, Box 711, Austin Office, JTP; and Lance Tarrance to Jim Leonard, October 19, 1966, Box 710, Austin Office, JTP.

20. "A Look at John G. Tower: Candidate for the United States Senate," Box 814, Campaign/Political: Washington Office, JTP.

21. Tower to Reagan, June 23, 1971, Box 451, JTP.

22. BW [full name unknown], memorandum to Nola Smith, n.d., Box 451, JTP; and Gary Bruner, memorandum to Nola Smith, re YAF, Box 451, JTP.

23. "A Research Proposal Presented to the Honorable John Tower, For the 1978 Senatorial Campaign," June 1977, Folder 19, Box 542; and "Decision Making Information Polls," September 1974, Folder 16, Box 638, JTP.

24. "Report on Campaign in Rural Texas: Texans for Tower-1972," Box 454, JTP.

25. Tower, statement to Mexican-Americans, May 5, 1972, Box 450, JTP.

26. Humberto Aguirre, "The Mexican-American Vote in Texas: February 7, 1973," Box 454, JTP.

27. President Ford Committee–Texas, pro forma letter, April 3, 1976, Box 6, Peter Hannaford Papers, Hoover Institution.

28. Hannaford, memorandum to Reagan, April 13, 1976, Box 6, Miscellaneous Campaign Files, Hannaford Papers.

29. "Panama Canal: 1977–1978," Box 1339, Houston Office, JTP; Tower to Donald Dozer, August 11, 1966, Box 78, Donald M. Dozer Papers, Hoover Institution; and Tower to Carter, October 26, 1977, John Tower Name File, White House Central Files, Jimmy Carter Presidential Papers, Jimmy Carter Presidential Library, Atlanta, GA.

30. Tower, draft copy, op-ed, Folder 68, Box 17, Press Office, JTP; and "Texas Briefing: Office of Policy Coordination," Box 24, Annelise Graebner Anderson Papers, HI.

31. "Political Brief: Texas," Box 406, Political Operations—Jerry Carman Files, Ronald Reagan Presidential Library, Simi Valley, CA. The Tower-Krueger contest was one of the dirtiest in recent Texas history. Krueger actually began the fight about marital status by using Tower's recent divorce and allegations of womanizing against him. When Tower and his backers responded by questioning the Democrat's sexuality and singleness, Krueger began marketing himself as a conservative, using photos of himself with unidentified women, whom he called "family."

32. *Houston Post*, July 3, 1977; and Olien, *From Token to Triumph*, 247.

33. Reagan, direct mailing, June 1978, Box 572, Tower Senate Club, JTP; George H. W. Bush, direct mailing, December 1977, Box 572, Tower Senate Club, JTP; and Allan Shivers, direct mailing, n.d., Box 560, Tower Senate Club, JTP.

34. For more on Texas and the growth of Republican conservatism, see Sean P. Cunningham, *Cowboy Conservatism: Texas and the Rise of the Modern Right* (Lexington: University Press of Kentucky, 2010).

35. Robert L. Thornton, "Statement in Opposition to the Housing Provisions of the Administration's Proposed 'Civil Rights Act of 1966'—Prepared at the Request of John Tower," July 19, 1966, JTP; "Draft Remarks of Senator Tower," n.d., Box 250, JTP.

36. V. O. Key Jr., *Southern Politics in State and Nation* (New York: Knopf, 1949), 254–55.

37. For more on the growth of southern Republicanism, see also Byron E. Shafer and Richard Johnston, *The End of Southern Exceptionalism: Class, Race, and Partisan Change in the Postwar South* (Cambridge, MA: Harvard University Press, 2006).

CHAPTER 7

Uneasy Alliance

The Religious Right and the Republican Party

Robert Freedman

In late 1978, the Reverend Jerry Falwell declared to readers of his Thomas Road Baptist Church newspaper, "Fundamental Christianity and liberal politics cannot rightly mix, any more than oil and water. The two positions are poles apart."[1] A few months later, the Lynchburg, Virginia–based pastor launched a "Clean Up America" campaign, claiming that "our energy crisis, economic inflationary problems, increasing crime rate, 40% divorce rate, and weakened military stance as compared to Russia . . . can all be attributed to our national sins and our unwillingness to repent."

Falwell placed ballots in newspapers and periodicals ranging from *Christianity Today* to the *National Enquirer*, asking, "How do you stand on the issues of PORNOGRAPHIC TEXTBOOKS, ABORTION-ON-DEMAND, and SEX and VIOLENCE on television? . . . If you are against these sins, then Praise the Lord! *You are exactly the person I want on my team.*"[2]

When 95.8 percent of the 1,007,100 respondents "backed the stand on righteousness," Falwell declared, "We stand with the moral majority and they don't like the drift of our nation."[3] Encouraged by New Right luminaries Howard Phillips, Richard Viguerie, and Paul Weyrich, who were engaged in building a grassroots movement dedicated to social conservatism, he formed the Moral Majority in June 1979. The new organization became the emblem of the broader Religious Right that was a significant force in late twentieth-century American politics.

This chapter explores the role played by the Religious Right in the Republican revival of the 1970s that culminated in the election of a Republican president and Senate in 1980. The myriad groups within the umbrella movement widened the Republican social base beyond the WASP country club set through the development of a social issues agenda that cut across the income and class boundaries of the New Deal partisan order. Nevertheless, as this chapter suggests, the Religious Right and the Republican Party were uneasy bedfellows. Accordingly, GOP leaders like Ronald Reagan were careful to avoid the appearance of being controlled by a "moral majority" that was in fact never more than a vocal minority, and of prioritizing moral concerns that could never be satisfied by governmental policy alone.

The Religious Right was born from a combination of factors: the reduction of sectarian tensions that enabled different denominations to engage in common pursuit of moral reform via the political process; a religious revival, particularly among evangelicals; and a reaction against the growth of social liberalism in the 1970s.

Evangelicals were at the heart of the new Christian mobilization. Their forebears had played a decisive role in political movements from abolitionism to Prohibition. In the early twentieth century, a "fundamentalist" evangelicalism emerged to defend the "fundamentals" of biblical inerrancy, which was under intellectual siege from "higher criticism," which subjected the Bible to literary and historical investigation rather than accepting it as the literal word of God. Darwinism was another force that upended the old religious certainties and provoked the fundamentalist backlash. As one scholar observed of this inward-looking development, "When fundamentalism started dwelling on the negative, it changed from a religious movement to a religious mentality. It never developed an affirmative world view and made no effort to connect its convictions to the wider problems of society."[4] The perils of insularity and isolation were underlined in the 1925 "Scopes Monkey Trial," during which former Populist leader William Jennings Bryan denounced the teaching of evolution. Shaken by the resultant public ridicule, fundamentalists thereafter withdrew from public life for more than twenty years.[5]

After the Second World War, a steady reversion toward political engagement reached its peak in response to the social changes of the 1960s and early 1970s. Many evangelicals had migrated from the southern heartland to booming areas such as Southern California. They found spiritual continuity in such unfamiliar environments in the messages of "religious entrepreneurs," as historian Lisa McGirr dubbed the likes of Robert Schuller and his drive-in church. These evangelical leaders combined a defense of traditional moral values with apologetics for the new culture of consumerism.[6] More than anyone else, however, Billy Graham was the public face of a "neoevangelical" movement that fused fundamentalist beliefs with a recognition that evangelicals had a duty to participate in politics in support of their values. In 1952, he tacitly supported the Republican presidential ticket that polled well in the booming cities of the postwar South where his "crusades" were so popular.[7]

The concern felt by religious Americans of all faiths about the erosion of traditional values in public life increased markedly in the 1960s and beyond. They were outraged by a number of Supreme Court judgments in 1962–1963 ruling that neither organized prayer nor prescribed Bible reading was permitted in public schools. In 1966, Reverend Tim LaHaye (who would become famous and very rich from the "Left Behind" series of evangelical thrillers he coauthored beginning in the 1990s), later a prominent Religious Right leader, launched the California League for Enlist-

ing Action Now (CLEAN), to campaign against lax state obscenity laws, an effort
that enjoyed the support of GOP gubernatorial candidate Ronald Reagan.[8]

The 1973 *Roe v. Wade* decision, which partially legalized abortion nationwide,
was a major spur for the political movement that would become known as the Religious Right. America's Catholic bishops had created the National Right to Life
Committee in 1970, shortly after Pope Paul VI declared abortion as grounds for
excommunication.[9] Such traditionalist themes were common in the *Phyllis Schlafly
Report*, a conservative newsletter. A Catholic and longtime Republican activist,
Schlafly had found fame in 1964 as the author of the Goldwater movement manifesto *A Choice, Not an Echo*.[10] The *Phyllis Schlafly Report*'s account of pro-abortion
sentiment at the UN World Population Conference, hosted in communist Roma-
nia in 1974, typified her warnings of the encroaching dangers of social liberalism.
The article quoted at length from a piece entitled "Motherhood: An Occupation
Facing Decline" by the feminist Jeanne Binstock in the *Futurist* magazine in 1972.
Binstock declared that the world would be "throttled by the overproduction of babies. We thus face the need to demand that the ancient and honorable occupation
of motherhood fall into disrepute, and that women commit themselves to other
occupations. Women must be *'liberated'* to enjoy the fruits of other occupations,
whether they want to be or not."[11]

The Republicans, traditionally the party of the WASP establishment, were not
an obvious ally for an emergent Religious Right. President Dwight D. Eisenhower
believed sincerely in the need for a spiritual force in public life but had no prescription for the specific form of this spirituality. As he famously remarked, "Our government . . . makes no sense unless it is founded on a deeply felt religious faith—
and I don't care what it is."[12] Moreover, despite the GOP national ticket's good
showing in the booming suburban areas of the South in the 1950s, the southern
evangelical heartlands and urban enclaves of Catholic "ethnics" were solidly Democratic into the 1960s.

It was the Nixon administration that eventually pioneered electoral connections between Republicanism and conservative religiosity as part of its effort to
reach out to the "silent majority." Presidential speechwriter Patrick J. Buchanan argued that in addition to measures on crime, welfare, and busing, voters wanted
"religion and discipline restored to their public schools and value-free sex education
and Eldridge Cleaver thrown out."[13] In May 1970, Nixon and William E. Brock III,
the Republican challenger for Albert Gore Sr.'s Senate seat in Tennessee, attended a
Billy Graham crusade in Knoxville. Graham's public speeches echoed Nixon's "law
and order" stance throughout the campaign.[14] After the 1970 midterms, Nixon
told his chief of staff, H. R. Haldeman, "to remember that our primary source of
support [in the South] will be among the fundamentalist Protestants, and we can
probably broaden that base of support."[15]

In historian Steven Miller's assessment, "A range of elements—entrepreneurial-
ism, asserted racial progress, and traditional faith—combined to form what com-

mentators during the 1970s began calling the Sunbelt or, more specifically, the Sunbelt South."[16] Yet the transition was not a straightforward one. Kevin Phillips, the Nixon adviser who prophesied a Sunbelt-dominated Republican Party, recalled that "members of the Downtown Association and the Links Club were never enthusiastic about 'Joe Sixpack' and middle America, to say nothing of preachers such as Oral Roberts or the Tupelo, Mississippi, Assemblies of God."[17] Gary Jarmin, a leader of Christian Voice—a Religious Right organization—later described the internal Republican conflict as one between the "three-martini Episcopalians who compare golf scores at county meetings" and the "teetotaling, devout people who compare Scripture at county meetings."[18]

The conservative movement also had a strong libertarian, antistatist streak, as espoused by Barry Goldwater. Conservatives of this ilk had little time for using the state to enforce moral reform. In 1981, one Goldwater ally and now a Reagan supporter criticized Republican senator Jesse Helms of North Carolina, a standard-bearer of the Religious Right, asking, "How can a conservative even imagine passing laws on your private life—like abortion and prayer!"[19] Of course, the counterargument was that the Religious Right was merely seeking to restore the legal status of abortion and prayer to where they had been before the social tumult of the 1960s and 1970s.

In 1976, the first presidential election since *Roe v. Wade*, both parties courted social conservatives. Jimmy Carter epitomized the modern evangelical, rising from rural Georgia roots to become a reforming governor of that state. Yet Carter was torn between his socially conservative sensibilities and the expectations of socially liberal Democratic activists. Robert Malson, who went on to advise President Carter on domestic policy, argues that Carter "had a personal struggle and conflict" over abortion, but took the position that "under certain circumstances I would not oppose abortion, but I wouldn't pay for it."[20] The U.S. Catholic Conference declared the Georgian's refusal to condemn *Roe* as "deeply disturbing to those who hold the right to life to be sacred and inalienable."[21]

Some evangelicals expressed concerns to Carter directly about the lack of religiosity in his public agenda, but eventually supported him because of the evident sincerity of his Christian beliefs. One declared that his conscience told him to vote for Carter even though "many of your spending solutions to our problems would not be the answer." He concluded: "Jimmy, we need a man of your convictions, controlled by the Holy Spirit, that will call for a Spiritual Revival and not more Social Revolutions. FDR, HST, JFK, and LBJ, all had their pie in the sky 'great societies,' and all are dead and their dreams and empires lie in ruins. One thing they left out and that was God in their planning."[22]

On the other hand, some evangelicals doubted Carter's ability to live up to his religious ideals. Following Carter's controversial campaign-season interview with *Playboy*, Guy Archer Weniger, publisher of a prominent evangelical newsletter, attacked the Democratic candidate for "casually expressing a careless view of sin and adultery in the life of a professing Christian. . . . Evangelicals are overwhelmed that he would lend presidential respectability to one of the most wicked magazines of filth which has contributed so heavily to the moral decay of our nation."[23] Others, however, were willing to forgive this indiscretion. The Reverend Bailey Smith told the Southern Baptist Convention that the country needed "a born-again man in the White House . . . and his initials are the same as our Lord's."[24]

Republican candidates for the highest office were well aware that to ignore social conservatives was not an option. In 1975, *National Review* publisher William Rusher had attempted to set up a conservative third party that would reach out to new constituencies, including social conservatives. Pat Buchanan predicted that the new party would forge "a new unity between the economic conservatives of the Republican Party and the social conservatives of the Democratic Party." In the process, it would become a "new political tent to contain both William F. Buckley, Jr., listening to the C-Sharp Minor of Rachmaninoff, and George Corley Wallace's people, listening to Hank Williams."[25] A conservative newsletter reported that the putative party would benefit from the Democratic Party's "anti-life, pro-abortion stand," which threatened to "drive millions of Catholics from its ranks."[26]

The scheme won backing from New Right activists Richard Viguerie, Paul Weyrich, and Howard Phillips. According to Weyrich, founder of the Heritage Foundation think tank, "The very essence of the New Right is a morally based conservatism. . . . Our view is not based in economics but in a religious view."[27] In 1975, Phillips set up the Conservative Caucus, a grassroots campaigning organization that prioritized social issues such as abortion.[28] Yet neither Reagan nor any credible candidate would join the effort—unsurprisingly, given the lamentable historical failure of third parties.[29]

Social issues played little role in the subsequent battle between Reagan and President Gerald Ford for the Republican nomination, and Ford was uncertain of how to use social issues in the general election. Ford's advisers predicted that Carter's strong professions of faith would ultimately work against him: "The image of a 'holier than thou' re-born Christian imposing his personal brand of morality on the nation will 'wear thin' in an intense campaign with great numbers of Americans."[30] Nevertheless, the Ford campaign decided that Religious Right groups could not be ignored. Making overtures to evangelicals in particular, the president broadcast messages on the television shows of evangelists Pat Robertson and Jerry Falwell.[31] He also attacked the "rising tide of secularism" and the "increased irreverence for life" before a crowd of 100,000 Catholics assembled for the International Eucharistic Congress, and supported Jesse Helms's campaign for an anti-abortion constitutional amendment.[32] But evangelicals and other social conservatives scorned Ford's actions, particularly his nomination of feminist Bella Abzug to a commission for the UN's International Women's Year. Detecting the influence of known feminist Betty Ford, Schlafly remarked that the "women's libbers have a lobbyist right in the

White House itself who boasts in the press about how she gets her way by means of 'pillow talk.'"[33]

Ultimately Carter overcame doubts about his dedication to faith-based public policy. He won 56 percent of the white Baptist vote nationwide, helping him to carry Pennsylvania, Ohio, and every state in the South except Virginia.[34] Yet Carter's White House immediately courted controversy on social issues. Weeks after taking office, his openly gay public liaison chief, Margaret "Midge" Costanza, hosted a meeting with the National Gay Task Force (NGTF). Seizing on this, popular singer Anita Bryant declared that gays were "really asking to be blessed in their abnormal lifestyle by the office of the President of the United States."[35] In a move that fired up the emerging Christian Right but also created a "frontlash" from social liberals, she campaigned successfully to overturn a Miami gay rights ordinance that opponents claimed would force parents "to accept an obviously 'gay' *babysitter . . .* to subject your children to the influence of flagrantly homosexual *teachers . . . in short, a law that carries the concealed power to jam immoral outrages down the throats of every God-fearing American!*"[36]

Building on this victory for social conservatism, California Republican state senator John Briggs enlisted the Reverend Robert Grant in support of Proposition 6, a 1978 ballot initiative to fire all teachers "who publicly admit being homosexual or who promote homosexuality as a life-style."[37] Grant's organization, the American Christian Cause, mounted an impressive fundraising operation, making extensive use of the New Right's emblematic tactic of direct mail. Grant praised Bryant for speaking out "even at the expense of suffering public ridicule and intense pressure from gay groups to destroy her professional career." He avowed, "What Christians need to do is take a lesson from the radical militant organizations that have mobilized 'people power' to effect major changes."[38]

In the case of Proposition 6, the conservative grassroots campaign fell short of Bryant's success in Florida owing to the strength of bipartisan opposition. Carter voiced opposition to it after being reassured by California's Democratic governor Jerry Brown that "Ford and Reagan have both come out against it. So I think it's perfectly safe." The involvement of Republican leaders in the same cause insulated the president from the criticisms of fundamentalists like Guy Archer Weniger that his stance "cast grave doubt over the credibility of his confession of being born again by associating himself on the side of moral perversion and homosexual wickedness."[39] Indeed, gay rights magazine *The Advocate* adjudged Reagan's assertion that Proposition 6 had "the potential of infringing on basic rights of privacy and perhaps even constitutional rights" to be of critical importance in the victorious campaign against the initiative.[40]

In spite of this defeat, Grant's mobilization of churches was so successful that in January 1979 he started Christian Voice, the first national Religious Right organization.[41] Nevertheless, the Religious Right henceforth tended to frame opposition to gay rights in a defensive manner that did not make for conflict with the GOP leadership. In February 1979, preacher James Robison's television show was cancelled for violating the Federal Communications Commission's Fairness Doctrine when he "preached what the Bible says about homosexuality" without putting the opposite point of view. Robison avowed, "God is the solution to the problems that beset America. Faithful ministers must be allowed to proclaim—without apology or compromise—the greatest message in history, the message of God. And they must be allowed to do so on the greatest communications medium in history, the medium of television. . . . The issue is not a debatable governmental policy. The issue is freedom of speech—the right to preach."[42]

The Religious Right also sought to frame its position on women's rights in a manner compatible with the Republican emphasis on small government. The Equal Rights Amendment (ERA), part of the GOP platform since 1940, eventually went for state ratification after congressional passage in 1972. Phyllis Schlafly quickly assumed leadership of an antiratification campaign. To capitalize on moral conservatives' opposition to the *Roe* decision, she linked opposition to the ERA with opposition to abortion. Warning that abortion advocates "almost always" supported the ERA, Schlafly's group, founded in September 1972 and known as STOP ERA, focused particular animus on the National Organization for Women, which it claimed was "militantly pro-abortion and is working for government-financed abortion and to remove the tax-exemption of churches which oppose abortion."[43] Schlafly later described herself as "very tolerant," because she let "people oppose the ERA for the reason of their choice," including moral concerns or opposition to increasing the government's power.[44] On the latter theme, Jerry Falwell's church newsletter warned that ERA supporters' desire to use the amendment to "liberate" women from housework would mean that children "could be put in government run day schools and day care centers where Christian training would be prohibited."[45] Such critiques fitted neatly with the antistatist position that was common across the wider conservative political movement.

In November 1977, Schlafly organized a twenty-thousand-strong demonstration against the government-sponsored International Women's Year conference in Houston. She likened the controversy to the Battle of Midway, a "decisive turning point in the war between Women's Lib and those who are Pro-Family." "Women's Lib," she wrote, had "sealed its own doom by deliberately hanging around its own neck the albatrosses of abortion, lesbianism, pornography, and federal control" in conference resolutions.[46] *Phyllis Schlafly Report* readers were further educated by photographs of conference stands, including those of "The Bisexual Center," "Lesbians For Wages For Housework," and a "Dyke Vigil."[47] Schlafly argued that "they never got another state [for the ERA] after that, because the publicity turned the American people off. They got their publicity—but it turned out to be a negative."[48]

In recognition of the strength of conservative grassroots opposition, the 1980

Republican platform dropped support for the ERA, but Reagan was careful to avoid charges that he opposed women's rights. Seeking the middle ground to appease Republican feminists, he declared in his nomination acceptance address, "I know we've had a quarrel or two but only as to the method of attaining a goal. There was no argument here about the goal." Reagan promised to work with state governors to "eliminate, wherever it exists, discrimination against women," adding that he would "monitor Federal laws to insure their implementation and to add statutes if they are needed."[49]

Adapting anti-ERA tactics for their own purposes, economic conservatives looked to bind the nascent Religious Right to the broader conservative movement through use of social concerns to advance their small government agenda. The National Tax Limitation Committee, a leading force in the state "tax revolts" of the late 1970s, told potential contributors about a "grade school course" that taught "children that *wife-swapping, cannibalism*, and the *murder of infants and the elderly* are not necessarily wrong, just different 'life styles.'" The letter claimed that spending on such programs contributed to the government taking forty-two cents of every dollar earned, meaning that people had to work "till 11:00 a.m. on June 3rd just to feed the bureaucrats. Only after that could you start feeding yourself and your family."[50]

Despite the cross-fertilization of different conservative concerns at the grassroots level, the GOP leadership was initially skeptical of associating closely with the Religious Right. Viguerie likened its standing in Republican eyes to that of the embarrassing "country cousin" at a wedding, to be kept out of sight until needed.[51] In 1977, Paul Weyrich urged Republican National Committee chair Bill Brock to embrace religious conservatives, only to realize that such an attachment "was so foreign to him that it didn't make any sense."[52]

Other Republicans, however, were more willing to make use of the energetic new movement. Anti-abortion advocates claimed that their leafleting of church car parks on the Sunday before the midterm elections of 1978 dislodged Senator Dick Clark, a liberal Democrat, in Iowa.[53] The National Pro-Life Political Action Committee, which made common cause with groups connected to the Religious Right, claimed partial credit for Republican Gordon Humphrey's defeat of "caustic pro-abortion incumbent Senator Tom McIntyre" in New Hampshire.[54] Humphrey chaired his state's Conservative Caucus organization, and churches served as precinct organizations in his campaign.[55] Thereafter, long-standing GOP congressional supporters of social conservatism, such as Senators Jake Garn of Utah, Jesse Helms, and Paul Laxalt of Nevada, grew bolder in seeking to advance the Religious Right's agenda. A Mormon whose alliance with evangelical leaders illustrated the easing of sectarian hatreds, Laxalt introduced the Family Protection bill in 1979. This measure condemned homosexuality, "sex intermingling in sports and other school activities" and contraception advice for the unwed. Although it got nowhere in Congress, Weyrich somewhat hyperbolically hailed it as "the most significant battle of the age-old conflict between good and evil, between the forces of God and forces against God."[56]

The issue that spurred evangelicals to mass political action more than any other also strengthened their ties to the GOP. This was the 1978 decision of the Internal Revenue Service (IRS) to end the tax-exempt status of many Christian schools on the grounds that they were covert "segregation academies."[57] Although some institutions, especially in the South, were guilty on this score, many were not, and their supporters were furious. One told Carter that Christian schools were "necessary since the Bible reading, prayers and discipline was taken out of our public schools. . . . To continue to try to destroy the reading of God's Word, and the teachings of his ways, I feel, will cause us to lose his blessings (Psalms 33:12–15) which have made our country so great. . . . At the rate we are going in twenty years our country and Communism will be hard to tell apart."[58]

According to Richard Viguerie, the controversy "kicked a sleeping dog. . . . It galvanized the religious right. It was the episode that ignited the religious right's involvement in real politics."[59] Bob Billings, a Christian school leader recruited by Weyrich to organize opposition to the IRS ruling, claimed that IRS commissioner Jerome Kurtz had "done more to bring Christians together than any man since the Apostle Paul."[60] Further illustrating the significance of the issue for the Religious Right, Billings became the first president of the Moral Majority, and half of the new organization's state chairmen were affiliated with churches fighting the IRS regulations.[61]

Republicans fighting the IRS directive portrayed themselves as protecting religious believers from illegitimate state taxation. Richard B. "Dick" Dingman, executive director of the conservative Republican Study Committee in Congress, sent its members an article that argued, "Here is a vast engine for the expansion of government power—the assumption that, whatever private activity the IRS now does not tax, it, in effect, *refrains* from taxing."[62] The issue also provided grist for Ronald Reagan's charges that government bureaucracy posed a threat to individual liberty. In 1980, he pledged his opposition to forcing "all tax-exempt schools—including church schools—to abide by affirmative action orders drawn up by—who else?— IRS bureaucrats."[63]

Despite signs of the Religious Right's growing strength, the Reagan campaign remained uncertain in its early stages of how close a relationship to develop with it. A September 1979 memorandum from Reagan adviser Bill Gavin expressed enthusiasm for bringing new groups into the Republican coalition. It argued that "preachers in politics" were a "legitimate grassroots phenomenon, not the front-group for any New Right types. . . . With our emphasis on home, family, neighborhood, these folks should be our kind of people. . . . At the very least we should be thinking about how we can show the movement we are with them on social issues without, at the same time, alienating those who might be turned off by the 'style' of the movement's people, which can be a bit blunt at times."[64] Another Reagan aide, Peter Hannaford, responded skeptically, however: "RR has had some meetings with fundamentalist preacher groups with apparently satisfactory results so far. I agree with you that we need to be very careful in this area. Fundamentalists—at least the ones I've run into over the years—tend to be rigid, not very tolerant *and* highly tendentious."[65]

Unsure about its acceptance by the GOP, the Religious Right kept lines open to the Democrats. Appointed as Carter's special assistant for religious affairs in 1979, Southern Baptist preacher Bob Maddox later recalled that nobody close to the president "knew what bad trouble [he] was in on those issues, abortion, ERA, prayer in public schools because the White House staff was liberal." As such, they "tended to discount the numbers and the intensity that was out there."[66] In January 1980, Maddox arranged a breakfast between Carter and prominent televangelists, which only provoked a spat with Falwell over whether the president had advocated affirmative action for hiring gays at the White House.[67] Yet he still urged senior staff to "seize the initiative on these moral issues. The President's positions are right on target to reach the people who live on the broad, middle ground from which we must garner the bulk of our support."[68]

Maddox also pleaded with Catholics not to abandon his boss over abortion. A state Democratic representative from Minnesota told him: "Carter cannot afford to have massive defections of Catholic Democrats and Eastern European ethnics. I really believe that you folks have got to get the movie star vs. the solid, mid-western salt-of-the-earth image going once this campaign starts." This informant added that a "well-educated person and active in DFL [the Minnesota Democratic-Farmer-Labor party] politics was shocked when I told him Reagan once was divorced."[69]

By late 1979, it was evident that the Religious Right was a significant political force. Christian Voice claimed 126,000 members, including 1,200 Protestant ministers and 300 Catholic priests. It began rating congressmen on a "morality scale" according to their positions on homosexuality, government spending, and defense. Christian Voice lobbyist Gary Jarmin explained, "The beauty of it is that we don't have to organize these voters. . . . They already have their own television networks, publications, schools, meeting places and respected leaders who are sympathetic to our goals."[70] Moral Majority claimed some 300,000 members by mid-1980, and to have registered between four million and eight million voters for the elections; while this was undoubtedly an exaggeration, the registration drive would prove significant in the South.[71]

The Religious Right's strength lay in the fact that sectarian divisions had declined to the extent that different groups could work together in the secular political arena to pursue shared moral goals. *Conservative Digest* argued that "there may be nearly 100 million Americans—50 million born-again Protestants, 30 million morally conservative Catholics, 3 million Mormons and 2 million Orthodox

Jews—from which to draw members of a pro-family, Bible-believing coalition. . . . Overcoming age-old suspicions among Catholics, Protestants and Jews won't be easy, but threats to religious freedom make it necessary."[72]

The national GOP leadership finally woke up to the significance of the Religious Right on the eve of the election year. In December 1979, William Brock held discussions with the movement's leaders and introduced them to Republican presidential hopefuls.[73] The GOP's putative new constituency was not automatically in favor of Reagan, a Hollywood divorcé who had signed the most liberal abortion law in the nation while governor of California and who had opposed the Briggs Initiative. At first, many preferred John Connally, former Texas governor and Nixon's treasury secretary, who had long wooed the Religious Right. At the end of a 1979 meeting with movement leaders—including Falwell and Bob Billings—one participant commented that "some of those guys were ready to carry Connally out of there on their shoulders."[74] There were reports that evangelicals could swing several southern primaries from Reagan to Connally.[75]

On the other hand, Connally's record as something of an economic corporatist—he had bailed out Lockheed while treasury secretary—made him unacceptable to traditional antistatists within the Republican firmament. There was also concern that the Democrats would exploit his close links to business interests. As one journalist observed, "The nation's corporate fat cats haven't had such an unabashed champion of their point of view aiming for the presidency since Calvin Coolidge." He also noted, "If there's an oil company whose top brass hasn't kicked into the Connally coffers, it must be in the machine or olive oil business."[76] In essence, Reagan had far broader support within the GOP by dint of his personal appeal and antigovernment message. Taking nothing for granted, however, he undertook outreach activities to undercut his rival's apparent lead among religious conservatives. In December 1979, for example, he met with nearly fifty Christian businessmen and professionals, who pledged to raise $450,000 for him.[77]

The foreign policy stance of some Religious Right leaders also complemented Republican positions, particularly as articulated by Reagan. The leader of Catholics for Conservative Political Action, established in 1977, lamented the fact that many Catholic bishops were "accommodationists" on questions such as the Panama Canal treaties and Rhodesia, on which the Carter administration also took a conciliatory line.[78] Falwell's church newsletter ran a front-page article on South Korea in 1978, carrying a stark warning from Il Koon Chung, speaker of the country's national assembly: "Withdrawing American troops will mean certain death to the Christians of our nation."[79] Offering a "Christian perspective" against the second Strategic Arms Limitation Treaty (SALT II) negotiated by Carter and Soviet leader Leonid Brezhnev in 1979, Falwell warned, "America will be important to God only as she is committed to world evangelization. Should America lose her freedom, she could not keep her commitment to world evangelization."[80] Not all religious conservatives sang from the same hymn-sheet, however. In particular, Billy Graham claimed that the Moral Majority was not his "cup of tea" partly because he did "not intend to use what little moral influence I may have on secular, nonmoral issues," such as the Panama Canal Treaties. Despite a staunch record of anticommunism, Graham was unwilling to endorse some of the Religious Right's more far-fetched notions of what constituted legitimate "moral" issues.[81]

While its foreign policy stance was broadly in tune with that of the GOP, the Religious Right's fervor on social issues sowed discord in party ranks. Congressman John Buchanan of Alabama, a Baptist minister, had been a Goldwater Republican before moving to the center on issues such as women's rights. Conservative groups, including the Moral Majority, supported a former John Birch Society member against him in the 1980 primary, organizing church buses to get supporters to the polls. After his defeat, Buchanan commented, "They beat my brains out with Christian love."[82] *Moral Majority Report* claimed that a three-week tour of Alaska in April 1980 by state Moral Majority leader Jerry Prevo had left Alaska's Democratic and Republican parties "reeling in change." *Moral Majority Report* recounted with evident pride an overtly hostile report in an Alaskan newspaper that the Moral Majority had "taken over the Alaska Republican Party, and steamrolled over a families conference in Fairbanks, establishing the group's narrow list of concerns as those of the community." The newcomers had displaced "many long-time Republican Party workers and organizers. Some whose views were considered liberal and opposed to the group's objectives were turned out to pasture."[83]

Such instances of the Religious Right's influence at state level were unrepresentative, but they led to exaggerated claims of, and fears of, its nationwide political power. Unsurprisingly, movement leaders were not shy about asserting the role of religious conservatives in electing Ronald Reagan and a Republican Senate in 1980. Citing pollster Lou Harris as his source, Falwell made the dubious claim that "Reagan would have lost the election by one percentage point without the help of the Moral Majority."[84] Implicitly claiming credit for the outcome, Falwell's organization celebrated the election of Senators Jeremiah Denton of Alabama, Charles Grassley of Iowa, and Don Nickles of Oklahoma. Noting that these Republicans "strongly identified themselves with issues of morality and sanctity of the family," it interpreted their success as a victory for the "interests of the traditional family" over "the special interests of welfare bureaucrats."[85] Denton had founded the Coalition for Decency in 1977 to campaign against adultery and pornography.[86] In a particularly significant demonstration of interdenominational unity, nine hundred mostly fundamentalist churches registered over seventy-five thousand voters as part of the Moral Majority campaign for Don Nickles, a Catholic.[87] In the opinion of journalist E. J. Dionne Jr., "Thus did the Moral Majority help the nation overcome old denominational prejudices in the interest of a new conservative politics."[88] In Texas, Jack Fields crafted a clear message to mobilize religious conservatives in his defeat of the liberal-leaning Democratic incumbent, Congressman Bob Eckhardt. "Christian Voice rates him a zero," intoned a Fields campaign advertisement, "the

National Christian Action Coalition rates him an 11 out of a possible 100 and his votes on Christian issues are bad."[89]

According to Republican congressman Newt Gingrich of Georgia, the "moral issue was what put us over the top." Lending his support for this view, political scientist James Sundquist interpreted the 1980 result as vindication of the "[Kevin] Phillips-Rusher-Buchanan" strategy of building a conservative coalition. There was certainly clear evidence that sociomoral issues had played in favor of the GOP. Republican Alphonse D'Amato won the New York Senate race with the aid of over 150,000 Right to Life party ballots, which represented 2.4 percent of total votes cast and exceeded his margin of victory. Meanwhile, 39 percent of Democrats defecting to Reagan disapproved of the Equal Rights Amendment, and 26 percent disapproved of all abortions.[90] At first glance, Reagan's share of the white evangelical vote, 62 percent, was virtually identical to the 61 percent of all white votes he received.[91] Thomas Edsall and Mary Edsall argue, however, that 85 percent of the "most fundamentalist" voters supported Reagan. In several southern states, the white evangelical shift exceeded Reagan's 1.2 percent margin of victory.[92]

That the Religious Right was instrumental in the Republican revival by 1980 is not in doubt, but the extent of its contribution is open to debate. Assessments of its influence depend on how significant sociomoral issues actually were in the panoply of voter concerns. The CBS News/*New York Times* exit poll found that only 7 percent of voters cited "ERA/abortion" as one of the two main issues influencing their ballot choice. In contrast, 57 percent cited economic issues, 31 percent cited fiscal issues, and 30 percent cited foreign policy issues.[93] In an age of uncertainty for which the Democrats took the blame, issues like runaway inflation, recession, growing budget deficits, and relative U.S. decline had more weight in determining the outcome of the 1980 elections than the agenda of the Religious Right.

Recognizing what had put it in power, the new Reagan administration was committed to economic and military revitalization rather than moral renewal. Commenting off the record after the election, a Reagan activist predicted, "There isn't going to be an abortion amendment [to the Constitution], and Helms knows it. . . . You'd see lawlessness in this country to make Prohibition look like a picnic."[94] Such a view presaged the fortieth president's meager efforts on social issues.

Moreover, social conservative leaders did not endear themselves to Reagan's image-makers with some of their more outlandish proposals. Jeremiah Denton, in particular, caused a political stir in his first term by introducing the Adolescent Family Life Act (AFLA), dubbed the "teenage chastity bill" by opponents. "I don't care if they tickle where it itches," he remarked, "I'm talking about screwing."[95]

The stated aim of AFLA, which became law as part of the 1981 omnibus budget legislation, was to "promote chastity and self discipline" by funding both abstinence programs and pregnancy support services (the latter encouraged Senator Ted Kennedy of Massachusetts to support it). As a counterweight to the influence of

Planned Parenthood and other family planning services perceived as pro-abortion, the measure required that the federal government "should emphasize the provision of support by other family members and religious charitable organizations, voluntary associations and other groups." Many grants went to socially conservative religious groups, such as a Catholic hospital that formulated a program with segments such as "The Church's Teachings on Abortion" and "The Church's Teachings on Artificial Contraception." AFLA was litigated, and the courts eventually forced organizations to submit AFLA-funded materials to the Department of Health and Human Services for approval.

Perhaps aware that the Religious Right could embarrass Reagan by association, White House deputy chief of staff Michael Deaver let it be known early on that Religious Right leaders would only be allowed into the White House through the "back door."[96] Unease about the new relationship was not the sole preserve of the administration, however. After the election, some religious conservatives recognized that close identification with the Republicans might be unproductive if it meant that the Religious Right was taken for granted by the GOP and seen as unremittingly hostile by the Democrats. The Christian Action Council newsletter cited the view of Reagan budget director David Stockman that the "Moral Majority Agenda" should be deferred because it would "only unleash cross-cutting controversy and political pressures which would undermine the fundamental administration and congressional GOP economic task." It went on to pose a fundamental question: "Can the abortion issue be won if it becomes the preserve of the conservative leadership of this nation, whether traditional or 'new right'? Obviously not." The movement could not "allow people with broader political goals to chart our course. . . . The challenge is to appreciate and preserve the conservative Republican commitment to the issue, while at the same time fostering a similar commitment among Democrats and their constituencies."[97]

In summary, the Religious Right helped to mobilize grassroots support for the Republicans, notably among constituencies with a pro-Democratic tradition. This was an important but not the dominant factor in the Republican revival of the 1970s. Far from being a marriage made in heaven, the Republicans and their new partners had an uneasy alliance of necessity.

The Religious Right became a "blocking minority" within the Republican Party—a vital infusion of passion into a party that had seemed doomed in the wake of Watergate, but also an obstacle to reaching moderate voters. By the end of President George W. Bush's term in office, evangelicals formed almost 40 percent of the Republican presidential electorate. Historian Daniel Williams writes that it "became impossible for any Republican presidential candidate to ignore the Christian Right's demands on abortion, gay rights, and other social issues."[98] A good example of the essentially negative power held by the Religious Right was that they were unable to stop Senator Bob Dole of Kansas, a moderate on social issues, from receiving the 1996 Republican nomination, but they were able, through organizations such as the Christian Coalition, to frustrate Dole's efforts to formally acknowledge Republicans' differences over abortion in the party platform.[99]

Movement leaders fumed at being taken for granted by GOP leaders who (justifiably) believed that the Religious Right constituency had "nowhere else to go." Concessionary scraps, such as Reagan's remote audio addresses to the annual "March for Life" rally in Washington (he never attended in person, despite personal pleas from the March for Life leader, Nellie Gray) never satisfied their moral hunger.[100] Not until the first decade of the twenty-first century, when a tight electoral environment induced GOP leaders to pursue a base mobilization strategy, would the Religious Right finally sup at the party's high table. Whether the outcome of this closer relationship works to the mutual benefit of party and movement remains to be seen.

NOTES

1. "Why Fundamentalists Are Conservative," *Thomas Road Family Journal-Champion* 1, no. 12 (October 13, 1978), Folder "Thomas Road Family Journal-Champion January 12, 1978–October 13, 1978," Thomas Road Family Journal-Champion Box 1, University of Iowa Social Documents Collection (hereafter SDC), University of Iowa, Iowa City, IA.

2. Jerry Falwell, direct mail letter, April 30, 1979, Folder "Falwell, Jerry," SDC. Emphases in the original.

3. *Thomas Road Family Journal-Champion* 2, no. 1 (May 4, 1979), Thomas Road Family Journal-Champion Box 1, SDC.

4. Sharon Linzey Georgianna, *The Moral Majority and Fundamentalism: Plausibility and Dissonance* (Lewiston, NY: Mellen, 1989), 7, 15.

5. James A. Speer, "The New Christian Right and Its Parent Company: A Study in Political Contrasts," in *New Christian Politics*, ed. David G. Bromley and Anson Shupe (Macon, GA: Mercer University Press, 1984), 29–31.

6. Lisa McGirr, *Suburban Warriors: The Origins of the New American Right* (Princeton, NJ: Princeton University Press, 2001), 241–42, 251–54.

7. Steven P. Miller, *Billy Graham and the Rise of the Republican South* (Philadelphia: University of Pennsylvania Press, 2009), 72.

8. McGirr, *Suburban Warriors*, 226–30.

9. Michael W. Cuneo, "Life Battles: The Rise of Catholic Militancy within the American Pro-Life Movement," in *Being Right: Conservative Catholics in America*, ed. Mary Jo Weaver and R. Scott Appleby (Bloomington: Indiana University Press, 1995), 273; Kenneth D. Wald, *Religion and Politics in the United States* (Washington, DC: CQ Press, 1992), 294.

10. Carol Felsenthal, *The Sweetheart of the Silent Majority: The Biography of Phyllis Schlafly* (Garden City, NY: Doubleday, 1981), 164–67.

11. "E.R.A. Means Abortion and Population Shrinkage," *Phyllis Schlafly Report* 8, no. 5 (December 1974), Folder "The Equal Rights Amendment," SDC. Italics presumed to be an addition by the editors of the *Phyllis Schlafly Report*.

12. Quoted in Miller, *Billy Graham*, 15.

13. Patrick J. Buchanan, *Conservative Votes, Liberal Victories* (New York: New York Times Book Co., 1975), 172–73.

14. Miller, *Billy Graham*, 133–34, 142–43.

15. Ibid., 150.

16. Ibid., 156.

17. Kevin Phillips, "How the GOP Became God's Own Party," *Washington Post*, April 2, 2006.

18. Quoted in Julie Johnson, "Showing by Robertson in Iowa Race Buoys Conservatives," *New York Times*, February 12, 1988.

19. Peter Ross Range, "Thunder on the Right," *New York Times*, February 8, 1981.

20. Author's interview with Robert Malson, October 5, 2005.

21. Stuart E. Eizenstat to Patrick Riley, July 22, 1976, and press release from Catholic League for Religious and Civil Rights, July 15, 1976, both in Folder "Abortion [1]," Box 304, Jimmy Carter Papers—Pre-Presidential, 1976 Presidential Campaign, Director's Office—Urban Ethnic Affairs Catholic Desk—Terry Sundy Collection, Jimmy Carter Presidential Library (hereafter JCPL), Atlanta, GA .

22. W. James Norris to Jimmy Carter, September 8, 1976, Folder "Form Letter—Prot. I and Correspondence," Box 308, Jimmy Carter Papers—Pre-Presidential, 1976 Presidential Campaign, Director's Office—Religion Political Affairs Coord. Protestant Desk—David B. Graham Subject File, JCPL.

23. Guy Archer Weniger, "Jimmy Carter and the Evangelical Conscience," *Fundamental Baptist Fellowship Information Bulletin* 20, no. 2 (October 7, 1976): 1–3, Document 4485, Folder "Carter, James Earl," Bob Jones University Fundamentalism File (hereafter BJUFF), Bob Jones University, Greenville, SC.

24. William Martin, *With God on Our Side: The Rise of the Religious Right in America* (New York: Broadway Books, 1996), 156–57.

25. Buchanan, *Conservative Votes, Liberal Victories*, 170.

26. Paul Scott, "New Party Efforts," *Independent American* 22, no. 4 (July–August 1976), Folder "The Independent American," SDC.

27. James L. Sundquist, "Whither the American Party System? Revisited," *Political Science Quarterly* 98 (1983–1984): 573–93.

28. Robert Shogan, "Conservative Drive Begun" (clipping from unknown newspaper), originally published in the *Los Angeles Times*, January 20, 1975, Folder "Conservative Caucus," SDC.

29. See Robert Freedman, "American Populist Conservatism, 1977–88" (University of Cambridge PhD thesis, 2006), 4–6.

30. Kenneth J. Heineman, *God Is a Conservative: Religion, Politics, and Morality in Contemporary America* (New York: New York University Press, 1998), 89.

31. Heineman, *God Is a Conservative*, 76.

32. John D. Lofton Jr., "Ford on Abortion," source unknown, c. mid-1976, Folder "Abortion [1]," Box 304, Jimmy Carter Papers—Pre-Presidential, 1976 Presidential Campaign, Director's Office—Urban Ethnic Affairs Catholic Desk—Terry Sundy Collection, JCPL.

33. "The Ripoff of the Taxpayers Known as: The Commission on International Women's Year or, Bella Abzug's Boondoggle," *Phyllis Schlafly Report* 9, no. 6, (January 1976): section 2, Phyllis Schlafly Report Collection, SDC.

34. A. James Reichley, *Religion in American Public Life* (Washington, DC: Brookings Institution, 1985), 318.

35. United Press International, "Anita Bryant Scores White House Talk with Homosexuals," *New York Times*, March 28, 1977.

36. American Christian Cause, Pasadena, CA, direct mail letter, c. October–November 1978, Folder "American Christian Cause," SDC. Emphases in the original.

37. McGirr, *Suburban Warriors*, 257–58.

38. American Christian Cause, direct mail letter, c. October–November 1978. Emphasis in the original.

39. "Jimmy Carter Supports the Homosexuals," *Blu-Print* 29, no. 43 (November 7, 1978): 1, Document 2087, Folder "Carter, James Earl," BJUFF.

40. McGirr, *Suburban Warriors*, 258; "Opening Space," *Advocate*, 1980 (file clipping), Folder "Homosexuals/Gay Rights," Box 6, Doug Bandow Files, Ronald Reagan Presidential Library (hereafter RRPL), Simi Valley, CA.

41. McGirr, *Suburban Warriors*, 258.

42. James Robison, advertisement, *Thomas Road Family Journal-Champion* 2, no. 2, (May 18, 1979), Folder "Thomas Road Family Journal-Champion February 2, 1979–May 18, 1979," Thomas Road Family Journal-Champion Box 1, SDC.

43. Eagle Forum, "The Abortion Connection" (pamphlet), Folder "ERA [7]," Box 29, Staff Offices—Special Assistant (Women's Affairs)—ERA (Weddington) Collection, JCPL. Indeed, during a second attempt to pass the ERA in 1983, Republican congressman Henry Hyde noted that it would make sex a "suspect classification" like race. Therefore, refusal to fund abortions would be similar to refusal to treat minority-specific diseases such as sickle-cell anemia. In several states with their own ERAs, the American Civil Liberties Union had argued before courts that the amendments mandated abortion funding. See "Abortion and the Equal Rights Amendment—Is There a Connection?" (factsheet), November 5, 1983 (Washington, DC: National Right to Life Committee), Folder "ERA," Box 12, Series 2 (legislative) A (subject files—ERA), Mack Mattingly Papers, Richard B. Russell Library, University of Georgia, Athens, GA.

44. Social conservatives feared that the ERA could be used to enforce gay rights because it would be discriminatory if a woman could marry a man but a man could not marry a man. Author's interview with Phyllis Schlafly, January 14, 2005.

45. "Mrs. Overcast: ERA Is 'Ugly,'" *Thomas Road Family Journal-Champion* 1, no. 6 (July 21, 1978), Thomas Road Family Journal-Champion Box 1, SDC.

46. Phyllis Schlafly, "What Really Happened in Houston," *Phyllis Schlafly Report* 11, no. 5 (December 1977), Box "Phyllis Schlafly Report," SDC.

47. "E.R.A. Suffers 1978 Defeats," *Phyllis Schlafly Report* 11, no. 8 (March 1978), Box "Phyllis Schlafly Report," SDC.

48. Author's interview with Phyllis Schlafly, January 14, 2005.

49. Text of Reagan's acceptance of the Republican nomination for president, July 17, 1980, *www.cnn.com*.

50. Lewis K. Uhler, president, National Tax Limitation Committee, direct mail letter, c. 1978, Folder "National Tax Limitation Committee," SDC. Emphases in the original.

51. Author's interview with Richard Viguerie, January 11, 2005.

52. Author's interview with Paul Weyrich, February 20, 2003.

53. Barry Light, "Surge in Independent Campaign Spending," *Congressional Quarterly*, June 14, 1980, 1637, Folder "Campaign 1980—Litigation, 6/16-29/80," Box 57, Staff Offices—Counsel Collection, JCPL.

54. "1980—The Pro-Life Fight for the Senate," *Pro-Life Political Reporter* (published by the National Pro-Life Political Action Committee, Falls Church, VA) 2, no. 3 (July 1980),

Folder "[National Pro-Life Action Committee] POTUS—Pro Life Coalition—Cabinet Room—January 23, 1984," OA 12448, Morton Blackwell Files, RRPL.

55. Gillian Peele, *Revival and Reaction: The Right in Contemporary America* (Oxford: Clarendon Press, 1984), 109.

56. Range, "Thunder on the Right."

57. Freedman, "American Populist Conservatism," 39–50.

58. Ralph J. Keefes Jr. to Carter, October 17, 1978, Folder "FI34 (Gen)," Box F10-2, 9/21/78-12/3/78, WHCF-Subject File, JCPL.

59. Quoted in Thomas Byrne Edsall with Mary D. Edsall, *Chain Reaction: The Impact of Race, Rights, and Taxes on American Politics* (New York: Norton, 1991), 132–33.

60. Quoted in Edsall with Edsall, *Chain Reaction*, 133.

61. Freedman, "American Populist Conservatism," 61–63; Oldfield, *Right and the Righteous*, 101; Edsall with Edsall, *Chain Reaction*, 133.

62. "Taxing private schools," *Washington Star*, August 29, 1978, included with memorandum from Dick Dingman to RSC members, September 26, 1978, Folder "IRS—Schools," Box 5, Jo Ann Gasper Papers, Hoover Institution, Stanford University, Palo Alto, CA.

63. Quoted in Sara Diamond, *Not By Politics Alone: The Enduring Influence of the Christian Right* (New York: Guilford, 1998), 68.

64. Bill Gavin, memorandum to Peter Hannaford and Martin Anderson, September 19, 1979, Folder "Official File, Hannaford Company, Inc, 1979," Box 13, Deaver and Hannaford Inc. Records (hereafter DHR), Hoover Institution.

65. Hannaford, memorandum to Gavin and Anderson, October 9, 1979 (emphasis in the original), Folder "Memoranda—Gavin, William 1978–1979," Box 3, DHR.

66. Bob Maddox, exit interview, December 8, 1980, Exit Interview Project, JCPL.

67. Jim Roberts, "Carter Aide Denies Anti-Falwell Effort," *Richmond* (VA) *Times-Dispatch*, August 8, 1980, Document 7012, Folder "Falwell, Jerry—Political Activity," BJUFF.

68. Bob Maddox, memorandum to Anne Wexler, Dick Moe, and Linda Tarr-Whelan, c. June 1980, Folder "Memos," Box 10, Robert Maddox Papers, JCPL.

69. The Minnesota Democratic-Farmer-Labor Party is an affiliate of the national Democratic Party. Steve Wenzel, memorandum to Dick Moe, July 3, 1980, Folder "Abortion Letters," Box 6, Maddox Papers.

70. "Preachers in Politics," *U.S. News and World Report*, September 24, 1979, 37–41.

71. Diamond, *Not by Politics Alone*, 66–67.

72. James C. Roberts, *The Conservative Decade: Emerging Leaders of the 1980s* (Westport, CT: Arlington House, 1980), 94.

73. Duane Murray Oldfield, *The Right and the Righteous: The Christian Right Confronts the Republican Party* (Lanham, MD: Rowman and Littlefield, 1996), 116–17.

74. "Preachers in Politics," 37.

75. Maxwell Glen and Cody Shearer, "That Old-Time Religion Goes Political," *Los Angeles Herald Examiner*, December 5, 1979, Folder "Reagan for President Committee File—Clippings, 1979–1980," Box 6, DHR.

76. Jack Anderson, "Connally Big Business Ties Valuable," *Washington Post*, December 12, 1979.

77. John Dart, "50 Christians Agree to Raise Reagan Funds," *Los Angeles Times*, December 3, 1979.

78. Roberts, *Conservative Decade*, 95.

79. Elmer L. Towns, "Korea Is 'Showplace,'" *Thomas Road Family Journal-Champion*, June

23, 1978, Folder "Thomas Road Family Journal-Champion April 1, 1978–June 23, 1978," Thomas Road Family Journal-Champion Box 1, SDC.

80. Jerry Falwell, "Why Every American Should Oppose SALT II: A Christian Perspective," *Thomas Road Family Journal-Champion*, August 1979, Thomas Road Family Journal-Champion Box 1, SDC.

81. Miller, *Billy Graham*, 205–6.

82. Quoted in George J. Church, "Politics from the Pulpit: Fundamentalists Take Aim at Carter and Liberals Nationwide," *Time*, October 13, 1980, 35.

83. Harry Covert, "Alaska's Political Structure 'Stirred Up,'" *Moral Majority Report* 1, no. 4 (April 11, 1980), Box "Moral Majority Report," SDC.

84. Jerry Falwell, *Strength for the Journey: An Autobiography* (New York: Simon and Schuster, 1987), 366.

85. Louise Ropog, "New Legislation Will Help Traditional Families," *Moral Majority Report* 1, no. 15 (December 15, 1980), Box "Moral Majority Report," SDC.

86. Marsha Dubrow, "With the Victory for AWACS, Senate Hawk Jeremiah Denton Moves Up the Pecking Order," *People*, November 16, 1981.

87. Patrick B. McGuigan, "Religious Right Played Key Role in Many Races for U.S. Senate," *Conservative Digest*, January 1981, 9, Document 8442, Folder "Moral Majority—Elections," BJUFF.

88. E. J. Dionne Jr, *Why Americans Hate Politics* (New York: Simon and Schuster, 1991), 235.

89. Quoted in "Shift of Religious Voters Defeated Carter," *Conservative Digest*, January 1981. (According to *Conservative Digest*, this unsigned article was "excerpted from the postelection edition of *Washington and World Religion Report*, edited and published by Edward E. Plowman. The WWRR is located at: Washington Building, Washington, D.C. 20005.")

90. Sundquist, "Whither the American Party System?"

91. William B. Hixson Jr., *Search for the American Right Wing: An Analysis of the Social Science Record, 1955–1987* (Princeton, NJ: Princeton University Press, 1992), 256–59.

92. Edsall with Edsall, *Chain Reaction*, 154.

93. CBS News/*New York Times*, "National Election Day Survey," November 4, 1980, *www.ropercenter.uconn.edu/elections/common/exitpolls.html*.

94. Range, "Thunder from the Right."

95. Quoted in Dubrow, "With the Victory for AWACS."

96. Martin, *With God on Our Side*, 223.

97. *Action Line—Christian Action Council Newsletter* 5, no. 1 (January 22, 1981), Box "Action Line," SDC.

98. Daniel K. Williams, *God's Own Party: The Making of the Christian Right* (New York: Oxford University Press, 2010), 8.

99. Ibid., 239–40.

100. Nellie J. Gray to Ronald Reagan, January 12, 1987, Folder "Pro-Life (2)," OA 17955, Mariam Bell Files, RRPL.

CHAPTER 8

Building Consensus

The Republican Right and Foreign Policy, 1960–1980

Sandra Scanlon

During the early stages of the campaigns for the 1968 Republican presidential nomination, the conservative movement spearheaded by Barry Goldwater was reported to have "collapsed, leaving a bad taste in many mouths." According to one analyst, the "delay and bickering" among conservative activists were simply aiding the efforts of moderate and liberal Republicans such as George Romney to capture the nomination.[1] Goldwater's focus on winning the Senate seat that he had left to pursue the presidency in 1964 certainly diverted his attention from promoting a national conservative electoral strategy. While Ronald Reagan moved tentatively to fulfill Goldwater's role as a unifying figurehead for the diverse conservative movement, he did not possess sufficient political leverage to secure this goal in 1968. As such, while the lament in early 1968 for conservative activism may have been overstated, it reflected the weaknesses associated with public divisions among conservatives.

Scholarly explanations for the 1960s and 1970s Republican resurgence conventionally emphasize the role of conservatives in mobilizing grassroots activists and in popularizing antistatist ideas. These accounts usually neglect, however, the seriousness of the divisions that existed not only between Goldwater Republicans and moderate or liberal Republicans, but also among conservatives themselves. Such divisions were especially serious between the Republican Right—office-holding Republican politicians who were on the party's right—and movement conservatives, whose political engagement took place outside party politics, within extra-party organizations and publications. Divisions were most visible when Republicans were in power—when party loyalty dictated Republican support for the administration's agenda, but when the governing demands of pragmatism were most likely to disappoint principle-focused movement conservatives. Despite the importance of antistatism to modern American conservatism, divisions were sharpest in the realm of foreign policy. Such divisions, furthermore, represented a significant obstacle to conservative success in achieving influence within the Republican Party.

This chapter analyzes, first, the ideological and political significance of conservative divisions. Second, it argues that these divisions prevented the achievement of sustained influence during the "new majority" project of the Nixon years. Third, it explores how, after Nixon, the Republican Right and movement conservatives secured agreement on foreign policy in a way that successfully promoted their concerns both within the party and among the wider electorate. Ronald Reagan played an important role in leading conservatives toward such an agreement, but the disappointments in foreign policy during the Carter years created fertile ground for conservative progress. In this sense, conservative advance relied on liberal setbacks.

The search for consensus on the right was long-standing, and during the 1970s was born chiefly from practical political considerations learned from the debilitating effects of division during the Nixon administration. The Republican Right's embrace of the New Right was, as such, a means of achieving the key goal of purging the party of its moderate albatross. But the effort to build consensus on the right also encompassed the endeavor to promote a unified foreign policy, one that embraced the Republican Right's traditional commitment to fighting the Cold War and opposing détente, but which also responded to popular anxieties about the United States' position in the world. The conservative foreign policy consensus that was formed included the ideas of politicians and intellectuals preoccupied with the ideology of the early Cold War and also the emphasis on morality and American values promoted by the New Right. In many respects nothing more than a tenuous alliance of related viewpoints, the Republican Right's ability to harness a foreign policy consensus did much to extend its political leverage in the creation of a Republican majority.

The Nixon years represent a period of intense division among conservatives, but they are certainly not unique in this regard. The isolationist wing of the conservative movement was discredited by the intensification of the Cold War and by the appeal to nationalist conservatives of Dwight D. Eisenhower's embrace of both fiscal responsibility and internationalism. But the unifying power of anticommunism during the post-1945 period can be contested. Division existed over the degree to which the Cold War environment warranted the growth of the national security state and the American embrace of world leadership through such programs as the Marshall Plan and institutions like the United Nations. Veering between anti-interventionism and support for heightening Cold War activism, the Republican Right failed to formulate a consistent and unified position on foreign policy. In part, this situation was conditioned by conservative Republicans' political need to support publicly their party's leader, but also by their inability to proffer a viable alternative to the Eisenhower administration's broad foreign policy goals. As such, it was the wider conservative movement that provided the intellectual basis for the foreign policies that would come to dominate the Republican Right during the 1960s.

One of the key vehicles for disseminating a distinctly conservative foreign policy was the periodical founded by William F. Buckley Jr., *National Review*. Individuals such as *National Review*'s Buckley, James Burnham, Frank Meyer, and William Rusher sought to bridge the gap between academic exploration of conservatism and wider, if not mass, consumption of conservative principles and political goals. It was therefore necessary to overcome the inconsistencies and debilitating divisions within conservative thought. Such divisions, primarily between the pure libertarian ideals of individuals like Frank Chodorov and the more traditionalist conservatism sponsored by Russell Kirk, provided fertile ground for intellectual debate, but had frustrated attempts to combine the various strains of conservatism into a single political program.[2] The purpose of *National Review* had always been to consider, but also subsume, such divisions for the purpose of greater conservative cooperation in the political arena. Frank Meyer thus defined the loose alliance between libertarians and traditionalists based on a shared anticommunism, in the effort to create a viable political ideology. Meyer's focus on anticommunism reflected his personal philosophical and political journeys. Born in New York, Meyer became an active communist while studying at Oxford University and the London School of Economics. His rejection of communism led him to embrace conservatism wholeheartedly, which distinguished him from other former communists who embraced New Deal liberalism and established a commitment to the Democratic Party.[3]

Known as "fusionism," Meyer's philosophy was fully articulated in 1964, but had mainly practical origins, born in part from the political experiences of conservatives in the early 1960s, and from the recognition that a more coherent theoretical framework was required if the movement was to avoid the factionalism that had haunted earlier forays into politics. Fusionism was thus a distillation of the already implemented cooperative methods and ideas that had begun with the creation of *National Review* in 1955 and which climaxed with the 1960 and 1964 Draft Goldwater drives. It was the principal philosophy of not only *National Review*, but also the Washington-based conservative news journal *Human Events*; Young Americans for Freedom, which was founded in 1960 to mount an effective conservative campaign on America's university campuses; and the American Conservative Union (ACU), founded in 1965 to rally together the activists of the Goldwater presidential campaign.[4]

Fusionism was fundamentally an effort to make unequivocal opposition to international communism the basis of conservative political activism. While this would serve the practical purpose of reducing the significance of tensions over other intellectual debates, it also served its main protagonists' goals of heightening the importance of foreign policy in the conservatives' political agenda. Reflecting Meyer's thesis, the ACU charged that the "American commonwealth, as well as the civilization that illuminated it, is mortally threatened by the global Communist revolution." Its statement of principles denounced the possibility of "permanent co-existence with Communism" and asserted that "no sacrifices" were "too great" to avoid the fate of slavery that would inevitably ensue from any effort to achieve cooperation with the Soviet Union. The means of securing victory were also made clear: "We would parry the enemy's thrusts—but more: by maintaining American military superiority and exerting relentless pressure against the Communist empire, we would advance the frontiers of freedom."[5]

Meyer's focus on communism did not sit well with all conservatives. The eminent libertarian Murray Rothbard described Meyer as "an old and valued friend and mentor," but argued that his "being militantly pro-war [with regard to the international threat of communist expansion] also meant being in favor of U.S. imperialism and of all-out military statism in the U.S." Rothbard further claimed that Meyer's "devotion to the global crusade against communism and the Soviet Union" ensured that "the Enemy for him and for the conservative movement, was not statism and socialism but communism." Consequently, he argued, "it was under Frank's theoretical and strategic aegis that the conservative movement rushed to welcome and honor any species of dangerous socialist so long as they were certifiably anti-communist or anti-Soviet."[6] Rothbard's claims reveal the tensions within the conservative movement, particularly those created by the traditionalists' devotion to opposing the spread of communism abroad and their willingness to adopt big government measures in order to achieve this aim. Rothbard's challenge to Meyer and his adherents reflected the view that conservatives in the postwar period had weakened the movement's ideological foundations by adopting any and all measures, including those contrary to individual freedom and conservative economic doctrine, in order to focus on opposing international communism. Indeed, similar concerns had been more publicly articulated by President Eisenhower's warnings of the encroaching military-industrial complex. By making such issues secondary to a determined anticommunist foreign policy, conservative Republicans made clear their priorities and their determination to shift away from the military restraints associated with Taft's form of isolationism.

Despite libertarian protestations, anticommunism became a powerful symbol of unity within the conservative movement and allowed the *National Review* circle to assume a position of leadership. This position of leadership came not only from the role of *National Review* activists in the Draft Goldwater campaign, but also because of the journal's role in attempting to legitimize conservatives' domestic and foreign policies. Buckley stated that the purpose of *National Review* was "to articulate a position on world affairs which a conservative candidate can adhere to without fear of intellectual embarrassment or political surrealism."[7] Much of this effort thereby involved discarding the image of extremism—from either the isolationist perspective or from the advocacy of unlimited use of nuclear weapons—that appeared to have diminished conservative voices in foreign policy–making circles throughout the Eisenhower administration.

By the early 1960s, conservatives had moved away from the liberationist position that had preoccupied them as they formulated foreign policy during the immediate postwar period. In accepting containment of communism, however, they also promoted the necessity of engaging in smaller wars that would undermine and deter the Soviet Union's extension of its sphere of influence. Having railed against the hesitance in using force during the Bay of Pigs invasion and vociferously opposed the neutralization of Laos, conservatives looked principally to Cuba as the test case for engaging in "small" wars of liberation. Struggling to define the nature of small wars and emboldened by the Cuban leadership's demonstrable relationship with the Soviet Union, activists at *National Review*, *Human Events*, and the rightward-leaning think tank the American Security Council (ASC) argued that Cuba provided the most fortuitous means for the United States to demonstrate a liberationist policy regarding communism.[8] The Kennedy administration's resolution of the missile problem in Cuba was consistently attacked by conservatives. *Human Events* published a series of scathing assessments of the situation in Cuba and maintained that neither the missile problem nor the moral issue of U.S. failure to aid subjugated peoples had been resolved. Historian George Nash has argued that "as conservatives surveyed world crises in the late 1950s and the 1960s, one fundamental fact seemed paramount: the continuous, implacable assault on the West by messianic, revolutionary Communism."[9] Conservatives thus agreed with their liberal and moderate Republican counterparts, including Nelson Rockefeller, that the United States was losing the Cold War. The conservative solution emphasized both military intervention to stop the spread of communism and the paramount importance of United States military supremacy. Political objectives could not, however, be entirely ignored.

The recognition that Barry Goldwater's image as a Cold War extremist had undermined conservatives' political goals in 1964 certainly concerned the Republican Right and the broader conservative movement. *National Review* attempted to resolve this issue by "removing" such organizations as the John Birch Society (JBS) from the "responsible conservative" alliance. Buckley and Burnham succeeded in gaining a broad repudiation of the organization's leadership when, in 1965, JBS leader Robert Welch denounced the Vietnam War on libertarian grounds. Far from revising mainstream perceptions, however, the stratagem of making conservative foreign policy more palatable mainly served to arouse the ire of the grassroots Right. It also displeased conservative leaders who were more concerned by 1967 with criticizing the GOP for its apparent failure to fully challenge the administration on Vietnam and to assume a more principled stand on major international issues.[10] Meyer claimed that "a new form of opportunism threatens the integrity of the Republican Party." This opportunism, he asserted, "is the despicable proposal to truckle to the Left-liberal and radical ideologues who are kicking up a storm against the Vietnam war, and join with them in confusing the American people on the deadly issues of national interest and civilizational survival our prosecution of the war represents." He concluded: "It is here that the Republican attack on Johnson should be centered: not upon his stubborn prosecution of the war in Vietnam, which reflects his instinctive understanding of the Communist danger, but upon his failures—political, psychological, strategical—as commander-in-chief in the worldwide cold war against Communism. To pander to popular confusion by attacking the waging of the Vietnam war instead, would be, both for the Republican Party and the country, an act of destructive cynicism."[11]

Such attacks angered conservative Republicans, many of whom were reluctant to challenge openly the president's Vietnam strategies for fear of eroding public support for military engagement. In this regard, it can perhaps be a mistake to overestimate the degree of unity on the Right during the 1960s regarding foreign policy; Frank Meyer's fusionism was by no means a political quick fix, but neither was it indicative of a deeply held consensus regarding the best means of winning either the Cold War or a conservative political majority. The ideological consistency that was apparent during the Democratic years was, however, challenged by the political sensitivities that accompanied a Republican administration.

Conservative support for Richard Nixon's presidential candidacy in 1968 was decisive in securing his nomination. While conservative activists were divided over whether or not to promote Ronald Reagan's nomination at the Republican National Convention in Miami Beach, conservatives within the GOP ultimately backed Nixon. Foreign policy played only a minor role in determining this outcome. Goldwater had openly supported Nixon's candidacy since 1965, in part because of the latter's vociferous campaigning efforts on his behalf in 1964. Conservative ideologues such as Bill Buckley had also made clear their practical, if not ideological, preference for Nixon. The key to Nixon's success among conservatives at Miami Beach, however, was his ability to gain the support of the South's delegates. The dual attacks from the Left and the Right—from Nelson Rockefeller and renegade Democrat George Wallace—hastened conservative willingness to support Nixon over Reagan. Senator Strom Thurmond's political aide, Harry Dent, warned that support for Reagan would simply divide the conservative vote, thus giving the nomination to Rockefeller, and the southern conservative vote in 1968 to Wallace.[12] Declaring in June 1968 that Nixon "offers America the best hope of recovering from domestic lawlessness; a bloody no-win war in Southeast Asia; . . . strategic military inferiority; [and] loss of influence in world affairs," Thurmond made clear that a sizable and influential element of the emerging conservative political movement was relying on Nixon to achieve its foreign policy aims.[13] Certainly, Nixon's reputation as a Cold Warrior and hawk on the Vietnam War influenced the *National Review* circle's willingness to favor his candidacy.

The Reagan campaign served an important function as a means of publicizing conservative activism and pushing Nixon to the right, if only rhetorically, but it could not achieve the conservative goal of more immediate political power. Reagan staked his claim as an anticommunist hard-liner during his address to the platform committee. Rejecting the Kennedy-Johnson approach to foreign policy, particularly regarding military strategy in Vietnam, he called for reengagement with the Cold War.[14] Nixon also proffered the possibility of forging a new approach to foreign policy. Strength in diplomacy, Nixon made clear during his private meeting with southern Republicans, was to be founded on military and economic power: "What we've got to do is walk softly and carry a big stick and we can have peace in this world. And that is what we are going to do." Hinting at the potential use of U.S. power, he declared: "I'll tell you one thing. I played a little poker when I was in the Navy. . . . I learned something. . . . When a guy didn't have the cards, he talked awfully big. But when he had the cards, he just sat there—had that cold look in his eyes. Now we've got the cards."[15] The differences between Reagan and Nixon on foreign policy certainly reflected divergent views on U.S. international strength during this period and the best means of taking advantage of the international environment. Nixon, however, was also convinced of the need to appeal to a broad political base and the importance of achieving intraparty consensus—so vividly and detrimentally absent in 1964—going into the 1968 election.

Unity among conservatives proved harder to maintain when Republicans were in power. Nixon's rhetoric may have convinced conservatives that he would use the strength of the United States to best advantage, but it was the recognition of his political strength that won over conservatives more ideologically attuned to a Reagan candidacy. Under the guidance of Republican congressman John Ashbrook of Ohio, the ACU had supported firmly Reagan's candidacy but offered unqualified support for Nixon during the campaign. "In the field of foreign affairs," the organization stated, "he will hold a firm line against the forces of totalitarianism and international Communism which continue to threaten the peace of the world.[16] The prospect of political victory thus united much of the conservative movement behind Nixon.

Early conservative challenges to the Nixon administration's choice of appointments, in particular the failure to overhaul the State Department, were indicative of later divisions over foreign policy. When the ACU labeled the first six weeks of the administration "disappointing," Harry Dent withdrew from the organization, while Barry Goldwater charged that responsible conservatives were applauding, not criticizing, the president.[17] The ACU, while stating that it did not regret endorsing Nixon, lamented the fact that "the foreign policy of America is being administered by many faceless and some notorious liberals who have been in control since the New Deal."[18] Goldwater's refusal to challenge publicly the administration was also a feature of the conservative movement's response to Nixon's foreign policies that would be repeated time and again. Conservatives were eager to promote the image of unity and aware of the need to associate with Nixon in order to secure political legitimacy. Nixon's popular credibility as a hawk on foreign policy ensured that any effort to push him from the right risked making conservatives look extreme. Goldwater privately complained, however, that there were in the State and Defense Departments individuals "whose only interest is the disarmament of our country."[19]

Henry Kissinger's appointment also attracted some conservative criticism, because of both his association with Rockefeller and his previously stated realist perspective on international relations. The national security adviser garnered praise from *National Review*, however, which stated that he would "render great service."[20] Broadly speaking, the Republican Right was keen to support the new administration's foreign policy agenda, particularly after the announcement in March of plans for the development of an anti-ballistic missile system. This provided the opportunity for gaining some "mileage" with the "conservative element," White House chief of staff H. R. Haldeman privately commented.[21] Indeed, the Republican Right increasingly focused on deterrence as the basis of U.S. strategic strength, a shift from an earlier emphasis on overwhelming military strength, brought about by the changed military balance between the Soviet Union and the United States. Meyer, in a barbed attack on the Nixon administration's defense budget, would later lament what he saw as the failure to recognize that "the credibility of our deterrent" and "the maintenance of an unquestionable deterrent power must be the first charge on our revenues."[22]

Vietnamization, which conservatives interpreted as a means of affording the South Vietnamese the opportunity to escalate the war, had become almost their solitary area of support for the administration's overall foreign policy by late 1970. They were particularly critical regarding the inadequacy of defense expenditures, especially in missile research and development, and the opening of the Strategic Arms Limitations Talks (SALT) in 1970. Instead of producing a united conservative challenge to administration policy as seen in the Johnson years, however, Nixon's policies resulted in debilitating divisions within the conservative movement. This was nowhere more evident than in the Right's responses to the president's revelation in July 1971 that Kissinger had been in secret negotiations with leaders of the People's Republic of China. Nixon's shock announcement that he would visit Beijing within a year caused further disarray among conservatives.

White House aide Patrick J. Buchanan, whose involvement in conservative political campaigns led to his unofficial role as liaison with conservative leaders, had warned in January that "we have a serious political problem developing on the Right." He stated that the "originally localized . . . infection is spreading and now being broadcast, through the press, to the party structure nationally."[23] Reflecting conservative fears with regard to the strategic defense capability of the United States, Buchanan warned against the administration's tendency to "congratulate ourselves on each new cut in the defense budget."[24] Publicly, the ACU argued that the Nixon line amounted to little more than a continuation of liberals' flawed interpretation of international affairs: "Appease Red China. Encourage Red trade. SALT talks forever. Cut defense costs to the bone. Get out of Vietnam, with only the pace of withdrawals the issue. Victory? Barry Goldwater's beloved blockading of Haiphong? No, sir."[25]

With the exception of ACU chair John Ashbrook, the GOP Right refused to follow this line of argument. Publicly, Goldwater offered a resounding endorsement of the administration, a position that was in large part followed by the leadership of the conservative movement at the annual Conservative Awards dinner in February. Buchanan urged conservative Republicans to emphasize the president's strong stand in Vietnam as a means of undermining challenges to his foreign policy. He focused on one of the administration's greatest strengths in this area: the president's refusal to assuage the demands of the antiwar faction in Congress. "Despite national opposition," Buchanan commented, "*he has hung in there in Vietnam.*" Buchanan described Nixon as possessing "the courage to do what Rusk and Johnson would not do," referencing Nixon's invasion of Cambodia "*to wipe out the sanctuaries.*" Nixon "has stayed the course," Buchanan concluded, "against massive media pressure."[26] Conservative supporters of the administration thereby used specific aspects of the administration's foreign policy record to demand overall support for the president's policy agenda.[27] Although many were beginning to question such issues as lessening trade and travel restrictions regarding communist China and the continuation of SALT, the dominant position of the Republican Right was one of support for Nixon's foreign policy.

It was becoming clear, however, that such support could not be sustained for much longer. Agreeing with the ACU's line of argument in June, the ASC's Stefan Possony charged the administration with "playing an extremely dangerous game of Russian roulette which could cost the United States dearly." Possony concluded that "for the past three years . . . the Soviets have been striving for global military superiority while simultaneously inducing the United States to emasculate its own military might."[28] The "*Human Events* line" had become dominant among conservatives by June 1971. Buckley warned that if Soviet concessions were not forthcoming at SALT, Nixon "won't win again," an implicit threat about conservative intentions regarding the 1972 election.[29]

Nixon's "China shock" of July 15, 1971, when he announced his intention to visit the People's Republic of China (PRC) by May 1972, brought about the climax of conservative opposition to the administration. Asked in 1970 to describe the event or development of the previous decade that had been most influential, Bill Buckley simply declared, "The philosophical acceptance of coexistence by the West."[30] The United States had, in Buckley's view, lost a measure of its moral legitimacy through its reliance on containment. Recognition of the PRC would thus serve only to foster the weakening moral position of the United States. Buckley's rhetoric resembled that of Democratic challengers to détente, increasingly referred to as neoconservatives, who opposed détente for its failure to convey U.S. foreign policy in terms of the ideological conflict between East and West, between communism and freedom. The emphasis on morality in foreign policy was pursued with more ideological consistency by neoconservatives, and indeed by antimilitarist "new internationalists" in Congress, although it would not become a prominent basis of foreign policy arguments until the final years of the Nixon administration.[31] The question of morality suggested, however, an early area of convergence between the Republican Right and disaffected Democrats that would prove significant by the end of the decade.

Nixon's China initiative pushed Buckley and Burnham into the opposition camp, although they remained reluctant to repudiate Nixon fully. In a statement issued by a group of conservatives opposed to the China move, Buckley insisted, "We consider that our defection is an act of loyalty to the Nixon we supported in 1968."[32] He and Burnham were again fearful of devastating any remaining conservative influence and extending the image of extremism on the Right. For much of the conservative movement, however, the China initiative was confirmation of the ACU's oft-repeated concerns about the trajectory of Nixon's foreign policies.[33]

The White House was anxious to head off attacks from the Right in the buildup to the China announcement. Despite vociferous opposition from *National Review* and the old China lobby, it managed to retain the support, albeit reluctant and cautious, of the Republican Right. Others habitually loyal to the *National Review* line also desisted from supporting it in this instance for fear of undermining conservative influence on administration policy. One activist warned "that on the China issue conservatives will paint themselves into a corner."[34] This concern was shared by conservative anticommunist luminaries like Goldwater; Reagan; Republican senator John Tower of Texas; Thurmond; and Senator James Buckley, brother of Bill and the sole congressional representative of the New York Conservative Party. They not only withheld judgment on Nixon's China initiative until after the visit, but also condemned the public position of those at *National Review* and the ACU.

Rather than provide the forum for a renewed debate on administration foreign policy, the China issue divided the conservative movement more extensively than ever before. Senator Buckley disagreed with some of the conservatives' specific analyses, "perhaps," he explained, "because during these past six months I have occupied a position from which I have been able to gain a better appreciation of the political constraints within which the President is required to operate."[35] Taking a similar line, Goldwater and Reagan also expressed confidence that Nixon was intent on increasing defense expenditure and, more significantly, that his China initiative would not weaken America's international position. The Arizona senator returned to the familiar refrain of blaming the previous Democratic administration "for any deficiency that exists in our military system." In parallel with this, he condemned the current Democratic Congress for thwarting White House preferences for higher defense outlays.[36]

The conservative divide was most obvious between *National Review* and the ACU on the one hand, and the Republican Right on the other.[37] Party loyalty thus played a key role in limiting conservative Republicans' dissent regarding Nixon's policies. Buckley continued to attack Goldwater's position on the China summit during 1972: "If Senator Goldwater doesn't believe that we have made a major concession of a hard psychological substance, he is living in his own world."[38] Goldwater then accused Buckley of thinking him "some kind of idiot" for accepting the assurances that nothing had been lost as a result of the Beijing summit.[39] Indicting Goldwater and Reagan for "dancing attendance on Richard Nixon," the ACU labeled them "partisan apologists for Cold War accommodation."[40] Ashbrook and Burnham judged Goldwater guilty of sin by omission because of his failure to disavow the China trip publicly. Goldwater, in turn, called on conservatives to be realistic, but also based his stance on a long-standing personal faith in Nixon. "If I cannot believe my president," he wrote privately, "then I have lost all my faith in men, in friends and in leadership." In reference to Nixon's assurances that nothing was compromised by the visit to China, Goldwater noted, "I think he has told us the truth."[41]

Neither the *National Review* conservatives nor Reagan was quite so convinced, although the California governor refrained from publicly voicing his anxieties. The Republican Right's bold rhetoric could not disguise the reality that its influence had significantly diminished by early 1972 compared to four years previously. Not only was Nixon free from the fear that a conservative contender of Reagan's strength would challenge his nomination, but also his foreign policy enjoyed widespread, if ultimately shallow, public support. As Robert Mason discusses in Chapter 9, Nixon's promise of "peace with honor" and mobilization of the "silent majority"—especially in opposition to the radical antiwar movement—proved to be successful in electoral terms, as were the détente initiatives that he framed in terms of patriotic concerns. The Republican Right was primarily motivated by party political considerations. While recognizing the need to induce the Soviet Union in particular to cooperate in such efforts at ending the Vietnam War, conservative Republicans were no less opposed to détente than their counterparts at *National Review*. The ACU/*National Review* insurgency may have highlighted conservative anxieties but ultimately it revealed the weakness of a divided Right. In these circumstances, a conservative challenge for the Republican nomination seemed a waste of already limited political capital.

Nixon's resignation in 1974 coincided with broader public questioning of the trajectory of American foreign policy, which was exacerbated by the dismal conclusion to the Vietnam War in 1975. As the Ford administration rejected the rhetoric, if not necessarily the substance, of détente, Democrats succeeded in presenting viable, if divergent, policy alternatives. Liberals' emphasis on reinvigorating American policy with an emphasis on human rights contrasted with the apparent failure of détente to consider the ethical dimensions of U.S. policy. Neoconservatives, led on Capitol Hill in principle if not in name by Washington's Democratic senator Henry "Scoop" Jackson, shared liberals' focus on regaining America's moral mission in the world. Their emphasis on ideology and determination to revive the U.S. role in protecting and projecting freedom was closer, however, to conservatives' calls for revitalizing American strength in the continuing Cold War. The waning role of the Republican Right in representing the hard line in foreign policy was suggested by the emergence of bipartisan groups such as the Committee on the Present Danger (CPD) during the mid-1970s. While the CPD promoted many of the ideas originally conceived by the conservative-dominated ASC, its close association with the Coalition for a Democratic Majority indicated the prominence of hard-line Democrats, rather than the Republican Right, in the new organization.

Conservative Republicans certainly did much in the immediate post-Vietnam period to emphasize the Soviet danger and continued to focus on the need for an intense program of rearmament. The conservative movement's political hopes largely rested with Ronald Reagan, who focused, however, on achieving consensus among Republicans and on projecting an image of moderation regarding foreign policy. As one commentator noted in 1979, Reagan was determined to demonstrate that he "was not another Barry Goldwater."[42] Winning over Democrats of the CPD vein was thus a clear element of his 1980 election strategy to demonstrate that the Republican Right had embraced more moderate positions on foreign policy. This did not entail acceptance of the now broadly discredited policies of détente or reduced focus on the military threat posed by the Soviet Union's strategic capabilities. Instead, Reagan's approach was to emphasize peace through strength rather than the need to challenge Soviet expansionism through military interventions such as Vietnam. It also embraced patriotism as a means of justifying foreign policy priorities. The Reagan game plan owed much to Nixon's 1972 campaign, but its embrace of nationalism provided a more traditional conservative twist. In emphasizing America's capacity to reclaim dominance in international relations, it blamed U.S. decline not only on successive Democratic administrations but also on the misguided pursuit of détente.

Much as neoconservative ideology incorporated the moral dimensions of America's international leadership, the Republican Right emphasized the need for the United States to embrace its international capabilities and reaffirm its position of international leadership. This effort involved an unprecedented appeal, certainly in the postwar period, to national pride. Conservative politicians emphasized the importance of America's international strength and prestige to its domestic economic and social recovery. In theoretical and political terms, this process involved lobbying for increased defense expenditure. In popular terms, conservative politicians utilized key international issues to discredit liberals and to undermine the image of extremism associated with conservatives' foreign policies. This initiative was demonstrated throughout the Cold War and became a useful political tool during the Korean War in particular.[43]

During the Vietnam War, conservatives related support for the effort to thwart communist expansion in Southeast Asia to patriotism, despite genuine beliefs that such issues were irrelevant to the rationale for supporting the U.S. military engagement in Southeast Asia. In 1966, Goldwater asserted that he was "ashamed to . . . see [Democrats] telling the American people that our power has made America arrogant and self-righteous and expansionist and immoral." "No American," he asserted, "has the right to or the justification to level such charges against his country."[44] Conservatives thus reoriented much of their propaganda offensive to associate their agenda with that of those opposing the radicalism of the antiwar movement. Historian David Levy notes that many liberal policy intellectuals drifted rightward in response to both the "lukewarm conduct of military operations" and the protest; the latter "seemed to represent profoundly troubling attacks upon the values, the institutions, the faiths that had made America the most successful country in history."[45] This shift to the right, symbolized by the development of such publications as *The Public Interest* in 1965, signified a broader attack on the nature of liberalism during this period and was initially motivated by opposition to the Great Society. It was also evidence, however, of the increasing presentation of conservative goals in opposition to those of antiwar protestors and politicians.

A series of foreign policy reverses under Jimmy Carter added grist to the conservative case. The Democratic administration's ultimately unsuccessful effort to prevent the success of the leftist Sandinista revolution in Nicaragua was seen as clear evidence of America's decline under liberalism. Seizing on this, conservatives framed the Nicaraguan crisis to leave Carter "with the blame for 'selling out an ally to the communists,' rather than with the credit for allowing Nicaraguans to remove their dictator."[46] The debates over the Panama Canal Treaty also allowed the Republican Right and the emerging New Right to unite their political forces around a populist foreign policy issue.

Congressional conservatives sought to undermine Kissinger's efforts to renegotiate the treaty with Panama as soon as the issue was raised in 1974. Conservative intellectuals and politicians were not wholly united on this issue; both Goldwater and Buckley opposed the Right's challenge to President Gerald Ford's policy. Reagan, supported by newly prominent conservative Republicans such as Senator Jesse Helms of North Carolina, turned the treaty into a "hot-button cause," declaring in his stump speeches for the 1976 Republican presidential nomination, "We built it, we paid for it, it's ours . . . [and] we are going to keep it."[47] Senators Thurmond and Helms launched vociferous attacks on the treaties negotiated by the Carter administration in 1977, while the ACU established a Task Force to Defeat Ratification.

The momentum of opposition, and thus the perhaps flawed appearance of conservative strength, was exacerbated by purely political calculations in Congress. As Robert David Johnson aptly notes, "Few foreign policy issues in U.S history have presented so stark a choice between serving the national interest and reflecting constituency wishes."[48] The issue brought together conservative activists and much of the Republican Right, uniting them on a foreign policy issue for largely political purposes. While the ACU emphasized the strategic implications of allowing the canal to become a neutral zone, much of the Right's campaign emphasized the weakness associated with the administration's policy, using such terms as "abandonment" and "retreat" to signify the trajectory of liberals' foreign policy agenda. By emphasizing the need to reassert America's international strength, conservatives offered a policy alternative that was appealing, rather than frightening. In a time of domestic and international vulnerability, the message was powerful.[49]

The search for a conservative foreign policy consensus in the postwar period initially focused on overcoming policy differences between distinct ideological strands of the conservative alliance and subsequently on overcoming the divisions between the *National Review* circle and leading conservative Republicans during the Nixon administration. By the late 1960s, such divisions were often determined by politics rather than policy. Republican conservatives demonstrated acceptance of party loyalty and recognition of the political necessity of supporting the popular policies of the Nixon administration. In the wake of the Vietnam War, the Republican Right rallied to promote a new foreign policy consensus, one based on popular appeals to patriotism as much as on intellectual analyses of America's strategic position in the Cold War. The willingness of conservative activists and ideologues to challenge the positions of their party counterparts did not evaporate, but the political appeal of unity became more evident. The changed domestic and international environments, not least the discrediting of détente, provided the context in which conservatives could assume a more prominent voice in foreign policy debates. The growth of the New Right, with its focus on moral and social issues, and the emergence of a neoconservatism as an influential policy force, influenced the rhetoric of the Republican Right. The recognition that internal divisions and the image of extremism had undermined conservatives' ability to achieve their foreign policy goals was also significant in uniting the conservative movement during the late 1970s.

Reagan's description of Vietnam as a "noble cause" in 1980 was, perhaps, the climax of this search for common ground on the right. It was part of a broader effort that sought to harness both popular anxieties about America's international weakness and popular hopes for its future. While the conservative consensus on international issues may have been limited and short-lived, it served a significant function in presenting conservatives as creators of more viable—and indeed, preferable—foreign policies than those promoted by their liberal counterparts.

NOTES

1. Robert S. Boyd, "Hard Sailing for Old Goldwater Movement," *St. Petersburg* (FL) *Times*, January 8, 1967.

2. John P. East, *The American Conservative Movement: The Philosophical Founders* (Chicago: Regnery, 1986), 19, 36.

3. Meyer's ideas were articulated in his books *The Moulding of Communists: The Training of the Communist Cadre* (New York: Harcourt, Brace, 1961) and *In Defense of Freedom: A Conservative Credo* (Chicago: Regnery, 1962). For a discussion of the origins of neoconservatism, see Jacob Heilbrunn, *They Knew They Were Right: The Rise of the Neocons* (New York: Doubleday, 2008), and Murray Friedman, *The Neoconservative Revolution: Jewish Intellectuals and the Shaping of Public Policy* (New York: Cambridge University Press, 2005).

4. The ACU was allied with the *National Review* circle. Its founding members included

Frank Meyer; William Rusher, who chaired the committee on political action; and Professor Stefan Possony, who chaired the committee on foreign and military policy.

5. ACU statement of principles, April 1965, Box 5, Thomas A. Lane Papers, Hoover Institution, Stanford University, Palo Alto, CA.

6. Murray N. Rothbard, "Frank Meyer and Sydney Hook," in *The Irrepressible Rothbard: The Rothbard-Rockwell Report Essays of Murray N. Rothbard* (Burlingame, CA: Center for Libertarian Studies, 2000), 20–26.

7. William F. Buckley Jr. cited in Rick Perlstein, *Before the Storm: Barry Goldwater and the Unmaking of the American Consensus* (New York: Hill and Wang, 2001), 155.

8. See, for example, "Cuba: JFK Leaves Much Unanswered," December 1, 1962; "Senators Still Have Doubts on Cuba," January 12, 1963; "Cuba: New Crisis Looms," February 2, 1963; "Cuba: Another Soviet Hoax," March 2, 1963; "We May Be Creating More Cubas," April 13, 1963; all in *Human Events*.

9. George Nash, *The Conservative Intellectual Movement in America since 1945*, 2nd ed. (Wilmington, DE: Intercollegiate Studies Institute, 1998), 238.

10. David Levy argues that the Vietnam War did not create a substantial divide for the Republican Party during the 1960s, but was rather used as a means of attacking the Democratic Party. David Levy, *The Debate over Vietnam*, 2nd ed. (Baltimore: Johns Hopkins University Press, 1995), 77. This was largely the case during the Johnson administration, but the war also did much to fragment the old Republican consensus, contributing to the rise of conservative influence within the party.

11. Frank Meyer, "Principles and Heresies: Republican Bug-out," *National Review*, October 31, 1967.

12. Nadine Cohodas, *Strom Thurmond and the Politics of Southern Change* (Macon, GA: Mercer University Press, 1994), 397–98. Thurmond's consequent support of Nixon was based on assurances that he would not be disappointed by the Nixon administration.

13. Strom Thurmond, "Endorsing Former Vice President Richard M. Nixon for President" (statement), Columbia, SC, June 22, 1968, Box 31, Strom Thurmond Papers, Strom Thurmond Institute, Clemson University, SC.

14. Ronald Reagan, speech before Platform Committee, Republican National Convention, July 31, 1968, Box 2, Ronald Reagan Subject Collection, Hoover Institution.

15. Jeffrey Kimball, *The Vietnam War Files: Uncovering the Secret History of Nixon-Era Strategy* (Lawrence: University Press of Kansas, 2004), 64–65.

16. ACU, "Aims and Principles," 1965, Box 131, William A. Rusher Papers, Manuscript Division, Library of Congress, Washington, DC.

17. "Mr. Nixon, Thus Far, Disappoints," *Republican Battle Line*, February–March 1969, Box 135, Rusher Papers; Senator Barry Goldwater Senate, early March 1969, reported in letter, Bob Kephart to William Rusher, mid-March 1969, Box 41, Rusher Papers.

18. *Republican Battle Line*, April 1969, Box 135, Rusher Papers.

19. Barry Goldwater, diary entry, February 8, 1969, Box 9, Personal/Political 1 series, Barry M. Goldwater Papers, Arizona Historical Foundation, Arizona State University, Tempe, AZ. Goldwater wrote also of "growing dissatisfaction among the members of Congress" because of the Nixon staff's failure to inform them of the status of their recommendations for appointments.

20. John B. Judis, *William F. Buckley, Jr.: Patron Saint of the Conservatives* (New York: Simon and Schuster, 1988), 302.

21. H. R. Haldeman, memorandum to Patrick J. Buchanan, March 13, 1969, Box 49, White House Special Files: Staff Member and Office Files—H. R. Haldeman, Nixon Presidential Materials Project (NPMP), National Archives, College Park, MD.

22. Frank Meyer, "Mr. Nixon's Course?," *National Review*, January 26, 1971.

23. Patrick J. Buchanan, memorandum to the president, January 6, 1971, Box 52, White House Special Files: Staff Member and Office Files—Charles W. Colson Files, NPMP.

24. Patrick J. Buchanan, memorandum to H. R. Haldeman, January 14, 1971, ibid.

25. Nick Thimmesch, "Conservatives Complain about Nixon," *Newsday*, January 5, 1971, in Box 71, Haldeman Files.

26. Patrick J. Buchanan, memorandum to the Committee of Six (Middle America Group), February 3, 1971, Box 73, Haldeman Files. Emphases in the original.

27. Patrick J. Buchanan, memorandum to H. R. Haldeman, February 8, 1971, Box 52, Colson Files. Both Senators Crane and Buckley "urged conservatives to back this Administration," according to Buchanan's record of the event.

28. "Inside Washington: Expert on USSR defense warns of SALT dangers," *Human Events*, June 19, 1971. *Human Events* argued that if immediate measures to increase US military strength were not enacted, the Soviets would achieve military *superiority* by the mid-1970s. "Joint Chiefs warn of USSR superiority by mid-'70s," *Human Events*, March 20, 1971.

29. H. R. Haldeman, memorandum to Patrick J. Buchanan, June 3, 1971, Box 80, Haldeman Files. Kissinger was subsequently asked by Haldeman to talk with Buckley and other conservative columnists. Haldeman claimed that the president "feels you should lay it on the line with no quarter given as to why they should be strongly defending the President on foreign policy instead of nit-picking here and there on every little thing." H. R. Haldeman, memorandum to Henry Kissinger, June 8, 1971, Box 80, Haldeman Files.

30. William F. Buckley Jr., cited in Mark R. Winchell, *William F. Buckley, Jr.* (Boston: Twayne Publishers, 1984), 22.

31. See Robert David Johnson, *Congress and the Cold War* (New York: Cambridge University Press, 2006), chaps. 5 and 6.

32. William Rusher, "Prominent conservative leaders 'suspend' support of President Nixon" (news release), July 29, 1971, Box 168, Rusher Papers.

33. David W. Reinhard, *The Republican Right since 1945* (Lexington: University Press of Kentucky, 1983), 224.

34. Ernst van den Haag to William Rusher, August 9, 1971, Box 94, Rusher Papers.

35. Senator James Buckley, press release, August 1, 1971, Box 13, Rusher Papers.

36. Senator Barry Goldwater, press release, December 29, 1971, Box 52, Colson Files.

37. The ACU and YAF were particularly critical of Goldwater's continued support of Nixon. Columns, Box 121, Rusher Papers.

38. Buckley was one of the official news media representatives who accompanied the president to the PRC. Despite being granted privileges by the White House, he continued to charge that the visit was a national disgrace.

39. Senator Barry Goldwater, column, mid-March 1972 [copy sent to William F. Buckley Jr., March 13, 1972], Box 121, Rusher Papers.

40. *Battle Line*, April 1972, Box 135, Rusher Papers.

41. Goldwater cited in Robert A. Goldberg, *Barry Goldwater* (New Haven, CT: Yale University Press, 1995), 266. Ashbrook and Burnham feared that Goldwater was too eager to satisfy the moderate or "regular" wing of the Republican Party.

42. Mary McGrory, "Reagan Finds Moderation," *Boca Raton* (FL) *News*, January 31, 1979.

43. Steven Casey, *Selling the Korean War: Propaganda, Politics, and Public Opinion in the United States, 1950–1953* (New York: Oxford University Press, 2007).

44. Goldwater cited in Goldberg, *Goldwater*, 245.

45. Levy, *Debate over Vietnam*, 86.
46. Derek N. Buckaloo, "Carter's Nicaragua and Other Democratic Quagmires," in *Rightward Bound: Making America Conservative in the 1970s*, ed. Bruce J. Schulman and Julian E. Zelizer (Cambridge, MA: Harvard University Press, 2008), 260.
47. Sean Wilentz, *The Age of Reagan: A History, 1974–2008* (New York: HarperCollins, 2008), 67.
48. Johnson, *Congress and the Cold War*, 235.
49. Philip Jenkins argues that the spread of radical movements, including terrorist organizations, throughout the globe during the 1970s also contributed to domestic pessimism and the "amazing appeal" of Ronald Reagan. "In the summer of 1977," he claims, "it did not seem far-fetched to imagine a systematic collapse of US influence much along the lines of what actually befell the Soviet bloc in 1989." Jenkins, *Decade of Nightmares: The End of the Sixties and the Making of Eighties America* (New York: Oxford University Press, 2006), 74, 62.

CHAPTER 9

Foreign Policy and the
Republican Quest for a New Majority

Robert Mason

O ne of the 1976 presidential campaign's most memorable moments took place at the first-ever vice presidential debate, between Senators Robert J. Dole of Kansas and Walter F. Mondale of Minnesota, respectively the Republican and Democratic candidates. Asked about Watergate's salience as an election issue, Dole responded that the scandal had no more relevance in 1976 than did the past failings of the Democrats as custodians of the nation's foreign policy. Characterizing World War I, World War II, the Korean War, and the Vietnam War as "all Democrat wars," Dole said, "I figured up the other day if we added up the killed and wounded in Democrat wars in this century, it would be about 1.6 million Americans, enough to fill the city of Detroit."[1]

This was a moment that not only helped to define Dole as an unusually aggressive and partisan politician but also provided an insight regarding his party's view of electoral politics during this period. Many leading Republicans saw foreign policy as the Democrats' area of greatest vulnerability because public confidence in their record in this sphere nowhere near matched the popularity of their domestic agenda. For much of the Cold War, opinion polls did indeed reveal that national security was a strong issue for the GOP. The Republican problem, however, was that the party considered better at maintaining prosperity tended to beat the party considered better at maintaining peace. The salience of concerns pertaining to New Deal liberalism tended to be greater than those involving Cold War internationalism. Moreover, the interparty difference on bread-and-butter issues was usually greater than that on foreign policy. In consequence, foreign policy largely remained a latent advantage that could not be fully mobilized to Republican benefit.

Republican leaders succeeded in turning foreign policy into a more actively positive advantage during the era of their party's revitalization. This chapter analyzes the importance of foreign policy in explaining the GOP revival. It contends that its role was significant—at the national level, at least—but one underappreciated so far by historians. Scholarly work on the Republican resurgence usually explores the importance of opposition to racial progress, of social and cultural upheavals, and of economic problems. Historians are right to emphasize the importance of these issues, but are wrong to neglect the Cold War's weighty impact on the era's electoral politics. Foreign policy certainly garners attention as a factor in Richard Nixon's 1968 victory (when Nixon promised "peace with honor" in Vietnam) and, especially, in Ronald Reagan's 1980 triumph (when Reagan attacked the Carter record on Afghanistan and Iran). It receives short shrift in explanations of broader party success, however.[2]

To demonstrate foreign policy's increasing importance to Republican fortunes, this chapter first explores how the Vietnam War and détente shaped Nixon's 1972 "new majority." Second, it considers Republican reliance on foreign policy as an answer to one of the key puzzles that scholars encounter when seeking to explain the party's resurgence—the phenomenon of "divided government," or the distinction that existed between the party's presidential and congressional fortunes. Finally, the chapter investigates the theme of continuity rather than change. The Republicans' foreign policy advantage was not a new development of the Vietnam era, since the GOP had enjoyed a popular reputation as the party of peace for much of the Cold War. Foreign policy's contribution to Republican revitalization did not, then, involve a transformation, but instead an evolution; an existing advantage became more advantageous at the polls.

This change took place during the Nixon administration. It represented success for Richard Nixon in his pursuit of a new majority as president. According to polls, foreign policy was the most important reason for his 1972 reelection landslide; as U.S. involvement in the Vietnam War faded away, Nixon voters were a majority that rallied around the flag. But Nixon's dependence on foreign policy for this success resulted from a failure to realize his larger vision of an electoral realignment to the Republicans' benefit. His agenda for the party's revitalization was initially more wide-ranging and ambitious, involving a wholesale transformation of its relationship with the electorate—rather than the more narrowly focused evolution in this relationship that took place in 1972, especially involving foreign policy.

At the end of the 1960s, it was clear that serious disarray within the Democratic coalition had created an opportunity for Republican growth. The strongest manifestation of new support for Nixon took place in response to his "silent majority" speech of November 1969. Intended to undercut the growth of antiwar sentiment that threatened the pursuit of his Vietnam policy, the nationally televised address not only achieved this goal, but also identified a large group of Americans who embraced the "silent majority" label and continued to do so long afterward. Nixon sought to deepen their support for the administration by widening its foundation beyond sympathy for "peace with honor" and the patriotic internationalism of his rationale against speedy withdrawal from Vietnam. By March 1970, Nixon was thinking of referring to the silent majority as his "new majority" instead—an indication of the grand electoral ambition animating his presidency.[3]

These efforts to broaden the silent majority's support for Nixon beyond foreign policy experienced limited success, however. In the 1970 midterms, the White House engineered a national strategy to exploit what Richard M. Scammon and Ben J. Wattenberg called the "Social Issue" in their book of that year, *The Real Majority*, as a way to undermine the salience of the "Economic Issue," which mainly benefited the Democrats.[4] Vietnam strongly informed the administration's Social Issue campaign. In demonizing many Democrats as "radical liberals," it attacked their views on Vietnam and sought to associate them with unpatriotic antiwar protests. Nixon spoke of his need for a supportive Congress in order to pursue his Vietnam policy effectively, and he condemned the protest movement as un-American, suggesting that the "radical liberals" condoned destructive criticism of the national purpose. But the definition of "radical liberalism" extended to opposition to the Nixon agenda in many other areas, including the contemporary buzzword issues of "permissiveness" and "law and order," which for Scammon and Wattenberg played a large role in defining the Social Issue.

This emphasis on the Social Issue did not, however, eclipse the salience of the Economic Issue. The sluggish economy of fall 1970 did not create a promising context for the Social Issue argument, but many Democratic candidates proved successful anyway in shrugging off the "radical-liberal" tag. Although the midterm results were open to an interpretation of qualified optimism for the Nixon cause—there were a few Senate gains, and House losses were lower than usual for the White House party—the president viewed them with disappointment. Administration polling suggested that the effort to promote "radical liberalism" as a key distinction between supportive and nonsupportive candidates had not affected the way in which most voters perceived the shape of political conflict. The effort to mobilize the "silent majority" at the polls by deepening and diversifying the foundations of its support for the administration had evidently failed to activate the electoral realignment that Nixon coveted.[5]

A few months later, the 1971 State of the Union address launched a fresh effort to revitalize the Republican Party. Nixon's "new American revolution" of programmatic innovation tackled an array of domestic issues with a boldness intended to transform popular understanding of the party. Electoral advantage figured prominently in the case that he made to win congressional Republican support for this agenda. Nixon argued that the GOP had depended on Democratic shortcomings for its few post–New Deal victories, and it had failed to develop any positive alternative to New Deal liberalism. Together with a Republican disinclination to outspend the Democrats, this reliance on opposition accounted for the party's minority status, according to Nixon.[6] Nixon failed to mobilize adequate Republican enthusiasm for the new American revolution, however; his own commitment proved half-hearted.

Although parts of the agenda achieved legislative enactment, the results of this reform impetus were not substantial enough to transform the GOP into what

Nixon had wishfully projected as "the party of change" and "the party of imagination, of innovation."[7] In June 1972, aides Patrick J. Buchanan and Kenneth Khachigian observed that despite "countless hours and unrecorded effort selling the bold dynamic 'New American Revolution,'" the results were "not encouraging," thereby making it pointless to emphasize the theme in the fall campaign.[8] Theirs was the voice of reform skeptics, but they were right to conclude that the rhetoric of reform had far outstripped the reality of its achievements, with disappointing implications for Nixon's plans for Republican revitalization.

As his reelection test approached, Nixon looked elsewhere for electoral advantage—in particular, at foreign policy.[9] This was his principal field of political interest and presidential effort anyway, but the failure of the 1970 midterm strategy and the 1971 legislative agenda to advance the Republican cause encouraged reliance on foreign policy. Nixon's key initiatives of 1972 were his visits to China and Moscow, and they became one of his major claims for support among voters. The electoral potential of détente intrigued Nixon, and opinion polls confirmed this promise.[10] Shortly after the announcement of his Moscow plans, he observed that "we should really go to work playing the 'Man of Peace' issue all the time, move all the other issues to a lower level and really build that one up, because it's our issue and we have to use it," according to his chief of staff H. R. Haldeman.[11] While in Moscow, he discussed with Haldeman "the general political approach that it's not domestic issues that we should spend our time on, that's their issue, not ours." Recommending against any domestic focus, Nixon said it was preferable instead to "concentrate on the international, which is where we make the gains."[12] This insight encouraged Nixon to ensure that these visits were carefully designed to achieve a maximum of electoral benefit. As Dominic Sandbrook has written, the China and Moscow visits "were so closely interwoven with his reelection drive as to become virtually indistinguishable from campaign events."[13]

Although Nixon identified détente as a route to victory, these initiatives were also powerful in alienating existing support, especially among conservatives. In late 1971 and early 1972, the "Manhattan Twelve" mobilized against the administration, first suspending their support for Nixon, and then switching this support to Representative John Ashbrook of Ohio for the party's presidential nomination. This elite group of leading conservatives had many disagreements with Nixon, encompassing domestic as well as foreign affairs, but crucial in precipitating their shift from discontent to active opposition was détente, in particular the administration's China policy.[14]

This opposition did not deflect Nixon's commitment to improve U.S. relations with the communist powers, and the Ashbrook candidacy posed no real challenge to his renomination. Nevertheless, the episode demonstrates the importance of internal party dynamics to Republican efforts to seek a new majority (a theme that Sandra Scanlon explores in the previous chapter). It also underscores the tensions between conservatism and Nixon's vision for the Republican future; despite the increasing vitality of grassroots conservatism, Nixon saw a conservative emphasis as helpful only in mobilizing activists and actually unhelpful in winning votes.

In using foreign policy to mobilize electoral support in 1972, Nixon stressed the Vietnam War as well as détente, framing the debate about policy options in terms of opposition to or sympathy for the antiwar movement. Just as the promise of "peace with honor" had helped him achieve a narrow victory against the incumbent Democrats in 1968, the war proved to be a campaign asset four years later. Within a platform of wide-ranging liberalism, the presidential campaign of Senator George McGovern of South Dakota challenged the logic of containment that formed the core of Cold War orthodoxy. With opposition to the Vietnam War the inspiration for his candidacy, he made speedy withdrawal a key position. Thus McGovern directly represented the antiwar views against which Nixon had rallied the "silent majority" in 1969.[15] The president relished the chance to frame the campaign along these lines. In his election-eve address, he told voters that their choice was one between "peace with honor" and "peace with surrender," between "a strong America" and "a weak America."[16] According to Nixon's pollster, Robert Teeter, the administration's conduct of the Vietnam War was "truely [sic] the gut issue in the campaign."[17] His poll analysis suggested that the most important factor explaining Nixon's 1972 victory was the war, and that détente was the second. This was the interpretation of public opinion that Nixon embraced as indicating the way to beat McGovern and later as the way to understand his victory.[18]

The case for reelection that the Nixon campaign advanced did not, of course, rely on foreign policy alone. Attacks on McGovern also insisted that his ideas about a whole host of issues—welfare and affirmative action, among many others—were excessively liberal, and out of step with majority sentiment. And foreign policy did not operate simply as a pro-Nixon issue. Its impact was polarizing. Patrick H. Caddell, who ran opinion surveying for the McGovern campaign, later said that Vietnam was the main reason why voters switched from Nixon to his candidate during the summer. Nevertheless, he acknowledged, "From May on, in terms of the war, the President was doing pretty well overall." Despite its polarizing effect, Vietnam helped Nixon much more than it hurt him. In the estimate of Nixon aides, McGovern's charges that the president had unnecessarily extended a conflict in a manner inimical to America's values and national interest boosted support for their candidate. "The more the McGovern side tried to say that the President was in *favor* of the war, the more it worked to our advantage," said Peter H. Dailey, who was responsible for the reelection campaign's advertising, noting that Nixon had persuaded most voters that he was working hard to end the war.[19]

Nixon's effort to mobilize his new majority stressed foreign policy because he identified achievements in this area as his presidency's most compelling strength and considered his Cold War approach as a clear-cut contrast with McGovern's. He also recognized foreign policy's power in challenging existing voter loyalties to the Democratic Party—something of critical significance for the goal of Republican resurgence. This was evident in the Nixon campaign's television incarnation. An especially powerful element was a commercial in the name of Democrats for Nixon—the organization established to foster the support of disaffected Democrats—that featured John Connally, a Texas Democrat and until recently Nixon's secretary of the treasury, and offered a vitriolic denunciation of McGovern on defense.[20]

Nixon regarded foreign policy as particularly useful in winning support from the key Democratic groups that he targeted for Republican cultivation, notably white southerners (though he by no means neglected their other concerns, as demonstrated by his Supreme Court nominations). Throughout the Cold War, polls tended to suggest that southerners were more supportive than other Americans of an assertive approach to superpower relations, sometimes by a margin of considerable significance. This support included opinion on the Vietnam War, which also boosted the salience of such concerns.[21] Such hawkish views aligned southern Democrats with Nixon and against McGovern. Foreign policy also assisted Nixon in his efforts to gain support from organized labor. George Meany, president of the American Federation of Labor and Congress of Industrial Organizations (AFL–CIO), praised Nixon's Vietnam and defense policies, and the organization's executive issued statements supportive of administration foreign policy.[22] Such support did not extend to bread-and-butter concerns, where common ground remained between Democrats and labor. Nixon perceived organized labor and, in particular, the South as strongly patriotic, a quality that he regarded as a key characteristic of his putative new majority.[23] Following a conversation with Senator Richard Russell of Georgia, for example, Nixon "mused quite a bit . . . about the fact that patriotism is so much higher in the South," noted H. R. Haldeman.[24]

Nixon's focus on foreign policy in mobilizing his new majority helped to lead him away from the larger goal of party revitalization, bolstering his impulse instead to concentrate on the maximization of his own reelection victory. He was reluctant to oppose those congressional Democrats who had supported him on Vietnam—especially numerous among the southern contingent—and he even looked for ways to assist them. For example, he encouraged his daughter Tricia Nixon Cox to endorse the candidacies of leading Democratic senators James Eastland of Mississippi and John McClellan of Arkansas during a visit to the South. More significantly, the president asked the National Republican Congressional Committee to withhold campaign efforts against a lengthy list of supportive Democrats.[25] Certainly, across much of the South, the prospects of a Republican candidate opposing a conservative Democrat remained feeble, and many districts still lacked a Republican challenger. However, the operational logic of Nixon's new majority effort actually pushed him away from a challenge to the status quo, thereby weakening his commitment to Republican revitalization. Only after polling day, once his own reelection was secure, did he rediscover an interest in this larger goal. By then, the zenith of new majority-related mobilization was in the past, and the Watergate crisis soon killed off White House efforts to boost party fortunes.[26]

The emphasis on foreign policy helps to explain why Nixon's landslide in 1972 had disappointing coattail benefits for the Republican Party as a whole. The 1968 elections returned 192 Republicans to the House and 43 to the Senate; in 1972, the numbers were 192 and 42. To be sure, other factors were also important in encouraging this divergence of outcomes, including the power of Capitol Hill incumbency; the policy distinctions between George McGovern and many congressional Democrats, which encompassed many issues beyond foreign policy; and the Republicans' continued weakness in congressional contests across much of the South.

But it was difficult to craft a party advantage on the foundations of a foreign policy emphasis. This was partly because Nixon did not wish to oppose Democrats who supported him on foreign policy, and partly because through Democrats for Nixon his campaign promoted the message that a vote against McGovern, especially relating to foreign policy concerns, was not inconsistent with Democratic loyalties. The institutional dimensions of electoral politics also diminished the party-building strength of foreign policy. As political scientist Byron Shafer argues, this issue domain had greater relevance to presidential rather than congressional contests, thanks to the president's responsibilities as commander in chief. Nixon's campaign emphasis on foreign policy thus helps to explain the arrival of a "divided government" era during his presidency.[27] The outcome of the 1972 elections, then, partly reflected Nixon's decision to stress foreign policy in ways that created a personal rather than party argument for his reelection. But this decision reflected an institutional reality of presidential responsibility for foreign policy, one with electoral consequences for the Republican Party's fortunes.

Nixon's reliance on foreign policy to mobilize his new majority qualified the extent of its newness. Foreign policy as an area of Republican advantage was not a new phenomenon of the Nixon administration and of the Vietnam era. In 1960, when he first sought the presidency against John F. Kennedy, Nixon observed that "if you ever let [the Democrats] campaign only on domestic issues, they'll beat us—our only hope is to keep it on foreign policy."[28] In this sense, there is a significant parallel between Nixon's 1960 conceptualization of interparty competition and that of 1972. In view of the social and political upheavals that the United States had experienced during the intervening period, which fostered talk of realignment during the Nixon administration, this continuity is noteworthy. It suggests that Nixon's thinking as an electoral strategist was not as adventurous and innovative as is often believed. As president, he did try out new ideas to boost Republican fortunes, notably in the 1970 campaign and the "new American revolution" agenda, but he relied on a safer, tested formula when his own reelection was at stake.

It was in 1952, during the Korean War, that the Republicans' foreign policy advantage first became significant. Dwight D. Eisenhower's promise to end the war was probably the crucial factor in his victory over Adlai Stevenson.[29] But the advantage predated Eisenhower's candidacy and the setbacks in Korea. It was, instead, emergent at the very start of the Cold War. Polling evidence suggests that in 1948 foreign policy was much more important to voters than domestic policy and that Republicans were at least slightly preferred to Democrats in this regard. Thomas E. Dewey, however, failed to exploit this potential advantage in his campaign for the presidency. Instead, he remained largely supportive of the Truman administration's foreign policy.[30] Adopting a different understanding of the bipartisan consensus in favor of containing communism, subsequent Cold War Republican presidential candidates, by contrast, developed a critique of their Democratic opponents as inadequate managers of the nation's foreign policy.

Sometimes assumed to be a concern that was usually marginal to voters by comparison with domestic issues, foreign policy remained important to many for most of the Cold War.[31] Admittedly, it was a secondary concern, other than in exceptional circumstances of crisis and war, and interparty difference with regard to such issues was much less significant than with regard to the issues in the tradition of New Deal liberalism. As a consequence, a voter's views on foreign policy did not determine party loyalty. Indeed, there was no discernible difference between the foreign policy views of a Republican voter and those of a Democratic voter.[32] In other words, the Republican advantage often remained latent and failed to inspire voter attachment to the party.

Reinforcing this feature, the Cold War may have been a pressing concern in presidential contests, but it was usually quite marginal at the congressional level.[33] Owing to its presidential focus, the GOP foreign policy advantage may at first seem to involve personalities—the relative strengths of individual politicians—rather than the party. In 1952 and 1956, Dwight D. Eisenhower clearly had immaculate credentials for gaining the trust of voters on issues of war and peace. In 1960 and 1968, Richard Nixon's credentials in this regard were less impeccable, but he had carefully burnished his reputation as an expert in foreign policy, enabling him to argue that he was the more knowledgeable and experienced candidate against first John F. Kennedy and then Hubert H. Humphrey.[34] For Nixon, that argument worked well against Humphrey in 1968, especially within the context of the Vietnam War. It was less effective in 1960, because of Kennedy's charge that a "missile gap" in favor of the Soviet Union had developed during the Eisenhower administration; the charge neutralized the favorable impact of Nixon's stress on his foreign policy expertise, in which he had invested his hopes for victory.[35] (In 1961, Republicans swiftly worked to regain lost ground; they countercharged that the missile gap was a myth.[36])

Barry Goldwater, by contrast, unequivocally lost the Republican edge on foreign policy in 1964 to Lyndon B. Johnson, whom opinion polls rated more favorably as the custodian of the nation's defenses.[37] This did not reflect any lack of effort by Goldwater, whose advisers had identified foreign policy as a promising focus

of attack on the president. During the Republican nomination campaign, he accused Johnson of weak leadership in this area, notably regarding support for South
Vietnam against communist insurgency.[38] This charge signaled Goldwater's larger
critique that the United States was not prosecuting the Cold War with adequate
vigor.[39] The carelessness with which Goldwater launched this attack, however, exposed him to attack from both Republican rivals and Democratic opponents for
being "trigger happy."[40] Goldwater never escaped that label, despite some efforts to
assert that the Republicans were the party of peace. "This nation has been prosper-
ous under *both* parties," he declared at the Illinois State Fair in August. "But this
nation has gone to war under the leaders of only *one* party."[41] These words made
little impact because Johnson's management of the recent Tonkin Gulf crisis, which
won widespread praise as a measured and effective response to the nation's escalating problems in Vietnam, helped to immunize him from Republican attacks on
his foreign policy.[42] According to the Goldwater campaign's internal analysis, the
trigger-happy image became "our greatest single liability," helping to explain slump-
ing support among Republican identifiers as well as the electorate as a whole. More
than one in four Republicans, for example, said that nuclear war was more likely
under their own candidate than Johnson.[43] Another internal poll indicated that
Goldwater's core concern on foreign policy, involving American weakness in the
Cold War, did not find a receptive audience; almost three out of four respondents
disagreed that U.S. defenses were weakening, and only 16 percent agreed.[44] As such,
Goldwater's misfortunes in 1964 confirm that individual candidacies consequen-
tially influenced voter evaluations with regard to foreign policy.

But explorations of public opinion during this period suggested that the foreign
policy advantage was a strength popularly associated with the Republican Party as a
whole, not simply with individual Republican politicians (as hinted at by Goldwater's campaign reference to the "party of peace"). According to polls, the Republican
Party often had the reputation as the party better able to maintain peace and more
skilled in running the Cold War.[45] Contemporary research on party identification
affirmed the persistence of the GOP's damaging Depression-era reputation for poor
economic management, but also discovered its widespread and profound association
as the party of peace.[46] When pollsters asked Americans for their views about the two
parties on issues of war and peace, pro-Republican or anti-Democratic comments
greatly outnumbered anti-Republican or pro-Democratic ones. In 1952, the proportion was more than seven to one, and in 1956 it was five times greater still.[47]

Such analysis intersected with the reality of political practice within the Republican Party; political practitioners were aware of this landscape of interparty
competition and its implications. When discussing plans for the 1956 campaign,
Eisenhower told Nixon that it was crucial to make the point that the Democrats
were the party of prosperity only because they were also the party of war—in other
words, Democratic administrations achieved economic growth by waging war.[48] As

outraged reaction to Dole's tarring of the Democrats as the war party two decades later showed, however, it was necessary to find a more indirect way to advance this incendiary claim. During the Eisenhower years, many Republicans promoted this "party of peace" identification (sometimes in contrast, nevertheless, with the "war party" charge) as the party's key claim to power in subpresidential as well as presidential contests.[49]

The persistence of the Republicans' foreign policy advantage suggests that dominant conceptualizations of twentieth-century electoral history are inadequate. These usually emphasize the existence of a New Deal order that ensured majority status for the Democrats and minority status for the Republicans. This understanding of electoral history necessarily relates the Republican revival that began in the late 1960s to the disintegration of the Democrats' New Deal coalition and to the decline of New Deal liberalism.[50] But this focus on the long-term implications of the New Deal for the party system often overlooks the impact of the Cold War on U.S. electoral politics during this period; the Cold War's impact was especially significant for the Republican Party, which in electoral terms tended to be the beneficiary of such discussions about foreign policy.

Although this Republican advantage emerged toward the start of the Cold War, it underwent an important transition during the Vietnam era and its aftermath. This transition took place for reasons of saliency, of divisions over principle, and of political calculation. First, and most obviously, the Vietnam War raised the importance of foreign policy for voters.[51] Second, it fractured the Cold War consensus, thereby widening partisan differences over foreign policy. Until then, interparty disagreements over the international struggle with communism generally involved policy detail rather than principle. The Republican advantage among voters did not reflect preference for their foreign policy ideas, which were hardly different from those of the Democrats. Instead, it was based on the popular perception that Republicans were more skilled in implementing these shared goals. Because the difference involved detail rather than principle, it was correspondingly less powerful in electoral terms, allowing individual candidacies such as John F. Kennedy's in 1960 and Lyndon B. Johnson's in 1964 to neutralize or even overwhelm the Republican advantage. Republican candidates for the presidency, by contrast, were never able to challenge the Democratic Party's bread-and-butter advantage of New Deal liberalism with similar success. In this area, partisan differences involved more than detail, and a majority of Americans did not prefer GOP ideas.

The controversies surrounding the Vietnam War were profound enough to challenge the Cold War consensus. When this debate moved from the antiwar movement to party politics, it took place within Democratic ranks; the Democratic Party experienced significant division between the supporters and the critics of the Cold War internationalist consensus. This contributed to the disaffection of the party's more conservative supporters and sometimes leading figures as well (such as Connally). It also enhanced Republican prospects of making gains among organized labor, white southerners, and other elements of the Democratic coalition—especially when Vietnam critic George McGovern secured the party's presidential nomination in 1972. The importance of these developments in fueling a Republican opportunity for gains at the polls demonstrates that the GOP revitalization of the 1960s and 1970s was at least partly a product of the Democratic Party's decline—its internal divisions and the incoherence of its electoral coalition.

But the final reason for the increased Republican foreign policy advantage was Richard Nixon's hard work in seeking electoral profit from the Democrats' problems. This strategy included positive initiatives to win more votes, exemplified by his attentiveness to the campaign dimension of the China and Moscow visits and his efforts to mobilize support for détente as the necessary next step in the Cold War to produce a "Generation of Peace." It also had a negative dimension that featured attack politics. In identifying patriotism as a key characteristic of his new majority, Nixon aimed to activate its electoral power by attacking his critics as unpatriotic. The president's reelection campaign attacked McGovern as dangerously radical, targeting in particular his views on foreign policy—especially his call for a swift end to the Vietnam War. Equating his proposals with "unconditional surrender," Secretary of Defense Melvin Laird called the Democratic candidate a "spokesman for the enemy," thus characterizing him as inadequately patriotic.[52] McGovern, by contrast, insisted that a swift end to the Vietnam War was a necessary consequence of patriotic concern.[53] It was, however, Senate minority leader Hugh Scott, Republican of Pennsylvania, who popularized perhaps the most famous attack on McGovern as the candidate of the "3 A's"—"acid, amnesty, and abortion."[54]

Reflecting on such rhetoric, journalist Sidney Blumenthal has written that "it was in the 1972 campaign that the social issue was melded with the national security issue."[55] This connection did not start with the attacks on McGovern, but dated back to the "silent majority" speech of November 1969. In this address, Nixon stressed patriotism as a rationale for support of his Vietnam policy and decried his opponents as counseling weakness. He said that "any hope the world has for the survival of peace and freedom will be determined by whether the American people have the moral stamina and the courage to meet the challenge of free world leadership."[56] The following April, to justify the extension of hostilities to Cambodia, he made a similar point still more bluntly. "If when the chips are down, the U.S. acts like a pitiful helpless giant, the forces of totalitarianism and anarchy will threaten free nations and free institutions throughout the world," he said.[57] Other administration officials were even more trenchant in their rhetoric. In a February 1972 television interview, chief of staff H. R. Haldeman said that Nixon's critics were "consciously aiding and abetting the enemy of the United States."[58] Vice President Spiro Agnew maintained a long-running series of attacks on Nixon's Vietnam opponents, reaching a concentrated height of vehemence during the 1970 midterms. "When a decision is required to keep America strong enough to encourage a peaceful world order, a little band of Senators can be counted upon to come down on the side of weakness," he said in one campaign address.[59]

Nixon's own contribution to campaign-time debate exemplified the transition. In 1968, he promised "peace with honor"; in 1972, he placed this pledge in contradistinction to his characterization of McGovern's policies as "peace with surrender." In his conceptualization of his new majority, Nixon blended the attributes of patriotism and antipermissiveness, as well as antielitism. During the 1972 campaign, he told aides that members of the new majority were "people who care about a strong United States, about patriotism, about moral and spiritual values."[60] Analysis of public opinion suggests that connections did exist between views on foreign policy and views on social issues. Those who took a more hawkish view on foreign policy were likely to be social conservatives; the more dovish were likelier to be social liberals.[61] By defining support for his foreign policy as patriotic—and opposition as unpatriotic—Nixon strengthened its electoral power.

The freshly controversial politics of foreign policy helped to build a new majority for Nixon in 1972. Nixon's new majority did not endure, however, as the 1976 presidential contest demonstrated. By then, Vietnam had ebbed away as an electoral concern. Lacking Nixon's zest for and experience in foreign policy, Gerald Ford also suffered from the disadvantage of being in office when détente faltered—when détente had apparently failed to deliver the "Generation of Peace" that Nixon had promised. It was also during the Ford administration that intraparty dissent about foreign policy became serious, culminating in an effective conservative challenge to the politics of détente. During the primary season, this challenge won a receptive audience among the party's supporters; it helped Ronald Reagan to come very close to triumph in his campaign against Ford for the Republicans' presidential nomination. "Under Messrs. Kissinger and Ford this nation has become Number Two in military power in a world where it is dangerous—if not fatal—to be second best," Reagan declared during the primary campaign. "All I can see is what other nations the world over see: collapse of the American will and the retreat of American power." He also seized on negotiations over the future of the Panama Canal Zone as a further opportunity to characterize Ford as weak.[62]

The constant attacks of his GOP challenger helped to dilute the foreign policy advantage that a Republican presidential incumbent could normally expect in the general election. Despite only recently emerging from political obscurity, Democratic candidate Jimmy Carter had higher foreign policy ratings than Ford at the start of the campaign. In the aftermath of Vietnam, Carter's emphasis on human rights in international relations seemed to offer a route to the positive reassertion of American values in global affairs.

When Bob Dole talked about "Democrat wars" during the vice presidential debate, the Ford campaign was involved in a serious effort to rescue the Republican advantage in foreign policy by stressing the president's experience as a statesman. Though not implying that Carter lacked patriotism, Ford commercials used an up-beat song that sought more positively, in the bicentennial year, to wrap the president's candidacy in the flag—"I'm feelin' good about America."[63] This strategy had some success. Internal polls suggested that by the end of the campaign, the GOP foreign policy advantage had returned, but only marginally, and of course not powerfully enough to save Ford from defeat.[64]

Even though the new majority campaign of 1972 had elevated foreign policy to a new degree of significance for Republican success, the near-disappearance of this advantage in 1976 suggested foreign policy's fragility in constructing the Republican revitalization. Of course, the uncertainties resulting from Watergate and the final collapse of South Vietnam in 1975 created an unusual context for electoral politics. Even so, the 1976 intraparty and interparty campaigns suggested that the GOP foreign policy advantage was volatile, because of its dependency on developments abroad. Foreign policy was much likelier to be salient and advantageous in the Vietnam-informed context of 1972 than the quieter conditions of 1976.

This did not mean, however, that foreign policy disappeared as a Republican advantage, or that the electoral association between foreign policy and patriotism pioneered by Nixon was defunct. As Dominic Sandbrook explores in his investigation of 1980's politics in Chapter 11, Ronald Reagan proved to be an especially skilled exponent of the promise that his candidacy would restore national greatness on the world stage as well as at home. Within the context of the international setbacks that America had suffered during the Carter presidency—in Afghanistan and Iran, most notably—this message found a receptive audience. Disappointments with Carter's foreign policy helped to fuel a rightward shift among voters in the late 1970s, in favor of U.S. power's reassertion in world affairs, which benefited Reagan in 1980.[65] This outlook was, in general, more manifest among male than female voters, thus constituting one of the elements that fostered the "gender gap," another characteristic of the Republican resurgence.[66] The emphasis on toughness meant that according to Gallup surveys, Republicans lost their traditional edge as the party of peace to the Democrats. (The party regained this label narrowly in 1984 and more decisively in 1988.)[67] Nevertheless, popular frustrations with Carter's record in foreign policy and dissatisfaction with his economic policy combined to benefit the GOP handsomely in 1980.[68]

The late 1970s also saw an effort to harness the foreign policy advantage at the congressional level. The Panama Canal Zone's future—a question exploited so successfully by Reagan in his 1976 challenge to Ford—remained the subject of intra-GOP disagreement between moderates and conservatives during Carter's presidency. Those who opposed any transfer of sovereignty to Panama framed the issue as involving patriotism, national strength, and American greatness. The New Right had been gaining in influence both within and beyond the Republican Party since the mid-1970s, and seized on the issue to boost its political forces.[69] The emergence of such organized activism elevated the potential significance of foreign policy in congressional contests, even with regard to issues of secondary importance, when they roused particular passions.[70] In 1978, congressional supporters of the Canal Zone treaties often faced noisy, well-funded New Right opposition in primaries as well as general elections. The impact of this campaign, however, was far less significant than its orchestrators claimed. The Panama Canal treaties only became a key issue in Gordon Humphrey's 1978 defeat of Senator Tom McIntyre in New Hampshire and John P. East's 1980 defeat of Senator Robert B. Morgan in North Carolina—in both cases a Republican gain. Their lack of significance in other races broadly confirmed the limited direct importance of foreign policy in Senate and House races.[71] As Sean P. Cunningham's analysis of Texas politics in Chapter 6 shows, subpresidential Republicans did not neglect the politics of patriotism in seeking to construct a productive electoral distinction from their Democratic rivals. In most cases, however, incumbency and economic indicators were more important in shaping election outcomes.

This does not consign the New Right's Panama Canal campaign to irrelevance. Its success in using the issue to organize and fundraise in support of conservative candidates provides evidence of the foreign policy advantage's indirect role in helping congressional Republicans. Ample funding assisted the Republicans' House advance and Senate takeover in 1980, as did the climate of party unity. In both cases, opposition to Carter's record in foreign policy was important, though so, too, were the continuing economic problems of stagflation.[72] But the conditions that fostered the 1980 surge did not endure, and—even in this indirect form—the significance of the foreign policy advantage retreated at the congressional level.[73]

Foreign policy therefore helps to explain the Republican Party's electoral revitalization in the late 1960s and 1970s. Richard Nixon was especially successful in making Cold War internationalism an active, significant issue of advantage. Forged in the context of Vietnam and presented within the rationale of patriotism, this defense of America's role overseas made an important contribution to his effort to mobilize a new majority. This was by no means the only issue that Nixon used to build his majority, but it formed a larger role in his design of electoral strategy than is often assumed. The limitations of foreign policy's electoral power, however, are as notable as its strengths. First, though often significant in contests for the presidency, it was less important in congressional races and far less so in state and local elections. Second, its salience was related to geopolitical developments. Whereas an international crisis could assist Republicans in exploiting the foreign policy advantage, quieter conditions were likely to reduce its electoral significance. Third, the Republican focus on patriotic toughness alienated some voters even while it attracted others—especially visible in the phenomenon of the gender gap. For these reasons, an understanding of foreign policy's role in fueling the GOP resurgence of the 1970s helps to explain not only Republican success in seeking a new majority but also the limits of the party's revitalization at the polls.

NOTES

For their helpful comments in response to earlier drafts of this chapter, I would like to thank Pertti Ahonen, Fabian Hilfrich, this book's anonymous readers, and the participants in the 2009 London-Edinburgh conference on the Republican Party during the 1960s and the 1970s.

1. Jules Witcover, *Marathon: The Pursuit of the Presidency, 1972–1976* (New York: Viking, 1977), 614.
2. For a strong analysis of the party's approach to foreign policy during this period, see Colin Dueck, *Hard Line: The Republican Party and U.S. Foreign Policy since World War II* (Princeton, NJ: Princeton University Press, 2010). On Republicans and Vietnam, a valuable investigation is offered by Andrew L. Johns, *Vietnam's Second Front: Domestic Politics, the Republican Party, and the War* (Lexington: University Press of Kentucky, 2010).
3. Richard Nixon, memorandum to H. R. Haldeman, March 2, 1970, Box 2, White House Special Files—Staff Member and Office Files (hereafter WHSF-SMOF): President's Personal Files, Nixon Presidential Library and Museum, Yorba Linda, CA.
4. Richard M. Scammon and Ben J. Wattenberg, *The Real Majority* (New York: Coward-McCann, 1970).
5. Robert Mason, *Richard Nixon and the Quest for a New Majority* (Chapel Hill: University of North Carolina Press, 2004), 77–112.
6. Patrick J. Buchanan, memorandum to Ronald Ziegler, January 29, 1971, Box 1, WHSF-SMOF: Patrick J. Buchanan.
7. Ray Price and Noel Koch, "Congressional Breakfast," January 27, 1971, Box 84, WHSF-SMOF: President's Office Files.
8. Patrick J. Buchanan and Kenneth Khachigian, memorandum to H. R. Haldeman, June 18, 1972, Box 299, WHSF-SMOF: H. R. Haldeman.
9. Dominic Sandbrook, "Salesmanship and Substance: The Influence of Domestic Policy and Watergate," in *Nixon in the World: American Foreign Relations, 1969–1977*, ed. Frederik Logevall and Andrew Preston (New York: Oxford University Press, 2008), 88.
10. William P. Bundy, *A Tangled Web: The Making of Foreign Policy in the Nixon Presidency* (New York: Hill and Wang, 1998), 240–41, 331–32.
11. H. R. Haldeman, *The Haldeman Diaries: Inside the Nixon White House*, complete multimedia ed. (Santa Monica, CA: Sony Imagesoft, 1994), entry for October 12, 1971.
12. Haldeman, *Haldeman Diaries*, May 27, 1972.
13. Sandbrook, "Salesmanship and Substance," 94.
14. Mason, *New Majority*, 137–39.
15. Herbert S. Parmet, *The Democrats: The Years after FDR* (1976; New York: Oxford University Press, 1977), 300–4.
16. Richard Nixon, *Public Papers of the Presidents of the United States: Richard Nixon, 1972* (Washington, DC: U.S. Government Printing Office, 1974), 1138–39.
17. Robert Teeter, memorandum to H. R. Haldeman, August 15, 1972, Box 1, Robert M. Teeter Papers, Gerald R. Ford Presidential Library, Ann Arbor, MI.
18. Frederick T. Steeper and Robert M. Teeter, "Comment on 'A Majority Party in Disarray,'" *American Political Science Review* 70 (1976): 806–13.

19. Ernest R. May and Janet Fraser, eds., *Campaign '72: The Managers Speak* (Cambridge, MA: Harvard University Press, 1973), 229–30.

20. Kathleen Hall Jamieson, *Packaging the Presidency: A History and Criticism of Presidential Campaign Advertising*, 2nd ed. (New York: Oxford University Press, 1992), 304–5; Michael Barone, *Our Country: The Shaping of America from Roosevelt to Reagan* (New York: Free Press, 1990), 507; and Mason, *New Majority*, 184–85.

21. Everett Carll Ladd Jr. and Charles D. Hadley, *Transformations of the American Party System: Political Coalitions from the New Deal to the 1970s*, 2nd ed. (New York: Norton, 1978), 169–71; John Kenneth White, *Still Seeing Red: How the Cold War Shapes the New American Politics*, updated and expanded ed. (1997; Boulder, CO: Westview, 1998), 132–37.

22. Charles W. Colson, memorandum to H. R. Haldeman, July 28, 1970, Box 61, WHSF-SMOF: H. R. Haldeman.

23. Raymond Price, *With Nixon* (New York: Viking, 1977), 120–22; Haldeman, *Haldeman Diaries*, October 14, 1972. In fact, southern opinion on the Cold War sometimes edged toward a unilateralism out of step with Nixon. Charles O. Lerche, *The Uncertain South: Its Changing Patterns of Politics in Foreign Policy* (Chicago: Quadrangle, 1964). Still, it was the South's support for the Cold War and its emphasis on a patriotic rationale for such support that were important for Nixon.

24. Haldeman, *Haldeman Diaries*, December 19, 1970. For a discussion of connections between patriotism and labor, see Haldeman, *Haldeman Diaries*, July 21, 1971.

25. Mason, *New Majority*, 173–74.

26. Robert Mason, "'I Was Going to Build a New Republican Party and a New Majority': Richard Nixon as Party Leader, 1969–73," *Journal of American Studies* 39 (2005): 478–81.

27. Byron E. Shafer, "The Notion of an Electoral Order: The Structure of Electoral Politics at the Accession of George Bush," in *The End of Realignment? Interpreting American Electoral Eras*, ed. Byron E. Shafer (Madison: University of Wisconsin Press, 1991), 37–84. See also White, *Still Seeing Red*, 144–47, 195.

28. Stephen Hess, "Foreign Policy and Presidential Campaigns," *Foreign Policy* 8 (Autumn 1972): 3.

29. Samuel Lubell, *Revolt of the Moderates* (New York: Harper, 1956), 37–43.

30. Elmo Roper reported at the start of September that "international affairs and foreign relations" were more important to 49.0 percent and "domestic affairs" to 29.8 percent. RNC Research Division, "Summary of Chief Political Polls: Week Ending Sept 5, 1948," September 7, 1948, in *Papers of the Republican Party*, part 2: *Reports and Memoranda of the Research Division of the Headquarters of the Republican National Committee, 1938–1980*, ed. Paul L. Kesaris (Frederick, MD: University Publications of America, 1986), Reel 1. On the Republican advantage in foreign policy and Dewey's failure to exploit this potential advantage, see Robert A. Divine, *Foreign Policy and U.S. Presidential Elections, 1940–1948* (New York: New Viewpoints, 1974), 200–201, 206–8, 223–26, 245–47; and H. Bradford Westerfield, *Foreign Policy and Party Politics: Pearl Harbor to Korea* (New Haven, CT: Yale University Press, 1955), 296–324.

31. John H. Aldrich, John L. Sullivan, and Eugene Borgida, "Foreign Affairs and Issue Voting: Do Presidential Candidates 'Waltz before a Blind Audience?,'" *American Political Science Review* 83 (1989): 123–41.

32. Ole R. Hosti, *Public Opinion and American Foreign Policy* (Ann Arbor: University of Michigan Press, 1996), 31, 55, 133–34, 187–88.

33. Malcolm E. Jewell, *Senatorial Politics and Foreign Policy* ([Lexington:] University Press of Kentucky, 1962), 193–96.

34. David Greenberg, "Nixon as Statesman: The Failed Campaign," in Logevall and Preston, *Nixon and the World*, 49–51.

35. Robert Mason, *The Republican Party and American Politics from Hoover to Reagan* (New York: Cambridge University Press, 2012), 176–80, 210.

36. "Missile Gap Bared as Democratic Campaign Fraud," *Battle Line* (Republican National Committee newsletter), February 8, 1961; "Missile Gap, Missile Gap, Who Has the Missile Gap?," *Battle Line*, February 9, 1961; and "Missile Gap: Fourth Version Filed," *Battle Line*, February 20, 1961.

37. Philip E. Converse, Aage R. Clausen, and Warren E. Miller, "Electoral Myth and Reality: The 1964 Election," *American Political Science Review* 59 (1965): 331–32; Leon D. Epstein and Austin Ranney, "Who Voted for Goldwater: The Wisconsin Case," *Political Science Quarterly* 81 (1966): 87–88.

38. Barry Goldwater, speech, March 19, 1964, Box W3, Barry Goldwater Papers, Arizona Historical Foundation, Arizona State University, Tempe, AZ; William B. Prendergast, "Summary of Discussion on Defense Policy," April 9, 1964, Box W7, Goldwater Papers; and William B. Prendergast, "Summary of Discussion of Foreign Policy," April 20, 1964, Box W7, Goldwater Papers.

39. Robert Alan Goldberg, *Barry Goldwater* (New Haven, CT: Yale University Press, 1995), 140–42.

40. Ibid., 183–92, 225–26.

41. Barry Goldwater, speech, August 19, 1964, Box W5, Goldwater Papers.

42. Robert David Johnson, *All the Way with LBJ: The 1964 Presidential Election* (New York: Cambridge University Press, 2009), 156–57, 230–31; Rick Perlstein, *Before the Storm: Barry Goldwater and the Unmaking of the American Consensus* (New York: Hill and Wang, 2001), 400.

43. "Strategy analysis of campaign survey," unsigned, n.d., Box 4, Goldwater Papers.

44. "October 5 campaign survey," unsigned, [1964,] Box 8, Goldwater Papers.

45. White, *Still Seeing Red*, 107–50.

46. Angus Campbell, Philip E. Converse, Warren E. Miller, and Donald E. Stokes, *The American Voter* (New York: Wiley, 1960), 48–50, 198–99.

47. Donald E. Stokes, Angus Campbell, and Warren E. Miller, "Components of Electoral Decision," *American Political Science Review* 52 (1958): 375.

48. Richard Nixon, notes, September 12, 1956, PPS 324.92, Vice Presidential Collection, Nixon Presidential Library and Museum.

49. Marquis Childs, "Washington Calling," *Ocala* (FL) *Star-Banner*, November 24, 1954; and Childs, "Republican Strategists to Pitch Campaign on 'Peace,'" *Florence* (AL) *Times*, April 1, 1958.

50. Some examples of important works that consider political parties and electoral politics during this period almost purely in terms of New Deal liberalism, to the exclusion of Cold War internationalism, are Ladd and Hadley, *Transformations of the American Party System*; and James L. Sundquist, *Dynamics of the Party System: Alignment and Realignment of Political Parties in the United States*, rev. ed. (Washington, DC: Brookings Institution, 1983). According to Stephen Hess and Michael Nelson, by contrast, during this period foreign policy was often "dominant" in presidential campaigns but rarely "decisive"; only in 1952, 1972, and 1980 did foreign policy become more important. Stephen Hess and Michael Nelson, "Foreign Policy: Dominance and

Decisiveness in Presidential Elections," in *The Elections of 1984*, ed. Michael Nelson (Washington, DC: CQ Press, 1985), 129–54.

51. Byron E. Shafer and William J. M. Claggett, *The Two Majorities: The Issue Context of Modern American Politics* (Baltimore: Johns Hopkins University Press, 1995), 13.

52. Mason, *New Majority*, 184.

53. Bruce Miroff, *The Liberals' Moment: The McGovern Insurgency and the Identity Crisis of the Democratic Party* (Lawrence: University Press of Kansas, 2007), 109.

54. Miroff, *Liberals' Moment*, 121. This tag was not a Republican invention; one of McGovern's Democratic rivals, Hubert Humphrey, coined it during the primary season, an indication of the significance of the party's divisions.

55. Sidney Blumenthal, *Pledging Allegiance: The Last Campaign of the Cold War* (1990; New York: HarperPerennial, 1991), 114.

56. William Safire, *Before the Fall: An Inside View of the Pre-Watergate White House* (Garden City, NY: Doubleday, 1975), 175.

57. Ibid., 187.

58. Haldeman quoted in James Reston, "White House Tries to Blitz Critics," *Modesto* (CA) *Bee*, February 9, 1972.

59. John R. Coyne Jr., *The Impudent Snobs: Agnew vs. the Intellectual Establishment* (New Rochelle, NY: Arlington House, 1972), 380.

60. Raymond Price, *With Nixon* (New York: Viking, 1977), 121.

61. Shafer and Claggett, *Two Majorities*.

62. Reagan quoted in Mason, *New Majority*, 221–22; and Adam Clymer, *Drawing the Line at the Big Ditch: The Panama Canal Treaties and the Rise of the Right* (Lawrence: University Press of Kansas, 2008), 19–39.

63. Jamieson, *Packaging the Presidency*, 369.

64. Martin Schram, *Running for President 1976: The Carter Campaign* (New York: Stein and Day, 1977), 269–70, 367.

65. William G. Mayer, *The Changing American Mind: How and Why American Public Opinion Changed between 1960 and 1988* (Ann Arbor: University of Michigan Press, 1992), 45–73.

66. Martin Gilens, "Gender and Support for Reagan: A Comprehensive Model of Presidential Approval," *American Journal of Political Science* 32 (1988): 19–49.

67. Nelson W. Polsby and Aaron Wildavsky, *Presidential Elections: Contemporary Strategies of American Electoral Politics*, 8th ed. (New York: Free Press, 1991), 234–35.

68. Miroslav Nincic and Barbara Hinckley, "Foreign Policy and the Evaluation of Presidential Candidates," *Journal of Conflict Resolution* 35 (1991): 345–47; and Everett Carll Ladd Jr., "The Brittle Mandate: Electoral Dealignment and the 1980 Presidential Election," *Political Science Quarterly* 96 (1981): 23–24. On the significance of foreign policy to voter evaluations of the Republican Party since 1980, see Shana Kushner Gadarian, "Foreign Policy at the Ballot Box: How Citizens Use Foreign Policy to Judge and Choose Candidates," *Journal of Politics* 72 (2010): 1046–62.

69. Godfrey Hodgson, *The World Turned Right Side Up: A History of the Conservative Ascendancy in America* (Boston: Houghton Mifflin, 1996), 225–30.

70. Charles W. Whalen Jr., *The House and Foreign Policy: The Irony of Congressional Reform* (Chapel Hill: University of North Carolina Press, 1982), 129–49.

71. Clymer, *Drawing the Line*, 106–29, 140–96.

72. Neil MacNeil, "The New Conservative House of Representatives," in *A Tide of Discontent: The 1980 Elections and Their Meaning*, ed. Ellis Sandoz and Cecil V. Crabb

Jr. (Washington, DC: CQ Press, 1981), 65–87; and Charles O. Jones, "The New, New Senate," in Sandoz and Crabb, *Tide of Discontent*, 89–111.

73. John A. Ferejohn and Morris P. Fiorina, "Incumbency and Realignment in Congressional Elections," in *The New Direction in American Politics*, ed. John E. Chubb and Paul E. Peterson (Washington, DC: Brookings Institution, 1985), 91–115; Albert R. Hunt, "National Politics and the 1982 Campaign," in *The American Elections of 1982*, ed. Thomas E. Mann and Norman J. Ornstein (Washington, DC: American Enterprise Institute, 1983), 1–43; and Norman J. Ornstein, "The Elections for Congress," in *The American Elections of 1984*, ed. Austin Ranney (Durham, NC: Duke University Press, 1985), 245–76.

CHAPTER 10

Taxation as a Republican Issue
in the Era of Stagflation

Iwan Morgan

In 2004, when George W. Bush's presidency was in full tax-cutting pomp, Stephen Moore—conservative activist and head of the Washington-based Club for Growth—remarked on the transformation of the GOP since the early 1960s. "It has evolved over the past forty years," he declared, "from being a party of Eisenhower balanced-budget Republicans into a party of Reaganite pro-growth advocates."[1] The second half of the 1970s was the critical era in this metamorphosis, and commitment to tax reduction as the prescription for economic growth was the catalyst for change. This essay considers that development in relationship to the Republican quest for a new majority. Its argument is twofold. First, tax reduction was significant in the Republican revival of the late 1970s as a party-defining issue. In essence, it became an agency of party unity, provided the party with a positive alternative to Democratic statism, and aligned the party with new economic ideas that were challenging the intellectual hegemony of Keynesianism. Nevertheless, this chapter also contends that the public did not embrace reduction of federal taxes as the panacea for the economic ills of the 1970s as readily as did the Republicans. Despite the GOP's electoral success in 1980, its new dedication to across-the-board tax cuts did not become a big vote-winner for the party until the mid-1980s.

Republicans had long called for tax reduction before the late 1970s, of course, but had rarely justified this primarily in terms of the benefits for economic growth. In their eyes, the foremost purpose of tax reduction in the post-1945 era was to rein in the expansion of federal expenditure that was underwritten by the broad-based income tax system created in World War II. In fiscal year (FY) 1940, federal income taxes, including corporate taxes, constituted only 16 percent of tax receipts collected by all levels of government, but they amounted to 51 percent ten years later. The bountiful revenues delivered by the new tax regime amid peacetime prosperity provided the wherewithal to fund federal spending that was vastly in excess of New Deal–era expenditure. In FY 1940, outlays and receipts respectively amounted to $9.5 billion (9.8 percent of gross domestic product [GDP]) and $6.5 billion (6.8

percent GDP), but the corollary figures in FY 1960 were $92.2 billion and $92.5 billion (both 17.8 percent GDP).[2]

GOP leaders in the Republican-controlled 80th Congress of 1947–1948 certainly extolled the Revenue Act of 1948, the party's principal tax-cutting success between the end of World War II and the Economic Recovery Tax Act of 1981, as necessary to create incentives and spur production in the postwar economy. Nevertheless, its expected benefits in constraining the growth of government held the main appeal for them. As Congressman Harold Knutson of Minnesota, chair of the Ways and Means Committee, affirmed, "For years we Republicans have been warning that the short-haired women and long-haired men of alien minds in the administrative branch of government were trying to wreck the American way of life and install a hybrid oligarchy in Washington through confiscatory taxation." In like vein, Senate majority leader Robert Taft of Ohio responded to Harry Truman's opposition to the bill: "The president's real reason for retaining the taxes is to have more money to spend. The best reason to reduce taxes is to reduce our ideas of the number of dollars the government can properly spend in a year."[3] Just over a decade later, Arizona senator Barry Goldwater's best-selling book, *The Conscience of a Conservative*, included a chapter entitled "Taxes and Spending." Far from justifying federal income tax cuts as an economic stimulant, however, the future GOP presidential candidate asserted the need for them in terms of safeguarding personal liberty from the confiscatory taxation levied to pay for excessive government spending.[4]

Significantly, the GOP had promoted tax reduction in 1947–1948 when the federal budget was operating at a surplus, and Goldwater's book appeared when surpluses were not the endangered species that they would soon become. For many Republicans, however, elimination of deficits took precedence over tax reduction in the quarter-century after World War II. Dwight D. Eisenhower's horror of unbalanced budgets as a source of inflation was widely—if not universally—shared by Republicans. In 1959, Ike had enjoyed a post–Modern Republican rapprochement with the GOP Right in energizing the bipartisan conservative coalition in Congress to support his opposition to the ambitious spending programs sought by the congressional Democrats in the wake of their recent midterm election success. Less to conservative liking was the president's insistence in 1960 on investing the projected FY 1961 surplus in debt reduction for fear that cutting taxes would fuel inflation.[5] In September 1963, however, a majority of House Republicans voted against the Kennedy tax cut bill out of concern that it would enlarge the budget deficit currently being operated. The GOP contingent voted 126–48 against the bill, while only twenty-six Democrats (all but three of them southerners) were nays. Republican senators were more supportive of the measure when the upper chamber considered it in early 1964, but deficit concerns still prompted a third of them (ten nays and twenty-one ayes) to vote against it.[6]

Significantly, the main GOP advocate of pro-growth policies in the late 1950s and early 1960s was Governor Nelson Rockefeller of New York, a liberal Republican whose limited following in the party ensured that his ambition to run for the 1960 presidential nomination was stillborn. Drawing on a Rockefeller Brothers Panel report, he promoted the view that tax reduction and increased spending on defense and domestic investment programs for education, urban renewal, highways, and the like would boost economic growth rates.[7]

Richard Nixon had also promoted himself as a growth candidate for president in 1960. In an effort to distance himself from Eisenhower's fiscal conservatism, the vice president had sounded very much like a supply-sider long before the term was invented. To boost the economy out of recession in 1958, he had publicly advocated reduction of corporation and high-earner personal income taxes to spur investment and business revival. The expansionary effects, he declared in a speech at Harvard in September 1958, "would lead to more rather than less [federal] revenue." The idea that incentive-boosting tax reduction would "lift the ceiling over personal opportunity" was also a key theme of Nixon's major economic policy address in the presidential election campaign, delivered at New York University on October 20, 1960. Unfortunately for the Republican candidate, the onset of a mild recession shortly before the election—the result of Eisenhower's deficit-conscious refusal to boost recovery from the previous downturn with a strong dose of fiscal stimulus—undercut his claims to be the champion of economic growth.[8]

Nixon himself lacked the ideological conviction to champion pro-growth tax reduction when he eventually became president amid conditions of rising inflation. Seeking revenues to balance his first budget as a way to demonstrate commitment to price stability, he secured a six-month extension of Lyndon B. Johnson's 1968 tax surcharge and got involved in a dogfight with congressional Democrats over the tax relief provisions that they wrote into the 1969 tax reform bill. So great was Nixon's determination to achieve a balanced budget that he seriously considered repealing Kennedy's 1962 investment credit. In contrast to his stand in the 1958 recession, the president also held back from proposing tax cuts as an economic stimulant during the downturn of 1970 out of concern that these could not be reversed with the advent of recovery. Accordingly, the administration's expansionary fiscal measures focused on the expenditure rather than the revenue side of the budget.[9]

Both Nixon and his successor, Gerald Ford, failed to establish a distinctively Republican economics because of their various U-turns when faced with the conundrum of stagflation. Typifying this, one of Ford's first acts as president was to call for a tax surcharge to counter consumer price inflation, which was heading toward an annual rate of 11 percent in 1974, but he shifted ground to propose an antirecession tax reduction funded from spending cuts in 1975. Concern about the effect of a growing budget imbalance on rising prices remained a preoccupation both for the administration and for Republican congressional leaders, however. When asked by House Minority Leader John J. Rhodes of Arizona at a White House legislative leaders meeting what would happen if taxes were cut without expenditure savings, Council of Economic Advisers (CEA) chairman Alan Greenspan re-

sponded, "Severe problems. . . . This type of budget deficit will bring chaotic infla-
tion." Speaking for many of his GOP colleagues, Rhodes commented in response,
"How can we bring revenue into line with expenditures when we are cutting taxes?
That will be hard to sell."[10]

When seeking reelection in 1976, Ford did promise a modest tax cut for
middle-income families to highlight differences with Jimmy Carter, who had only
promised not to raise taxes. He did not give this much emphasis in the campaign,
however, for fear that consumers would anticipate rising inflation from a growing
deficit. The Ford White House also ensured that the Republican platform committee resisted calls for the inclusion of the Jobs Creation bill, a pro-growth measure
promoted by Representative Jack Kemp of New York to enhance capital formation
through tax incentives for business and high earners, in the party's 1976 platform.
Disillusioned with Republican resistance to tax-cutting in the name of budget-
balancing, Kemp later commented, "I have come to realize that the real enemy is
my own party. . . . We're the ones who have said to the people, 'Don't come to our
table for dinner. All we're going to do is tighten your belt.'"[11]

In 1980, by contrast, the Republican presidential candidate and the congressional party stood united in support of tax cuts as their common economic priority
at a time of growing deficits. A long-standing campaigner for lower taxes, Ronald
Reagan had endorsed the so-called Kemp-Roth bill, a supply-side pro-growth measure proposing a 30 percent across-the-board cut in income taxes in three annual
installments of 10 percent, which already had substantial support among congressional Republicans. This was part of a deal struck early in his campaign—for Jack
Kemp to support Reagan's candidacy instead of running for president himself. Reagan's putative rival had virtually no chance of winning the nomination because he
lacked funds, organization, and widespread name recognition. Nevertheless, Reagan aides feared that Kemp could still damage their boss by drawing votes from
the conservative base.[12] As well as shoring up his right flank, the GOP presidential
front-runner's approval of the congressional GOP initiative marked the evolution
of his personal crusade for tax reduction into the paramount cause of the Republican Party.

Reagan's prepresidential dedication to tax reduction has been the subject of
considerable historical analysis in relationship to his conservative ideology.[13] The
economic justification for this took center stage in his thinking only in the second
half of the 1970s. As California governor from 1967 to 1975, Reagan had justified
tax reduction in traditional Republican terms of denying fiscal oxygen to big government. Typifying this, he avowed in a 1973 message to the state assembly that the
taxpayer had "become a pawn in a deadly game of government monopoly whose
only purpose is to serve the confiscatory appetites of runaway government spending."[14] Later that same year, he promoted an unsuccessful ballot initiative, Proposition 1, to limit California taxes to a fixed percentage of total personal income. Cur-

tailing "government's allowance," he declared, was "the only way we will ever bring government spending under control."[15]

The shift of his ambition toward the presidency amid the nation's worsening economic problems impelled Reagan to lace his advocacy of tax cuts with a pro-growth rationale. In an October 1977 radio address, for example, he asserted that enactment of Kemp-Roth "would reduce the deficit which causes inflation because the tax base would be *broadened* by increased prosperity." While Reagan continued to link tax reduction to smaller government, the growth benefits received increasing emphasis in his 1980 campaign rhetoric as the Republicans targeted stagflation-weary voters. To this end, his major election address on economic policy was entitled "A Strategy for Growth: The American Economy in the 1980s." As Republican National Committee chair William Brock later testified with regard to the 1980 campaign, "The basic aim of the policy we were trying to implement was to restore growth."[16]

The congressional GOP's parallel journey in the same cause is less well known than Reagan's anti-tax odyssey. The conventional narrative, which is largely the work of those claiming the credit, presents this as a three-stage process. First, supply-side ideas were developed in academia, notably by Robert Mundell of Columbia University and later in more high-profile fashion by Arthur Laffer of the University of Southern California. Rejecting the aggregative demand–orientation of Keynesianism, these scholars contended that tax reduction would enhance the incentive of individuals to save, invest, and work harder by allowing them to keep more of the wealth they created. Their ideas were then popularized by Jude Wanniski and championed by Robert Bartley, respectively columnist and editor of the *Wall Street Journal.* Finally, these media policy entrepreneurs found their congressional policy promoter in Jack Kemp, the former Buffalo Bills quarterback who had represented a suburban Buffalo district since 1971.[17]

In reality, supply-side doctrine's permeation through congressional Republican ranks was more complex than this story allows. Laffer, Wanniski, and Kemp all had important roles, of course, but others played equally significant if underrecognized parts. Indeed, it could be argued that this stellar trio was not always helpful to the cause. The Laffer curve theory that low tax rates would produce a reflow of revenue to government allowed critics of supply-side to focus attention on its consequences for the deficit rather than economic growth. Wanniski's excessive championing of the relatively junior Kemp as the supply-side hero and Kemp's eager embrace of this mantle ruffled many feathers in the congressional GOP. Particularly objectionable was Wanniski's *Wall Street Journal* editorial "JFK Strikes Again," which presented Kemp as a bold and visionary advocate of tax reduction in the mold of John F. Kennedy, whose initials he shared.[18]

A confluence of factors promoted the transformation of the congressional GOP into a pro-growth tax-cutting party in the late 1970s. Without doubt, the incidence of stagflation made it receptive to the new thinking that a host of supply-siders were producing on the economy. The inability of conventional Keynesian prescriptions to work their magic against the combination of stagnation and inflation legitimized the long-standing belief of conservative Republicans that these were just a recipe for ruinous big spending by government. However, the availability of new ideas gave them something to be for rather than merely against.[19]

It was through the legislature's labyrinthine staff system that the novel doctrines gained support within the congressional GOP. If there was an unsung hero in the process of transformation, it was Paul Craig Roberts, someone not even mentioned by Jack Kemp in his own supply-side tract, *An American Renaissance: A Strategy for the 1980s* (written with Wanniski's assistance). Born in Atlanta in 1939, Roberts was a trained economist with a PhD from the University of Virginia, one of the few citadels of conservative economics in the era of Keynesian ascendancy within the profession. He had been a senior fellow at Stanford University's Hoover Institution in the early 1970s and then an associate editor of the *Wall Street Journal* before joining Kemp's staff in 1975.

Roberts was instrumental in fashioning Kemp's job creation bill with the aid of economics consultant Norman Ture, for whom he obtained a Business Roundtable grant to develop an econometrics model demonstrating the supply benefits of business tax reduction.[20] Both these economists would later serve as assistant secretaries of the treasury in the Reagan administration and both would resign in the spring of 1982 in disagreement with the White House's acceptance of a tax increase to control the burgeoning deficit. Roberts was also the principal drafter of what became known as the Kemp-Roth tax reduction bill. Analysis of the econometric benefits of the business-oriented tax cuts in the job creation bill convinced him that a broader-based tax reduction would have even greater consequences for economic growth. Equally important, a committed partisan, he feared that a solely business-oriented measure would not "open up any new political ground to the Republicans."[21]

In late 1976, Roberts left Kemp's staff to become aide to the minority Republicans on the recently created House Budget Committee, a position that gave him greater strategic influence in shaping congressional party thinking. Once the House Budget Committee Republicans had become attuned to supply-side thinking, he took up another new post as aide to Senator Orrin Hatch of Utah, a member of both the Senate Budget Committee and the Joint Economic Committee (JEC). The contacts he made in these various positions put Roberts at the center of the developing network of like-minded GOP aides who proved useful in spreading the supply-side message to their bosses, particularly Steve Entin of the JEC.[22] In addition, his academic pedigree allowed him to recruit a host of conservative professional economists to testify before congressional committees in opposition to the Keynesian luminaries who had hitherto had a virtually free run. It also enabled him to pen rebuttals to the efforts of Keynesian economists like former Kennedy-

Johnson CEA chair Walter Heller and critical conservative economists like former Nixon CEA chair Herbert Stein to rubbish the new doctrine in the print media.[23]

It took more than ideas and individuals to persuade the congressional Republicans to set aside their hang-up about the deficit, however. Fiscal realities and partisan calculation were essential to this particular transformation. The budget was only in balance once between FY 1960 and FY 1980. With the exception of the peak Vietnam-War deficit in FY 1968, fiscal imbalances had been small in the 1960s. In the second half of the 1970s, despite withdrawal from Vietnam and recovery from the 1974–1975 recession, deficits were routinely at a level (percentage of GDP) that had been deemed exceptional in the quarter-century after World War II. In Republican estimation, the root cause of these unbalanced budgets was federal spending on domestic programs. The shift that had taken place in the composition of the budget added grist to their case. Total outlays in FY 1977–FY 1979 averaged the same in GDP terms as in FY 1968, even though defense spending now constituted only half of its FY 1968 level of 9.4 percent GDP.[24]

This development facilitated the GOP embrace of tax reduction in two ways. First, Democratic accusations that cutting taxes would enlarge the deficit struck Republicans as a hypocritical defense of opposition expenditure priorities that had caused the deficit in the first place. This did much to move their focus away from the deficit to the component elements of the budget. Few Republicans were as willing to downplay the significance of fiscal responsibility as Kemp, who famously declared in 1981 that the GOP "no longer worships at the altar of a balanced budget." It was likely, however, that many Republicans would have agreed in retrospect with remarks made by Jude Wanniski in 1976: "The political tension in the marketplace of ideas must be between tax reduction and spending increases, and as long as Republicans have insisted on balanced budgets, their interests as a party have shriveled, and budgets have been imbalanced."[25]

In addition, the view that total government spending did far more than the deficit level to generate stagflation gained increasing legitimacy within the congressional GOP. Free-enterprise champion Milton Friedman, who was particularly influential in party circles, offered considerable reassurance on this score. "I would far rather have total spending at $200 billion with a deficit of $100 billion," he asserted, "than a balanced budget of $500 billion." A host of other conservative economists delivered a similar message in congressional testimony in a variety of hearings on Kemp-Roth. Speaking before the House Ways and Means committee, former Nixon CEA chair Paul McCracken declared that the "primary case" for the measure "is a growing conviction that Government has been allocating too much of the national income to itself, and that the time has come to change this."[26]

House Republicans were particularly angry at the growth of expenditure-led deficits. Many had voted in defiance of Richard Nixon to establish the new congressional budget process mandated by the Congressional Budget and Impoundment Control Act of 1974 in the belief that this would control spending. In their view, budget reform had instead become a smokescreen to permit the congressional majority to push spending ever higher. Adding to their resentment, Democrat Alice Rivlin, the first director of the nonpartisan Congressional Budget Office created by the 1974 legislation as a counterweight to the executive's Office of Management and Budget (OMB), admitted that there were no Republican economists on its staff but claimed in justification that she could not find any. House Budget Committee Republicans took further offense at her adamant refusal to consider the possibility that taxes had any effect on work effort, saving, and investment.[27]

The final straw for House Republicans was the Democratic decision, in defiance of the new budget rules, to seek a third budget resolution in early 1977 as a way of authorizing new president Jimmy Carter's economic stimulus initiatives in the current fiscal year. This proposed to raise the FY 1977 deficit from $50 billion as initially forecast to $70 billion. Abetted by Roberts, however, Budget Committee members John Rousselot of California and Marjorie Holt of Maryland proposed a minority budget resolution for the first time in response to this breach of procedural orthodoxy. Instead of Carter's $50 tax rebate, the GOP initiative advocated a permanent 5 percent across-the-board marginal tax cut. Rousselot justified this in pure supply-side terms: "The purpose of a permanent tax reduction is to reduce the tax bias against work, saving and investment." Equally significantly, he claimed that the permanent tax cut would expand the projected deficit by less than $8 billion, compared to $20 billion for the Carter program, because its expansionary benefits for the economy would recoup much of the revenue cost.[28]

Although the Rousselot-Holt initiative had no chance of enactment, it generated almost unanimous support from House Republicans, with 128 backing it and only 10 against in a floor vote on February 7, 1977. Within days, ranking minority member of the Ways and Means Committee Barber Conable of New York won 140–1 Republican support for another proposal to substitute a permanent tax cut for the Carter tax rebate. From that juncture onwards, the House Republicans showed remarkable unity in supporting alternative budget resolutions and tax cut proposals. This development opened the way for the introduction on July 14, 1977, of the Kemp-Roth tax reduction bill, the foundation for what would eventually become Ronald Reagan's Economic Recovery Tax Act of 1981. This soon had the sponsorship of virtually every House Republican, including the party leadership, and by the end of 1977 had received Republican National Committee endorsement.[29]

Senate Republicans, by contrast, were much slower to jump on the supply-side bandwagon because deficit concerns were stronger in the upper chamber in spite of Senator William Roth of Delaware having joined forces with Kemp. Not until the election year of 1980 did their bill receive the official endorsement of the GOP Senate leadership. By then Reagan had formally endorsed Kemp-Roth and there appeared to be a danger that Jimmy Carter was contemplating stealing his thunder by proposing a major tax cut of his own in advance of the presidential campaign. Moreover, Senator Lloyd Bentsen of Texas, the Democratic chair of the JEC, had grown increasingly vociferous in support of tax cuts that reduced barriers to work and production, as advocated by the Special Study of Economic Change undertaken by his committee staff.[30]

To stake out the Republicans' unequivocal identity as a tax-cutting party, Senator Robert J. Dole of Kansas—as part of a maneuver agreed with Reagan—sought to amend a routine debt ceiling extension by adding to it a proposed 10 percent across-the-board individual tax cut and depreciation allowances, effective January 1, 1981. In essence this was the first installment of the Kemp-Roth plan, even if it was never called that in order to ensure unanimous GOP support. As anticipated, the Democrats banded together to defeat it, handing the Republicans a propaganda victory that enabled them to label the opposition as the tax-and-spend party in the election campaign.[31]

The GOP's adoption of pro-growth tax reduction in place of their habitual fiscal prioritization of budgetary restraint and deficit control strengthened the party in a number of important ways. First, it united the Republicans on an issue that defined their partisan identity. They went into the 1980 elections agreed on a positive agenda in marked contrast to the divisions between Carter and Kennedy Democrats. Signifying this, Reagan met with 285 Republican congressional candidates in September to issue the Capitol Compact of common commitment to reduce government, cut taxes, and expand defense. The RNC was already making every effort to join the presidential and congressional races in the minds of voters through its "Vote Republican—for a Change" campaign. In addition to publicizing the core program, the campaign also sought to educate voters that the Democrats had controlled Congress for twenty-five years. In 1979, party polling showed that only 68 percent of respondents knew this—by June 1980, 80 percent did so.[32]

Second, the Republicans' embrace of supply-side tax reduction made them look modern, innovative, and optimistic. Fearful that the Democrats looked outmoded by comparison, Senator Daniel Patrick Moynihan of New York warned in July 1980, "Of a sudden, the GOP has become a party of ideas."[33] The linkage of tax reduction with economic growth played particularly well with Republicans from the South, a region with a new pro-growth outlook in the post–civil rights era of Sunbelt expansion. Significantly, in 1978, Newt Gingrich won election on his third try at becoming the representative of an Atlanta suburban district—making him the sole GOP House victor in the Peach State—with a campaign that pronounced support for Kemp-Roth as one of his core commitments.[34]

Finally, the embrace of supply-side tax measures that offered a gamut of benefits for business and investment and a 20 percent reduction in the top rate of personal income tax helped boost GOP coffers with increased contributions from the corporate community. The link between the party and business was personified by Charls Walker, who was instrumental in getting Senate Republicans to write depreciation allowances and other benefits into their 1980 tax initiative. Formerly an advocate of revenue-raising taxes as an undersecretary in the Nixon Department of the Treasury, he was now a fervent tax-cutter, first as a Washington lobbyist who counted top corporations and the Business Roundtable among his clients, then as chair of the American Council for Capital Formation. A trained economist with a doctoral pedigree, Walker had effectively drafted the investment-incentive tax cut amendment offered by Representative William Steiger of Wisconsin, which the House Ways and Means Committee adopted in place of Jimmy Carter's tax reform proposal. Eventually enacted as the Revenue Act of 1978 with the support of every Republican and large numbers of conservative and moderate Democrats, this measure went down in conservative lore as the first supply-side legislative success. Walker also served on the cadre of economic advisers who counseled Reagan in the 1980 campaign and was instrumental in ensuring that a 10-5-3 depreciation allowance was written into the Republican platform at the national convention.[35]

What the GOP's new stand on taxation meant for its electoral prospects was less clear-cut, however. At first sight, the issue seemed a guaranteed vote-winner. A national Roper Poll conducted shortly after California voters approved the Proposition 13 state-tax limitation initiative in mid-1978 showed support for a one-third cut in federal income taxes as proposed by Kemp-Roth running at two-to-one. In light of this, Kemp and other Republicans, not least Ronald Reagan, made every effort to present this measure as the national equivalent of Proposition 13.[36]

Spiraling state taxes on property and income that resulted from the inflationary conditions of the 1970s had generated a grassroots tax revolt in California, which soon spread to other states. The bracket-creep effect of inflation had a similar impact on personal income tax liabilities at federal level. In 1961, marginal rates of income tax in the federal code varied from 20 percent to 91 percent, but 88 percent of tax returns paid between 20 and 22 percent, while only 2 percent paid over 32 percent. By the end of the 1970s, however, 45 percent of taxpayers paid marginal tax rates over 22 percent. By 1981, the federal income tax burden of the middle income quintile was at its peak level (8.3 percent of household income) since the income tax's transformation into a mass tax in World War II. After two decades of largely Republican-driven tax reduction, it reached a historic low in 2003, and has crept up only slightly since then (to 3 percent in 2006, according to the most recently available data).[37]

Nevertheless, the evidence for the Republicans riding to power in the White House, capturing control of the Senate, and slashing the Democratic majority in the House in the 1980 elections on the back of the tax-cut issue is unconvincing. Certainly the polls showed a broad popular belief that federal taxes were too high, but once pollsters asked questions that posed other considerations or trade-offs, the results were more complex. As Table 1 indicates, in response to a 1978 Gallup poll asking whether cutting taxes was more important than balancing the budget, 39 percent opted for the former and 53 percent the latter (with 8 percent having no

Table 1. Attitudes toward the trade-off between deficits and taxes
(in percentages of sample)

QUESTIONS:

1946, 1953—"What is more important in the coming year, a balanced
budget or cutting taxes?"

1947—"The U.S. has a $1 billion surplus. Should we cut taxes or reduce the
national debt?"

1978—"It has been said that tax cuts would lead to a bigger deficit in the
federal budget and would make it very difficult for the president to
fulfill his promise to balance the budget by 1981. Do you think it is
more important to work toward balancing the budget or to cut taxes at
this time?"

	1946	1947	1953	1978
Cut taxes	20	38	25	39
Balance budget/ Reduce debt	71	53	69	53
No opinion	9	9	6	8

Source: *The Gallup Poll* (New York: Random House, 1946, 1947, 1953, and 1978).

opinion). This was almost exactly the level of response to a 1947 Gallup poll asking whether the surplus should be invested in tax reduction or debt reduction (38 percent, 53 percent, and 9 percent).[38]

Significantly, as Table 2 shows, the CBS News/*New York Times* exit poll for the 1980 presidential election found that the issues of main concern to voters (when asked to rank their top two) were inflation and the economy (33 percent), jobs (24 percent), and balancing the budget (21 percent). Only 10 percent cited taxes—though the 14.5 percent swing of voters from Democrat to Republican in 1980 compared to 1976 was nearly as high on this issue as on balancing the budget (15 percent) and inflation (16.5 percent). Nonetheless, these returns indicate that the tax issue was at best a contributory rather than critical factor in Reagan's victory.[39]

Nor did poll results show the public overwhelmingly in favor of cutting government services as the price for tax reduction. As indicated in Table 3, the Advisory Commission on Intergovernmental Relations tracked opinion on this issue throughout the latter part of the 1970s. In 1980, it found that 38 percent of respondents on average favored this trade-off, 45 percent wanted taxes and services maintained at their current level, 6 percent wanted increased services paid for by tax increases, and 11 percent had no opinion. There had been some movement on this score since 1976 but by no means was it a truly dramatic shift.[40]

The public mind on taxation was not difficult to fathom. With the return of

Table 2. Issues and the 1980 vote

		Percentage of 1980 Vote			
	1980 % of Electorate	Carter	Reagan	Anderson	% swing to GOP, 1976–1980*
All voters	100	41	50	7	11.5

Which issues were most important in deciding how you voted today? (up to 2 answers)

Inflation and economy	33	28	61	9	16.5
Jobs and unemployment	24	48	42	7	13.0
Balancing the budget	21	27	65	6	15.0
US prestige round the world	16	31	61	7	16.0
Crisis in Iran	14	63	31	4	4.0
Reducing federal income taxes	10	29	64	4	14.5
ERA/abortion	7	50	38	10	14.0
Needs of big cities	2	77	13	7	1.0
Don't know/none	20	45	46	7	8.0

Cutting taxes is more important than balancing the federal budget.

Agree	30	42	50	6	15.0
Disagree	53	37	53	9	11.0

*Swing is defined as the average of the Republican gain and the Democratic loss, 1976–1980, in each group. The 1976 vote is measured by voter recall, which overstates Carter's support at 57 percent to 43 percent for Ford.
Note: *N* = 12,782
Source: CBS News/*New York Times*, "National Election Day Survey," November 4, 1980, *www.ropercenter.uconn.edu/elections/common/exitpolls.html.*

double-digit inflation in 1979–1980, price stability had become the main concern of most Americans. This was exacerbated by the ratcheting up of interest rates as a result of the money-stock control strategy pursued by Paul Volcker's Federal Reserve in late 1979 and early 1980 and the limitations on credit card borrowing introduced in the spring of 1980. The general—if mistaken—popular belief was that a rising federal budget deficit was to blame for skyrocketing inflation, leading twice as many voters to prioritize balancing the budget over tax reduction as a major concern in 1980. The double whammy of higher prices and massive increases in borrowing costs hurt most Americans far more than the deepening bite of federal income tax. When a new round of money-stock restraint generated a deep recession

Table 3. Attitudes toward the trade-off between services and taxes, 1975–1980 (percentages in sample)

QUESTION: "Considering all government services on the one hand and taxes on the other, which of the following statements comes closest to your views?"

	1975	1976	1977	1979	1980
Decrease services and taxes	38	30	31	39	38
Keep taxes and services about where they are	45	51	52	46	45
Increase services and raise taxes	5	5	4	6	6
No opinion	12	14	13	9	11

Source: *Changing Public Attitudes on Government and Taxes* (Washington, DC: Advisory Commission on Intergovernmental Relations, 1981), 16.

in 1981–1982, a Reagan OMB official counseled the White House not to condemn Volcker's draconian cure for inflation with the budget currently heading deep into the red. "Scapegoating the Fed while we struggle with triple-digit deficits will do the administration a lot of harm," he warned. In his view, it would have no credibility with the average voter, who blamed price instability on the deficit rather than the money supply.[41]

Moreover, voters' attitude to spending showed that the general disillusion with government did not translate into a desire to reduce or eliminate services. Polls were consistent in showing that when presented with a list of where cuts should be made, Americans tended only to opt for foreign aid and public welfare assistance. In general, voters who wanted to reduce federal spending thought this could be done painlessly for them through the elimination of fraud, waste, and abuse in government. Significantly, polls leading up to the election consistently showed that around 70 percent of respondents believed that the budget could be balanced if government was more efficient. The Center for Political Studies found that 77 percent of respondents answered affirmatively that government wasted a lot of money that was paid in taxes compared with just 43 percent twenty years earlier. Gallup polls taken between 1977 and 1981 asking respondents to estimate the proportion of every tax dollar that the federal government wasted elicited a median response of forty-eight cents (compared with thirty cents and twenty-four cents for state and local government respectively). Such findings suggested that Americans wanted better government rather than less government.[42]

All this is not to deny that tax reduction did eventually become a potent agency of the Republican quest to build a new majority, at least in presidential terms, in the 1980s. When the Kemp-Roth bill was effectively enacted as the Economic Recovery Tax Act of 1981, this reduced the top marginal rate of income tax from 70 percent to 50 percent, effective January 1, 1982, but phased in the cuts for other income groups in annual tranches of 5 percent, 10 percent, and 10 percent. Amid the deep recession of 1981–1982, polls found that majorities of three-to-one wanted a balanced budget and were prepared to surrender or defer the second and third tranches of the Reagan tax cut to pay for it. Not until the latter part of 1983 and the first half of 1984, by when lower interest rates had produced economic recovery, did they show a steady reversal of this opinion to the point where three-to-one majorities refused to surrender the tax cuts to balance a budget that was now heading for a record peacetime deficit of 6 percent GDP.[43]

A case can be made for the mass public's rational perspective to explain this change. In the early 1980s, the large deficit was popularly regarded as the main source of inflation that the recession-inducing high interest rates were intended to combat. By late 1982, however, the battle against inflation was largely won, so the Fed began a steady relaxation of monetary policy that laid the foundations for economic recovery. Hence the association of deficits with high interest rates and inflation in the public mind was broken. Moreover, from January 1, 1984, the final tranche of the Reagan tax cuts had become operational. From this point on, Americans would have to accept higher taxes to reduce the deficit rather than surrender something they did not yet have, as in 1982.

In 1987, political scientist Aaron Wildavsky observed, "In the past, as the party of responsible finance, Republicans had tried to cut spending and deficits; generally they were successful at neither. Under Reagan they have abandoned the tasks at which they failed in the past in favor of others that are easier to accomplish."[44] Without doubt, GOP support for tax reduction was instrumental in a succession of presidential election victories in 1984, 1988, 2000, and 2004, and in the capture of both houses of Congress for the first time in forty years in 1994. It can also be argued, however, that there was a disjunction between partisan success and good public policy. The consequence of massive tax reduction without corollary expenditure retrenchment has been the steady escalation of the deficit to the point that the public debt may become unsustainable without a correction of budgetary course. Sooner or later the need to avert calamity in the national finances is likely to have a crowding out effect on GOP partisan calculation. Having used tax reduction as a fundamental instrument of their advance toward the goal of creating a new majority in the late twentieth century—even if this political holy grail was never fully grasped—the Republicans' continued deployment of this issue into the twenty-first century risks running aground on the rocks of fiscal reality.

NOTES

1.   Quoted in John Cassidy, "Tax Code," *New Yorker*, June 9, 2004, 9.
2.   Calculations based on Office of Management and Budget, *Budget of the United States Government Fiscal Year 2009: Historical Tables* (hereafter *Historical Tables*) (Washington, DC: White House, 2008). For review of the new tax regime, see John F.

Witte, *The Politics and Development of the Federal Income Tax* (Madison: University of Wisconsin Press, 1981), 110–30; and W. Elliott Brownlee, *Federal Taxation in America: A Short History* (New York: Cambridge University Press, 1996), 89–109.

3. *Congressional Record*, 80th Congress, 1st session, 2726; Taft quoted in *New York Times*, August 1, 1947.

4. Barry M. Goldwater, *The Conscience of a Conservative* (Lexington, KY: Victor Books, 1960), chap. 7.

5. See, for example, *1960 Economic Report* (Washington, DC: U.S. Government Printing Office, 1960), 5–7; cabinet paper, June 4, 1960, Ann Whitman File–Cabinet Series, Box 15, Dwight D. Eisenhower Presidential Library (hereafter DDEPL), Abilene, KS. On Eisenhower's battles with Congress, see Iwan W. Morgan, *Eisenhower versus "the Spenders": The Eisenhower Administration, the Democrats and the Budget, 1953–60* (New York: St. Martin's Press, 1990), chaps. 6 and 7.

6. *Congressional Record*, 88th Congress, 1st Session, 18,119. See also Witte, *Politics and Development*, 160–65.

7. See Rockefeller Brothers Fund, *Prospect for America: The Rockefeller Panel Reports* (Garden City, NY: Doubleday, 1961), especially 264–65, 275–82.

8. Morgan, *Eisenhower versus "the Spenders,"* 169–71. Nixon's guidance notes to 1960 speechwriters also emphasize the significance of linking tax reduction and economic growth: see, in particular, Richard Nixon, "Memorandum to Speech Team," October 11, 1960, Frederick Seaton Papers, 1960 Campaign Series, Box 2, DDEPL.

9. Allen J. Matusow, *Nixon's Economy: Booms, Busts, Dollars, and Votes* (Lawrence; University Press of Kansas, 1999), 39–51; and A. James Reichley, *Conservatives in an Age of Change: The Nixon and Ford Administrations* (Washington, DC: Brookings Institution, 1981), 205–31.

10. Transcript of GOP Leadership Meeting, October 7, 1975, America since Hoover Collection, Box 11, Gerald R. Ford Presidential Library (hereafter GRFPL), Ann Arbor, MI. For analysis of Ford's economic policies, see Yanek Mieczkowski, *Gerald Ford and the Challenges of the 1970s* (Lexington: University Press of Kentucky, 2005), 95–194; Herbert Stein, *Presidential Economics: The Making of Economic Policy from Roosevelt to Clinton*, 3rd rev. ed. (Washington, DC: American Enterprise Institute, 1994), 133–218; and Andrew Moran, "Gerald R. Ford and the 1975 Tax Cut," *Presidential Studies Quarterly* 26 (Summer 1996): 738–54.

11. "Campaign Strategy for President Ford, 1976," August 1976, Robert Teeter Papers, Box 54, GRFPL; Bruce Bartlett, *"Reaganomics": Supply-Side Economics in Action* (Westport, CT: Arlington House, 1981), 127; Kemp quoted in David Broder, *Changing the Guard: Power and Leadership in America* (New York: Simon and Schuster, 1980), 171.

12. Martin Anderson, *Revolution* (San Diego: Harcourt Brace Jovanovich), 161–63.

13. See, for example, Lou Cannon, *President Reagan: The Role of a Lifetime* (New York: Simon and Schuster, 1991), 88–92, and *Governor Reagan: His Rise to Power* (New York: PublicAffairs, 2003), 368–79; Robert Collins, *More: The Politics of Economic Growth in Postwar America* (New York: Oxford University Press, 2000), 191–210; and Hugh Heclo, "Ronald Reagan and the American Public Philosophy," in *The Reagan Presidency: Pragmatic Conservatism and Its Legacies*, ed. Elliot Brownlee and Hugh Davis Graham (Lawrence: University Press of Kansas, 2003), 17–39.

14. "Revenue Control and Tax Deduction, submitted to the California Legislature by Governor Ronald Reagan," March 12, 1973.

15. "Address to the American Textile Manufacturers Institute," March 29, 1973, in *A Time*

for Choosing: The Speeches of Ronald Reagan, 1961–1982 (Washington, DC: Regnery, 1983), 118.

16. "Taxes," October 18, 1977, in *Reagan: In His Own Hand*, ed. Kiron K. Skinner, Annelise Anderson, and Martin Anderson (New York: Free Press, 2001), 277; Anderson, *Revolution*, 122–39; Brock quoted in *The Reagan Presidency: Ten Intimate Perspectives of Ronald Reagan*, ed. Kenneth W. Thompson (Lanham, MD: University Press of America, 1997), 114.

17. See, for example, Jude Wanniski, "The Mundell-Laffer Hypothesis: A New View of the World Economy," *Public Interest*, Spring 1975, 31–52; Jude Wanniski, *The Way the World Works*, 3rd ed. (Morristown, NJ: Polyconomics, 1989), 345–46; Robert L. Bartley, "Jack Kemp's Intellectual Blitz," *Wall Street Journal*, November 29, 1979; Robert L. Bartley, *The Seven Fat Years: And How to Do It Again*, updated ed. (New York: Free Press, 1995), 44–45, 54–58; and Jack Kemp, *An American Renaissance: A Strategy for the 1980s* (New York: Harper and Row, 1980), 37–39. For a scholarly history of supply-side economists and their ideas, see Brian Domitrovic, *Econoclasts: The Rebels Who Sparked the Supply-Side Revolution and Restored American Prosperity* (Wilmington, DE: Intercollegiate Studies Institute, 2009). Also illuminating on the impact of this doctrine are Paul Krugman, *Peddling Prosperity: Economic Sense and Nonsense in the Age of Diminished Expectations* (New York: Norton, 1994), 82–103; and Godfrey Hodgson, *The World Turned Right Side Up: A History of the Conservative Ascendancy in America* (Boston: Houghton Mifflin, 1996), chap. 8.

18. Jude Wanniski, "JFK Strikes Again," *Wall Street Journal*, February 23, 1977. For other media profiles of Kemp, see Irwin Ross, "Jack Kemp Wants to Cut Your Taxes—a Lot," *Fortune*, April 10, 1978; Paul Hendrickson, "Jack Kemp: From 70-Yard Spirals to Laffer Curves," *Washington Post*, June 22, 1978; Martin Tolchin, "Jack Kemp's Bootleg Run to the Right," *Esquire*, October 24, 1978, 59–69; and Adam Clymer, "Washington: Quarterbacking for the GOP," *Atlantic Monthly*, December 1978, 14–21. For the problematic consequences of Kemp's high profile, see Paul Craig Roberts, *The Supply-Side Revolution: An Insider's Account of Policymaking in Washington* (Cambridge, MA: Harvard University Press, 1984), 29–30.

19. Paul Craig Roberts, "The Breakdown of the Keynesian Model," *Public Interest*, Summer 1978, 20–33; Water Guzzari Jr., "The New Down-to-Earth Economics," *Fortune*, December 31, 1978, 72–79; "Why Supply-Side Economics Is Suddenly Popular," *Business Week*, September 17, 1979, 116–18.

20. For Ture's economic ideas, see Norman Ture and Kenneth Sanden, *The Effects of Tax Policy on Capital Formation* (New York: Financial Executives Research Foundation, 1977); "Norman B. Ture: Books, Papers, Speeches, Conference Presentations, and Congressional Testimony," Institute for Research on the Economics of Taxation, *www. iret.org*; Domitrovic, *Econoclasts*, 128–33.

21. Roberts, *Supply-Side Revolution*, 32–33. Roberts's political position would shift in the post-Reagan era to embrace a curious mix of New Left ideas on the corporate-government link and Pat Buchanan–style economic nationalism. A trenchant critic of George W. Bush's economic policy and the Iraq War, he declared that had he known what the GOP would become, he would never have helped the party's rise to power in the 1970s. See Paul Craig Roberts, "The Mother of All Messes: The Greatest Threat America has ever faced: The GOP?," July 23, 2008, *www.counterpunch.org*.

22. Roberts, *Supply-Side Revolution*, chaps. 1–3; and Bartley, *Seven Fat Years*, 73–75.

23. For a selection of newspaper and journal articles penned by Roberts, see "Disguising the Tax Burden," *Harper's*, March 1978, 32–38; "Some Tax Myths: Who Pays What,"

National Review, April 28, 1978; "The Tax Reform Fraud," *Policy Review*, Summer 1979, 121–39 (coauthored by Richard Wagner); and "Caricatures of Tax-Cutting," *Wall Street Journal*, April 24, 1980. For his response to criticisms by Walter Heller and Herbert Stein of the revenue benefits of supply-side tax cuts, see Bartley, *Seven Fat Years*, 73–74.

24. Office of Management and Budget, *Historical Tables*, Table 1.2, Table 6.1.

25. Kemp statement in testimony before the House Budget Committee, March 21, 1981, quoted in James Savage, *Balanced Budget and American Politics* (Ithaca, NY: Cornell University Press, 1988), 226; and Jude Wanniski, "Taxes and a Two-Santa Theory," *National Observer*, March 6, 1976.

26. Milton Friedman, "The Limitations of Tax Limitation," *Policy Review*, Summer 1978, 11–12; U.S. Congress, Committee on Ways and Means, House of Representatives, *Tax Reductions: Economists' Comments on H.R. 8333 and S. 1860, Bills to Provide for Permanent Tax Rate Reductions for Individuals and Businesses*, 95th Congress, 2nd Session (Washington, DC: U.S. Government Printing Office, 1978), 68. See also U.S. Congress, Committee on the Budget, House of Representatives and Senate, *Leading Economists' View of Kemp-Roth*, 95th Congress, 2nd Session (Washington, DC: U.S. Government Printing Office, 1978).

27. Bartlett, "*Reaganomics*," 131; Domitrovic, *Econoclasts*, 13–14, 127.

28. Roberts, *Supply-Side Revolution*, 9–20.

29. Bartlett, "*Reaganomics*," 18–29.

30. Collins, *More*, 188–89. For the committee report, see "Special Study on Economic Change: Committee Report," Robert Ash Wallace Papers, Box 2, Jimmy Carter Presidential Library (hereafter JCPL), Atlanta, GA.

31. "Reagan's Tax Cut Ploy," *Newsweek*, July 7, 1980, 20; "Opening the Tax Battle," *Time*, July 7, 1980, 8–9; and Joseph White and Aaron Wildavsky, *The Deficit and the Public Interest: the Search for Responsible Budgeting in the 1980s* (Berkeley: University of California Press; New York: Russell Sage Foundation, 1989), 54.

32. Iwan Morgan, *Beyond the Liberal Consensus: A Political History of the United States since 1965* (New York: St. Martin's, 1994), 184–85; Andrew E. Busch, *Reagan's Victory: The Presidential Election of 1980 and the Rise of the Right* (Lawrence: University Press of Kansas, 2005), 149–52.

33. Daniel Patrick Moynihan, *Miles to Go: A Personal History of Social Policy* (Cambridge, MA: Harvard University Press, 1996), 10.

34. Mel Steely, *The Gentleman from Georgia: A Biography of Newt Gingrich* (Macon, GA: Mercer University Press, 2000), 101–2. For the significance of tax reduction issues in the emergence of Republicanism elsewhere in the South, see Amos L. Esty, "North Carolina Republicans and the Conservative Revival, 1964–1968," *North Carolina Historical Review* 1 (2005): 1–32; Joseph Crespino, *In Search of Another Country: Mississippi and the Conservative Counterrevolution* (Princeton, NJ: Princeton University Press, 2009); and Sean P. Cunningham, *Cowboy Conservatism: Texas and the Rise of the Modern American Right* (Lexington: University Press of Kentucky, 2010).

35. Hodgson, *World Turned Right Side Up*, 208–9, 212; Matusow, *Nixon's Economy*, 41; and Witte, *Politics and Development*, 218–19. For White House discomfiture about business lobbying to GOP advantage over the 1978 tax cut, see Bob Ginsburg to Stuart Eizenstat, "Campaign against Steiger Proposal," and Michael Blumenthal, memorandum for the president, "Status of the Tax Bill," September 20, 1978, Domestic Policy Staff–Stuart Eizenstat, Box 289, JCPL.

36. U.S. Congress, *Roper Opinion Poll: Hearings Before the Committee on Finance, United*

States Senate, 95th Congress, 2nd Session (Washington, DC: U.S. Government Printing Office, 1978), 25; Robert Samuelson, "Son of Proposition 13?," *National Journal*, June 17, 1978, 974; and Jack Kemp, "Prop 13 Fever," *New York Daily News*, July 23, 1978.

37. Robert E. Hall and Alvin Rabushka, *The Flat Tax* (Palo Alto, CA: Hoover Institution, 1985), 36; Bartlett, "*Reaganomics*," 222; and Lori Montgomery, "Americans' Tax Burden Near Historic Low," *Washington Post*, April 16, 2009.

38. Data from *The Gallup Poll, 1938–1971* (New York: Random House, 1972). For similar findings for the late 1970s, see H&R Block, *The American Public and the Income Tax System* (Kansas City: H&R Block, 1978), 33.

39. CBS News/*New York Times*, "National Election Day Survey," November 4, 1980. *www.ropercenter.uconn.edu/elections/common/exitpolls.html*. For analysis, see William Schneider, "The November 4 Vote for President: What Did It Mean?" in *The American Elections of 1980*, ed. Austin Ranney (Washington, DC: American Enterprise Institute, 1981), 212–63.

40. *Changing Public Attitudes on Government and Taxes* (Washington, DC: Advisory Commission on Intergovernmental Relations, 1981), 16. Polls that asked about tax fairness also revealed the ambiguity of the public mind on tax cuts. A three-year Roper study found that 74 percent of respondents in 1978 thought that taxes were too high for middle-income families but 76 percent thought that high-income families should pay more in taxes and 72 percent thought large business corporations should do so as well.

41. Laurence Kudlow to James Baker, "Monetary Discussion," January 23, 1982, White House Staff Office Collections (WHOSC)–Craig Fuller Files, OA1092, Ronald Reagan Presidential Library (RRPL), Simi Valley, CA. For further analysis of the perceived link between inflation and deficits in 1980, see Iwan Morgan, *The Age of Deficits: Presidents and Unbalanced Budgets from Jimmy Carter to George W. Bush* (Lawrence: University Press of Kansas, 2009), chap. 3.

42. H&R Block, *American Public*, 29; Seymour M. Lipset and William Schneider, "The Decline of Confidence in American Institutions," *Political Science Quarterly* 98 (Fall 1983): 83–84. For insightful analysis of popular attitudes on government, see Everett Carll Ladd Jr., *Where Have All the Voters Gone? The Fracturing of America's Political Parties*, 2nd ed. (New York: Norton, 1982).

43. Richard Wirthlin to Edwin Meese, James Baker, and Michael Deaver, "Federal Deficits," August 30, 1982, WHOSC–Michael Deaver files, OA11584, RRPL; Richard Wirthlin to James Baker et al., "Major Findings of the July National Survey," July 30, 1984, WHOSC–James Baker Files, Box 8, RRPL.

44. Aaron Wildavsky, "President Reagan as Political Strategist," *Society* (May–June, 1987), 58.

CHAPTER 11

Rendezvous with Destiny

The Republican Party and the 1980 Election

Dominic Sandbrook

On Thursday, August 19, 1976, the day after his epic campaign for the Republican presidential nomination had ended in defeat, Ronald Reagan bade farewell to his campaign staff in the ballroom of the Alameda Plaza in Kansas City. The room was packed to bursting point, and the air crackled with sadness and regret, but Reagan had rarely been in more moving form. As his young supporters stood there with their hats and their banners, he reassured them that "the cause goes on." "We're going to stay in there and you stay in there with me," he said, as the tears began to flow in his audience. "Don't get cynical," he went on, his voice almost breaking. "Don't get cynical, because, look at what you were willing to do and recognize that there are millions and millions of Americans out there who want what you want, that want it to be that way, that want it to be a shining city on a hill." It was a familiar line, but he had never delivered it with such feeling. At his side, Nancy turned her back on the cameras to hide her tears. Then Reagan himself turned aside, his eyes glistening, and abruptly walked away.[1]

At that moment, the prospect of Ronald Reagan ever becoming president of the United States seemed about as likely as a group of Midwestern amateurs beating the Russians to win hockey gold at the next Winter Olympics. Yet fast-forward just over four years, to Pacific Palisades, California, and although the cast was the same, the scene was very different. Late on the afternoon of November 4, 1980, with the air still warm and the skies crystal-clear, Reagan was taking a shower when, through the steam, he saw Nancy coming into the bathroom. Swathed in towels and a robe, she shouted that there was someone on the telephone. "It's Jimmy Carter," she said. Reagan turned off the shower, shook water from his hair, and reached for a towel. Then he picked up the extension, while Nancy stood by his side, her eyes fixed on her husband. Reagan said nothing, just listened; then, finally, he said, "Thank you, Mr. President," and hung up. He turned to his wife and said simply, "He conceded." "Standing in my bathroom with a towel wrapped around me, my hair dripping with water," Reagan wrote later, "I had just learned I was going to be the fortieth president of the United States."[2]

Reagan's admirers often present his road to the White House as smooth and straight, and the election of 1980 as not just a victory for his personal charm and good humor, but a vindication of his uncompromising right-wing agenda and a culmination of social and economic forces that had been building for decades, from the rise of the suburbs and the Sunbelt to the public rejection of secular humanism and Great Society liberalism. And yet, as numerous historians have pointed out, this is a very unconvincing explanation of Reagan's success. As is well known, Reagan did not pull away from the discredited Jimmy Carter in the opinion polls until the very eve of the election, while exit polls and surveys found little evidence of any major public shift to the right on the issues, or even any sense that the election represented a mandate for conservatism. Of course it would be ridiculous to argue that his victory was merely the result of contingency or luck: if we widen our focus from the United States to the West in general, it is clear that conservatism was the most dynamic political force in the democratic world.

It is no coincidence that Reagan's victory was preceded by Margaret Thatcher's accession to power in Britain eighteen months previously; neither is it an accident that it was followed by the victories of Helmut Kohl in West Germany in 1982 and Brian Mulroney in Canada in 1984, or by the adoption of free-market economic policies even by the center-left governments of New Zealand, Australia, and (whisper it softly) France. In an age of high inflation, cutthroat international competition, and increasingly globalized capital markets, the pendulum had clearly swung away from the pseudo-Keynesianism of the 1950s and 1960s. To some extent, therefore, the Reagan ascendancy was merely the American manifestation of a worldwide phenomenon. But there were, of course, purely local, parochial factors, too. To explain Reagan's victory, therefore, it is necessary to strike a careful but precarious balance between the contingencies of the Carter presidency and the election campaign on the one hand, and deeper demographic and economic forces on the other. And to do that, we should start with the aftermath of Reagan's defeat in 1976.

When Reagan's disappointment at the Republican convention was followed by Gerald Ford's defeat in the presidential election, many observers thought that the game was up for the Republican Party. Humiliated by the Watergate scandal, hammered in the 1974 midterms, and bleeding from the long battle between Ford and Reagan, the party of Lincoln was apparently staggering toward irrelevance. In the *New York Times*, Warren Weaver wrote that the Republican Party was "perhaps closer to extinction than ever before in its 122-year history." The Republicans had "lost their grip on the American establishment," wrote distinguished political scientist Everett Carll Ladd, while elections expert Gerald Pomper forecast "the decline of the Republicans to a permanent minority or even their replacement by a new party." Conservative columnist Robert Novak predicted "the long descent of the Republican Party into irrelevance, defeat, and perhaps eventual disappearance," and even House Minority Leader John Rhodes, an Arizona Republican, publicly worried that his party would "go the way of the Whigs."[3]

In the Carter administration, meanwhile, there was an unmistakable sense of satisfaction, confidence, and even complacency. "When we turn to the Republicans," wrote Pat Caddell in his postelection report, "we find them in deep trouble. Their ideology is restrictive, they have few bright lights to offer the public. Given the antiquated machinery of the Republican Party, the rise of a moderate, attractive Republican in their primary process is hard to imagine. The Republican Party seems bent on self-destruction."[4]

What all of these experts underestimated, of course, was the rising appeal of conservatism. And yet conservatism had both a rich history and an extremely promising future. Its core themes—belief in private property and free enterprise; opposition to communism, socialism, and New Deal liberalism; a strong sense of American nationalism and manifest destiny; and commitment to traditional moral and cultural standards—were deeply rooted in the nation's past. And almost beneath the surface of political events, a new conservative generation had reached maturity: the generation of Pat Buchanan and George Will, the tens of thousands of college students who joined Young Americans for Freedom, the 100,000 subscribers who read William F. Buckley's *National Review*, the two million people who had voted for Barry Goldwater in the 1964 primaries, the twenty-seven million who had voted for the Arizonan on Election Day, and the thirty-nine million who, despite everything, had voted for Gerald Ford twelve years later.[5]

Despite the accusations of its opponents, the new conservatism of the postwar decades was not a business-funded conspiracy any more than it was an elite-driven enterprise directed from William F. Buckley's Connecticut estate. It was, above all, a grassroots movement, born in the mundane coffee mornings, study groups, and educational campaigns of innumerable anonymous local activists. In many places, suburban anticommunist groups laid the foundations; in others, the motivating themes may have been revulsion at cultural change or anger at high taxes. But as early as 1960, as a British reporter observed, there was "a whole structure of crusades, campaigns, radio stations, newsletters, storefronts, action groups, committees, lecture bureaus, lobbies, and assorted voluntary organizations of every kind."[6]

One of the biggest mistakes liberals ever made was to underestimate their adversaries as eccentrics or losers, blindly lashing out against progress and modernity. Even academic scholars, like the experts who contributed essays to Daniel Bell's collection *The New American Right* (1955), regarded conservatives as glorified psychiatric patients. Conservative beliefs, wrote political scientist Herbert McClosky, appealed to "the uninformed, the poorly educated and . . . the less intelligent"— to people "bewildered" by the modern world. And when Barry Goldwater won the Republican nomination, most scholars dismissed his success as an embarrassing fluke. His ideas, wrote Richard Hofstadter, were "so bizarre, so archaic, so self-confounding, so remote from the basic American consensus" that it was a miracle he had made it so far. His campaign was essentially "a kind of vocational therapy, without which [his supporters] might have to be committed."[7]

As we know, however, this was a complete misreading of the kind of people whose efforts gave the conservative movement its momentum. The activists who attended coffee mornings, stuffed envelopes, and wrote letters to local newspapers tended to be affluent, middle-class people, heading up the social ladder. They held managerial or professional positions associated with new industries like aerospace or computing, lived in pleasant suburban communities, and were personally happy and successful. They saw themselves as perfectly reasonable, modern people, and to them, conservatism simply made sense. They liked its emphasis on hard work and competition, which seemed to have brought them so many rewards. They liked its libertarian, individualistic themes, which matched their love of suburban privacy and self-improvement. They liked its strict Christian piety, which reminded them of the moral values they had learned as children. And they liked its sense of "coherence, community, and commitment," which they found in the suburban churches and volunteer groups that gave them a sense of belonging. They were not cranks or losers; they were ordinary homeowners, parents, and taxpayers. As one of their great champions, who first ran for political office in 1974, remarked of his suburban Atlanta constituents, they lived in "a sort of Norman Rockwell world with fiber-optic computers and jet airplanes." It was a world that would later be named after him: Newtland.[8]

Two other developments, both taking place outside the structure of the Republican Party, have often monopolized the attention of historians writing about the late 1970s. The first was the development of what even at the time was called the New Right network, associated above all with ideological entrepreneurs like Richard Viguerie, Howard Phillips, and Paul Weyrich. Exactly how new it was, however, remains very doubtful. Viguerie had not only worked for Barry Goldwater in 1964, he had been the executive secretary of Young Americans for Freedom in 1961, when he was just twenty-eight. He was also precisely the kind of person one might expect to be involved in conservative politics, being the son of a Texas oilman and a long-standing admirer of Douglas MacArthur and Joe McCarthy.[9]

The same was true of the sleek, baby-faced Paul Weyrich, who had become involved with right-wing politics during the Goldwater campaign. Weyrich, too, was firmly rooted in the Old Right. His father, a conservative German Catholic, had idolized the Midwestern isolationist, Senator Robert Taft of Ohio, and young Paul claimed to have read everything that Taft wrote. Weyrich also acknowledged debts to the Catholic "radio priest" Father Charles Coughlin, another isolationist who fiercely denounced Franklin D. Roosevelt and the East Coast elite, and to Senator Joe McCarthy of Wisconsin, the darling of many Midwestern Germans and the master of scaremongering populism. And although his dream of a vast conservative coalition reaching across sectarian boundaries, welcoming West Coast libertarians and big-city Catholics, evangelical Christians and self-made tycoons, did represent something new, it crucially depended on the one thing that conservatives had always needed and that opponents had always claimed that they stood for—

money, and lots of it, provided in this case by the Colorado beer magnate Joseph Coors.[10]

The second development, of course, was the growth of a new kind of moral populism, associated above all with evangelical Christianity and with outspoken antiestablishment firebrands such as Phyllis Schlafly and Jerry Falwell. But was it really so new? Whatever Falwell himself liked to think, he was far from the first evangelical preacher to become involved in politics; indeed, as late as 1965, he had told his flock that preachers were not called to "reform externals," adding that his mission was to "regenerate the inside," not "clean up the outside." "Believing the Bible as I do," Falwell said, "I would find it impossible to stop preaching the pure saving gospel of Jesus Christ, and begin doing anything else—including fighting Communism, or participating in civil-rights reforms."[11]

Yet preachers had long been involved with politics and current affairs, from Charles Grandison Finney in the antebellum era to Billy Sunday during World War I. Even during the postwar decades, when fundamentalism was supposed to have gone underground, evangelical political involvement was still alive and well. The anticommunist fundamentalist Billy James Hargis, for instance, would have been right at home in the mid-1970s. Speaking to millions on radio and television in the 1950s and 1960s, he denounced federal officials as devil-worshippers, accused the Beatles of spreading communism, and toured rural states in a customized bus on his "Christian Anti-Communist Crusade." When Hargis denounced the "anti-God Liberal Establishment," or sent out computer-generated letters asking readers to send money to fight "moral decay," he sounded like a rudimentary version of Jerry Falwell, only two decades too early. Alas, the wheels fell off his bus in 1974 when he faced accusations of having sexually molested members of his youth choir: another precedent for more than a few televangelists of the future.[12]

In many ways, the language of moral populism is one of the keys to understanding American politics and society in the era of Nixon and Reagan. In a comparative context, it is interesting to note that when the Western world was hit by oil shocks, inflation, and recession in the 1970s, different countries fell back on different traditions. Whereas British politics in this era was saturated with class consciousness and the rhetoric of class warfare, American politics was correspondingly steeped in a much more class*less* or class-blind language of antiestablishment, anti-Washington populism. Through the Moral Majority, Weyrich and Falwell came to embody this supposedly new development, but they certainly did not invent it. It was there, for instance, in the Kanawha County textbook protests in West Virginia in 1974; it was there in the battles over school busing that tore Boston apart in the mid-seventies; it was there in Phyllis Schlafly's campaign against the ERA; and of course it was there in Anita Bryant's campaign against gay rights in Miami–Dade County in 1977.

Revealingly, in each case a strong and strident woman took the leading role, almost always describing herself (misleadingly) as an ordinary housewife: Alice

Moore in Kanawha County, Louise Day Hicks in Boston, Schlafly with the ERA, and Bryant in Florida, each unwittingly looking back to a long tradition of activist women functioning as the moral guardians of the republic. And their rhetoric was so alike as to be almost interchangeable. Alice Moore, for example, was fighting a battle between "the parents and taxpayers and the people who live here" and "the administrators, the people from other places who have been trying to tell us what is best for our children." Louise Day Hicks said that she was fighting a "small band of racial agitators, non-native to Boston, and a few college radicals who have joined in the conspiracy to tell the people of Boston how to run their schools, their city, and their lives." And Anita Bryant warned that the homosexual conspiracy was "highly financed and highly organized"—a "recruitment plan" to corrupt the children of the "straight-thinking normal majority."[13]

Yet neither of these developments—the growth of the New Right network, and the increasingly strident rhetoric of moral populism—was obviously bound to benefit the Republican Party. Many New Right activists, for example, deeply distrusted the Republicans, whom they associated with Richard Nixon, Nelson Rockefeller, and Wall Street. In 1976, the direct-mail entrepreneur Richard Viguerie worked not for Reagan or Ford but for the Democrat George Wallace, and when the defeated governor refused to run as an independent, Viguerie even flirted with running himself. It would never be possible "successfully to market the word 'Republican,'" he once said. "You could as easily sell Edsel or Typhoid Mary." And Weyrich remained suspicious even of Ronald Reagan, the darling of the conservative grass roots, whom he regarded—correctly, in my view—not as an ideological champion but as merely another cautious professional politician. New Right activists, he said, could expect "no input in [a Reagan] administration," and in many ways, of course, he was right.[14]

It was also far from obvious that the Republicans, traditionally the party of big business and the old Ivy League elites, were the obvious vehicle for the insurgent politics of moral populism. Richard Nixon had striven hard to turn piety into a political asset, hosting regular prayer breakfasts and Sunday services, and ordering his pet bulldog Charles Colson to "develop a list of rich people with strong religious interest to be invited to the White House church services." Revealingly, however, his Republican successor ignored his advisers' suggestions to take a harder moral line in the 1976 election. In September 1975, one of Ford's advisers suggested that he try to mobilize the "silent majority" on the grounds of "neighborhood, community and family." According to this stratagem, the president should put more effort into attacking "strange or offensive textbooks," "sex education," and the "liberal chic, women's lib content" imposed on "traditional educational programs." And yet even though Ford was a devout Christian, he was uncomfortable campaigning on cultural issues, not least because it would mean coming out against his own outspoken and free-thinking wife. Even when his favorite preacher, Billy Zeoli (who conducted locker-room services for the NFL, which is probably why Ford liked him), offered to put together a book about their spiritual relationship, Ford turned him down. He had no wish, he said, "to name Jesus as my running mate."[15]

Ford, however, represented the GOP past. By the mid-1970s the Republican Party was clearly changing. Not only was its center of gravity shifting to the South and West—in other words, to regions where affluent, suburban voters placed a high political premium on individualism and personal morality—but a new generation of corporate executives, horrified by the collapse of profits during the recession of 1974–1975, was engaged in an increasingly vigorous counterattack against federal taxes and regulations. The business campaign left its mark even on Ford: throughout his short presidency, he pushed hard for the transfer of money and power to the states and a bonfire of government regulations, rather belying his ill-deserved image as a woolly moderate. But it was not really until the midterm elections of 1978—arguably one of the most significant congressional election years in modern political history—that the contours of the new Republican Party really became apparent.[16]

By this point, it was almost impossible to be picked as a Republican congressional candidate without voicing strong support for low taxes, tough sentences, and Christian values. Even Barry Goldwater, who had backed Ford over Reagan in 1976, was horrified by the New Right's intolerant views on abortion and homosexuality. Religious issues, he declared, had "little or nothing" to do with conservatism, and he vowed to "fight them every step of the way if they try to dictate their moral convictions to all Americans in the name of conservatism." But by this point even Goldwater had been left behind: no longer a hero to younger Republicans, he was now dismissed in conservative publications as "lazy" and "soft."[17]

Cultural issues had played a role in congressional elections before, of course, but they had never been so pronounced as in 1978. Mail to Democratic congressmen, one lobbyist reported, was running "ten-to-one, a hundred-to-one, against busing, abortion, gay rights. They believe that 'lifestyle' issues will re-elect them or defeat them, and so they're voting with the antis." But it was not only Democrats who had something to fear. Moderate GOP senators such as Edward Brooke of Massachusetts and Charles Percy of Illinois faced debilitating primary challenges from conservatives who hammered at their records on abortion, busing, the Panama Canal treaties, and the ERA. Although news of the Camp David accords blunted the impact of the Republican campaign, the GOP still picked up fifteen House seats, seven governorships and three hundred state legislature seats. In the Senate, the New Right helped to elect three new populist conservatives, Gordon Humphrey of New Hampshire, Roger Jepsen of Iowa, and William Armstrong of Colorado. In the new House, meanwhile, Weyrich could command the attention of about forty representatives, both Republicans and Democrats. Conservatism even seemed to be on the march in hitherto liberal states. In Minnesota, the home of Hubert Humphrey and Eugene McCarthy, the Republicans took both Senate seats and the statehouse; in Massachusetts, Michael Dukakis was kicked out of the governor's mansion after raising taxes.[18]

By playing on Panama, taxes, and abortion, the Republicans had made significant inroads into the white evangelical and small-town votes. And in the Kemp-Roth tax reduction plan, they also boasted a powerful weapon, or perhaps bribe, to win over voters worried about inflation, bracket creep, and stagnating living standards. While twelve states approved Proposition 13–style tax-reduction measures, eight out of ten voters agreed that government was "spending too much." "The real message of the election returns," said *Newsweek*, was a new "consensus on inflation as the priority target and tax-and-spend government as the primary villain." And the real triumph of conservatism, the magazine argued, was "often vicarious—the pride of authorship in a new politics in which Democrats talk like Republicans to survive."[19]

What all this meant was that as conservatives looked forward to the next presidential election, they felt a palpable quickening of the blood—a sense that if they picked the right candidate and events fell in their favor, they might just see a true believer in the White House. Crucially, the very image of conservatism had changed: once fusty and eccentric, it now seemed young, confident, and aggressive—the creed of the Sunbelt and the suburbs, the wave of the future. The GOP had become a "party of ideas," said Senator Daniel Patrick Moynihan, Democrat of New York, "a party of the People arrayed against a Democratic Party of the State."[20]

A nice illustration of what had happened to the Republican Party by 1980 was the presidential campaign of George H. W. Bush, who was generally seen at the time as the candidate of the party's moderate, eastern wing. With a stunning résumé, taking in the House of Representatives, the United Nations, the Republican National Committee, China, and the CIA, Bush had accumulated a vast list of friends and contacts. His campaign staff was dominated by Ford veterans and moderate Republicans from his New England stomping ground, while he boasted early support from Henry Cabot Lodge, Clare Boothe Luce, and Elliot Richardson—a roll-call of the old Yankee elite. Journalists joked that his staff "looked as if they'd been picked from the Harvard and Yale crew rosters of the past twenty years." And as the candidate of the so-called establishment, Bush had a reputation for gentlemanly moderation: one commentator remarked that his politics were "slightly to the center of center," while his own nephew said that he had "no political ideology."[21]

And yet what is really striking about Bush's campaign (which effectively fizzled out after he lost the second contest in New Hampshire) was not how moderate it was, but how conservative. While his platform called for increased defense spending and dramatic welfare cuts, Bush himself echoed Reagan's nationalistic sentiments about the Panama Canal, denounced the "Marxist-Leninist" advance in Central America, and promised to fire "McGovern-type regulators." And although he famously called Reagan's supply-side plan "voodoo economics," his own economic plan also called for tax cuts, just smaller ones. He was "the Tweed Reagan," quipped *National Review*, while his liberal rival John Anderson nicknamed him "Ronald Reagan in Brooks Brother suits." Indeed, the reason he failed to catch fire with Republican activists outside Iowa was not his platform but his style, for it was a long time since the Republicans had nominated a genuine country-club patrician. "We have the Schlitz drinkers; Bush has the sherry drinkers," quipped one Reagan aide. But by 1980, very few sherry drinkers voted in the Republican primaries.[22]

Paradoxically, while Bush was more conservative than we often remember, his victorious rival was actually a lot more moderate than is conventionally recalled. It is simply not true that Reagan beat Bush in 1980 because he outflanked him to the right; rather, he won because his campaign was better managed and financed, because he was a more accomplished performer on the campaign trail, and because he had a much dearer place in the hearts of Republican activists. Soon after his defeat in 1976, in fact, Reagan had begun moving toward the center. As his foreign policy adviser Richard Allen put it, he needed to get rid of his old image as a "saber-rattler" and to stop "scaring the hell out of people." Although Allen knew Reagan hated to be "fuzzy, indefinite and 'political-sounding' on issues" he felt strongly about, he nevertheless told his boss that there must be "a deliberate attempt to soften the delivery of your message."[23]

Reagan's willingness to follow Allen's advice, and that of his Machiavellian campaign director, John Sears, was one of the least recognized elements of his rise to power. He deliberately accepted speaking engagements in the Northeast and Midwest, where his support was weakest, and he refused to support the anti-gay Briggs Initiative in California in 1978. "I know I'm supposed to be a terrible right-wing person," he told the *Wall Street Journal*, "but I just wish people who think that would look at my record in California." There, he pointed out, he had introduced conjugal visits for convicted felons, made the income tax "more progressive," and increased welfare payments to the "truly needy." Not surprisingly, this attempt at a makeover stunned some conservatives. "Gone is the would-be charismatic insurgent of several years ago," wrote Kevin Phillips. "Now we have in his place a 67-year-old party regular preaching unity while aides hint he'd serve only one term."[24]

This explains, of course, why New Right activists like Viguerie and Weyrich were so reluctant to support Reagan in the months before the presidential primaries, and why they flirted for so long with alternative candidates such as Congressman Jack Kemp of New York. But it should hardly surprise us. Reagan's record in California, after all, was hardly that of a fire-breathing ideologue: during his time in Sacramento, he had signed the biggest tax increase in the history of any state, and, despite all his criticisms of students and professors, increased spending on state universities and student grants. He approved stricter regulations for home insurance, real estate, retailing, doctors, dentists, and auto repairs; he signed the nation's toughest water pollution controls; he agreed to a welfare deal that gave higher pay-ments to eight out of ten recipients; and he even blocked the Dos Rios dam and trans-Sierra highway projects, saving vast tracts of wilderness from development. Most remarkably, he signed the nation's most progressive abortion law, permitting more legal abortions than in any other state before *Roe v. Wade*—a fact that most conservatives still like to forget.[25]

This also explains Reagan's behavior at the Republican convention in Detroit. In stark contrast to his unusually uncompromising rhetoric in 1976, this time he explicitly reached out to floating voters and Democrats, most famously invoking the record and spirit of Franklin D. Roosevelt in his acceptance address. This was not just a bit of rhetorical trickery: throughout his life, Reagan remained an ardent admirer of the father of the New Deal, and even the speech for Barry Goldwa-ter that launched his political career in 1964 borrowed FDR's words about Ameri-cans having a rendezvous with destiny. The most striking sign of his willingness to compromise, however, was his bid to attract Gerald Ford as his vice president (or co-president, as the press described it), which suggested not only that he was much more pragmatic than many people believed, but also that he was much less secure, feeling the need to balance his ticket with an experienced party moderate. In many ways, he had a lucky escape: a Reagan-Ford ticket would have been ex-tremely popular, but it would also have left Reagan's authority compromised and his message confused. Instead, of course, he went with Bush. Poor Ford had to con-sole himself with a cameo appearance on *Dynasty*, chatting to the Carringtons at a charity ball while Henry Kissinger flirts with Joan Collins's Alexis.[26]

This is not to say, of course, that Reagan did not run on a distinctly right-wing platform in 1980, or that the American people did not perceive him as highly con-servative. But it is to point out that at bottom, Reagan was a careful, pragmatic politician, and that his conservatism was always more nuanced, even more under-stated, than many people now realize. On foreign policy, for example, he took care to soften the sharp edges that had been so pronounced in 1976: during his presi-dential debate with Jimmy Carter, he used the word "peace" over and over again, and even began his first answer with the words, "I'm only here to tell you that I believe with all my heart that our first priority must be world peace."[27]

And while his economic platform promised drastic tax and spending cuts, it is not at all clear that Reagan himself was a doctrinaire supply-sider. After briefing the candidate about the new supply-side gospel, the cult's high priest Jude Wanniski "was alarmed at how shallow the guy seemed," while Reagan's future budget chief David Stockman, who prepared him for the presidential debate, thought that he "had only the foggiest idea of what supply-side was all about." Most Republicans, in fact, backed supply-side because it provided a new rationale for their old faith in cutting taxes, not because they shared Wanniski's messianic faith in supply-side as a recipe for eternal growth. As Stockman himself put it, supply-side was "a Trojan horse," providing "new clothes for the unpopular doctrine of the old Republican orthodoxy." "It's kind of hard to sell 'trickle down,'" he said, "so the supply-side formula was the only way to get a tax policy that was really 'trickle down.'"[28]

It is not quite true that there was no right turn *at all* at the end of the 1970s. The OPEC oil shock, military defeat in Vietnam, and the humiliation of the Iranian hostage crisis had all left powerful scars in the nation's self-esteem, and there was clearly a pronounced public appetite for a leader who would walk tall abroad and carry a big stick. Crime was another obvious area where public sentiments had moved rightward: by the end of the decade, polls showed increasing impatience with liberal judges, no sympathy for poor criminals, and a firm belief that prison sentences should be much tougher.[29]

As Reagan's pollster Richard Wirthlin argued, however, it was "very difficult" to make the case that Americans were "moving in a more conservative direction." True, cutting taxes and spending more on defense won more support than "five or ten years ago." But the trends, he said, did not present "a nice, neat picture." On specific issues such as food stamps and health insurance, Wirthlin noted, Americans "frequently opt for the liberal choice." They did "want to take care of the needy, and they are clearly more liberal on the life-style issues, like the use of drugs, the ERA, abortion, gay rights, and their attitudes toward marriage." Gerald Ford's old pollster Bob Teeter agreed. While the public clearly held more conservative views on tax, crime, and welfare, he also said that "when the problems are fair housing and getting black kids an education, those same people look more liberal."[30]

Looking at the astonishing election results in November 1980, many observers concluded that liberalism was finished. "Basically, the New Deal died yesterday," said Paul Tsongas, the young Democratic senator from Massachusetts. To have any chance of surviving, he added, "liberalism must extricate itself from the 1960s" and "find a new rationale." If it failed, "then the last meeting of liberals will inevitably be held in an old people's home." In some ways, he was right. Having put their faith in economic growth for so long, liberals had never come up with coherent answers to the stagflation of the seventies, which pitted class against class, put a brake on rising living standards, and drastically curtailed government's ability to tax and spend. Polls in 1980 showed that 68 percent of voters thought their taxes were too high, while half agreed that the power of government was too strong. Inflation, unemployment, crime, taxes, delinquency, abortion, homosexuality, feminism, Vietnam, Iran: all seemed to be pushing the American electorate into the arms of the Republicans.[31]

And yet it is surely wrong to think of 1980 as a conservative realignment when fewer than one in three voters described themselves as "conservative," and when only one in ten Reagan voters said they had been swayed by the candidate's ideology. Polls showed that most Americans still believed in activist government and federal spending. The vast majority still supported Social Security and Medicare, most still supported abortion and the Equal Rights Amendment, and most were moving toward more liberal positions on race, homosexuality, and women's rights. Indeed, for all the talk of a "Reagan Revolution," only 22 percent of Americans supported a federal tax cut, only 36 percent supported cuts in domestic spending, and only 19 percent opposed a new arms limitation deal with the Soviet Union. Most people remained smack in the middle of the ideological spectrum. "There was no party realignment in 1980," said Reagan's pollster Richard Wirthlin, who knew what he was talking about.[32]

In many ways, in fact, the real story of 1980 was not Reagan's victory but Carter's defeat. In a *Time* magazine poll, only one in four voters thought the election was a "mandate for more conservative policies," while 63 percent agreed that the election was "mostly a rejection of President Carter." And the single most important issue was not abortion, crime, or even Iran, but the economy—which is why Reagan's "Are you better off than you were four years ago?" refrain in the presidential candidates' only debate struck such a chord. No incumbent president had ever won reelection with such a poor economic record. "We never had a chance of winning that campaign," Hamilton Jordan admitted many years later. "It was only ultimately a nagging doubt about Ronald Reagan that kept that race close up until the final days."[33]

Since any election is, to an extent, a referendum on the incumbent, there is a case that Reagan won in 1980 merely because Carter's presidency had been such a fiasco. And yet that does not explain why so many people at the time thought that the election had been a watershed, or why the Republicans had such spectacular success at kicking out established liberal Democrats such as Senators Birch Bayh of Indiana, Frank Church of Idaho, and George McGovern of South Dakota, or why they had done so well in 1978, or why the Democrats would struggle to regain their former glory in the 1980s. To focus merely on Carter's mistakes, and to conclude that Reagan won only because of luck or the turn of events, is to miss the point that American politics had actually *already* shifted rightward, thanks to the elections of 1968, 1972, and 1976. It was not Reagan but Carter who insisted that big-government liberalism should be consigned to history, launched the great wave of deregulation, and began cutting welfare budgets. It was Carter who lectured the Soviet leaders about human rights, began sending aid to the insurgents in Afghanistan, and asked for more defense spending to meet the challenge of a renewed Cold War. If, by some fluke, Carter had won in 1980, he would have taken the election as a mandate for confrontation abroad and conservatism at home. His reelection would not have been a victory of liberalism over Reaganism; it would have been the victory of Reaganism-lite.

What emerges, therefore, is an extremely messy, complicated picture that defies easy categorization. Although we are often quick to divide political history into discrete eras—the New Deal, the Great Society, the Reagan Revolution—the example of the 1970s and 1980s is a good illustration of just how misleading this can be. In some ways, to be sure, this was an increasingly conservative age, in which Americans turned their backs on progressive taxation and welfare spending, took a hard line on crime and moral issues, prioritized inflation over unemployment, and retreated from the promise of the environmental, feminist, and other social movements. And yet, at the same time, this was also an age in which overt political racism evaporated and affirmative action became embedded in the fabric of American life. It was an age in which women, racial minorities, gays and lesbians, illegal immigrants, migrant farmworkers, the poor, the handicapped, prisoners, the mentally retarded, and even atheists and pornographers all enjoyed new rights—and rights, crucially, that often survived the Reagan and Bush years unscathed and even enhanced. The miserable failure of Edward Kennedy's presidential campaign in 1980, as well as that of Walter Mondale's four years later, is a reminder that "traditional" sub-Keynesian liberalism, in so far as there was such a thing, was no longer a very effective vote-winner. But liberalism itself was far from dead; in some ways, it was more deeply woven into American life than ever.

That it was Reagan who came to dominate this era is a testament less to the importance of his backers in the New Right or the Moral Majority—who never wielded the influence they liked to boast about—than to his own skill in appealing simultaneously to right and center. With his gospel of low taxes, economic growth, and strong defense, he naturally appealed to the Republican Party's heartlands, which by now included the booming Sunbelt South. But Reagan was also a master of exploiting the inconsistencies of a society poised between liberalism and conservatism. That a divorced Hollywood actor with a history of dating nubile starlets and a bottomless fund of dirty jokes could become the candidate of the Religious Right was merely the least of his political accomplishments; even more striking was the fact that a Californian millionaire with expensive tastes and a family life torn from the script of *Dynasty* could win election as the incarnation of latter-day populism. But when Reagan took that call from Jimmy Carter, his hair dripping with water, and he heard the words he had long dreamed about, it was not just a victory for a refurbished Republican Party, or for a newly confident conservative movement, but for a candidate whose personal and political contradictions embodied the ambiguities of his times.

NOTES

1. *New York Times*, August 20, 1976; *Washington Post*, August 20, 1976; and Lou Cannon, *Governor Reagan: His Rise to Power* (New York: PublicAffairs, 2003), 432–33.
2. Ronald Reagan, *An American Life* (New York: Simon and Schuster, 1990), 222.
3. *New York Times*, November 24, 1976; Everett Carll Ladd Jr. with Charles D. Hadley, *Transformations of the American Party System: Political Coalitions from the New Deal to the 1970s*, 2nd ed. (New York: Norton, 1978), 258–59; and Gerald Pomper, "The

Presidential Election," in *The Election of 1976: Results and Interpretations*, ed. Gerald Pomper (New York: David McKay, 1977), 82; and *Time*, August 23, 1976.

4. Pat Caddell to Jimmy Carter, "Initial Working Paper on Political Strategy," December 10, 1976, quoted in Thomas Byrne Edsall with Mary D. Edsall, *Chain Reaction: The Impact of Race, Rights, and Taxes on American Politics* (New York: Norton, 1992), 103.

5. George H. Nash, *The Conservative Intellectual Movement in America*, updated ed. (Wilmington, DE: Intercollegiate Studies Institute, 1996), 134–71, 321–24. See also John B. Judis, *William F. Buckley, Jr.: Patron Saint of the Conservatives* (New York: Simon and Schuster, 1988).

6. Godfrey Hodgson, *The World Turned Right Side Up: A History of the Conservative Ascendancy in America* (Boston: Houghton Mifflin, 1996), 62; Donald T. Critchlow, *Phyllis Schlafly and Grassroots Conservatism: A Woman's Crusade* (Princeton, NJ: Princeton University Press, 2005), 6.

7. Daniel Bell, ed., *The New American Right* (New York: Criterion, 1955); Herbert McClosky, "Conservatism and Personality," *American Political Science Review* 52 (March 1958): 27–45; Herbert McClosky, "Conservatism and Personality," *Saturday Evening Post*, September 29, 1964; Rick Perlstein, *Before the Storm: Barry Goldwater and the Unmaking of the American Consensus* (New York: Hill and Wang, 2001), xiii; and Richard Hofstader, "A Long View: Goldwater in History," *New York Review of Books*, October 8, 1964.

8. Lisa McGirr, *Suburban Warriors: The Origins of the New American Right* (Princeton, NJ: Princeton University Press, 2001), 83, 94, 8–9; Matthew D. Lassiter, *The Silent Majority: Suburban Politics in the Sunbelt South* (Princeton, NJ: Princeton University Press, 2005), 7–8; and Peter Appleborne, *Dixie Rising: How the South Is Shaping American Values, Politics, and Culture* (New York: Times, 1996), 27, 44–45.

9. Alan Crawford, *Thunder on the Right: The "New Right" and the Politics of Resentment* (New York: Pantheon, 1980), 43; E. J. Dionne Jr., *Why Americans Hate Politics* (New York: Simon and Schuster, 1992), 229; David S. Broder, *Changing of the Guard: Power and Leadership in America* (New York: Penguin, 1981), 183; and Perlstein, *Before the Storm*, 162–63.

10. Crawford, *Thunder on the Right*, 270; and Russ Bellant, *The Coors Connection: How Coors Family Philanthropy Undermines Democratic Pluralism* (Boston: South End, 1991), xiii–xv, 2.

11. Jerry Falwell, "Ministers and Marchers" [March 21, 1965], reprinted in Perry Deane Young, *God's Bullies: Native Reflections on Preachers and Politics* (New York: Holt, Rinehart and Winston, 1982), 310–11.

12. Dan T. Carter, *The Politics of Rage: George Wallace, the Origins of the New Conservatism and the Transformation of American Politics* (New York: Simon and Schuster, 1995), 298–99, 346, 460–61.

13. James Moffett, *Storm in the Mountains: A Case Study of Censorship, Conflict and Consciousness* (Carbondale: Southern Illinois University Press, 1988), 54; *Human Events*, July 29, 1978; William Martin, *With God on Our Side: The Rise of the Religious Right in America* (New York: Broadway, 2005), 132; Peggy Lamson, "The White Northerner's Choice: Mrs. Hicks of Boston," *Atlantic Monthly*, June 1966, 58–62; Ronald P. Formisano, *Boston against Busing: Race, Class, and Ethnicity in the 1960s and 1970s* (1991; Chapel Hill: University of North Carolina Press, 2004), 39; J. Anthony Lukas, *Common Ground: A Turbulent Decade in the Lives of Three American Families* (New York: Knopf, 1985), 129–30, 134–35; *New York Times*, May 10, 1977; Anita

Bryant, *The Anita Bryant Story* (Old Tappan, NJ: Revell, 1977), 42–43, 90, 16; and Crawford, *Thunder on the Right*, 52.

14. Crawford, *Thunder on the Right*, 118, 23–37.

15. Martin, *With God on Our Side*, 97–98; *New York Times*, October 10, 1976; *Time*, January 2, 2007; Gil Troy, *Affairs of State: The Rise and Rejection of the Presidential Couple since World War II* (New York: Free Press, 1997), 230, 232–33.

16. See Yanek Mieczkowski, *Gerald Ford and the Challenges of the 1970s* (Lexington: University Press of Kentucky, 2005).

17. *Congressional Record*, September 16, 1981, 97th Congress, 1st Session, 757–58; and Crawford, *Thunder on the Right*, 113–17.

18. Crawford, *Thunder on the Right*, 267–68, 277; and Michael Barone, *Our Country: The Shaping of America from Roosevelt to Reagan* (New York: Free Press, 1990), 576.

19. *Newsweek*, November 20, 1978. See also Robert Kuttner, *Revolt of the Haves: Tax Rebellions and Hard Times* (New York: Simon and Schuster, 1980); Edsall with Edsall, *Chain Reaction*, 134; and Critchlow, *Phyllis Schlafly and Grassroots Conservatism*, 263.

20. *New York Times*, July 7, 1980.

21. Theodore H. White, *America in Search of Itself: The Making of the President, 1956–1980* (New York: Harper and Row, 1982), 238, 302; and Andrew E. Busch, *Reagan's Victory: The Presidential Election of 1980 and the Rise of the Right* (Lawrence: University Press of Kansas, 2005), 46–47.

22. Peter Schweizer and Rochelle Schweizer, *The Bushes: Portrait of a Dynasty* (New York: Doubleday, 2004), 279; *National Review*, February 22, 1980; Jack W. Germond and Jules Witcover, *Blue Smoke and Mirrors: How Reagan Won and Why Carter Lost the Election of 1980* (New York: Viking, 1981), 117–18; Steven F. Hayward, *The Age of Reagan: The Fall of the Old Liberal Order, 1964–1980* (Roseville, CA: Forum, 2001), 625; and Herbert S. Parmet, *George Bush: The Life of a Lone-Star Yankee* (New York: Scribner, 1997), 226.

23. Hayward, *Age of Reagan (Fall)*, 614, 597.

24. *Wall Street Journal*, July 19, 1978; and Crawford, *Thunder on the Right*, 120.

25. See Cannon, *Governor Reagan*.

26. *Washington Post*, July 18, 1980; Germond and Witcover, *Blue Smoke and Mirrors*, 167–72, 174–83, 187–88; and Cannon, *Governor Reagan*, 472–75.

27. Transcript of the presidential debate, October 28, 1980, online at *www.debates.org*.

28. David A. Stockman, *The Triumph of Politics: How the Reagan Revolution Failed* (New York: Harper and Row, 1986), 44–47; Sidney Blumenthal, *The Rise of the Counter-Establishment: From Conservative Ideology to Political Power* (New York: Times, 1986), 224; and William Greider, "The Education of David Stockman," *Atlantic Monthly*, December 1981, 27–54.

29. Edsall with Edsall, *Chain Reaction*, 45; Daniel Patrick Moynihan, *Maximum Feasible Misunderstanding: Community Action in the War on Poverty* (New York: Free Press, 1969), xii–xiii; Morris Janowitz, *The Last Half Century: Societal Change and Politics in America* (Chicago: University of Chicago Press, 1978), 377; and Jonathan Rieder, *Canarsie: The Jews and Italians of Brooklyn against Liberalism* (Cambridge, MA: Harvard University Press, 1985), 180.

30. Thomas Ferguson and Joel Rogers, *Right Turn: The Decline of the Democrats and the Future of American Politics* (New York: Hill and Wang, 1986), 14–15, 18–19; Edsall with Edsall, *Chain Reaction*, 152; Michael Schaller, *Right Turn: American Life in the Reagan-Bush Era, 1980–1992* (New York: Oxford University Press, 2007), 41; and Broder, *Changing of the Guard*, 411–12.

31. Hayward, *Age of Reagan (Fall)*, 714; *Washington Post*, November 6, 1980; Broder, *Changing of the Guard*, 6; Edsall with Edsall, *Chain Reaction*, 3–5, 101–3, 152, 181; Dionne, *Why Americans Hate Politics*, 136; and Busch, *Reagan's Victory*, 143.

32. Dionne, *Why Americans Hate Politics*, 136; Gil Troy, *Morning in America: How Ronald Reagan Invented the 1980s* (Princeton, NJ: Princeton University Press, 2005), 49; John Ehrman, *The Eighties: America in the Age of Reagan* (New Haven, CT: Yale University Press, 2005), 47–48; *Time*, February 2, 1981; and Broder, *Changing of the Guard*, 2.

33. *Time*, February 2, 1981; W. Carl Biven, *Jimmy Carter's Economy: Policy in an Age of Limits* (Chapel Hill: University of North Carolina Press, 2002), 3, 13; Burton I. Kaufman, *The Presidency of James Earl Carter, Jr.* (Lawrence: University Press of Kansas, 1993), 206; and Kenneth E. Morris, *Jimmy Carter: American Moralist* (Athens: University of Georgia Press, 1996), 287.

EPILOGUE

The Ongoing Republican Search for a New Majority since 1980

Robert Mason and Iwan Morgan

The outcome of the 1980 elections encouraged Republicans to believe that they were on the verge of establishing themselves as the new majority party in American politics, but this proved to be another false dawn in the wake of the disappointments of the Nixon era. The pattern of hopes raised and promise unfulfilled would become a common one for the GOP over the next thirty years. Whenever the party appeared close to breaking through to majority status, contingency, overreach, or miscalculation—whether singly or in combination—put this achievement beyond its grasp. Accordingly, the Republicans never attained the sustained domination of national politics that the Democrats had enjoyed from the 1930s through the 1960s. Despite sometimes holding the upper hand, they had to settle in the main for what GOP pollster Richard Wirthlin called "parity status" in a habitually tight electoral environment.[1]

Republican hopes of shifting America's center of political gravity in the direction of conservatism also fell short of party expectations and ambitions. As historian Julian Zelizer notes, the nation's right turn in the late twentieth century and beyond was only partial in nature and liberalism remained more powerful than is often assumed. The GOP counted tax reduction, deregulation, domestic program cutbacks, and retrenchment of labor union rights among its conservative successes, but other elements of its agenda, notably antistatism as a whole and sociomoral traditionalism, had more limited popular appeal.[2] That said, it is undeniable that conservatism has carried greater policy influence and electoral weight since 1980 than was the case during the long period of Democratic Party dominance that started with the New Deal. This was in part because Republicans succeeded in making conservative ideas and issues more relevant to voter interests and in part because Democrats failed to update aspects of liberalism in appealing fashion.

The GOP's hope that Ronald Reagan would lead it to the Promised Land of partisan ascendancy proved short-lived. Having slashed the Democratic majority in the House of Representatives from 119 seats to 51 to go with their capture of the Senate in 1980, Republicans were confident of soon taking control of the entire

Congress. The deep recession of 1981–1982, the product of the Federal Reserve's castor-oil monetarist cure for inflation, put paid to that prospect. Many stagflation-weary Democratic voters in states that had gone to Reagan two years earlier reverted to their habitual loyalty in the 1982 midterm elections, which saw the Republicans lose twenty-five House seats. At least the GOP kept its Senate majority of nine intact, but the National Conservative Political Action Committee's failure to unseat any liberal Democratic senators with a repeat of its 1980 electoral blitzkrieg suggested that pocketbook issues were more important than sociomoral values to the party's electoral success. Four years later, the Republicans also lost their Senate majority due to a combination of factors, notably farm state dissatisfaction about the rural economy, the shallowness of the economic recovery in some industrial states, and a Democratic campaign that targeted freshman GOP senators from the class of 1980.[3]

Overall, the Reagan era was a period of progress but not ascendancy for the GOP. Notwithstanding his somewhat personalized reelection campaign, which had short coattails for congressional Republicans in 1984, the president was a considerable asset to his party. One political science study posited that Reagan's personal popularity was worth three percentage points in the growth of Republican Party identifiers during the 1980s. Reagan was usually generous in his support for the party's candidates, he worked to build on the organizational improvements initiated during William Brock's tenure as Republican National Committee chair in 1977–1981, and he articulated a message of optimistic conservatism that appealed to many blue-collar Democrats. If Reagan could not fully transfer his personal popularity to his party, he helped to ensure that it would not undergo temporary decline after he left office in the manner of the post-Eisenhower GOP. Despite the bitterness of the 1988 battle for the Republican presidential nomination, which testified to ideological and personality rifts within party ranks and among his would-be successors, the fortieth president established strong foundations, both in policy and organizational terms, for the GOP's future success.[4]

The second instance when a Republican majority seemed imminent was in the mid-1990s. In the 1994 elections, the GOP achieved a historic breakthrough to take control of both houses of the legislature for the first time since 1952 and then sustained this for more than one Congress for the first time since the 1920s.[5] The midterm gain of fifty-six House and ten Senate seats, the party's greatest advance in any congressional election since 1946, instilled confidence that a Republican would recapture the presidency in 1996.[6] At this juncture, it seemed certain that Bill Clinton would be a one-term president. He had sullied his centrist "New Democrat" credentials by promoting higher taxes in 1993 and a failed health-care initiative in 1994, both of which made him look like just another "tax-and-spend" liberal. He had also presided over a sluggish recovery from the recession that had initially helped him capture the White House in 1992, albeit with the smallest winning share of the popular vote since 1912. Nevertheless, he went on to be reelected by a comfortable margin, thanks in part to GOP leaders of the 104th Congress of 1995–1996 overreaching in their dealings with him.

With the putative "Republican revolution" of 1994, Congress replaced the presidency as the primary focus of party revitalization under the energetic leadership of the new House Speaker, Representative Newt Gingrich of Georgia. First elected in 1978 as a beneficiary of the party's new strength in the suburban South, Gingrich disdained the minority mindset that seemingly gripped longer-established GOP legislators from the Northeast and Midwest and questioned what the party had gained from their habitual willingness to engage in the politics of compromise. In 1983 he joined with other young Turks of similar outlook to form the Conservative Opportunity Society (COS) as the first step in building a new Republican majority. The group's reputation was initially defined by attack rhetoric and confrontational stands, rather than its policy ideas. As one of its founding members, Representative Vin Weber of Minnesota, acknowledged in 1990, COS devoted excessive attention to "wedge issues against the Democrats, without also creating magnet issues that would attract the public." The development of the "Contract with America" in readiness for the 1994 midterm elections marked a change of approach. Adopted by 367 Republican candidates as their common platform, this conservative manifesto established a set of policy goals predicated on the belief that the GOP now had "the chance, after four decades of one-party control, to bring the House a new majority that will transform the way Congress works."[7]

Heady with victory, House Republicans made the mistake of interpreting their election success as a mandate for the Contract with America agenda, rather than an expression of voter dissatisfaction with the president and his party. Pulling GOP Senate leaders along in his wake, Gingrich headed the charge to enact its ambitious aims. The principal Republican goal was a sweeping proposal to balance the budget over seven years through massive expenditure retrenchment that would also pay for huge tax cuts. Confident that Clinton was now the lamest of lame ducks, the congressional GOP refused to agree a budget unless he accepted its fiscal plan. Adopting a "triangulation" strategy that aimed to restore his centrist identity through acceptance of popular Republican issues, the president agreed to balance the budget but insisted on doing so over a ten-year period to soften social program retrenchment. Faced with his determined resistance, congressional Republicans precipitated two partial shutdowns of government to force his acquiescence to their budget plan. This enabled Clinton to denounce them for putting ideology ahead of national interest in refusing to negotiate a settlement. Polls indicated that most Americans preferred compromise to confrontation between the two branches of government and blamed the Republicans for the shutdowns. Aware that they had a public relations disaster on their hands, GOP leaders retreated to accept White House terms, but the episode saddled their party with an extremist image. Continuing to pursue triangulation, the president then undercut Republican distinctiveness on their other popular issues of welfare reform and anticrime measures by integrating these into his own agenda. Adding to the GOP's woes, the party's 1996 presidential candidate, Robert J. Dole, lacked Clinton's charisma and campaigning skill, and the gathering pace of economic recovery limited the appeal of his banner proposal for a supply-side tax cut, targeted primarily at high earners, to spur investment and jobs.[8]

Unable to defeat Clinton at the polls, the GOP then sought to impeach him for perjury and obstruction of justice in covering up his affair with White House intern Monica Lewinsky. Although hearings did not start until after the 1998 midterms, scandal-focused Republican attacks on Clinton in the campaign proved a miscalculation of the first order. Opinion polls showed that a significant majority of the public made a distinction between the president's private misconduct and his job effectiveness, notably in helping to promote the strongest period of economic growth since the 1960s. As a result, the Democrats achieved a small net gain of seats in the 1998 midterm elections, the first time since 1822 that a president's party had increased its congressional representation in his sixth year of office.[9]

The next instance that a new Republican majority appeared at hand was when the War on Terror changed American politics to the party's advantage during George W. Bush's presidency. Prior to the 9/11 attacks on New York and Washington, the GOP had seemed to be slipping back in the quest for the elusive goal. Although the party recaptured the White House in 2000, Bush was the first president since 1888 to have won office without a popular vote majority and owed his Electoral College victory to the disputed votes of Florida, awarded to him by the Supreme Court in the *Bush v. Gore* decision. The congressional GOP also had its House majority further reduced and depended on the casting vote of Vice President Dick Cheney to retain control of an evenly divided Senate, which was soon lost when James Jeffords of Vermont abandoned his party affiliation to assume status as an independent in mid-2001. These developments suggested the emergence of a "fifty-fifty nation"—an equilibrium between the so-called Red America of Republican supporters and the Blue America of Democratic supporters that was seemingly an exact manifestation of Richard Wirthlin's parity concept.[10] Whether this deadlock could be broken and to whose advantage became a major topic of early twenty-first-century political debate.[11]

Seeing an enduring Republican majority as necessary to promote its agenda and sustain its legacy, the Bush White House instituted a systematic quest to establish one. Although senior political adviser Karl Rove was the architect of this ambitious strategy, the president was energetic in its promotion. He campaigned enthusiastically for Republican candidates and supported organizational improvements to identify and mobilize GOP voters. As political scientists Sidney Milkis and Jesse Rhodes commented, "Bush's partisan leadership marks the most systematic effort by a modern president to create a strong national party."[12]

The initial Rove-Bush strategy, which came to be characterized as "compassionate conservatism," involved an often uneasy balance between conservative goals and governmental activism. Consciously designed to achieve electoral realignment, this agenda recognized the danger of appearing hostile to social-welfare concerns in the manner of the Contract with America. It entailed promotion of nationalized education standards; government support for faith-based organizations providing social services; the partial privatization of Social Security; the introduction of a private alternative to Medicare; and immigration reform. These measures were intended to appeal to existing Republican constituencies and to woo new ones. "It's hard to think of any analogue in American history to what Karl Rove was trying to do," said political scientist David Mayhew, author of a skeptical book about realignments. In fact, Bush's adviser had a historical precedent in mind since he believed that his boss could emulate the success of a distant Republican predecessor, President William McKinley, in reaching out to disaffected Democrats. The policy agenda of compassionate conservatism, however, proved difficult to enact, had limited electoral effect, and fomented conflict between the White House and congressional Republicans.[13]

In the post-9/11 political environment, Bush downplayed compassionate conservatism to turn the 2002 elections into a referendum on his leadership in the War on Terror and the strengthening of homeland security. In so doing, he reactivated the Republican Party's foreign policy advantage that had been visible during the Cold War. The GOP's consequent success in increasing its House majority and recapturing control of the Senate was the first time since 1934 that a president's party had increased its congressional representation in the midterm contests of his first term. Building on this achievement, the Republicans retained the presidency and both houses of Congress in 2004, the first time they had achieved this feat since 1928.[14]

Buoyed by this outcome, House Majority Leader Tom DeLay of Texas triumphantly proclaimed, "The Republican Party is a permanent majority for the future of this country. . . . We are going to be able to lead this country in the direction we've been dreaming of for years."[15] Such confidence exaggerated the scope of the GOP's 2004 electoral success, however. Political scientists Earl Black and Merle Black more accurately judged its success "solid but not overwhelming." Bush's 51 to 48 percent popular-vote triumph was low by the historic standards of presidential reelection margins. Exit polls reported, moreover, that the GOP lead over the Democrats in terms of party identification among voters was a mere 39 to 38 percent.[16] Aware that the election did not mark the final emergence of a Republican majority but confident that it was an important staging post on the way to one, Karl Rove characterized the victory as "part of the rolling realignment."[17] Even this assessment overstated the significance of what was just another moment of unfulfilled promise for the GOP.

Over the next four years, the Republican Party failed to consolidate, much less expand, the gains made during Bush's first term. The president's inept management of the Hurricane Katrina disaster, the unpopularity of the Iraq War, the political fallout from the unsuccessful initiative to reform Social Security, and the series of scandals that hit the congressional party all contributed to the reversal of the Republican advance. In the 2006 midterms, the GOP surrendered control of Congress, losing thirty seats in the House (its largest loss since 1974) and six in the Senate (the largest since 1986). It also lost six governorships and over three hundred state legislature seats nationwide. Two years later, the 2008 elections turned into a virtual referendum on the Bush presidency in the midst of the worst economic crisis since the Great Depression—with predictably dire consequences for the president's party. Not only did the Republicans lose the White House but further losses of House and Senate seats reduced their congressional representation to what it had been before the great leap forward of 1994. This outcome ended all talk for the time being of a GOP majority.[18]

Despite this denouement, the Republicans had not slipped back to the status quo ante 1980. In the intervening period, the GOP had enhanced some of the strengths that underwrote its initial revival. Most significantly, the transition in its regional base that had started in the 1970s had undergone completion. Although their growing support in the South occupied much media and scholarly attention in this earlier era, the Republicans remained more powerful in the traditional bastions of the West, Midwest, and parts of the Northeast. Indeed it was not until the 1990s that they truly established ascendancy over what had formerly been the Democrats' "Solid South." In presidential terms, the GOP enhanced its grip on the electoral college votes of the South in elections of the 1980s, but the same was not true with regard to Congress. In 1989, it only held seven of the region's Senate seats and thirty-nine of its House seats, compared with eleven and forty in 1981. Not until 1994 did the Republicans capture a majority of Dixie's seats in both chambers for the first time in U.S. history. Thereafter, the region was the fundamental core of the party's strength at presidential and congressional levels—a reliable bastion that was resistant to the Democratic national sweeps of 2006 and 2008.[19]

Critical to Republicans' success in the South was their growing appeal to evangelical voters, Christians who saw themselves as saved by their personal relationship to Jesus Christ. The Christian Right, an important element within but by no means the whole of the evangelical milieu, had initially mobilized to oppose the sociocultural changes of the 1960s and early 1970s through political engagement in support of the GOP. Its activism was in relative decline in the late 1980s because of failure to advance its substantive agenda, particularly in terms of outlawing abortion. Within a short time, however, a second wave of mobilization developed in response to the election of Bill Clinton and resultant controversies over gays in the military and abortion rights. Christian Right support helped the Republican capture of Congress in 1994, but evangelical activism receded once more as a result of limited policy achievements and, particularly, the failure to impeach Clinton. Nevertheless, the second mobilization left an important legacy of influence within the structure of the GOP. According to one estimate, the Christian Right by 2000 had a strong

influence (measured as 50 percent or more of the seats on the GOP central committee) in eighteen states and moderate influence (measured as 25 to 49 percent of
seats) in twenty-six states.[20]

The 68 percent share of the evangelical vote that George W. Bush won in 2000
was crucial to his election as president. In spite of this, the new president's campaign team identified failure to mobilize a larger turnout of this constituency as a
critical factor in his lack of a popular-vote majority. Under Karl Rove's leadership,
the Bush White House undertook a concerted effort to maximize evangelical voter
participation in the 2004 election. This strategy found expression in the appointment of John Ashcroft as attorney general, the nomination of federal judges sympathetic to evangelical concerns on abortion and gay marriage, and the president's fre-
quent addresses to evangelical audiences. In addition, Tim Goeglein was appointed
deputy director of the Office of Public Liaison with a specific brief to forge a close
relationship with evangelical organizations. Richard Land of the Southern Baptist
Convention subsequently remarked: "In the Reagan administration, they would
usually return our phone calls. In the Bush 41 administration, they often would return our phone calls, but not as quickly. . . . In this administration, they call us."[21]

While Bush's reelection campaign continued to emphasize the War on Terror
leadership issue that had reaped success in 2002, his determination to appeal to
evangelicals in particular and moral traditionalists in general endowed the 2004
presidential race with a "values election" dimension. This helped Bush to win a 78
percent share of a much larger evangelical turnout that represented 23 percent of
all voters. Four years later, despite disappointment with Republican policy achievements—particularly the failure to promote a constitutional amendment prohibit-
ing gay marriage, doubts that John McCain was a true believer in their cause, and
heightened economic concerns—evangelicals still gave the Republican presidential
candidate 73 percent of their votes. However, this slight fall-off in support, combined with the much steeper ones among Catholics and the religiously unaffiliated,
tipped the scales in favor of Barack Obama.[22]

Intertwined with the growth of Republican support in the South and in the
evangelical constituency was the rightward shift in the self-identity of the electorate
at the expense of centrists. In the aggregate of national surveys held in the month
prior to the 1980 presidential election, 55 percent of voters considered themselves
moderate, 25 percent conservative, and 18 percent liberal. By 1992, the respective
tallies in Gallup surveys were 43 percent, 36 percent, and 17 percent. Conservative
identifiers increased over the next decade to exceed moderates in 2003–2004 for
the first time, but the two groups returned to even standing at 37 percent by 2008,
with liberals up to 22 percent. As conservatives became a more significant element
in the electorate, they also grew more Republican in appreciation of the GOP's
antistatism on fiscal and economic issues and sociomoral traditionalism. In 2008,
70 percent of these considered themselves as Republicans compared to 62 percent
in 2000.[23]

Meanwhile, the GOP consolidated its hold on the votes of white Americans, presently the largest group in the entire electorate but undergoing relative decline in the long term. Following John F. Kennedy's creditable 49 percent share of white votes in 1960, LBJ's 59 percent plurality in 1964 was the last time the Democrats carried a majority of this demographic in a presidential election. Thereafter, their support among whites fell away, a trend that became particularly marked from 1980 onward. With the exception of the independent candidate–affected contests of 1992 and 1996, Republicans have won strong pluralities of white ballots in every presidential election since Reagan's initial triumph. Winning the presidency in 2008 amid the kind of hard times that had brought many white voters flocking into the Democratic column in the 1930s, memory of which had kept them loyal for years afterward to the party of FDR, Barack Obama won only 43 percent of white ballots. This was just 2 percent more than John Kerry had won in the less advantageous circumstances of 2004.[24]

The Republicans' hold on the white vote partly reflected their appeal to the South, evangelicals, and conservatives, but it was also built on the foundations of socioeconomic class. In broad terms, the GOP held the ascendancy with voters in the upper half of the income distribution, a lead that grew in the top two quintiles. Its advocacy of tax cuts that particularly benefited the overwhelmingly white up-per income and upper-middle income groups was a critical factor in consolidating their support. Initially promoted by the Reagan administration and carried forward by the congressional Republicans in the 1990s, this strategy reached a new peak in George W. Bush's tax program, which was heavily skewed toward the wealthy. Some analysts regarded the 2001 and 2003 tax cuts as a fundamental effort to maximize Republican support among this base in the highly competitive electoral environment of the early twenty-first century. Others considered them part of a base-broadening strategy to appeal to the investor class that had grown in size and significance from the second half of the 1990s onward. According to pollster John Zogby, 46 percent of voters in the 2004 elections were self-identified investors, and this group went for Bush by 61 to 39 percent, whereas noninvestors voted for his Democratic opponent by 57 to 42 percent.[25]

Notwithstanding these considerable strengths, the post-1980 Republican Party also had significant weaknesses that limited its prospects of establishing majority status—and are likely to continue to do so into the second decade of the twenty-first century. One of its problems is the difficulty of pleasing its conservative base without alienating the critical group of moderate voters whose support is essential to the development of a majoritarian electoral coalition. Ronald Reagan's combi-nation of conviction and flexibility enabled him to set a new conservative agenda while displaying pragmatism in its pursuit, particularly on social program retrench-ment and sociomoral issues, but this approach became difficult to sustain as the party grew more conservative in his wake. George H. W. Bush's willingness to com-promise his "no new taxes" pledge in the interest of deficit control produced a damaging split with the GOP Right in 1990.[26] Five years later, the newly ascendant conservatives in the congressional wing of the party were taught a lesson about the dangers of being perceived as ideologically extreme in their budget battle with Bill Clinton.

Although George W. Bush's drive for compassionate conservatism had limited base-broadening success, he remained skeptical about the political appeal of antistatism. Accordingly, he chose to accept the reality of big government but redirected its focus through such programs as education reform, prescription drug benefits, and farm subsidies to benefit Republican constituencies rather than Democratic ones. This approach found its ultimate expression in his administration's intervention to save the financial system from collapse in 2008. Bush's big-government conservatism alienated many conservative Republicans, however, as a betrayal of the supposed Reagan Revolution, thereby ensuring that it did not offer a long-term solution to the problem of bridging the center and the right of the political spectrum.[27]

The GOP has a relatively homogenous base in comparison to the Democrats, which facilitated organizational efforts to mobilize the base, but the downside of this advantage is the consequent difficulty of broadening its base without alienating core constituencies that are part of it. Most obviously, the party's success in mobilizing evangelical voters complicates its efforts to win over social moderates. Similarly, its appeal to wealthier Americans is sometimes in conflict with its need to win support from lower echelons of the income distribution, namely the contemporary equivalents of the "middle Americans" that Nixon targeted and the "Reagan Democrats" of the 1980s. In this regard, Ross Douthat and Reihan Salam, writing in 2008, identified an agenda of appeal to the non–college educated as key to Republican growth.[28]

Republicans also had problems in appealing to other important groups in the electorate. The continued preference of women voters for the Democrats, often giving the opposition their margin of victory, indicated the continuation of the gender gap that GOP strategists had begun to worry about in the 1980s—particularly with regard to unmarried women. Poll data suggested that women were less likely than men to identify with the Republican stand on social program cutbacks, punitive criminal justice, abortion, and foreign military interventions in particular. The gender gap in voting worked to Bill Clinton's advantage in 1992 and again in 1996 (when Dole easily outran him among white males despite a lackluster campaign) and limited the scope of George W. Bush's popular vote in 2000 and 2004. In 2008, Barack Obama ran ahead of John McCain among women voters by 56 to 43 percent compared to his 49 to 48 percent lead among male voters. The trend was also evident in congressional elections, even when the GOP won sweeping nationwide victories. Despite recording their best midterm performance since 1946 in the 2010 elections, the Republicans ran markedly better with men than women. According to one analysis, gender gaps spreading from four to seventeen percentage points were evident in twenty-five of the twenty-six Senate races for which exit polls were conducted.[29]

Even clearer than the gender gap was the racial polarization of the electorate. African Americans had been an integral constituency of the New Deal coalition but prior to the civil rights revolution of the 1960s the Republicans could still draw support from a not insignificant number of black voters as a result of their support for civil rights initiatives. Dwight D. Eisenhower took 39 percent of African American ballots in 1956 and Richard Nixon captured 32 percent in 1960. However, the Johnson administration's promotion of the landmark civil rights legislation of 1964–1965 resulted in the collapse of black Republican support.

Thereafter the GOP faced a constant dilemma of how to boost its share of the black vote without alienating white voters, particularly those in the increasingly important South. From the 1980s onward, this largely resulted in Republicans laying more emphasis on symbolic gestures pertaining to appointments of African Americans to federal posts than substantive promotion of affirmative action policies, civil rights initiatives, and improved welfare provision. On occasion, too, Republicans used racialized appeals, albeit in coded terms that did not mention race, to maximize support from whites in both presidential and congressional elections. The most controversial instance of this occurred during George H. W. Bush's 1988 run for president, when the campaign used the case of Willie Horton, a convicted murderer who committed rape while on weekend furlough from prison in Massachusetts, to demonize liberalism as being soft on crime; for most observers, the suggested connection between criminality and race was clear. Paradoxically, Lee Atwater, the campaign aide who developed this strategy, still recognized that the GOP needed at least 20 percent of African American ballots "if we want to become a majority party." In fact, the Republicans have never captured more than 13 percent of black votes in presidential elections since 1960 and their support has several times been in single digits.[30]

Of potentially greatest significance for the Republicans' future prospects is their hitherto underdeveloped support among Latinos, whose demographic importance will grow as the twenty-first century progresses. By and large the GOP looked to appeal to this group through a combination of symbolic appointments and an emphasis on family values that supposedly bound together the party's Protestant base and Roman Catholic Latinos. This strategy attracted 37 percent of Latino voters to Reagan in 1984, but thereafter the GOP has only once got over this baseline when 44 percent went for George W. Bush in the "values election" of 2004. With economic issues eclipsing all else in 2008, the Latino support level for John McCain fell back to one in three voters. If the Democrats sustain their clear advantage with this group, it spells danger for the GOP, even allowing for the reality that high numbers of the young and the noncitizens among Latinos have so far ensured that their proportion of the electorate falls far short of their share of the overall population.

The nation's two largest states are now majority-minority states; California, once solidly Republican in the 1970s and 1980s, has effectively switched into the Democratic column in national politics, and there are predictions that demographic trends will eventually result in Texas replicating this pattern. Significantly, the Latino population is also growing across other parts of the South where the Republicans currently enjoy dominance. Responding to its expansion represents one of the greatest electoral challenges for the GOP in the medium to long term. As in the case of African Americans, the Republicans face difficulties in striking a balance between building Latino support and retaining their white base. Indicative of this is the hard line that many GOP legislators have taken on illegal immigration in the 1990s and early twenty-first century. This is also a source of intraparty tensions with Republicans who are sympathetic to the influx of Latinos, whether out of economic or political calculation.[31]

In the short term, however, the GOP's prospects looked considerably better as a result of the 2010 elections than two years earlier. The outcome discouraged speculation of a new Democratic majority emerging out of the electoral successes of 2006 and 2008. The Republicans made a net gain of sixty-four seats to regain control of the House and picked up six seats in the Senate, an outcome that was broadly attributable to the combination of four factors. The presidential party was exposed to adverse economic conditions; there was extraordinary animosity and anger among Republican identifiers that made them more likely to vote than Democrats; GOP leaders succeeded in nationalizing the election into a referendum on Barack Obama's presidency; and the Democrats failed to persuade the nation of the significance of their legislative successes. The rise of the Tea Party, essentially an alliance of angry, antistatist, conservative whites, and its success in penetrating the ranks of the House GOP also made for arguably the most divisive elections of the last twenty years.[32]

Without doubt, the Republican success put the Obama White House and the Democrats on the defensive on domestic policy during the 112th Congress. Beyond that, its significance was more difficult to gauge in the shorter term. Allied with the advantages of redistricting and the electoral efficiency of the well-dispersed Republican vote, the 2010 result augured well for the continuation of GOP control of the House and seemingly offered the party hope of soon recapturing the Senate. However, the election signified more what the Republicans were against rather than what they were for. In parallel with this, the referendum nature of the election made it more a vote against the Obama record, particularly on the economy, rather than a positive endorsement of the GOP. Moreover, the growing influence of the Tea Party promised to energize the Republican base and reflected the increasing ascendancy of self-identified conservatives in the electorate (who had opened a 42 to 35 percent lead over moderates in the mid-2010 Gallup survey of political opinion). Such conservative influence, however, threatens to offend the all-important center in a manner reminiscent of the Contract with America Republicans in the mid-

1990s.[33] Finally, whatever the short-term benefits arising out of the 2010 midterm gains, the makeup of Republican support in those elections only reaffirmed that the party's strength lies among groups that are declining in demographic significance rather than those of growing importance.[34]

Moreover, the context of politics in the second decade of the twenty-first century and beyond militates against any assumption that angry conservatism offers the party a viable platform for building a Republican majority. The new problems facing the United States are highly challenging in their scope and complexity. Economic recovery from the Great Recession remains far from complete. The rising challenge of China, India, and Brazil is bringing about an increasingly perceptible shift in the global economic balance of power that America needs to address. Most worryingly, perhaps, the United States must preempt the threat of fiscal unsustainability by bringing its escalating public debt under control. It remains to be seen whether the Republicans will adapt to these new circumstances, which will ultimately put a premium on political compromise and constructive bipartisanship in policy development, or stay wedded to the old politics in their ongoing pursuit of majority party status.

NOTES

1. Wirthlin coined this term as Reagan's time in the White House progressed, modifying his earlier assertion that a "creeping realignment was in progress." See his comments quoted in Kevin P. Phillips, *Post-Conservative America: People, Politics, and Ideology in a Time of Crisis* (New York: Vintage, 1983), 220; and Hedrick Smith, "Congress: Will There Be a Realignment?," in *Beyond Reagan: The Politics of Upheaval*, ed. Paul Duke (New York: Warner, 1986), 162.

2. Julian E. Zelizer, "Rethinking the History of American Conservatism," *Reviews in American History* 38 (2010): 371–87.

3. For overviews of the GOP in the 1980s, see Daniel J. Galvin, *Presidential Party Building: Dwight D. Eisenhower to George W. Bush* (Princeton, NJ: Princeton University Press, 2010), 120–42; and Robert Mason, "Ronald Reagan and the Republican Party: Responses to Realignment," in *Ronald Reagan and the 1980s: Perceptions, Policies, Legacies*, ed. Cheryl Hudson and Gareth Davies (New York: Palgrave, 2008), 151–72. The various elections are covered in Thomas E. Mann and Norman J. Ornstein, eds., *The American Elections of 1982* (Washington, DC: American Enterprise Institute, 1983); Michael Nelson, ed., *The Elections of 1984* (Washington, DC: CQ Press, 1985); Pippa Norris, "1986 US Elections: National Issues or Pluralistic Diversity," *Political Quarterly* 58 (1987): 194–207; and Michael Nelson, ed., *The Elections of 1988* (Washington, DC: CQ Press, 1989).

4. Paul Allen Beck, "Incomplete Realignment: The Reagan Legacy for Parties and Elections," in *The Reagan Legacy: Promise and Performance*, ed. Charles O. Jones (Chatham, NJ: Chatham House, 1988), 145–71; William Mishler, Marilyn Hoskin, and Roy E. Fitzgerald, "Hunting the Snark: Or Searching for Evidence of That Widely Touted but Highly Elusive Resurgence of Public Support for Conservative Parties in Britain, Canada, and the United States," in *The Resurgence of Conservatism in Anglo-American Democracies*, ed. Barry Cooper, Allan Kornberg, and William Mischler

(Durham, NC: Duke University Press, 1988), 85–86; Galvin, *Presidential Party Building*, 120–42; and Sidney M. Milkis and Jesse H. Rhodes, "George W. Bush, the Republican Party, and the 'New' American Party System," *Perspectives on Politics* 5 (2007): 464–67.

5. The Republicans kept control of Congress from 1995 through 2006, except for the brief loss of the Senate for a nineteen-month period beginning in mid-2001 as a result of the assumption of independent status by James Jeffords of Vermont. This was the first period of prolonged GOP control of both houses since 1919–1931. The Democrats controlled the House and Senate from 1933 through 1994 except for short-lived Republican majorities in 1947–1948 and 1953–1954; there was also a Republican majority in the Senate in 1981–1987.

6. Harold W. Stanley, "The Parties, the President, and the 1994 Midterm Elections," in *The Clinton Presidency: First Appraisals*, ed. Colin Campbell and Bert A. Rockman (Chatham, NJ: Chatham House, 1996), 188–211; Philip A. Klinkner, ed., *Midterm: The Elections of 1994 in Context* (Boulder, CO: Westview Press, 1996); and Jeffrey Stonecraft and Mack D. Mariani, "GOP Gains in the House in the 1994 Elections: Class Polarization in American Politics," *Political Science Quarterly* 116 (Spring 2000): 93–113.

7. Robert Mason, *The Republican Party and American Politics from Hoover to Reagan* (New York: Cambridge University Press, 2012), 247–81; Adam Meyerson, "Wedges and Magnets: Vin Weber on Conservative Opportunities," *Policy Review*, Spring 1990, 38; and James T. Patterson, *Restless Giant: The United States from Watergate to Bush v. Gore* (New York: Oxford University Press, 2005), 343.

8. Iwan Morgan, *The Age of Deficits: Presidents and Unbalanced Budgets from Jimmy Carter to George W. Bush* (Lawrence: University Press of Kansas, 2009), 178–93; James W. Ceaser and Andrew E. Busch, eds., *Losing to Win: The 1996 Elections and American Politics* (Lanham, MD: Rowman and Littlefield, 1997); and Michael Nelson, ed., *The 1996 Elections* (Washington, DC: CQ Press, 1997).

9. Gary C. Jacobsen, "Impeachment Politics in the 1998 Congressional Elections," *Political Science Quarterly* 114 (Spring 1999): 31–51.

10. Andrew J. Taylor, *Elephant's Edge: The Republicans as a Ruling Party* (Westport, CT: Praeger, 2005), 6.

11. John B. Judis and Ruy Teixeira, *The Emerging Democratic Majority* (New York: Scribner, 2002); Taylor, *Elephant's Edge*; and John Micklethwait and Adrian Wooldridge, *The Right Nation: Conservative Power in America* (New York: Penguin, 2004).

12. Milkis and Rhodes, "George W. Bush," 467–75.

13. Joshua Green, "The Rove Presidency," *Atlantic*, September 2007, reprinted in Royce Flippin, ed., *The Best American Political Writing 2008* (New York: PublicAffairs, 2008), 253–74; and David R. Mayhew, *Electoral Realignments: A Critique of an American Genre* (New Haven, CT: Yale University Press, 2002).

14. Gary C. Jacobson, "Terror, Terrain, and Turnout: The 2002 Midterm Election," *Political Science Quarterly* 118 (May 2003): 1–22; James E. Campbell, "The 2002 Midterm Election: A Typical or an Atypical Moment," *PS: Political Science and Politics* 36 (April 2003): 203–7; Taylor, *Elephant's Edge*, 103–25; Kevin Fullam and Alan R. Gitelson, "A Lasting Republican Majority? George W. Bush's Electoral Strategy," in *Assessing the George W. Bush Presidency: A Tale of Two Terms*, ed. Andrew Wroe and Jon Herbert (Edinburgh: Edinburgh University Press, 2009), 245–48; Philip Davies, "A New Republican Majority?," in *Right On? Political Change and Continuity in George W.*

Bush's America, ed. Iwan Morgan and Philip Davies (London: Institute for the Study of the Americas, 2006), 184–203.

15. John F. Harris and James VandeHei, "Doubts about Mandate for Bush, GOP," *Washington Post*, May 2, 2005.

16. Earl Black and Merle Black, *Divided America: The Ferocious Power Struggle in American Politics* (New York: Simon and Schuster, 2007), 2–8.

17. Taylor, *Elephant's Edge*, 14.

18. Gary C. Jacobson, "The 2008 Presidential Elections: Anti-Bush Referendum and Prospects for the Democratic Majority," *Political Science Quarterly* 124 (Spring 2009): 1–30; Gary C. Jacobson, "George W. Bush, the Iraq War and the Election of Barack Obama," *Presidential Studies Quarterly* 40 (June 2010): 207–24; and Philip John Davies, "Bush's Partisan Legacy and the 2008 Elections," in *Assessing George W. Bush's Legacy: The Right Man?*, ed. Iwan Morgan and Philip John Davies (New York: Palgrave, 2010), 201–21.

19. Earl Black and Merle Black, *The Rise of Southern Republicans* (Cambridge, MA: Harvard University Press, 2003); Charles S. Bullock III and Mark J. Rozell, eds., *The New Politics of the Old South: An Introduction to Southern Politics*, 3rd ed. (Lanham, MD: Rowman and Littlefield, 2007); and Ronald Brownstein, "For GOP, a Southern Exposure," *National Journal*, May 23, 2009, *www.nationaljournal.com*.

20. Daniel K. Williams, "Reagan's Religious Right: The Unlikely Alliance between Southern Evangelicals and a California Conservative," in Hudson and Davies, *Ronald Reagan and the 1980s*, 135–50; Robert Boston, *Close Encounters with the Religious Right* (Amherst, MA: Prometheus Books, 2000); and Kimberley H. Conger and John C. Green, "Spreading Out and Digging In: Christian Conservatives and State Republican Parties," *Campaigns and Elections* 23 (February 2002): 58–60, 64–65.

21. Martin Durham, "Evangelicals and the Politics of Red America," in Morgan and Davies, *Right On?*, 204–18; and "The Jesus Factor: Interview Richard Land," *Frontline*, 2004, *www.pbs.org*.

22. John C. Green, Mark J. Rozell, and Clyde Wilcox, eds., *The Values Campaign? The Christian Right and the 2004 Elections* (Washington, DC: Georgetown University Press, 2006); and Pew Forum on Religion and Public Life, "How the Faithful Voted," November 10, 2008, *pewforum.org*.

23. Everett Carll Ladd Jr., *Where Have All the Voters Gone? The Fracturing of America's Political Parties* (New York: Norton, 1982); and Gallup, "In 2010, Conservatives Still Outnumber Moderates, Liberals," June 25, 2010, *www.gallup.com*.

24. Davies, "Bush's Partisan Legacy," 218.

25. Morgan, *Age of Deficits*, 220–31; Jacob S. Hacker and Paul Pierson, *Off Center: The Republican Revolution and the Erosion of Democracy* (New Haven, CT: Yale University Press, 2005), 48–49; and Thomas B. Edsall, *Building Red America: The New Conservative Coalition and the Drive for Permanent Power* (New York: Basic Books, 2006), 43–44.

26. For commentary on Reagan's pragmatic conservatism, see W. Elliott Brownlee and Hugh Davies Graham, eds., *The Reagan Presidency: Pragmatic Conservatism and Its Legacies* (Lawrence: University Press of Kansas, 2003); and Robert M. Collins, *Transforming America: Politics and Culture during the Reagan Years* (New York: Columbia University Press, 2007), 29–57. The 1990 GOP split on taxes is analyzed in Morgan, *Age of Deficits*, 137–49.

27. Fred Barnes, "'Big Government Conservatism': George Bush Style," *Wall Street Journal*, August 15, 2003, and Barnes, *Rebel-in-Chief: Inside the Bold and Controversial*

Presidency of George W. Bush (New York: Crown Forum, 2006); Dan Casse, "Is Bush a Conservative?," *Commentary*, February 2004, 19–26; and Alex Waddan, "Bush and Big Government Conservatism," in Morgan and Davies, *Assessing George W. Bush's Legacy*, 165–84. For examples of conservative hostility, see Richard A. Viguerie, *Conservatives Betrayed: How George W. Bush and Other Big-Government Republicans Hijacked the Conservative Cause* (Los Angeles: Bonus Books, 2006); and Michael D. Tanner, *Leviathan on the Right: How Big-Government Conservatism Brought Down the Republican Revolution* (Washington, DC: Cato Institute, 2007).

28. Black and Black, *Divided America*, 91; and Ross Douthat and Reihan Salam, *Grand New Party: How Republicans Can Win the Working Class and Save the American Dream* (New York: Doubleday, 2008).

29. For analysis over time, see Jeff Manza and Clem Brooks, "The Gender Gap in US Presidential Elections: When? Why? Implications?," *American Journal of Sociology* 103 (1998): 1235–66. For data on and analysis of elections from 2000 to the present, consult the Election Watch reports and commentaries of the Center for Women in American Politics, Rutgers University, at *www.cawp.rutgers.edu*. See in particular "Gender Gap Widespread in 2010 Elections: Women Less Likely Than Men to Support Republican Candidates," November 4, 2010.

30. Louis Bolce, Gerald de Maio, and Douglas Muzzio, "Blacks and the Republican Party: The 20 Percent Solution," *Political Science Quarterly* 107 (Spring 1992): 63–79; and Michael K. Fauntroy, *Republicans and the Black Vote* (Boulder, CO: Lynne Rienner, 2006).

31. Mason, "Ronald Reagan and the Republican Party," 164, 172; David L. Leal, Matt A. Barreto, Jongho Lee, and Rodolfo O. de la Garza, "The Latino Vote in the 2004 Elections," *PS: Political Science and Politics* 38 (January 2005): 41–49; Dowell Myers, "California and the Third Great Transition: Immigrant Incorporation, Ethnic Change, and Population Aging, 1970–2030," in *America's Americans: Population Issues in U.S. Society and Politics*, ed. Philip Davies and Iwan Morgan (London: Institute for the Study of the Americas, 2007), 346–82; Ruy Texeira, "Demographic Change and the Future of the Parties" (working paper), Center for American Progress Action Fund, June 2010, *www.americanprogressaction.org*; and Andrew Wroe, *The Republican Party and Immigration Politics: From Proposition 187 to George W. Bush* (New York: Palgrave, 2008).

32. Gary C. Jacobson, "The Republican Resurgence in 2010," *Political Science Quarterly* 127 (Spring 2011): 27–52; Jamie L. Carson and Stephen Pettigrew, "Strategic Politicians, the Great Recession, and the Tea Party Movement: Evaluating the 2010 Midterm Elections" (paper prepared for the 2011 Midwest Political Science Association meeting), *www.mpsanet.org*.

33. Gallup, "In 2010."

34. For discussion of this, see Philip A. Klinkner and Thomas Schaller, "LBJ's Revenge: The 2008 Election and the Rise of the Great Society Coalition," *Forum* 6, no. 4 (2008), article 9, *www.bepress.com/forum*.

CONTRIBUTORS

Donald T. Critchlow is the Goldwater Chair of American Institutions at Arizona State University. The founding editor of the *Journal of Policy History*, he is the author of numerous books, including *Debating the American Conservative Movement: 1945 to the Present* (with Nancy MacLean; Rowman and Littlefield, 2009), *The Conservative Ascendancy: How the GOP Right Made Political History* (Harvard University Press, 2007), and *Phyllis Schlafly and Grassroots Conservatism: A Woman's Crusade* (Princeton University Press, 2005).

Sean P. Cunningham is assistant professor of history at Texas Tech University. He is the author of *Cowboy Conservatism: Texas and the Rise of the Modern Right* (University Press of Kentucky, 2010) and is working on a synthesis of Sunbelt political history since 1945.

Robert Freedman received his doctorate from the University of Cambridge for his analysis of the New Right's impact on American politics in the Carter and Reagan eras. He has published articles in both journals and newspapers on this subject.

Robert Mason is senior lecturer in history at the University of Edinburgh. He is the author of *Richard Nixon and the Quest for a New Majority* (University of North Carolina Press, 2004) and *The Republican Party and American Politics from Hoover to Reagan* (Cambridge University Press, 2012).

Joe Merton is lecturer in U.S. history at the University of Nottingham. His doctorate is on the rise and decline of white ethnic politics from 1964 to 1984, on which he has written numerous journal articles.

Iwan Morgan is professor of U.S. studies at the Institute of the Americas, University College London. His publications include *Eisenhower versus "the Spenders": The Eisenhower Administration, the Democrats and the Budget, 1953–60* (St. Martin's Press, 1990), *Nixon* (Arnold, 2002), and (coedited with Michael Genovese) *Remembering Watergate: Its Legacy for American Politics* (Palgrave, 2012). His monograph *The Age of Deficits: Presidents and Unbalanced Budgets from Jimmy*

Carter to George W. Bush (University Press of Kansas, 2009), won the Richard Neustadt Prize of the American Politics Group.

Catherine E. Rymph is associate professor of history at the University of Missouri—Columbia. She is the author of *Republican Women: Feminism and Conservatism from Suffrage through the Rise of the New Right* (University of North Carolina Press, 2006). She has written on gender and on nation building after World War II and is writing a book on the history of the U.S. foster care system.

Dominic Sandbrook is the author, most recently, of *Mad as Hell: The Crisis of the 1970s and the Rise of the Populist Right* (Knopf, 2011) and *Seasons in the Sun: The Battle for Britain, 1974–1979* (Allen Lane, 2012). His other books are *Eugene McCarthy: The Rise and Fall of Postwar American Liberalism* (Knopf, 2004), *Never Had It So Good: A History of Britain from Suez to the Beatles* (Little, Brown, 2005), *White Heat: A History of Britain in the Swinging Sixties* (Little, Brown, 2006), and *State of Emergency: The Way We Were—Britain, 1970–1974* (Allen Lane, 2010).

Sandra Scanlon is lecturer in American history at University College Dublin. Her academic specialism focuses on the linkage between domestic politics and foreign policy in the Cold War, the subject of her Cambridge doctorate. In addition to having written numerous articles, she is the coeditor of *Reform and Renewal: Transatlantic Relations in the 1960s and 1970s* (Cambridge Scholars, 2008) and the author of *The Pro-War Movement: Vietnam and the Rise of Modern American Conservatism* (University of Massachusetts Press, forthcoming).

Timothy Stanley is a Leverhulme Research Fellow at Royal Holloway, University of London. He is the author of *Kennedy vs. Carter: The 1980 Battle for the Democratic Party's Soul* (University Press of Kansas, 2010) and *The Crusader: The Life and Tumultuous Times of Patrick Buchanan* (Thomas Dunne Books, 2012), and coeditor of *Making Sense of American Liberalism* (University of Illinois Press, 2012).

Timothy N. Thurber is associate professor of history at Virginia Commonwealth University. He is the author of *The Politics of Equality: Hubert Humphrey and the African American Freedom Struggle, 1945–1978* (Columbia University Press, 1998), and he is writing a book about the Republican Party and civil rights from 1945 to 1980.

Index